Mastering KVM Virtualization

Dive in to the cutting edge techniques of Linux KVM
virtualization, and build the virtualization solutions your
datacentre demands

Humble Devassy Chirammal

Prasad Mukhedkar

Anil Vettathu

[PACKT] open source✻
PUBLISHING   community experience distilled

BIRMINGHAM - MUMBAI

Mastering KVM Virtualization

First published: August 2016

Production reference: 2180816

Published by Packt Publishing Ltd.
Livery Place
35 Livery Street
Birmingham B3 2PB, UK.

ISBN 978-1-78439-905-4

www.packtpub.com

Credits

Authors
Humble Devassy Chirammal
Prasad Mukhedkar
Anil Vettathu

Reviewers
Aric Pedersen
Ranjith Rajaram
Amit Shah

Commissioning Editor
Kunal Parikh

Acquisition Editor
Shaon Basu

Content Development Editor
Shweta Pant

Technical Editor
Saurabh Malhotra

Copy Editors
Sneha Singh
Stephen Copestake

Project Coordinator
Kinjal Bari

Proofreader
Safis Editing

Indexer
Hemangini Bari

Graphics
Disha Haria
Kirk D'Penha

Production Coordinator
Shantanu N. Zagade

Cover Work
Shantanu N. Zagade

About the Authors

Humble Devassy Chirammal works as a senior software engineer at Red Hat in the Storage Engineering team. He has more than 10 years of IT experience and his area of expertise is in knowing the full stack of an ecosystem and architecting the solutions based on the demand. These days, he primarily concentrates on GlusterFS and emerging technologies, such as IaaS, PaaS solutions in Cloud, and Containers. He has worked on intrusion detection systems, clusters, and virtualization. He is an Open Source advocate. He actively organizes meetups on Virtualization, CentOS, Openshift, and GlusterFS. His Twitter handle is @hchiramm and his website is http://www.humblec.com/.

I would like to dedicate this book in the loving memory of my parents, C.O.Devassy and Elsy Devassy, whose steady, balanced, and loving upbringing has given me the strength and determination to be the person I am today. I would like to thank my wife, Anitha, for standing beside me throughout my career and for the effort she put in taking care of our son Heaven while I was writing this book. Also, I would like to thank my brothers Sible and Fr. Able Chirammal, without whose constant support this book would not have been possible.

Finally, a special thanks to Ulrich Obergfell for being an inspiration, which helped me enrich my knowledge in virtualization.

Prasad Mukhedkar is a senior technical support engineer at Red Hat. His area of expertise is designing, building, and supporting IT infrastructure for workloads, especially large virtualization environments and cloud IaaS using open source technologies. He is skilled in KVM virtualization with continuous working experience from its very early stages, possesses extensive hands-on and technical knowledge of Red Hat Enterprise Virtualization. These days, he concentrates primarily on OpenStack and Cloudforms platforms. His other area of interest includes Linux performance tuning, designing highly scalable open source identity management solutions, and enterprise IT security. He is a huge fan of the Linux "GNU Screen" utility.

Anil Vettathu started his association with Linux in college and began his career as a Linux System Administrator soon after. He is a generalist and is interested in Open Source technologies. He has hands on experience in designing and implementing large scale virtualization environments using open source technologies and has extensive knowledge in libvirt and KVM. These days he primarily works on Red Hat Enterprise Virtualization, containers and real time performance tuning. Currently, he is working as a Technical Account Manager for Red Hat. His website is http://anilv.in.

I'd like to thank my beloved wife, Chandni, for her unconditional support. She took the pain of looking after our two naughtiest kids, while I enjoyed writing this book. I'd like also like to thank my parents, Dr Annieamma & Dr George Vettathu, for their guidance and to push me hard to study something new in life. Finally, I would like to thank my sister Dr. Wilma for her guidance and my brother Vimal.

About the Reviewers

Aric Pedersen is the author of *cPanel User Guide and Tutorial* and *Web Host Manager Administration Guide*, both written for Packt Publishing. He has also served as a reviewer for *CUPS Administrative Guide*, *Linux E-mail*, and *Linux Shell Scripting Cookbook*, published by Packt Publishing.

He has over 11 years of experience working as a systems administrator. He currently works for `http://www.hostdime.com/`, the world-class web host and global data center provider, and also for `https://netenberg.com/`, the makers of Fantastico, the world's most popular web script installer for cPanel servers.

> I would like to thank Dennis and Nicky, who have helped me in innumerable ways with their friendship over the past several years.
>
> I'd also like to thank my mother and the rest of my family, Allen, Ken, Steve, and Michael, because without them, nothing I've done would have been possible.

Ranjith Rajaram works as a Senior Principle Technical Support Engineer at a leading open source Enterprise Linux company. He started his career by providing support to web hosting companies and managing servers remotely. He has also provided technical support to their end customers. Early in his career, he has worked on Linux, Unix, and FreeBSD platforms.

For the past 12 years, he has been continuously learning something new. This is what he likes and admires about technical support. As a mark of respect to all his fellow technical support engineers, he has included "developing software is humane but supporting them is divine" in his e-mail signature.

At his current organization, he is involved in implementing, installing, and troubleshooting Linux environment networks. Apart from this, he is also an active contributor to the Linux container space, especially using Docker-formatted containers.

As a reviewer this is his second book. His earlier book was *Learning RHEL Networking* from Packt Publishing.

Amit Shah has been working on FOSS since 2001, and QEMU/KVM virtualization since 2007. He currently works as a senior software engineer in Red Hat. He has reviewed KVM Internals and Performance Tuning chapters.

www.PacktPub.com

eBooks, discount offers, and more

Did you know that Packt offers eBook versions of every book published, with PDF and ePub files available? You can upgrade to the eBook version at www.PacktPub.com and as a print book customer, you are entitled to a discount on the eBook copy. Get in touch with us at customercare@packtpub.com for more details.

At www.PacktPub.com, you can also read a collection of free technical articles, sign up for a range of free newsletters and receive exclusive discounts and offers on Packt books and eBooks.

https://www2.packtpub.com/books/subscription/packtlib

Do you need instant solutions to your IT questions? PacktLib is Packt's online digital book library. Here, you can search, access, and read Packt's entire library of books.

Why subscribe?

- Fully searchable across every book published by Packt
- Copy and paste, print, and bookmark content
- On demand and accessible via a web browser

A big thank you to the KVM, QEMU, libvirt & oVirt community for wonderful opensource projects.

We would also thank our reviewers and readers for supporting us.

Table of Contents

Preface

Mastering KVM Virtualization is a culmination of all the knowledge that we have gained by troubleshooting, configuring, and fixing the bug on KVM virtualization. We have authored this book for system administrators, DevOps practitioners, and developers who have a good hands-on knowledge of Linux and would like to sharpen their open source virtualization skills. The chapters in this book are written with a focus on practical examples that should help you deploy a robust virtualization environment, suiting your organization's needs. We expect that, once you finish the book, you should have a good understanding of KVM virtualization internals, the technologies around it, and the tools to build and manage diverse virtualization environments. You should also be able to contribute to the awesome KVM community.

What this book covers

Chapter 1, *Understanding Linux Virtualization*, talks about the prevailing technologies used in Linux virtualization and their advantages over others. It starts with basic concepts of Linux virtualization and advantages of Linux-based virtualization platforms and then moves on to hypervisor/VMM. This chapter ends with how Linux is being used in private and public cloud infrastructures.

Chapter 2, *KVM Internals*, covers the important data structures and functions which define the internal implementation of libvirt, qemu, and KVM. You will also go through the life cycle of vCPU execution and how qemu and KVM perform together to run a guest operating system in the host CPU.

Chapter 3, Setting Up Standalone KVM Virtualization, tells you how to set up your Linux server to use KVM (Kernel-based Virtual Machine) and libvirt. KVM is for virtualization and libvirt is for managing the virtualization environment. You will also learn how to determine the right system requirements (CPU, memory, storage, and networking) to create your own virtual environment.

Chapter 4, Getting Started with libvirt and Creating Your First Virtual Machines, will tell you more about libvirt and its supported tools, such as virt-manager and virsh. You will dig more into the default configurations available in libvirt. You will install a new virtual machine using virt-manager as well virt-install and also learn about advanced virtual machine deployment tools, such as virt-builder and oz.

Chapter 5, Network and Storage, is one of the most important chapters that teaches you about virtual networking and storage, which determine the QoS of your virtual machine deployments. In virtual networking, you will learn in detail about bridging, different bridging concepts, and the methods you can adopt for a fault tolerant network layer for virtual machines. You will understand how to segregate the network with the use of tagged vLan bridges. In storage, you will learn how to create storage pools for our virtual machines from storage backends such as fiber channel (FC), ISCSI, NFS, local storage, and so on. You will also learn how to determine the right storage backend for your virtual machines.

Chapter 6, Virtual Machine Lifecycle Management, discusses the tasks of managing virtual machines. You will learn about the different statuses of virtual machines and methods to access a virtual machine that includes spice and VNC. You will understand the use of guest agents. You will also learn how to perform offline and live migration of virtual machines.

Chapter 7, Templates and Snapshots, tells us how to create templates of Windows and Linux for rapid VMs provisioning. The chapter will also teach us how to create external and internal snapshots and when to use which snapshot. Snapshot management, including merge and deletion is also covered with snapshot best practice.

Chapter 8, Kimchi, An HTML5-Based Management Tool for KVM/libvirt, explains how to manage KVM virtualization infrastructure remotely, using libvirt-based web management tools. You will learn how to create new virtual machines, remotely adjust an existing VM's resource allocation, implement user access controls, and so on over the Internet using Kimchi WebUI. It also introduces VM-King, an Android application that lets you manage KVM virtual machines remotely from your Android mobile or tablet.

Chapter 9, Software-Defined Networking for KVM Virtualization, covers the use of SDN approach in KVM virtualization using Open vSwitch and supporting tools that include OpenDayLight SDN controller. You will learn about Open vSwitch installation and setup, creating vLans for KVM virtual machines, applying granular traffic and policy control to KVM VMs, creating overlay networks, and port mirroring and SPAN. You will also learn how to manage Open vSwitch using OpenDayLight SDN controller.

Chapter 10, Installing and Configuring the Virtual Datacenter Using oVirt, oVirt is a virtual datacenter manager and is considered as the open source replacement of VMware vCenter. It manages virtual machines, hosts, storage, and virtualized networks. It provides a powerful web management interface. In this chapter, we will cover oVirt architecture, oVirt engine installation, and oVirt node installation.

Chapter 11, Starting Your First Virtual Machine in oVirt, tells us how to initiate an oVirt datacenter in order to start your first virtual machine. This initialization process will walk you through creating a datacenter, adding a host to datacenter, adding storage domains, and its backend. You will learn about configuring networking.

Chapter 12, Deploying OpenStack Private Cloud backed by KVM Virtualization, covers the most popular open source software platform to create and manage public and private IaaS cloud. We will explain the different components of OpenStack. You will set up an OpenStack environment and will start your first instance on it.

Chapter 13, Performance Tuning and Best Practices in KVM, tells us how performance tuning can be done on a KVM setup. It will also discuss the best practices that can be applied in a KVM setup to improve the performance.

Chapter 14, V2V and P2V Migration Tools, will tell you how to migrate your existing virtual machines that are running on proprietary hypervisors to a truly open source KVM hypervisor using virt-v2v tool. You will also learn how to migrate physical machines to virtual machines and run them on the cloud.

Appendix, Converting a Virtual Machine into a Hypervisor, this will tell you how you can turn a VM into a hypervisor by using specific method.

What you need for this book

This book is heavily focused on practical examples; due to the nature of the content, we recommend that you have a test machine installed with Fedora 22 or later to perform the tasks laid out in the book. This test machine should have a minimum of 6 GB memory with an Intel or AMD processor that supports virtualization. You should be able to do most of the examples using nested virtual machines.

Who this book for

This book is for system administrators, DevOps practitioners and developers who have a good hands-on knowledge of Linux and would like to sharpen their skills of open source virtualization.

Conventions

In this book, you will find a number of text styles that distinguish between different kinds of information. Here are some examples of these styles and an explanation of their meaning.

Code words in text, database table names, folder names, filenames, file extensions, pathnames, dummy URLs, user input, and Twitter handles are shown as follows: "These `ioctls()` fundamentally map to the system KVM level, VM level, and vCPU level ."

A block of code is set as follows:

```
switch (run->exit_reason) {
        case KVM_EXIT_IO:
                DPRINTF("handle_io\n");
                  /* Called outside BQL */
                kvm_handle_io(run->io.port, attrs,
                                (uint8_t *)run + run->io.data_offset,
                            run->io.direction,
                             run->io.size,
                             run->io.count);
             ret = 0;
          break;
```

When we wish to draw your attention to a particular part of a code block, the relevant lines or items are set in bold:

```
include/linux/kvm_host.h :

struct kvm {
        struct mm_struct *mm; /* userspace tied to this vm */
        struct kvm_vcpu *vcpus[KVM_MAX_VCPUS];
        struct kvm_io_bus *buses[KVM_NR_BUSES];
        struct kvm_coalesced_mmio_ring *coalesced_mmio_ring;
}
```

Any command-line input or output is written as follows:

```
#git clone git://git.qemu-project.org/qemu.git
```

New terms and **important words** are shown in bold. Words that you see on the screen, for example, in menus or dialog boxes, appear in the text like this: "If you want to connect to the remote hypervisor, check **Connect to remote host** and fill the details."

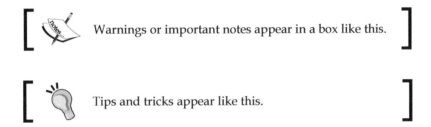

Warnings or important notes appear in a box like this.

Tips and tricks appear like this.

Reader feedback

Feedback from our readers is always welcome. Let us know what you think about this book—what you liked or disliked. Reader feedback is important for us as it helps us develop titles that you will really get the most out of.

To send us general feedback, simply e-mail feedback@packtpub.com, and mention the book's title in the subject of your message.

If there is a topic that you have expertise in and you are interested in either writing or contributing to a book, see our author guide at www.packtpub.com/authors.

Customer support

Now that you are the proud owner of a Packt book, we have a number of things to help you to get the most from your purchase.

Downloading the color images of this book

We also provide you with a PDF file that has color images of the screenshots/diagrams used in this book. The color images will help you better understand the changes in the output. You can download this file from `http://www.packtpub.com/sites/default/files/downloads/Mastering_KVM_Virtualization_ColorImages.pdf`.

Errata

Although we have taken every care to ensure the accuracy of our content, mistakes do happen. If you find a mistake in one of our books—maybe a mistake in the text or the code—we would be grateful if you could report this to us. By doing so, you can save other readers from frustration and help us improve subsequent versions of this book. If you find any errata, please report them by visiting `http://www.packtpub.com/submit-errata`, selecting your book, clicking on the **Errata Submission Form** link, and entering the details of your errata. Once your errata are verified, your submission will be accepted and the errata will be uploaded to our website or added to any list of existing errata under the Errata section of that title.

To view the previously submitted errata, go to `https://www.packtpub.com/books/content/support` and enter the name of the book in the search field. The required information will appear under the **Errata** section.

Piracy

Piracy of copyrighted material on the Internet is an ongoing problem across all media. At Packt, we take the protection of our copyright and licenses very seriously. If you come across any illegal copies of our works in any form on the Internet, please provide us with the location address or website name immediately so that we can pursue a remedy.

Please contact us at `copyright@packtpub.com` with a link to the suspected pirated material.

We appreciate your help in protecting our authors and our ability to bring you valuable content.

Questions

If you have a problem with any aspect of this book, you can contact us at
questions@packtpub.com, and we will do our best to address the problem.

1

Understanding Linux Virtualization

This chapter provides the reader with an insight into the prevailing technologies in Linux virtualization and their advantage over others. There are a total of 14 chapters in this book, which are lined up to cover all the important aspects of KVM virtualization, starting from KVM internals and advanced topics such as software defined networking, performance tuning, and optimization, to physical to virtual migration.

In this chapter, we will cover the following topics:

- Linux virtualization and its basic concepts
- Why you should use Linux virtualization
- Hypervisor/VMM
- What Linux virtualization offers you in the cloud
- Public and private clouds

 Before you start, check out the homepage of the book `http://bit.ly/ mkvmvirt` to see the new updates, tips and version changes.

What is virtualization?

In philosophy, virtual means "something that is not real". In computer science, virtual means "a hardware environment that is not real". Here, we duplicate the functions of physical hardware and present them to an operating system. The technology that is used to create this environment can be called **virtualization technology**, in short, virtualization. The physical system that runs the virtualization software (hypervisor or Virtual Machine Monitor) is called a host and the virtual machines installed on top of the hypervisor are called guests.

Why should I use Linux virtualization?

Virtualization first appeared in Linux in the form of **User-mode Linux** (**UML**) and it started the revolution required to bring Linux into the virtualization race. Today, there is a wide array of virtualization options available in Linux to convert a single computer into multiple ones. Popular Linux virtualization solutions include KVM, Xen, QEMU, and VirtualBox. In this book, we will be focusing on KVM virtualization.

Openness, flexibility, and performance are some of the major factors that attract users to Linux virtualization. Just like any other open source software, virtualization software in Linux is developed in a collaborative manner; this indirectly brings users the advantages of the open source model. For example, compared to closed source, open source receives wider input from the community and indirectly helps reduce research and development costs, improves efficiency, and performance and productivity. The open source model always encourages innovation. The following are some of the other features that open source provides:

- User-driven solutions for real problems
- Support from the community and a user base who help fellow users to solve problems
- Provides choice of infrastructure
- Control of data and security, as the code is freely available to read, understand, and modify when required
- Avoid lock-in flexibility to migrate the entire load with comparable product and stay free from vendor lock-in

Types of virtualization

Simply put, virtualization is the process of virtualizing something such as hardware, network, storage, application, access, and so on. Thus, virtualization can happen to any of the components.

Refer to the *Advantages of virtualization* section for more details on different possibilities in virtualization.

For example:

- **SDN** or **Software-Defined Networking,** https://en.wikipedia.org/wiki/Software-defined_networking. These techniques are examples of network virtualization, https://en.wikipedia.org/wiki/Network_virtualization.
- **Software Defined Storage (SDS),** https://en.wikipedia.org/wiki/Software-defined_storage. This is part of storage virtualization, https://en.wikipedia.org/wiki/Storage_virtualization.
- The application streaming, remote desktop service, and desktop virtualization techniques fall into the category of application virtualization, https://en.wikipedia.org/wiki/Application_virtualization.

However, in the context of our book, we will discuss virtualization mainly in terms of software (hypervisor-based) virtualization. From this angle, virtualization is the process of hiding the underlying physical hardware so that it can be shared and used by multiple operating systems. This is also known as platform virtualization. In short, this action introduces a layer called a **hypervisor/VMM** between the underlying hardware and the operating systems running on top of it. The operating system running on top of the hypervisor is called the guest or virtual machine.

Advantages of virtualization

Let's discuss some of the advantages of virtualization:

- **Server consolidation**: It is well understood that virtualization helps in saving power and having a smaller energy footprint. Server consolidation with virtualization will also reduce the overall footprint of the entire data center. Virtualization reduces the number of physical or bare metal servers, reducing networking stack components and other physical components, such as racks. Ultimately, this leads to reduced floor space, power savings, and so on. This can save you more money and also help with energy utilization. Does it also ensure increased hardware utilization? Yes, it does. We can provision virtual machines with the exact amount of CPU, memory, and storage resources that they need and this will in turn make sure that hardware utilization is increased.

- **Service isolation**: Suppose no virtualization exists; in this scenario, what's the solution to achieve service isolation? Isn't it that we need to run one application per physical server? Yes, this can make sure that we achieve service isolation; however, will it not cause physical server sprawl, underutilized servers, and increased costs? Without any doubt, I can say that it does. The server virtualization helps application isolation and also removes application compatibility issues by consolidating many of these virtual machines across fewer physical servers. In short, service isolation technique this brings the advantage of simplified administration of services.

- **Faster server provisioning**: Provisioning a bare metal system will consume some time, even if we have some automated process in the path. But in case of virtualization, you can spawn a virtual machine from prebuilt images (templates) or from snapshots. It's that quick, as you can imagine. Also, you really don't have to worry about physical resource configuration, such as "network stack", which comes as a burden for physical or bare metal server provisioning.

- **Disaster recovery**: Disaster recovery becomes really easy when you have a virtualized data center. Virtualization allows you to take up-to-date snapshots of virtual machines. These snapshots can be quickly redeployed so you can reach to a state where everything was working fine. Also, virtualization offers features such as online and offline VM migration techniques so that you can always move those virtual machines elsewhere in your data center. This flexibility assists with a better disaster recovery plan that's easier to enact and has a higher success rate.

- **Dynamic load balancing**: Well, this depends on the policies you set. As server workloads vary, virtualization provides the ability for virtual machines, which are overutilizing the resources of a server, to be moved (live migration) to underutilized servers, based on the policies you set. Most of the virtualization solutions come with such policies for the user. This dynamic load balancing creates efficient utilization of server resources.

- **Faster development and test environment**: Think of this, if you want to test environment in a temporary manner. It's really difficult to deploy it in physical servers, isn't it? Also, it won't be of much worth if you set up this environment in a temporary manner. But it's really easy to set up a development or test environment with virtualization. Using a guest operating system/VM enables rapid deployment by isolating the application in a known and controlled environment. It also eliminates lots of unknown factors, such as mixed libraries, caused by numerous installs. Especially, if it's a development or test environment, we can expect severe crashes due to the experiments happening with the setup. It then requires hours of reinstallation, if we are on physical or bare metal servers. However, in case of VMs, it's all about simply copying a virtual image and trying again.

- **Improved system reliability and security**: A virtualization solution adds a layer of abstraction between the virtual machine and the underlying physical hardware. It's common for data on your physical hard disk to get corrupted due to some reason and affect the entire server. However, if it is stored in a virtual machine hard disk, the physical hard disk in the host system will be intact, and there's no need to worry about replacing the virtual hard disk. In any other instance, virtualization can prevent system crashes due to memory corruption caused by software such as the device drivers. The admin has the privilege to configure virtual machines in an independent and isolated environment. This sandbox deployment of virtual machines can give more security to the infrastructure because the admin has the flexibility to choose the configuration that is best suited for this setup. If the admin decides that a particular VM doesn't need access to the Internet or to other production networks, the virtual machine can be easily configured behind the network hop with a completely isolated network configuration and restrict the access to the rest of the world. This helps reduce risks caused by the infection of a single system that then affects numerous production computers or virtual machines.

- **OS independence or a reduced hardware vendor lock-in**: Virtualization is all about creating an abstraction layer between the underlying hardware and presenting a virtual hardware to the guest operating systems running on top of the stack. Virtualization eliminates the hardware vendor lock-in, doesn't it? That being said, with virtualization the setup has to be tied down to one particular vendor/platform/server, especially when the virtual machines don't really care about the hardware they run on. Thus, data center admins have a lot more flexibility when it comes to the server equipment they can choose from. In short, the advantage of virtualization technology is its hardware independence and encapsulation. These features enhance availability and business continuity. One of the nice things about virtualization is the abstraction between software and hardware.

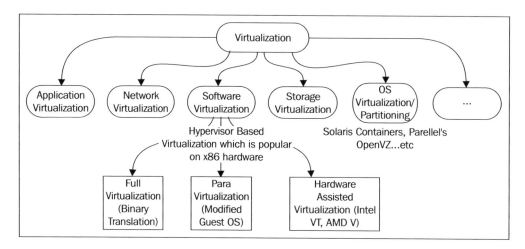

As we discussed in the preceding section, even though virtualization can be achieved in different areas, I would like to talk more about operating system virtualization and software virtualization.

Operating system virtualization/ partitioning

The operating system virtualization technique allows the same physical host to serve different workloads and isolate each of the workloads. Please note that these workloads operate independently on the same OS. This allows a physical server to run multiple isolated operating system instances, called **containers**. There is nothing wrong if we call it container-based virtualization. The advantage of this type of virtualization is that the host operating system does not need to emulate system call interfaces for operating systems that differ from it. Since the mentioned interfaces are not present, alternative operating systems cannot be virtualized or accommodated in this type of virtualization. This is a common and well-understood limitation of this type of virtualization. Solaris containers, FreeBSD jails, and Parallel's OpenVZ fall into this category of virtualization. While using this approach, all of the workloads run on a single system. The process isolation and resource management is provided by the kernel. Even though all the virtual machines/containers are running under the same kernel, they have their own file system, processes, memory, devices, and so on. From another angle, a mixture of Windows, Unix, and Linux workloads on the same physical host are not a part of this type of virtualization. The limitations of this technology are outweighed by the benefits to performance and efficiency, because one operating system is supporting all the virtual environments. Furthermore, switching from one partition to another is very fast.

Before we discuss virtualization further and dive into the next type of virtualization, (hypervisor-based/software virtualization) it would be useful to be aware of some jargon in computer science. That being said, let's start with something called "protection rings". In computer science, various hierarchical protection domains/privileged rings exist. These are the mechanisms that protect data or faults based on the security enforced when accessing the resources in a computer system. These protection domains contribute to the security of a computer system.

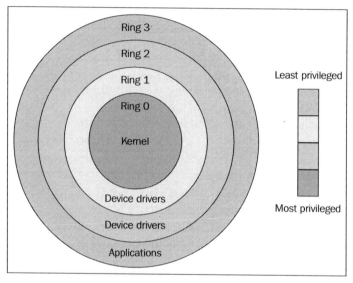

Source: https://en.wikipedia.org/wiki/Protection_ring

As shown in the preceding figure, the protection rings are numbered from the most privileged to the least privileged. Ring 0 is the level with the most privileges and it interacts directly with physical hardware, such as the CPU and memory. The resources, such as memory, I/O ports, and CPU instructions are protected via these privileged rings. Ring 1 and 2 are mostly unused. Most of the general purpose systems use only two rings, even if the hardware they run on provides more CPU modes (https://en.m.wikipedia.org/wiki/CPU_modes) than that. The main two CPU modes are the kernel mode and user mode. From an operating system's point of view, Ring 0 is called the kernel mode/supervisor mode and Ring 3 is the user mode. As you assumed, applications run in Ring 3.

Operating systems, such as Linux and Windows use supervisor/kernel and user mode. A user mode can do almost nothing to the outside world without calling on the kernel or without its help, due to its restricted access to memory, CPU, and I/O ports. The kernels can run in privileged mode, which means that they can run on ring 0. To perform specialized functions, the user mode code (all the applications run in ring 3) must perform a system call (`https://en.m.wikipedia.org/wiki/System_call`) to the supervisor mode or even to the kernel space, where a trusted code of the operating system will perform the needed task and return the execution back to the user space. In short, the operating system runs in ring 0 in a normal environment. It needs the most privileged level to do resource management and provide access to the hardware. The following image explains this:

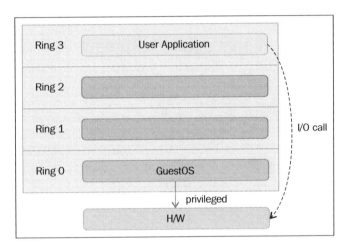

The rings above 0 run instructions in a processor mode called unprotected. The hypervisor/**Virtual Machine Monitor (VMM)** needs to access the memory, CPU, and I/O devices of the host. Since, only the code running in ring 0 is allowed to perform these operations, it needs to run in the most privileged ring, which is Ring 0, and has to be placed next to the kernel. Without specific hardware virtualization support, the hypervisor or VMM runs in ring 0; this basically blocks the virtual machine's operating system in ring-0. So the VM's operating system has to reside in Ring 1. An operating system installed in a VM is also expected to access all the resources as it's unaware of the virtualization layer; to achieve this, it has to run in Ring 0 similar to the VMM. Due to the fact that only one kernel can run in Ring 0 at a time, the guest operating systems have to run in another ring with fewer privileges or have to be modified to run in user mode.

This has resulted in the introduction of a couple of virtualization methods called full virtualization and paravirtualization, which we will discuss in the following sections.

Full virtualization

In full virtualization, privileged instructions are emulated to overcome the limitations arising from the guest operating system running in ring 1 and VMM runnning in Ring 0. Full virtualization was implemented in first-generation x86 VMMs. It relies on techniques, such as binary translation (`https://en.wikipedia.org/wiki/Binary_translation`) to trap and virtualize the execution of certain sensitive and non-virtualizable instructions. This being said, in binary translation, some system calls are interpreted and dynamically rewritten. Following diagram depicts how Guest OS access the host computer hardware through Ring 1 for privileged instructions and how un-privileged instructions are executed without the involvement of Ring 1:

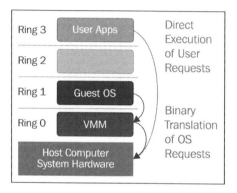

With this approach, the critical instructions are discovered (statically or dynamically at runtime) and replaced with traps into the VMM that are to be emulated in software. A binary translation can incur a large performance overhead in comparison to a virtual machine running on natively virtualized architectures.

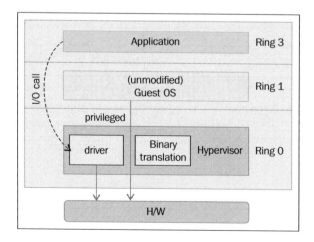

However, as shown in the preceding image, when we use full virtualization we can use the unmodified guest operating systems. This means that we don't have to alter the guest kernel to run on a VMM. When the guest kernel executes privileged operations, the VMM provides the CPU emulation to handle and modify the protected CPU operations, but as mentioned earlier, this causes performance overhead compared to the other mode of virtualization, called paravirtualization.

Paravirtualization

In paravirtualization, the guest operating system needs to be modified in order to allow those instructions to access Ring 0. In other words, the operating system needs to be modified to communicate between the VMM/hypervisor and the guest through the "backend" (hypercalls) path.

 Please note that we can also call VMM a hypervisor.

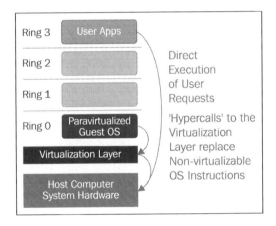

Paravirtualization (https://en.wikipedia.org/wiki/Paravirtualization) is a technique in which the hypervisor provides an API and the OS of the guest virtual machine calls that API which require host operating system modifications. Privileged instruction calls are exchanged with the API functions provided by the VMM. In this case, the modified guest operating system can run in ring 0.

As you can see, under this technique the guest kernel is modified to run on the VMM. In other terms, the guest kernel knows that it's been virtualized. The privileged instructions/operations that are supposed to run in ring 0 have been replaced with calls known as hypercalls, which talk to the VMM. The hypercalls invoke the VMM to perform the task on behalf of the guest kernel. As the guest kernel has the ability to communicate directly with the VMM via hypercalls, this technique results in greater performance compared to full virtualization. However, This requires specialized guest kernel which is aware of para virtualization technique and come with needed software support.

Hardware assisted virtualization

Intel and AMD realized that full virtualization and paravirtualization are the major challenges of virtualization on the x86 architecture (as the scope of this book is limited to x86 architecture, we will mainly discuss the evolution of this architecture here) due to the performance overhead and complexity in designing and maintaining the solution. Intel and AMD independently created new processor extensions of the x86 architecture, called Intel VT-x and AMD-V respectively. On the Itanium architecture, hardware-assisted virtualization is known as VT-i. Hardware assisted virtualization is a platform virtualization method designed to efficiently use full virtualization with the hardware capabilities. Various vendors call this technology by different names, including accelerated virtualization, hardware virtual machine, and native virtualization.

For better support of for virtualization, Intel and AMD introduced **Virtualization Technology (VT)** and **Secure Virtual Machine (SVM)**, respectively, as extensions of the IA-32 instruction set. These extensions allow the VMM/hypervisor to run a guest OS that expects to run in kernel mode, in lower privileged rings. Hardware assisted virtualization not only proposes new instructions, but also introduces a new privileged access level, called ring -1, where the hypervisor/VMM can run. Hence, guest virtual machines can run in ring 0. With hardware-assisted virtualization, the operating system has direct access to resources without any emulation or OS modification. The hypervisor or VMM can now run at the newly introduced privilege level, Ring -1, with the guest operating systems running on Ring 0. Also, with hardware assisted virtualization, the VMM/hypervisor is relaxed and needs to perform less work compared to the other techniques mentioned, which reduces the performance overhead.

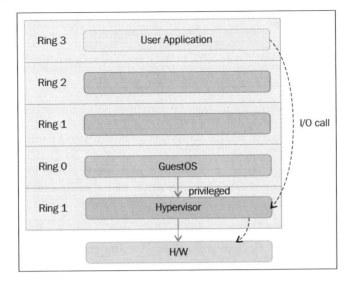

In simple terms, this virtualization-aware hardware provides the support to build the VMM and also ensures the isolation of a guest operating system. This helps to achieve better performance and avoid the complexity of designing a virtualization solution. Modern virtualization techniques make use of this feature to provide virtualization. One example is KVM, which we are going to discuss in detail in the scope of this book.

Introducing VMM/hypervisor

As its name suggests, the VMM or hypervisor is a piece of software that is responsible for monitoring and controlling virtual machines or guest operating systems. The hypervisor/VMM is responsible for ensuring different virtualization management tasks, such as providing virtual hardware, VM life cycle management, migrating of VMs, allocating resources in real time, defining policies for virtual machine management, and so on. The VMM/hypervisor is also responsible for efficiently controlling physical platform resources, such as memory translation and I/O mapping. One of the main advantages of virtualization software is its capability to run multiple guests operating on the same physical system or hardware. The multiple guest systems can be on the same operating system or different ones. For example, there can be multiple Linux guest systems running as guests on the same physical system. The VMM is responsible to allocate the resources requested by these guest operating systems. The system hardware, such as the processor, memory, and so on has to be allocated to these guest operating systems according to their configuration, and VMM can take care of this task. Due to this, VMM is a critical component in a virtualization environment.

Depending on the location of the VMM/hypervisor and where it's placed, it is categorized either as type 1 or type 2.

Type 1 and Type 2 hypervisors

Hypervisors are mainly categorized as either Type 1 or Type 2 hypervisors, based on where they reside in the system or, in other terms, whether the underlying operating system is present in the system or not. But there is no clear or standard definition of Type 1 and Type 2 hypervisors. If the VMM/hypervisor runs directly on top of the hardware, its generally considered to be a Type 1 hypervisor. If there is an operating system present, and if the VMM/hypervisor operates as a separate layer, it will be considered as a Type 2 hypervisor. Once again, this concept is open to debate and there is no standard definition for this.

A Type 1 hypervisor directly interacts with the system hardware; it does not need any host operating system. You can directly install it on a bare metal system and make it ready to host virtual machines. Type 1 hypervisors are also called **Bare Metal**, **Embedded**, or **Native Hypervisors**.

oVirt-node is an example of a Type 1 Linux hypervisor. The following figure provides an illustration of the Type 1 hypervisor design concept:

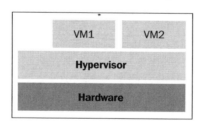

Here are the advantages of Type 1 hypervisors:

- Easy to install and configure
- Small in size, optimized to give most of the physical resources to the hosted guest (virtual machines)
- Generates less overhead, as it comes with only the applications needed to run virtual machines
- More secure, because problems in one guest system do not affect the other guest systems running on the hypervisor

However, a type 1 hypervisor doesn't favor customization. Generally, you will not be allowed to install any third party applications or drivers on it.

On the other hand, a Type 2 hypervisor resides on top of the operating system, allowing you to do numerous customizations. Type 2 hypervisors are also known as hosted hypervisors. Type 2 hypervisors are dependent on the host operating system for their operations. The main advantage of Type 2 hypervisors is the wide range of hardware support, because the underlying host OS is controlling hardware access. The following figure provides an illustration of the Type 2 hypervisor design concept:

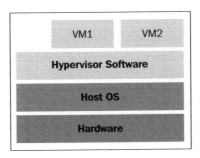

Deciding on the type of hypervisor to use mainly depends on the infrastructure of where you are going to deploy virtualization.

Also, there is a concept that Type 1 hypervisors perform better when compared to Type 2 hypervisors, as they are placed directly on top of the hardware. It does not make much sense to evaluate performance without a formal definition of Type 1 and Type 2 hypervisors.

Open source virtualization projects

The following table is a list of open source virtualization projects in Linux:

Project	Virtualization Type	Project URL
KVM (Kernel-based Virtual Machine)	Full virtualization	`http://www.linux-kvm.org/`
VirtualBox	Full virtualization	`https://www.virtualbox.org/`
Xen	Full and paravirtualization	`http://www.xenproject.org/`
Lguest	Paravirtualization	`http://lguest.ozlabs.org/`
UML (User Mode Linux)		`http://user-mode-linux.sourceforge.net/`
Linux-VServer		`http://www.linux-vserver.org/Welcome_to_Linux-VServer.org`

In upcoming sections, we will discuss Xen and KVM, which are the leading open source virtualization solutions in Linux.

Xen

Xen originated at the University of Cambridge as a research project. The first public release of Xen was in 2003. Later, the leader of this project at the University of Cambridge, Ian Pratt, co-founded a company called XenSource with Simon Crosby (also of the University of Cambridge). This company started to develop the project in an open source fashion. On 15 April 2013, the Xen project was moved to the Linux Foundation as a collaborative project. The Linux Foundation launched a new trademark for the Xen Project to differentiate the project from any commercial use of the older Xen trademark. More details about this can be found at xenproject. org website.

Xen hypervisor has been ported to a number of processor families, for example, Intel IA-32/64, x86_64, PowerPC,ARM, MIPS, and so on.

Xen can operate on both para virtualization and **Hardware-assisted or Full Virtualization (HVM)**, which allow unmodified guests. A Xen hypervisor runs guest operating systems called **Domains**. There are mainly two types of domains in Xen:

- Dom 0
- Dom U

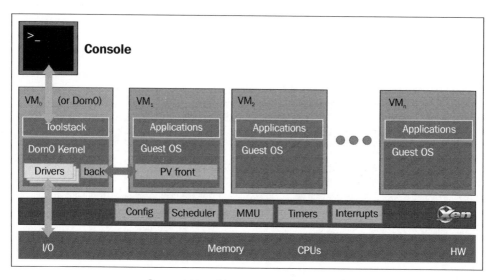

Source: http://www.xenproject.org/

Dom Us are the unprivileged domains or guest systems. Dom 0 is also known as the privileged domain or the special guest and has extended capabilities. The Dom Us or guest systems are controlled by Dom 0. That said Dom 0 contains the drivers for all the devices in the system. Dom 0 also contains a control stack to manage virtual machine creation, destruction, and configuration. Dom 0 also has the privilege to directly access the hardware; it can handle all the access to the system's I/O functions and can interact with the other Virtual Machines. Dom 0 sets the Dom Us, communication path with hardware devices using virtual drivers. It also exposes a control interface to the outside world, through which the system is controlled. Dom 0 is the first VM started by the system and it's a must-have domain for a Xen Project hypervisor.

 If you want to know more about the Xen project, please refer to `http://wiki.xenproject.org/wiki/Xen_Overview` or `http://xenproject.org`

Introducing KVM

Kernel-based Virtual Machine (KVM) represents the latest generation of open source virtualization. The goal of the project was to create a modern hypervisor that builds on the experience of previous generations of technologies and leverages the modern hardware available today (VT-x, AMD-V).

KVM simply turns the Linux kernel into a hypervisor when you install the KVM kernel module. However, as the standard Linux kernel is the hypervisor, it benefits from the changes to the standard kernel (memory support, scheduler, and so on). Optimizations to these Linux components (such as the new scheduler in the 3.1 kernel) benefit both the hypervisor (the host operating system) and the Linux guest operating systems. For I/O emulations, KVM uses a userland software, QEMU; Qemu is a userland program that does hardware emulation.

It emulates the processor and a long list of peripheral devices: disk, network, VGA, PCI, USB, serial/parallel ports, and so on to build a complete virtual hardware on which the guest operating system can be installed and this emulation is powered by KVM.

High-level overview of KVM

The following figure gives us a high-level overview of the user mode and kernel mode components of a KVM:

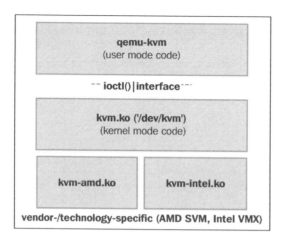

A separate qemu-kvm process is launched for each virtual machine by libvirtd at the request of system management utilities, such as virsh and virt-manager. The properties of the virtual machines (number of CPUs, memory size, I/O device configuration) are defined in separate XML files, which are located in the directory /etc/libvirt/qemu. libvirtd uses the details from these XML files to derive the argument list that is passed to the qemu-kvm process.

Here is an example:

```
qemu      14644  9.8  6.8 6138068 1078400 ?       Sl   03:14   97:29 /usr/
bin/qemu-system-x86_64 -machine accel=kvm -name guest1 -S -machine
pc--m 5000 -realtime mlock=off -smp 4,sockets=4,cores=1,threads=1
-uuid 7a615914-ea0d-7dab-e709-0533c00b921f -no-user-config
-nodefaults -chardev socket,id=charmonitor-drive file=/dev/vms/
hypervisor2,if=none,id=drive-virtio-disk0,format=raw,cache=none,aio=na
tive -device id=net0,mac=52:54:00:5d:be:06
```

Here, an argument similar to -m 5000 forms a 5 GB memory for the virtual machine, --smp = 4 points to a 4 vCPU that has a topology of four vSockets with one core for each socket.

Details about what libvirt and qemu are and how they communicate each other to provide virtualization, are explained in *Chapter 2, KVM Internals.*

What Linux virtualization offers you in the cloud

Over the years, Linux has become the first choice for developing cloud-based solutions. Many successful public cloud providers use Linux virtualization to power their underlying infrastructure. For example, Amazon, the largest IaaS cloud provider uses Xen virtualization to power their EC2 offering and similarly it's KVM that powers Digital Ocean. Digital Ocean is the third largest cloud provider in the world. Linux virtualizations are also dominating the private cloud arena.

The following is a list of open source cloud software that uses Linux virtualization for building IaaS software:

- **Openstack**: A fully open source cloud operating system, this consists of several open source sub-projects that provide all the building blocks to create an IaaS cloud. KVM (Linux Virtualization) is the most-used (and best-supported) hypervisor in OpenStack deployments. It's governed by the vendor-agnostic OpenStack Foundation. How to build an OpenStack cloud using KVM is explained in detail in *Chapter 6, Virtual Machine Lifecycle Management* and *Chapter 7, Templates and Snapshots*.

- **Cloudstack**: This is another open source **Apache Software Foundation (ASF)** controlled cloud project to build and manage highly-scalable multi-tenant IaaS cloud, which is fully compatible with EC2/S3 APIs. Although it supports all top-level Linux hypervisors. Most Cloudstack users choose Xen, as it is tightly integrated with Cloudstack.

- **Eucalyptus**: This is an AWS-compatible private cloud software for organizations to reduce their public cloud cost and regain control over security and performance. It supports both Xen and KVM as a computing resources provider.

Summary

In this chapter, you have learned about Linux virtualization, its advantages, and different types of virtualization methods. We also discussed the types of hypervisor and then went through the high-level architecture of Xen and KVM, and popular open source Linux virtualization technologies.

In the next chapter, we will discuss the internal workings of `libvirt`, `qemu`, and KVM, and will gain knowledge of how these components talk to each other to achieve virtualization.

2
KVM Internals

In this chapter, we will discuss the important data structures and the internal implementation of libvirt, QEMU, and KVM. Then we will dive into the execution flow of a vCPU in the KVM context.

In this chapter, we will cover:

- The internal workings of libvirt, QEMU, and KVM.
- Important data structures and code paths of libvirt, QEMU, and KVM.
- Execution flow of vCPUs
- How all these communicate with each other to provide virtualization

Getting acquainted with libvirt and its implementation

As discussed in a previous chapter, there is an extra management layer called libvirt which can talk to various hypervisors (for example: KVM/QEMU, LXC, OpenVZ, UML, and so on) underlying it. libvirt is an open source **Application Programming Interface (API)**. At the same time, it is a daemon and a management tool for managing different hypervisors as mentioned. libvirt is in use by various virtualization programs and platforms; for example, graphical user interfaces are provided by GNOME boxes and virt-manager (http://virt-manager.org/). Don't confuse this with virtual machine monitor/VMM which we discussed in *Chapter 1, Understanding Linux Virtualization.*

The command line client interface of libvirt is the binary called `virsh`. libvirt is also used by other higher-level management tools, such as oVirt (`www.ovirt.org`):

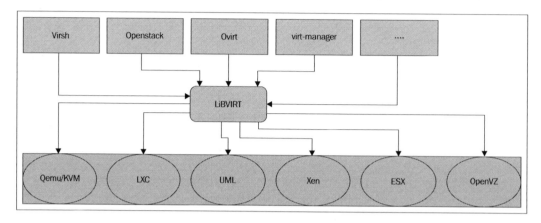

Most people think that libvirt is restricted to a single node or local node where it is running; it's not true. libvirt has remote support built into the library. So, any libvirt tool (for example virt-manager) can remotely connect to a libvirt daemon over the network, just by passing an extra `-connect` argument. One of libvirt's clients (the `virsh` binary provided by the libvirt-client package) is shipped in most distributions such as Fedora, CentOS, and so on.

As discussed earlier, the goal of the libvirt library is to provide a common and stable layer to manage VMs running on a hypervisor. In short, as a management layer it is responsible for providing the API that does management tasks such as virtual machine provision, creation, modification, monitoring, control, migration, and so on. In Linux, you will have noticed some of the processes are deamonized. The libvirt process is also deamonized, and it is called `libvirtd`. As with any other daemon process, the libvirtd provides services to its clients upon request. Let us try to understand what exactly happens when a libvirt client such as virsh or virt-manager requests a service from `libvirtd`. Based on the connection URI (discussed in the following section) passed by the client, libvirtd opens a connection to the hypervisor. This is how the clients virsh or virt-manager ask the libvirtd to start talking to the hypervisor. In the scope of this book, we are aiming at KVM virtualization technology. So, it would be better to think about it in terms of a QEMU/KVM hypervisor instead of discussing some other hypervisor communication from libvirtd. You may be a bit confused when you see QEMU/KVM as the underlying hypervisor name instead of either QEMU or KVM. But don't worry, all will become clear in due course. The connection between QEMU and KVM is discussed in the following. For now just know that there is a hypervisor that uses both the QEMU and KVM technologies.

Let us go back to the connection URI we passed with the libvirt client virsh. As we are concentrating on QEMU/KVM virtualization, the connection URI, which has been passed from the client has, strings of "QEMU", or will have the following skeleton when passed to libvirt to open a connection:

- `qemu://xxxx/system`
- `qemu://xxxx/session`

The former (`qemu://xxxx/system`) basically requests to connect locally as the 'root' to the daemon supervising QEMU and KVM domains or virtual machines. However, the latter (`qemu://xxxx/session`) requests to connect locally as a "normal user" to its own set of QEMU and KVM domains. Previously, I mentioned that libvirt also supports remote connections; luckily, to achieve this functionality, it is only required to have a small change in the connection URI. That said, it can establish a remote connection by changing some strings in the connection URI. For example, the common format for the connection URI is as follows:

```
driver[+transport]://[username@][hostname][:port]/[path]
[?extraparameters]
```

A simple command line example of a `virsh` binary for a remote connection would be as follows:

```
$ virsh --connect qemu+ssh://root@remoteserver.yourdomain.com/system list
--all
```

As shown in the `virsh` command example (`qemu+ssh://root@remoteserver.yourdomain.com/system`), remote URIs are formed by taking ordinary local URIs and adding a hostname and/or transport name:

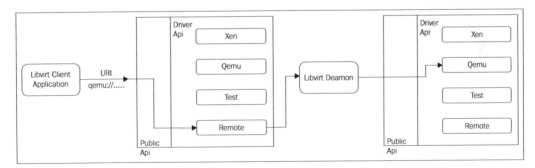

The preceding figure shows the remote connection established to talk to the libvirt running on a remote or other system. The details of the driver API or driver implementation follow later. When using a URI scheme of "remote", it will tell the remote libvirtd server to probe for the optimal hypervisor driver. The following sections will provide some details about "remote" drivers. Refer to the following URLs for more details on what options can be given for a remote connection URI:

- http://libvirt.org/remote.html#Remote_URI_reference
- http://libvirt.org/remote.html

To understand how libvirt really works, let us look at the code. This section contains some developer-oriented details; if you are not at all keen to know about how libvirt works internally, you can skip this part. If you are in half a mind, go through it!

Internal workings of libvirt

Let me give some details about the following libvirt source code. If you really want to know more about the implementation, it is good to poke around in the libvirt source code. Get the libvirt source code from the libvirt Git repository:

```
[root@node]# git clone git://libvirt.org/libvirt.git
```

Once you clone the repo, you can see the following hierarchy of files in the repo:

```
[humble-lap ]$ ls
AUTHORS.in        configure.ac      libvirt-admin.pc.in      po
autobuild.sh      COPYING           libvirt-lxc.pc.in        README
autogen.sh        COPYING.LESSER    libvirt.pc.in            README-hacking
bootstrap         daemon            libvirt-qemu.pc.in       run.in
bootstrap.conf    docs              libvirt.spec.in          src
build-aux         examples          m4                       tests
cfg.mk            gnulib            Makefile.am              TODO
ChangeLog-old     HACKING           Makefile.nonreentrant    tools
config-post.h     include          mingw-libvirt.spec.in
[humble-lap ]$
```

libvirt code is based on the C programming language; however, libvirt has language bindings in different languages such as C#, Java, OCaml, Perl, PHP, Python, Ruby, and so on. For more details on these bindings, please refer to: https://libvirt.org/bindings.html. The main (and few) directories in the source code are docs, daemon, src, and so on. The libvirt project is well documented and the documentation is available in the source code repo and also at http://libvirt.org.

Let us move on. If we look at the libvirt internals, we can see libvirt operates or starts the connection path based on driver modes. That said, different types or levels of driver are part of the libvirt implementation. At the time of initialization, these drivers are registered with libvirt. If you are confused by the term "drivers", they are basic building blocks for libvirt functionality to support the capability to handle specific hypervisor driver calls. These drivers are discovered and registration happens at the time of connection processing, as you can see at `http://libvirt.org/api.html`:

> *"Each driver has a registration API, which loads up the driver specific function references for the libvirt APIs to call. The following is a simplistic view of the hypervisor driver mechanism. Consider the stacked list of drivers as a series of modules that can be plugged into the architecture depending on how libvirt is configured to be built"*

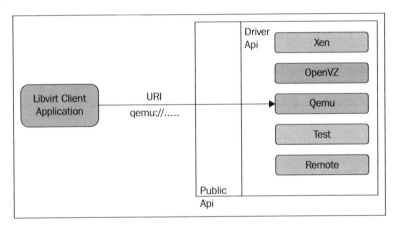

As in the preceding figure, there is a **Public API** that is exposed to the outside world. Depending on the connection URI (for example: `virsh --connect QEMU://xxxx/system`) passed by the clients, when initializing the library, this Public API delegates its implementation to one or more internal drivers. Yes, there are different categories of driver implementations in libvirt. For example, there are `hypervisor`, `interface`, `network`, `nodeDevice`, `nwfilter`, `secret`, `storage`, and so on. Refer to `driver.h` inside the libvirt source code to know about the driver data structures and other functions associated with the different drivers.

For example:

```
struct _virConnectDriver {
    virHypervisorDriverPtr hypervisorDriver;
    virInterfaceDriverPtr interfaceDriver;
    virNetworkDriverPtr networkDriver;
```

```
virNodeDeviceDriverPtr nodeDeviceDriver;
virNWFilterDriverPtr nwfilterDriver;
virSecretDriverPtr secretDriver;
virStorageDriverPtr storageDriver;
 };
```

`struct` fields are self-explanatory and convey which type of driver is represented by each of the field members. As you might have assumed, one of the important or main drivers is `hypervisor driver`, which is the driver implementation of different hypervisors supported by libvirt. The drivers are categorized as `primary` and `secondary` drivers. The hypervisor driver is a primary-level driver and there is always a hypervisor driver active. If the libvirt daemon is available, usually a network and storage driver are active as well. So, the libvirt code base is well segregated and for each supported hypervisor there is a driver implementation (or there should be). The following list gives us some idea about the hypervisors supported with libvirt. In other words, hypervisor-level driver implementations exist for the following hypervisors (`reference#` `README` and the libvirt source code):

- `bhyve`: The BSD hypervisor
- `esx/`: VMware ESX and GSX support using vSphere API over SOAP
- `hyperv/`: Microsoft Hyper-V support using WinRM
- `lxc/`: Linux Native Containers
- `openvz/`: OpenVZ containers using CLI tools
- `phyp/`: IBM Power Hypervisor using CLI tools over SSH
- `qemu/`: QEMU / KVM using QEMU CLI/monitor
- `remote/`: Generic libvirt native RPC client
- `test/`: A "mock" driver for testing
- `uml/`: User Mode Linux
- `vbox/`: Virtual Box using the native API
- `vmware/`: VMware Workstation and Player using the vmrun tool
- `xen/`: Xen using hypercalls, XenD SEXPR, and XenStore
- `xenapi`: Xen using libxenserver

Previously, I mentioned that there are secondary-level drivers as well. Not all, but some secondary drivers (see the following) are shared by several hypervisors. That said, currently these secondary drivers are used by hypervisors such as the LXC, OpenVZ, QEMU, UML, and Xen drivers. The ESX, Hyper-V, Power Hypervisor, Remote, Test, and VirtualBox drivers all implement secondary drivers directly.

Examples of secondary-level drivers include:

- `cpu/`: CPU feature management
- `interface/`: Host network interface management
- `network/`: Virtual NAT networking
- `nwfilter/`: Network traffic filtering rules
- `node_device/`: Host device enumeration
- `secret/`: Secret management
- `security/`: Mandatory access control drivers
- `storage/`: Storage management drivers

Node resource operations, which are needed for the management and provisioning of virtual machines (also known as guest domains), are also in the scope of the libvirt API. The secondary drivers are consumed to perform these operations, such as interface setup, firewall rules, storage management, and general provisioning of APIs. From `https://libvirt.org/api.html`:

> *"OnDevice the application obtains a virConnectPtr connection to the hypervisor it can then use it to manage the hypervisor's available domains and related virtualization resources, such as storage and networking. All those are exposed as first class objects and connected to the hypervisor connection (and the node or cluster where it is available)".*

The following figure shows the five main objects exported by the API and the connections between them:

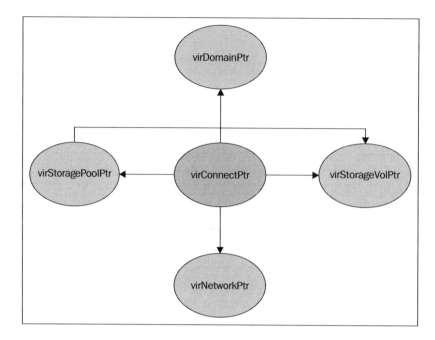

I will give some details about the main objects available in the libvirt code. Most functions inside libvirt make use of these objects for their operations:

- virConnectPtr: As we discussed earlier, libvirt has to connect to a hypervisor and act. The connection to the hypervisor has been represented as this object. This object is one of the core objects in libvirt's API.

- virDomainPtr: VMs or Guest systems are generally referred to as domains in libvirt code. virDomainPtr represents an object to an active/defined domain/VM.

- virStorageVolPtr: There are different storage volumes, exposed to the domains/guest systems. virStorageVolPtr generally represen20t one of the volumes.

- virStoragePoolPtr: The exported storage volumes are part of one of the storage pools. This object represents one of the storage pools.

- virNetworkPtr: In libvirt, we can define different networks. A single virtual network (active/defined status) is represented by the virNetworkPtr object.

You should now have some idea about the internal structure of libvirt
implementations; this can be expanded further:

```
[humble-lap ]$ cd src/qemu/
[humble-lap ]$ ls
EVENTHANDLERS.txt        qemu_cgroup.h      qemu_hostdev.h        qemu_monitor_json.h
libvirtd_qemu.aug        qemu_command.c     qemu_hotplug.c        qemu_monitor_text.c
MIGRATION.txt            qemu_command.h     qemu_hotplug.h        qemu_monitor_text.h
qemu_agent.c             qemu.conf          qemu_hotplugpriv.h    qemu_process.c
qemu_agent.h             qemu_conf.c        qemu_interface.c      qemu_process.h
qemu_blockjob.c          qemu_conf.h        qemu_interface.h      qemu_processpriv.h
qemu_blockjob.h          qemu_domain.c      qemu_migration.c      test_libvirtd_qemu.aug.in
qemu_capabilities.c      qemu_domain.h      qemu_migration.h      THREADS.txt
qemu_capabilities.h      qemu_driver.c      qemu_monitor.c
qemu_capspriv.h          qemu_driver.h      qemu_monitor.h
qemu_cgroup.c            qemu_hostdev.c     qemu_monitor_json.c
[humble-lap ]$
```

On different hypervisor driver implementation our area of interest is on QEMU/
KVM. So, let's explore it further. Inside the `src` directory of the libvirt source code
repository, there is a directory for QEMU hypervisor driver implementation code.

I would say, pay some attention to the source files, such as `qemu_driver.c`,
which carries core driver methods for managing QEMU guests.

For example:

```
static virDrvOpenStatus qemuConnectOpen(virConnectPtr conn,
                              virConnectAuthPtr auth ATTRIBUTE_UNUSED,
                              unsigned int flags
```

libvirt makes use of different driver codes to probe the underlying hypervisor/
emulator. In the context of this book, the component of libvirt responsible for finding
out the QEMU/KVM presence is the QEMU driver code. This driver probes for the
`qemu-kvm` binary and `/dev/kvm` device node to confirm the KVM fully-virtualized
hardware-accelerated guests are available. If these are not available, the possibility
of a QEMU emulator (without KVM) is verified with the presence of binaries such
as `qemu`, `qemu-system-x86_64`, `qemu-system-mips`, `qemu-system-microblaze`,
and so on.

The validation can be seen in `qemu-capabilities.c`:

```
from   (qemu-capabilities.c)


static int virQEMUCapsInitGuest ( ..,   .. ,   virArch hostarch,
virArch guestarch)
{
…..

binary = virQEMUCapsFindBinaryForArch (hostarch, guestarch);

   /* qemu-kvm/kvm binaries can only be used if
   *   - host & guest arches match
   *   - hostarch is x86_64 and guest arch is i686 (needs -cpu qemu32)
   *   - hostarch is aarch64 and guest arch is armv7l (needs -cpu
aarch64=off)
   *   - hostarch and guestarch are both ppc64*    */
native_kvm = (hostarch == guestarch);
x86_32on64_kvm = (hostarch == VIR_ARCH_X86_64 &&  guestarch == VIR_
ARCH_I686);


arm_32on64_kvm = (hostarch == VIR_ARCH_AARCH64 && guestarch== VIR_
ARCH_ARMV7L);


ppc64_kvm = (ARCH_IS_PPC64(hostarch) && ARCH_IS_PPC64(guestarch));


if (native_kvm || x86_32on64_kvm || arm_32on64_kvm || ppc64_kvm) {

    const char *kvmbins[] = {
        "/usr/libexec/qemu-kvm", /* RHEL */
        "qemu-kvm", /* Fedora */
        "kvm", /* Debian/Ubuntu */    …};
………
kvmbin = virFindFileInPath(kvmbins[i]);
…….
virQEMUCapsInitGuestFromBinary (caps, binary, qemubinCaps, kvmbin, kvm
binCaps,guestarch);
……
}
```

Then, KVM enablement is performed as shown in the following:

```
int virQEMUCapsInitGuestFromBinary(..., *binary, qemubinCaps, *kvmbin,
kvmbinCaps, guestarch)
{
…….. . .
```

```
    if (virFileExists("/dev/kvm") && (virQEMUCapsGet(qemubinCaps, QEMU_
CAPS_KVM) ||
        virQEMUCapsGet(qemubinCaps, QEMU_CAPS_ENABLE_KVM) ||
kvmbin))
        haskvm = true;
```

Even though it's self-explanatory, libvirt's QEMU driver is looking for different binaries in different distributions and in different paths—for example, qemu-kvm in RHEL/Fedora. Also it finds a suitable QEMU binary based on the architecture combination of both host and guest. If both the QEMU binary and KVM presence are found, then KVM is fully virtualized and hardware-accelerated guests will be available. It's also libvirt's responsibility to form the entire command line argument for the QEMU-KVM process. Finally, after forming the entire command (qemu-command.c) line arguments and inputs, libvirt calls exec() to create a QEMU-KVM process:

```
util/vircommand.c
static int virExec(virCommandPtr cmd) {
......
  if (cmd->env)
    execve(binary, cmd->args, cmd->env);
  else
    execv(binary, cmd->args);
```

In KVM land, there is a misconception that libvirt directly uses the device file (/dev/kvm) exposed by KVM kernel modules, and instructs KVM to do the virtualization via the different ioctls() available with KVM. This is indeed a misconception! As mentioned earlier, libvirt spawns the QEMU-KVM process and QEMU talks to the KVM kernel modules. In short, QEMU talks to the KVM via different ioctl() to the /dev/kvm device file exposed by the KVM kernel module. To create a VM (for example: virsh create), all libvirt does is to spawn a QEMU process, which in turns creates the virtual machine. Please note that a separate QEMU-KVM process is launched for each virtual machine by libvirtd. The properties of virtual machines (the number of CPUs, memory size, and I/O device configuration) are defined in separate XML files, which are located in the /etc/libvirt/qemu directory. libvirtd uses the details from these XML files to derive the argument list that is passed to the QEMU-KVM process. The libvirt clients issue requests via the AF_UNIX socket /var/run/libvirt/libvirt-sock on which libvirtd is listening.

Well, we discussed libvirt and its connection to QEMU/KVM; however, users/ developers periodically pose this question: Why do we need libvirt and what advantages does it bring? I would say this is best answered by Daniel P. Berrange, one of the core maintainers of libvirt, here: `https://www.berrange.com/ posts/2011/06/07/what-benefits-does-libvirt-offer-to-developers-targetting-QEMUKVM/`.

Time to think more about QEMU

Quick Emulator (QEMU) was written by Fabrice Bellard (creator of FFmpeg), and is free software and mainly licensed under GNU **General Public License (GPL)**.

QEMU is a generic and open source machine emulator and virtualizer. When used as a machine emulator, QEMU can run OSs and programs made for one machine (for example: an ARM board) on a different machine (for example: your own PC). By using dynamic translation, it achieves very good performance (see `www.QEMU.org`).

Let me rephrase the preceding paragraph and give a more specific explanation. QEMU is actually a hosted hypervisor/VMM that performs hardware virtualization. Are you confused? If yes, don't worry. You will get a better picture by the end of this chapter, especially when you go through each of the interrelated components and correlate the entire path used here to perform virtualization. QEMU can act as an Emulator or Virtualizer:

- **Qemu as an Emulator**: In *Chapter 1, Understanding Linux Virtualization*, we briefly discussed binary translation. When QEMU operates as an emulator, it is capable of running operating systems/programs made for one machine type on a different machine type. How is this possible? It just uses binary translation methods. In this mode, QEMU emulates CPUs through dynamic binary translation techniques and provides a set of device models. Thus, it is enabled to run different unmodified guest operating systems with different architectures. The binary translation is needed here because the guest code has to be executed in the host CPU. The binary translator that does this job is known as **Tiny Code Generator (TCG)**; it's a Just-In-Time compiler. It transforms the binary code written for a given processor to another one (for example: ARM in X86):

"The Tiny Code Generator (TCG) aims to remove the shortcoming of relying on a particular version of GCC or any compiler, instead incorporating the compiler (code generator) into other tasks performed by QEMU at run time. The whole translation task thus consists of two parts: blocks of target code (TBs) being rewritten in TCG ops - a kind of machine-independent intermediate notation, and subsequently this notation being compiled for the host's architecture by TCG. Optional optimisation passes are performed between them.

TCG requires dedicated code written to support every architecture it runs on."

(TCG info from Wikipedia `https://en.wikipedia.org/wiki/QEMU#Tiny_Code_Generator`)

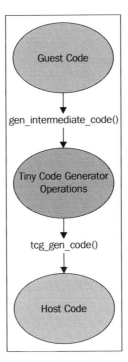

Tiny Code Generator in QEMU

- **Qemu as a virtualizer**: This is the mode where QEMU executes the guest code directly on the host CPU, thus achieving native performance. For example, when working under Xen/KVM hypervisors, QEMU can operate in this mode. If KVM is the underlying hypervisor, QEMU can virtualize embedded guests such as Power PC, S390, x86, and so on. In short, QEMU is capable of running without KVM, using the previously mentioned binary translation method. This execution will be slower when compared to the hardware-accelerated virtualization enabled by KVM. In any mode (either as a virtualizer or emulator), QEMU *DOES NOT ONLY* emulate the processor, it also emulates different peripherals, such as disks, networks, VGA, PCI, serial and parallel ports, USB, and so on. Apart from this I/O device emulation, when working with KVM, QEMU-KVM creates and initializes virtual machines. It also initializes different posix threads for each virtual CPU (refer to the following figure) of a guest. Also, it provides a framework to emulate the virtual machine's physical address space within the user mode address space of QEMU-KVM:

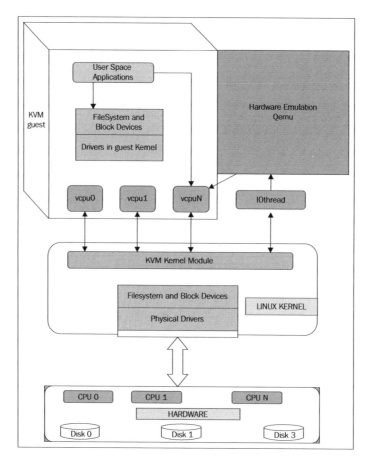

To execute the guest code in the physical CPU, QEMU makes use of `posix` threads. That said, the guest virtual CPUs are executed in the host kernel as `posix` threads. This itself brings lots of advantages, as these are just some processes for the host kernel in a high-level view. From another angle, the user space part of the KVM hypervisor is provided by QEMU. QEMU runs the guest code via the KVM kernel module. When working with KVM, QEMU also does I/O emulation, I/O device setup, live migration, and so on.

QEMU opens the device file (`/dev/kvm`) exposed by the KVM kernel module and executes `ioctls()` on it. Please refer to the next section on KVM to know more about these `ioctls()`. To conclude, KVM makes use of QEMU to become a complete hypervisor, and KVM is an accelerator or enabler of the hardware virtualization extensions (VMX or SVM) provided by the processor to be tightly coupled with the CPU architecture. Indirectly, this conveys that virtual systems also have to use the same architecture to make use of hardware virtualization extensions/capabilities. Once it is enabled, it will definitely give better performance than other techniques such as binary translation.

Qemu – KVM internals

Before we start looking into QEMU internals, let's clone the QEMU git repository:

```
#git clone git://git.qemu-project.org/qemu.git
```

Once it's cloned, you can see a hierarchy of files inside the repo, as shown in the following screenshot:

```
[ humble-lap ]$ ls
accel.c              fsdev                qdev-monitor.c          target-cris
aio-posix.c          gdbstub.c            qdict-test-data.txt     target-i386
aio-win32.c          gdb-xml              qemu-bridge-helper.c    target-lm32
arch_init.c          HACKING              qemu-char.c             target-m68k
async.c              hmp.c                qemu-doc.texi           target-microblaze
audio                hmp-commands.hx      qemu-ga.texi            target-mips
backends             hmp-commands-info.hx qemu-img.c              target-moxie
balloon.c            hmp.h                qemu-img-cmds.hx         target-openrisc
block                hw                   qemu-img.texi           target-ppc
block.c              include              qemu-io.c               target-s390x
blockdev.c           iohandler.c          qemu-io-cmds.c          target-sh4
blockdev-nbd.c       ioport.c             qemu-log.c              target-sparc
blockjob.c           iothread.c           qemu-nbd.c              target-tilegx
bootdevice.c         kvm-all.c            qemu-nbd.texi           target-tricore
bsd-user             kvm-stub.c           qemu.nsi                target-unicore32
bt-host.c            libdecnumber         qemu-options.h          target-xtensa
bt-vhci.c            LICENSE              qemu-options.hx         tcg
Changelog            linux-headers        qemu-options-wrapper.h  tcg-runtime.c
CODING_STYLE         linux-user           qemu.sasl               tci.c
configure            main-loop.c          qemu-seccomp.c          tests
contrib              MAINTAINERS          qemu-tech.texi          thread-pool.c
COPYING              Makefile             qemu-timer.c            thunk.c
COPYING.LIB          Makefile.objs        qga                     tpm.c
cpu-exec.c           Makefile.target      qjson.c                 trace
cpu-exec-common.c    memory.c             qmp.c                   trace-events
cpus.c               memory_mapping.c     qmp-commands.hx         translate-all.c
cputlb.c             migration            qobject                 translate-all.h
crypto               module-common.c      qom                     translate-common.c
cscope.out           monitor.c            qtest.c                 ui
default-configs      nbd.c                README                  user-exec.c
device-hotplug.c     net                  replay                  util
device_tree.c        numa.c               roms                    VERSION
disas                os-posix.c           rules.mak               version.rc
disas.c              os-win32.c           scripts                 vl.c
dma-helpers.c        page_cache.c         slirp                   xen-common.c
docs                 pc-bios              softmmu_template.h       xen-common-stub.c
dtc                  pixman               spice-qemu-char.c        xen-hvm.c
dump.c               po                   stubs                   xen-hvm-stub.c
exec.c               qapi                 target-alpha             xen-mapcache.c
fpu                  qapi-schema.json     target-arm
```

Some important data structures and `ioctls()` make up the QEMU userspace and KVM kernel space. Some of the important data structures are KVMState, CPU{X86} State, MachineState, and so on. Before we further explore the internals, I would like to point out that covering them in detail is beyond the scope of this book; however, I will give enough pointers to understand what is happening under the hood and give additional references for further explanation.

Data structures

In this section, we will discuss some of the important data structures of QEMU. The KVMState structure contains important file descriptors of VM representation in QEMU. For example it contains the virtual machine file descriptor, as shown in the following code:

```
struct KVMState        ( kvm-all.c )
{          .....
  int fd;
  int vmfd;
  int coalesced_mmio;
    struct kvm_coalesced_mmio_ring *coalesced_mmio_ring; ....}
```

QEMU-KVM maintains a list of CPUX86State structures, one structure for each virtual CPU. The content of general purpose registers (as well as RSP and RIP) is part of the CPUX86State:

```
struct CPUState {
.....
  int nr_cores;
  int nr_threads;
  ...
  int kvm_fd;
      ....
  struct KVMState *kvm_state;
  struct kvm_run *kvm_run
```

```
typedef struct CPUX86State (
target-i386/cpu.h )
  {
  /* standard registers */
  target_ulong regs[CPU_NB_REGS];
....
  uint64_t system_time_msr;
  uint64_t wall_clock_msr;
.......
  /* exception/interrupt handling */
  int error_code;
  int exception_is_int;
.....
  }
```

Various `ioctls()` exist: `kvm_ioctl()`, `kvm_vm_ioctl()`, `kvm_vcpu_ioctl()`, `kvm_device_ioctl()`, and so on. For function definitions, please visit `kvm-all.c` inside the QEMU source code repo. These `ioctls()` fundamentally map to the system KVM level, VM level, and vCPU level. These `ioctls()` are analogous to the `ioctls()` categorized by KVM. We will discuss this when we dig further into KVM internals. To get access to these `ioctls()` exposed by the KVM kernel module, QEMU-KVM has to open `/dev/kvm`, and the resulting file descriptor is stored in `KVMState->fd`:

- `kvm_ioctl()`: These `ioctl()`s mainly execute on the KVMState->fd parameter, where KVMState->fd carries the file descriptor obtained by opening `/dev/kvm`.

  For example:

  ```
  kvm_ioctl(s, KVM_CHECK_EXTENSION, extension);
  kvm_ioctl(s, KVM_CREATE_VM, type);
  ```

- `kvm_vm_ioctl()`: These `ioctl()`s mainly execute on the KVMState->vmfd parameter.

  For example:

  ```
  kvm_vm_ioctl(s, KVM_CREATE_VCPU, (void *)kvm_arch_vcpu_id(cpu));
  kvm_vm_ioctl(s, KVM_SET_USER_MEMORY_REGION, &mem);
  ```

- `kvm_vcpu_ioctl()`: These `ioctl()`s mainly execute on the CPUState->kvm_fd parameter, which is a vCPU file descriptor for KVM.

  For example:

  ```
  kvm_vcpu_ioctl(cpu, KVM_RUN, 0);
  ```

- `kvm_device_ioctl()`: These `ioctl()`s mainly execute on the device fd parameter.

  For example:

  ```
  kvm_device_ioctl(dev_fd, KVM_HAS_DEVICE_ATTR, &attribute) ? 0 : 1;
  ```

`kvm-all.c` is one of the important source files when considering QEMU KVM communication.

Now let us move on and see how a virtual machine and vCPUs are created and initialized by a QEMU in the context of KVM virtualization.

kvm_init() is the function that opens the KVM device file as shown in the following and it also fills fd [1] and vmfd [2] of KVMState:

```
static int kvm_init(MachineState *ms)
{
.....
KVMState *s;
     s = KVM_STATE(ms->accelerator);

     ...
     s->vmfd = -1;
     s->fd = qemu_open("/dev/kvm", O_RDWR);        --->[1]
   ..
   do {
        ret = kvm_ioctl(s, KVM_CREATE_VM, type); --->[2]
      } while (ret == -EINTR);
   s->vmfd = ret;
   ret = kvm_arch_init(ms, s);     ---> ( target-i386/kvm.c: )
  }
```

As you can see in the preceding code, the ioctl() with the KVM_CREATE_VM argument will return vmfd. Once QEMU has fd and vmfd, one more file descriptor has to be filled, which is just kvm_fd or vcpu fd. Let us see how this is filled by QEMU:

```
main() ->
         -> cpu_init(cpu_model);
    [#define cpu_init(cpu_model) CPU(cpu_x86_init(cpu_model)) ]
         ->cpu_x86_create()
         ->qemu_init_vcpu
         ->qemu_kvm_start_vcpu()
         ->qemu_thread_create
         ->qemu_kvm_cpu_thread_fn()
         ->kvm_init_vcpu(CPUState *cpu)
int kvm_init_vcpu(CPUState *cpu)
{
   KVMState *s = kvm_state;
   ret = kvm_vm_ioctl(s, KVM_CREATE_VCPU, (void *)kvm_arch_vcpu_id(cpu));
```

```
    cpu->kvm_fd = ret;    --->    [vCPU fd]
    ..
    mmap_size = kvm_ioctl(s, KVM_GET_VCPU_MMAP_SIZE, 0);
    cpu->kvm_run = mmap(NULL, mmap_size, PROT_READ | PROT_WRITE,
    MAP_SHARED,  cpu->kvm_fd, 0);   [3]
...
    ret = kvm_arch_init_vcpu(cpu);    [target-i386/kvm.c]
.....
}
```

Some of the memory pages are shared between the QEMU-KVM process and the KVM kernel modules. You can see such a mapping in the kvm_init_vcpu() function. That said, two host memory pages per vCPU make a channel for communication between the QEMU user space process and the KVM kernel modules: kvm_run and pio_data. Also understand that, during the execution of these ioctls() that return the preceding fds, the Linux kernel allocates a file structure and related anonymous nodes. We will discuss the kernel part later when discussing KVM.

We have seen that vCPUs are posix threads created by QEMU-KVM. To run guest code, these vCPU threads execute an ioctl() with KVM_RUN as its argument, as shown in the following code:

```
int kvm_cpu_exec(CPUState *cpu) {
    struct kvm_run *run = cpu->kvm_run;
    run_ret = kvm_vcpu_ioctl(cpu, KVM_RUN, 0);
    ...

}
```

The same function kvm_cpu_exec() also defines the actions that need to be taken when the control comes back to the QEMU-KVM user space from KVM with a VM exit. Even though we will discuss later on how KVM and QEMU communicate with each other to perform an operation on behalf of the guest, let me touch upon this here. KVM is an enabler of hardware extensions provided by vendors such as Intel and AMD with their virtualization extensions such as SVM and VMX. These extensions are used by the KVM to directly execute the guest code on host CPUs. However if there is an event, for example, as part of an operation guest kernel code access hardware device register which is emulated by the QEMU, KVM has to exit back to QEMU and pass control. Then QEMU can emulate the outcome of the operation. There are different exit reasons, as shown in the following code:

```
    switch (run->exit_reason) {
     case KVM_EXIT_IO:
             DPRINTF("handle_io\n");

     case KVM_EXIT_MMIO:
             DPRINTF("handle_mmio\n");

     case KVM_EXIT_IRQ_WINDOW_OPEN:
             DPRINTF("irq_window_open\n");

     case KVM_EXIT_SHUTDOWN:
             DPRINTF("shutdown\n");
     case KVM_EXIT_UNKNOWN:
 ...
     case KVM_EXIT_INTERNAL_ERROR:

 ...

     case KVM_EXIT_SYSTEM_EVENT:
             switch (run->system_event.type) {
                case KVM_SYSTEM_EVENT_SHUTDOWN:
                case KVM_SYSTEM_EVENT_RESET:
                case KVM_SYSTEM_EVENT_CRASH:
```

Threading models in QEMU

QEMU-KVM is a multithreaded, event-driven (with a big lock) application.
The important threads are:

- Main thread
- Worker threads for virtual disk I/O backend
- One thread for each virtual CPU

For each and every VM, there is a QEMU process running in the host system. If the guest system is shut down this process will be destroyed/exited. Apart from vCPU threads, there are dedicated iothreads running a select (2) event loop to process I/O such as network packets and disk I/O completion. IO threads are also spawned by QEMU. In short, the situation will look like this:

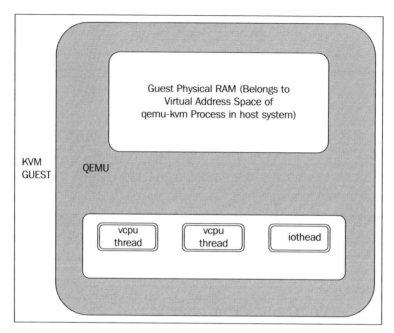

KVM Guest

Before we discuss this further, there is always a question about the physical memory of guest systems: Where is it located? Here is the deal: the guest RAM is assigned inside the QEMU process's virtual address space, as shown in the preceding figure. That said, the physical RAM of the guest is inside the QEMU Process Address space.

 More details about threading can be fetched from the threading model at: `blog.vmsplice.net/2011/03/qemu-internals-overall-architecutre-and-html?m=1`.

The event loop thread is also called `iothread`. Event loops are used for timers, file descriptor monitoring, and so on. `main_loop_wait()` is the QEMU main event loop thread, which is defined as shown in the following. This main event loop thread is responsible for, main loop services include file descriptor callbacks, bottom halves, and timers (defined in `qemu-timer.h`). Bottom halves are similar to timers that execute immediately, but have a lower overhead, and scheduling them is wait-free, thread-safe, and signal-safe.

File: `vl.c`

```
static void main_loop(void)  {
  bool nonblocking;
  int last_io = 0;
...
  do {
      nonblocking = !kvm_enabled() && !xen_enabled() && last_io > 0;
....
      last_io = main_loop_wait(nonblocking);
....
  } while (!main_loop_should_exit());
}
```

Before we leave the QEMU code base, I would like to point out that there are mainly two parts to device codes. For example, the directory `hw/block/` contains the host side of the block device code, and `hw/block/` contains the code for device emulation.

KVM in action

Time to discuss KVM! The fundamentals KVM developers followed were the same as the Linux kernel: "Don't reinvent the wheel". That said, they didn't try to change the kernel code to make a hypervisor; rather, the code was developed by following the new hardware assistance in virtualization (VMX and SVM) from hardware vendors as a loadable kernel module. There is a common kernel module called **kvm.ko** and there are hardware-based kernel modules such as **kvm-intel.ko** (Intel-based systems) or **kvm-amd.ko** (AMD-based systems). Accordingly, KVM will load the kvm-intel.ko (if the vmx flag is present) or kvm-amd.ko (if the svm flag is present) modules. This turns the Linux kernel into a hypervisor, thus achieving virtualization. The KVM is developed by qumranet and it has been part of the Linux kernel since version 2.6.20. Later qumranet was acquired by Red Hat.

KVM exposes a device file called `/dev/kvm` to applications to make use of the `ioctls()` provided. QEMU makes use of this device file to talk with KVM and to create, initialize, and manage the kernel mode context of virtual machines. Previously, we mentioned that the QEMU-KVM user space hosts the virtual machine's physical address space within the user mode address space of QEMU-KVM, which includes memory-mapped I/O. KVM helps to achieve that. There are more things achieved with the help of KVM. Below are some of those.

- Emulation of certain I/O devices, for example (via "mmio") the per-CPU local APIC and the system-wide IOAPIC.

- Emulation of certain "privileged" (R/W of system registers CR0, CR3 and CR4) instructions.

- The facilitation to run guest code via VMENTRY and handling of "intercepted events" at VMEXIT.

- "Injection" of events such as virtual interrupts and page faults into the flow of execution of the virtual machine and so on are also achieved with the help of KVM.

Once again, let me say that KVM is not a hypervisor! Are you lost? OK, then let me rephrase that. The KVM or kernel-based virtual machine is not a full hypervisor; however, with the help of QEMU and emulators (a slightly modified QEMU for I/O device emulation and BIOS), it can become one. KVM needs hardware virtualization-capable processors to operate. Using these capabilities, KVM turns the standard Linux kernel into a hypervisor. When KVM runs virtual machines, every VM is a normal Linux process, which can obviously be scheduled to run on a CPU by the host kernel as with any other process present in the host kernel. In *Chapter 1, Understanding Linux Virtualization*, we discussed different CPU modes of execution. If you recollect, there is mainly a USER mode and a Kernel/Supervisor mode. KVM is a virtualization feature in the Linux kernel that lets a program such as QEMU safely execute guest code directly on the host CPU. This is only possible when the target architecture is supported by the host CPU.

However, KVM introduced one more mode called the guest mode! In nutshell, guest mode is the execution of guest system code. It can either run the guest user or the kernel code. With the support of virtualization-aware hardware, KVM virtualizes the process states, memory management, and so on.

With its hardware virtualization capabilities, the processor manages the processor states by **Virtual Machine Control Structure (VMCS)** and **Virtual Machine Control Block (VMCB)** for the host and guest operating systems, and it also manages the I/O and interrupts on behalf of the virtualized operating system. That said, with the introduction of this type of hardware, tasks such as CPU instruction interception, register read/write support, memory management support (**Extended Page Tables (EPT)** and NPT), interrupt handling support (APICv), IOMMU, and so on, came in.

KVM uses the standard Linux scheduler, memory management, and other services. In short, what KVM does is help the user space program to make use of hardware virtualization capabilities. Here, you can treat QEMU as a user space program as it's well-integrated for different use cases. When I say "hardware-accelerated virtualization", I am mainly referring to Intel VT-X and AMD-Vs SVM. Introducing Virtualization Technology processors brought an extra instruction set called Virtual Machine Extensions or VMX.

With Intel's VT-x, the VMM runs in "VMX root operation mode", while the guests (which are unmodified OSs) run in "VMX non-root operation mode". This VMX brings additional virtualization-specific instructions to the CPU such as VMPTRLD, VMPTRST, VMCLEAR, VMREAD, VMWRITE, VMCALL, VMLAUNCH, VMRESUME, VMXOFF, and VMXON. The virtualization mode (VMX) is turned on by VMXON and can be disabled by VMXOFF. To execute the guest code, one has to use VMLAUNCH/VMRESUME instructions and leave VMEXIT. But wait, leave what? It's from nonroot operation to root operation. Obviously, when we do this transition, some information needs to be saved so that it can be fetched later. Intel provides a structure to facilitate this transition called **Virtual Machine Control Structure (VMCS)**; this handles much of the virtualization management functionality. For example, in the case of VMEXIT, the exit reason will be recorded inside this structure. Now, how do we read or write from this structure? VMREAD and VMWRITE instructions are used to read or write to the fields of VMCS structure.

There is also a feature available from recent Intel processors that allows each guest to have its own page table to keep track of memory addresses. Without EPT, the hypervisor has to exit the virtual machine to perform address translations and this reduces performance. As we noticed in Intel's virtualization-based processors' operating modes, AMD's **Secure Virtual Machine (SVM)** also has a couple of operating modes, which are nothing but Host mode and Guest mode. As you would have assumed, the hypervisor runs in Host mode and the guests run in Guest mode. Obviously, when in Guest mode, some instructions can cause VMEXIT and are handled in a manner that is specific to the way Guest mode is entered. There should be an equivalent structure of VMCS here, and it is called **Virtual Machine Control Block (VMCB)**; as discussed earlier, it contains the reason of VMEXIT. AMD added eight new instruction opcodes to support SVM. For example, the VMRUN instruction starts the operation of a guest OS, the VMLOAD instruction loads the processor state from the VMCB, and the VMSAVE instruction saves the processor state to the VMCB. Also, to improve the performance of Memory Management Unit, AMD introduced something called NPT (Nested Paging), which is similar to EPT in Intel.

KVM APIs

As mentioned earlier, there are three main types of ioctl()s.

Three sets of ioctl make up the KVM API. The KVM API is a set of ioctls that are issued to control various aspects of a virtual machine. These ioctls belong to three classes:

- System ioctls: These query and set global attributes, which affect the whole KVM subsystem. In addition, a system ioctl is used to create virtual machines.

- VM ioctls: These query and set attributes that affect an entire virtual machine—for example, memory layout. In addition, a VM ioctl is used to create virtual CPUs (vCPUs). It runs VM ioctls from the same process (address space) that was used to create the VM.

- Vcpu ioctls: These query and set attributes that control the operation of a single virtual CPU. They run vCPU ioctls from the same thread that was used to create the vCPU.

To know more about the `ioctls()` exposed by KVM and the `ioctl()`s that belong to a particular group of fd, please refer to KVM.h:

For example:

```
/*  ioctls for /dev/kvm fds: */
#define KVM_GET_API_VERSION      _IO(KVMIO,    0x00)
#define KVM_CREATE_VM            _IO(KVMIO,    0x01) /* returns a VM fd
*/
…..

/*  ioctls for VM fds */
#define KVM_SET_MEMORY_REGION    _IOW(KVMIO,   0x40, struct kvm_memory_
region)
#define KVM_CREATE_VCPU          _IO(KVMIO,    0x41)
…

/* ioctls for vcpu fds  */
#define KVM_RUN                   _IO(KVMIO,    0x80)
#define KVM_GET_REGS              _IOR(KVMIO,   0x81, struct kvm_regs)
#define KVM_SET_REGS              _IOW(KVMIO,   0x82, struct kvm_regs)
```

Anonymous inodes and file structures

Previously, when we discussed QEMU, we said the Linux kernel allocates file structures and sets its f_ops and anonymous inodes. Let's look into the kvm-main.c file:

```
static struct file_operations kvm_chardev_ops = {
        .unlocked_ioctl = kvm_dev_ioctl,
        .compat_ioctl   = kvm_dev_ioctl,
        .llseek         = noop_llseek,
};
  kvm_dev_ioctl ()
     switch (ioctl) {
          case KVM_GET_API_VERSION:
              if (arg)
                      goto out;
              r = KVM_API_VERSION;
              break;
          case KVM_CREATE_VM:
```

```
             r = kvm_dev_ioctl_create_vm(arg);
             break;
         case KVM_CHECK_EXTENSION:
             r = kvm_vm_ioctl_check_extension_generic(NULL, arg);
             break;
         case KVM_GET_VCPU_MMAP_SIZE:
     .    ..…
   }
```

As such as `kvm_chardev_fops`, **there exist** `kvm_vm_fops` and `kvm_vcpu_fops`:

```
static struct file_operations kvm_vm_fops = {
        .release        = kvm_vm_release,
        .unlocked_ioctl = kvm_vm_ioctl,
.…..

        .llseek         = noop_llseek,
};
static struct file_operations kvm_vcpu_fops = {
        .release        = kvm_vcpu_release,
        .unlocked_ioctl = kvm_vcpu_ioctl,
.…

        .mmap           = kvm_vcpu_mmap,
        .llseek         = noop_llseek,
};
```

An inode allocation may be seen as follows:

```
        anon_inode_getfd("kvm-vcpu", &kvm_vcpu_fops, vcpu, O_RDWR | O_
CLOEXEC);
```

Data structures

From the perspective of the KVM kernel modules, each virtual machine is represented by a `kvm` structure:

```
include/linux/kvm_host.h :

struct kvm {
   ...
        struct mm_struct *mm; /* userspace tied to this vm */
           ...
        struct kvm_vcpu *vcpus[KVM_MAX_VCPUS];
           ....
```

```
        struct kvm_io_bus *buses[KVM_NR_BUSES];
....
        struct kvm_coalesced_mmio_ring *coalesced_mmio_ring;
.....
}
```

As you can see in the preceding code, the kvm structure contains an array of pointers to kvm_vcpu structures, which are the counterparts of the CPUX86State structures in the QEMU-KVM user space. A kvm_vcpu structure consists of a common part and an x86 architecture-specific part, which includes the register content:

```
struct kvm_vcpu {
    . . .
        struct kvm *kvm;
        int cpu;
.....
        int vcpu_id;
.....
        struct kvm_run *run;
......
        struct kvm_vcpu_arch arch;
...
}
```

The x86 architecture-specific part of the kvm_vcpu structure contains fields to which the guest register state can be saved after a VM exit and from which the guest register state can be loaded before a VM entry:

arch/x86/include/asm/kvm_host.h
```
struct kvm_vcpu_arch {
..
        unsigned long regs[NR_VCPU_REGS];
        unsigned long cr0;
        unsigned long cr0_guest_owned_bits;
.....
struct kvm_lapic *apic;  /* kernel irqchip context */
    ..
struct kvm_mmu mmu;
..
struct kvm_pio_request pio;
void *pio_data;
..
/* emulate context */
```

```
    struct x86_emulate_ctxt emulate_ctxt;
    ...
    int (*complete_userspace_io)(struct kvm_vcpu *vcpu);
    ....
}
```

As you can see in the preceding code, kvm_vcpu has an associated kvm_run structure used for the communication (with pio_data) between the QEMU userspace and the KVM kernel module as mentioned earlier. For example, in the context of VMEXIT, to satisfy the emulation of virtual hardware access, KVM has to return to the QEMU user space process; KVM stores the information in the kvm_run structure for QEMU to fetch it:

/usr/include/linux/kvm.h:
```
/* for KVM_RUN, returned by mmap(vcpu_fd, offset=0) */
struct kvm_run {
        /* in */
        __u8 request_interrupt_window;
        __u8 padding1[7];

        /* out */
        __u32 exit_reason;
        __u8 ready_for_interrupt_injection;
        __u8 if_flag;
        __u8 padding2[2];

        union {
                /* KVM_EXIT_UNKNOWN */
                struct {
                        __u64 hardware_exit_reason;
                } hw;
                /* KVM_EXIT_FAIL_ENTRY */
                struct {
                        __u64 hardware_entry_failure_reason;
                } fail_entry;
                /* KVM_EXIT_EXCEPTION */
                struct {
                        __u32 exception;
                        __u32 error_code;
                } ex;
                /* KVM_EXIT_IO */
                struct {
#define KVM_EXIT_IO_IN  0
#define KVM_EXIT_IO_OUT 1
                        __u8 direction;
```

```
                        __u8 size; /* bytes */
                        __u16 port;
                        __u32 count;
                        __u64 data_offset; /* relative to kvm_run start
    */
                } io;
    ..
    }
```

The `kvm_run` struct is an important data structure; as you can see in the preceding code, the `union` contains many exit reasons, such as `KVM_EXIT_FAIL_ENTRY`, `KVM_EXIT_IO`, and so on.

When we discussed hardware virtualization extensions, we touched upon VMCS and VMCB. These are important data structures when we think about hardware-accelerated virtualization. These control blocks help especially in VMEXIT scenarios. Not every operation can be allowed for guests; at the same time, it's also difficult if the hypervisor does everything on behalf of the guest. Virtual machine control structures such as VMCS or VMCB control the behavior. Some operations are allowed for guests, such as changing some bits in shadowed control registers, but others are not. This clearly provides a fine-grained control over what guests are allowed to do and not do. VMCS control structures also provide control over interrupt delivery and exceptions. Previously, we said the exit reason of VMEXIT is recorded inside the VMCS; it also contains some data about it. For example, if a write access to a control register caused the exit, information about the source and destination registers is recorded there.

Let us see some of the important data structures before we dive into the vCPU execution flow.

The Intel-specific implementation is in `vmx.c` and the AMD-specific implementation is in `svm.c`, depending on the hardware we have. As you can see, the following `kvm_vcpu` is part of `vcpu_vmx`. The `kvm_vcpu` structure is mainly categorized as a common part and architecture specific part. The common part contains the data which is common to all supported architectures and architecture specific, for example, x86 architecture specific (guest's saved general purpose registers) part contains the data which is specific to a particular architecture. As discussed earlier, the `kvm_vcpus` `kvm_run` and `pio_data` are shared with the userspace.

The `vcpu_vmx` and `vcpu_svm` structures (mentioned next) have a `kvm_vcpu` structure, which consists of an x86-architecture-specific part (`struct 'kvm_vcpu_arch'`) and a common part and also, it points to the `vmcs` and `vmcb` structures accordingly:

vcpu_vmx structure	vcpu_svm structure
| ```
struct vcpu_vmx {
      struct kvm_vcpu
vcpu;
      ...
      struct loaded_vmcs
vmcs01;
      struct loaded_vmcs
*loaded_vmcs;
      ....
      }
``` | ```
struct vcpu_svm {
      struct kvm_vcpu vcpu;
      ...
      struct vmcb *vmcb;
....
      }
``` |

The `vcpu_vmx` or `vcpu_svm` structures are allocated by the following code path:

```
kvm_arch_vcpu_create()
       ->kvm_x86_ops->vcpu_create
                   ->vcpu_create()   [.vcpu_create = svm_create_vcpu,
.vcpu_create = vmx_create_vcpu,]
```

Please note that the VMCS or VMCB store guest configuration specifics such as machine control bits and processor register settings. I would suggest you examine the structure definitions from the source. These data structures are also used by the hypervisor to define events to monitor while the guest is executing. These events can be intercepted and these structures are in the host memory. At the time of VMEXIT, the guest state is saved in VMCS. As mentioned earlier the, VMREAD instruction reads the specified field from the VMCS and the VMWRITE instruction writes the specified field to the VMCS. Also note that there is one VMCS or VMCB per vCPU. These control structures are part of the host memory. The vCPU state is recorded in these control structures.

Execution flow of vCPU

Finally, we are into the vCPU execution flow which helps us to put everything together and understand what happens under the hood.

I hope you didn't forget that the QEMU creates a posix thread for a vCPU of the guest and `ioctl()`, which is responsible for running a CPU and has the KVM_RUN arg (`#define KVM_RUN_IO(KVMIO,    0x80)`). vCPU thread executes `ioctl(..,` `KVM_RUN,   ...)` to run the guest code. As these are posix threads, the Linux kernel can schedule these threads as with any other process/thread in the system.

Let us see how it all works:

```
Qemu-kvm User Space:
kvm_init_vcpu ()
    kvm_arch_init_vcpu()
        qemu_init_vcpu()
            qemu_kvm_start_vcpu()
                qemu_kvm_cpu_thread_fn()
    while (1) {
        if (cpu_can_run(cpu)) {
                r = kvm_cpu_exec(cpu);
                    }
        }
    }


kvm_cpu_exec (CPUState *cpu)
    ->          run_ret = kvm_vcpu_ioctl(cpu, KVM_RUN, 0);
```

According to the underlying architecture and hardware, different structures are initialized by the KVM kernel modules and one among them is `vmx_x86_ops/ svm_x86_ops` (owned by either the kvm-intel or kvm-amd module), as can be seen in the following. It defines different operations that need to be performed when the vCPU is in context. The KVM makes use of the `kvm_x86_ops` vector to point either of these vectors according to the KVM module (kvm-intel or kvm-amd) loaded for the hardware. The "run" pointer defines the function, which needs to be executed when the guest vCPU run is in action and `handle_exit` defines the actions needed to be performed at the time of a vmexit:

vcpu_vmx structure	vcpu_svm structure

`static struct kvm_x86_ops vmx_x86_ops = {`
 	
`...`
 	
`    .vcpu_create = vmx_create_vcpu,`
`    .run = vmx_vcpu_run,`
`    .handle_exit = vmx_handle_exit,`
`...`
`}`
	`static struct kvm_x86_ops svm_x86_ops = {`
	
	`    .vcpu_create = svm_create_vcpu,`
	`    .run = svm_vcpu_run,`
	`    .handle_exit = handle_exit,`
	`..`
	`}`

The run pointer points to vmx_vcpu_run or svm_vcpu_run accordingly. The functions svm_vcpu_run or vmx_vcpu_run do the job of saving KVM host registers, loading guest o/s registers, and SVM_VMLOAD instructions. We walked through the QEMU KVM user space code execution at the time of vcpu run, once it enters the kernel via syscall. Then, following the file operations structures, it calls kvm_vcpu_ioctl(); this defines the action to be taken according to the ioctl() it defines:

```
static long kvm_vcpu_ioctl(struct file *filp,
                unsigned int ioctl, unsigned long arg)   {
        switch (ioctl) {
          case KVM_RUN:
      ….
          kvm_arch_vcpu_ioctl_run(vcpu, vcpu->run);
              ->vcpu_load
              -> vmx_vcpu_load
              ->vcpu_run(vcpu);
              ->vcpu_enter_guest
              ->vmx_vcpu_run
      ….

    }
```

We will go through vcpu_run() to understand how it reaches vmx_vcpu_run or svm_vcpu_run:

```
static int vcpu_run(struct kvm_vcpu *vcpu) {
….

        for (;;) {
                if (kvm_vcpu_running(vcpu)) {
                        r = vcpu_enter_guest(vcpu);
                } else {
                        r = vcpu_block(kvm, vcpu);
                }
```

Once it's in vcpu_enter_guest(), you can see some of the important calls happening when it enters guest mode in the KVM:

```
static int vcpu_enter_guest(struct kvm_vcpu *vcpu) {
    ...
        kvm_x86_ops->prepare_guest_switch(vcpu);
        vcpu->mode = IN_GUEST_MODE;
        __kvm_guest_enter();
        kvm_x86_ops->run(vcpu);
```

```
                              [vmx_vcpu_run or svm_vcpu_run ]

        vcpu->mode = OUTSIDE_GUEST_MODE;
        kvm_guest_exit();
        r = kvm_x86_ops->handle_exit(vcpu);
                              [vmx_handle_exit or handle_exit ]

    ...
    }
```

You can see a high-level picture of VMENTRY and VMEXIT from the vcpu_enter_guest() function. That said, VMENTRY ([vmx_vcpu_run or svm_vcpu_run]) is just a guest operating system executing in the CPU; different intercepted events can occur at this stage, causing a VMEXIT. If this happens, any vmx_handle_exit or handle_exit will start looking into this exit cause. We have already discussed the reasons for VMEXIT in previous sections. Once there is a VMEXIT, the exit reason is analyzed and action is taken accordingly.

vmx_handle_exit() is the function responsible for handling the exit reason:

```
    / * The guest has exited.  See if we can fix it or if we need
    userspace
      assistance. */

    static int vmx_handle_exit(struct kvm_vcpu *vcpu)
    {
    .....

    /* The exit handlers return 1 if the exit was handled fully and guest
    execution
     may resume.  Otherwise they set the kvm_run parameter to indicate
    what needs
     to be done to userspace and return 0. */

    static int (*const kvm_vmx_exit_handlers[])(struct kvm_vcpu *vcpu) = {
        [EXIT_REASON_EXCEPTION_NMI]          = handle_exception,
        [EXIT_REASON_EXTERNAL_INTERRUPT]     = handle_external_interrupt,
        [EXIT_REASON_TRIPLE_FAULT]           = handle_triple_fault,
        [EXIT_REASON_IO_INSTRUCTION]         = handle_io,
        [EXIT_REASON_CR_ACCESS]              = handle_cr,
        [EXIT_REASON_VMCALL]                 = handle_vmcall,
        [EXIT_REASON_VMCLEAR]                = handle_vmclear,
        [EXIT_REASON_VMLAUNCH]                = handle_vmlaunch,

    ...
    }
```

`kvm_vmx_exit_handlers[]` is the table of VM exit handlers, indexed by "exit reason". Similar to Intel, the svm code has `handle_exit()`:

```
static int handle_exit(struct kvm_vcpu *vcpu)
{
        struct vcpu_svm *svm = to_svm(vcpu);
        struct kvm_run *kvm_run = vcpu->run;
        u32 exit_code = svm->vmcb->control.exit_code;

    ....

        return svm_exit_handlers[exit_code](svm);
}
```

`handle_exit()` has the `svm_exit_handler` array, as shown in the following section.

If needed KVM has to fall back to userspace (QEMU) to perform the emulation as some of the instructions has to be performed on the QEMU emulated devices. For example to emulate i/o port access, the control goes to userspace (QEMU):

`kvm-all.c`:

```
static int (*const svm_exit_handlers[])(struct vcpu_svm *svm) = {
        [SVM_EXIT_READ_CR0]                     = cr_interception,
        [SVM_EXIT_READ_CR3]                     = cr_interception,
        [SVM_EXIT_READ_CR4]                     = cr_interception,
        [SVM_EXIT_INTR]                         = intr_interception,
        [SVM_EXIT_NMI]                          = nmi_interception,
        [SVM_EXIT_SMI]                          = nop_on_interception,
        [SVM_EXIT_IOIO]                         = io_interception,
        [SVM_EXIT_VMRUN]                        = vmrun_interception,
        [SVM_EXIT_VMMCALL]                      = vmmcall_interception,
        [SVM_EXIT_VMLOAD]                       = vmload_interception,
        [SVM_EXIT_VMSAVE]                       = vmsave_interception,
    ....
}

switch (run->exit_reason) {
        case KVM_EXIT_IO:
                DPRINTF("handle_io\n");
                /* Called outside BQL */
                kvm_handle_io(run->io.port, attrs,
                                (uint8_t *)run + run->io.data_offset,
                              run->io.direction,
                              run->io.size,
                              run->io.count);
                ret = 0;
            break;
```

Summary

In this chapter, we discussed important data structures and functions that define the internal implementation of libvirt, QEMU, and KVM. We also discussed the vCPU execution life cycle and how QEMU and KVM perform together to run guest operating systems in host CPUs. We also discussed the hardware support for virtualization, the important concepts around it, and how it plays a role in KVM virtualization. With these concepts and illustrations in mind, we can explore KVM virtualization in greater detail.

In the next chapter, we will see how to set up a standalone KVM, along with libvirt management tools.

3

Setting Up Standalone
KVM Virtualization

In the second chapter, you learned about KVM internals; now in this chapter, you will learn about how to set up your Linux server as a virtualization host. We are talking about using KVM for virtualization and libvirt as the virtualization management engine.

KVM enables virtualization and readies your server or workstation to host the virtual machines. In technical terms, KVM is a set of kernel modules for an x86 architecture hardware with virtualization extensions; when loaded, it converts a Linux server into a virtualization server (hypervisor). The loadable modules are `kvm.ko`, which provides the core virtualization capabilities and a processor-specific module, `kvm-intel.ko` or `kvm-amd.ko`.

 According to `https://en.wikipedia.org/wiki/Hypervisor`. A hypervisor or **virtual machine monitor (VMM)** is a piece of computer software, firmware, or hardware that creates and runs virtual machines.

It is not enough to just load the KVM kernel modules to start your virtual machines. You need an emulator to emulate the hardware peripherals for your virtual machines. It is now time to introduce QEMU.

Quick Emulator (QEMU) is an open source machine emulator. This emulator will help you to run the operating systems that are designed to run one architecture on top of another one. For example, Qemu can run an OS created on the ARM platform on the x86 platform; however, there is a catch here. Since QEMU uses dynamic translation, which is a technique used to execute virtual machine instructions on the host machine, the VMs run slow.

If QEMU is slow, how can it run blazing fast KVM-based virtual machines at a near native speed? KVM developers thought about the problem and modified QEMU as a solution. This modified QEMU is called qemu-kvm, which can interact with KVM modules directly and safely execute instructions from the VM directly on the CPU without using dynamic translations. In short, we use qemu-kvm binary to run the KVM-based virtual machines.

It is getting more and more confusing, right? If qemu-kvm can run a virtual machine, then why do you need to use libvirt. The answer is simple, libvirt manages qemu-kvm and qemu-kvm runs the KVM virtual machines.

> The qemu-kvm binary is now deprecated and all of the codes in that are now merged with the qemu-system-x86_64 binary. For the purpose of understanding, we are using qemu-kvm. Some Linux distributions still carry qemu-kvm.

Without further ado, let us see what topics will be covered in this chapter:

- Introduction to libvirt
- libvirt management tools
- Hardware setup recommendations

Getting acquainted with libvirt

Libvirt is a set of API libraries that sits in between the end user and the hypervisor. The hypervisor can be built using any virtualization technology that libvirt supports. At the time of writing, libvirt supports the following hypervisors:

- The KVM/QEMU Linux hypervisor
- The Xen hypervisor on Linux and Solaris hosts
- The LXC Linux container system
- The OpenVZ Linux container system
- The User Mode Linux paravirtualized kernel
- The VirtualBox hypervisor
- The VMware ESX and GSX hypervisors
- The VMware Workstation and Player hypervisors
- The Microsoft Hyper-V hypervisor
- The IBM PowerVM hypervisor
- The Parallels hypervisor
- The Bhyve hypervisor

libvirt acts as a transparent layer that takes commands from users, modifies them based on the underlying virtualization technology, and then executes them on the hypervisor. This means that if you know how to use libvirt-based management tools, you should be able to manage the preceding set of hypervisors without knowing them individually. You can select any virtualization management technology. They all use libvirt as their backend infrastructure management layer, even though the frontend tools look different; for example, oVirt, **Red Hat Enterprise Virtualization (RHEV)**, OpenStack, Eucalyptus, and so on. This book is all about KVM libvirt and its tools.

In the following figure, we will summarize how everything is connected:

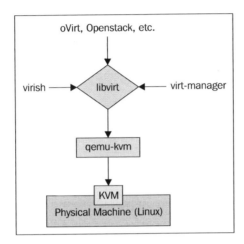

Libvirt will take care of the storage, networking, and virtual hardware requirements to start a virtual machine along with VM lifecycle management.

Here's how easy it is to start VM using libvirt. Here, we are starting a VM named TestVM using virsh.

```
# virsh start TestVM
```

> virsh is the frontend command line that interacts with the libvirt service and virt-manager is its GUI frontend. You will learn more about these tools later on in the book.

In the backend, you can see that libvirt initiated the qemu process with a bunch of options:

```
# qemu-system-x86_64 -machine accel=kvm -name TestVM -S -machine
pc-i440fx-1.6,accel=kvm,usb=off -m 4000 -realtime mlock=off -smp
2,sockets=2,cores=1,threads=1 -uuid 39ac4786-1eca-1092-034c-edb6f93d291c
-no-user-config -nodefaults -chardev socket,id=charmonitor,path=/var/lib/
libvirt/qemu/TestVM.monitor,server,nowait -mon chardev=charmonitor,id=mo
nitor,mode=control -rtc base=utc -no-shutdown -device piix3-usb-uhci,id=
usb,bus=pci.0,addr=0x1.0x2 -drive file=/dev/vms/TestVM,if=none,id=drive-
virtio-disk0,format=raw,cache=none,aio=native -device virtio-blk-pc
i,scsi=off,bus=pci.0,addr=0x4,drive=drive-virtio-disk0,id=virtio-
disk0,bootindex=2 -netdev tap,fd=27,id=hostnet0,vhost=on,vhostfd=28
-device virtio-net-pci,netdev=hostnet0,id=net0,mac=52:54:00:a5:cd:61,bu
s=pci.0,addr=0x3,bootindex=1 -chardev pty,id=charserial0 -device isa-se
rial,chardev=charserial0,id=serial0 -device usb-tablet,id=input0 -vnc
127.0.0.1:2 -device cirrus-vga,id=video0,bus=pci.0,addr=0x2 -device
virtio-balloon-pci,id=balloon0,bus=pci.0,addr=0x5
```

While introducing libvirt, we deliberately avoided mentioning many features of libvirt. This is done to make the concept clearer and focus on the key functions of libvirt. When you progress through the chapters, you will get introduced to those features.

Now, you are familiar with the key components required to use KVM-based virtualization. Before we learn how to set up the environment, we should take a look at the system requirements.

Host system requirements

A virtual machine needs a certain amount of CPU, memory, and storage to be assigned to it. This means that the number of virtual machines you are planning to run on that particular host decides the hardware requirements for the KVM hypervisor.

Let's start with the minimum requirements to start two simple virtual machines on KVM with 756 MB of RAM each:

- An Intel or AMD 64-bit CPU that has virtualization extension, VT-x for Intel and AMD-V for AMD.
- 2 GB RAM.
- 8 GB free disk space on KVM hypervisor after Linux OS installation.
- 100 Mbps network.

For the examples in the book, we are using Fedora 21. However, you are free to use any Linux distribution (Ubuntu, Debian, CentOS, and so on) that has KVM and libvirt support. We assume that you have already installed a Fedora 21 or a Linux distribution with all the basic configurations, including the networking.

Determining the right system requirements for your environment

This is a very important stage and we need to get this right. Having the right system configuration is the key to getting native-like performance from the virtual machines. Let us start with the CPU.

Physical CPU

An Intel or AMD 64-bit CPU that has virtualization extension, VT-x for Intel and AMD-V for AMD.

To determine whether your CPU supports the virtualization extension, you can check for the following flags:

```
# grep --color -Ew 'svm|vmx|lm' /proc/cpuinfo

flags       : fpu vme de pse tsc msr pae mce cx8 apic sep mtrr pge mca
cmov pat pse36 clflush dts acpi mmx fxsr sse sse2 ss ht tm pbe syscall
nx rdtscp lm constant_tsc arch_perfmon pebs bts rep_good nopl xtopology
nonstop_tsc aperfmperf pni dtes64 monitor ds_cpl vmx smx est tm2 ssse3
cx16 xtpr pdcm sse4_1 sse4_2 popcnt lahf_lm ida dtherm tpr_shadow vnmi
flexpriority ept vpid
```

The svm flag means that the CPU has AMD-V, vmx flag means that the CPU has VT-x, and lm means a 64-bit support.

If your CPU supports a virtualization extension, then your system is probably ready to host the KVM virtual machines. You will also notice that the appropriate KVM modules get loaded automatically with no additional configuration. To verify whether the modules are loaded or not, use following command:

```
# lsmod | grep kvm
kvm_intel           148081  9
kvm                 461126  1 kvm_intel
```

If the system is AMD, you will see `kvm_amd` instead of `kvm_intel`.

If you do not see the preceding CPU flags, or all the KVM modules are not loaded, but you are sure that the system supports virtualization extensions, then try the following troubleshooting steps:

1. Reboot the system and go to the BIOS.
2. Go to advanced options for CPU. Enable **Intel Virtualization Technology** or **Virtualization Extensions**. For AMD, it should be enabled by default. The exact words might be different depending on your BIOS.
3. Restart the machine.
4. You should now see the KVM modules loaded. If you still do not see them as loaded, then try loading them manually.

   `# modprobe kvm kvm_intel` or `modprobe kvm kvm_amd`

5. If you are able to load them manually but they still don't work, then it is time to involve your hardware vendor or double-check the processor details on respective Intel or AMD product pages.

In addition to the virtualization extension, you may need to enable Intel VT-d or AMD IOMMU (AMD-Vi) in the BIOS. These are required for direct PCI device assignment to virtual machines, for example, to assign a physical **Network Interface Card (NIC)** from the hypervisor to the virtual machine; we will be covering more about this in the upcoming chapters.

CPU cores

If you are planning to run server-class virtual machines, then one core per vCPU is recommended. When counting cores, do not count the hyperthreaded cores on the Intel CPUs, just the actual cores. Of course, you can overcommit the number of vCPUs available as more than the actual cores but it comes with a performance penalty.

If you are planning to run desktop-class virtual machines or less CPU-intensive virtual machines, then you can safely overcommit the CPU since the performance takes a back seat here and priority changes to VM density per hypervisor more than the performance.

 Overcommitting means assigning more virtual resources than the physical resources available.

There is no crystal clear definition of how many VMs you can run on a hypervisor. It all depends upon the type of workload inside the VMs and how much performance degradation you can afford. If all the VMs run CPU intensive tasks, then overcommitting vCPUs is a bad idea.

 Use the lscpu command to see your CPU topology.

Physical memory

A simple rule of thumb you can use to decide how much memory you need for the physical node is to add up all the memory you plan to assign to virtual machines and add an additional 2 GB of RAM for the hypervisor itself to use.

This is the expected configuration if you are planning to run memory intensive workloads.

Similar to the CPU, KVM also supports memory overcommitting. This means that you can assign more memory to the VMs than the hypervisor actually has, with the risk of running out of memory. Usually this type of allocation is done for desktop class virtual machines or test virtual machines.

You can use the following formulas to find how much RAM will be available to the VMs:

- For systems with memory up to 64 GB:

    RAM - 2 GB = Amount of RAM available to VMs in GBs

- For systems with memory above 64 GB:

    RAM - (2 GiB + .5* (RAM/64)) = Amount of RAM available to VMs in GBs

We are adding 500 MiB to every 64 GB added to the hypervisor + a mandatory 2 GB. Use this formula to get a rough idea of how much memory is available for the virtual machines. In some workloads, you may not need more than 5 GB of RAM space for the hypervisor, even if our formula suggests that you may need to keep 10 GB reserved for the hypervisor software on a system with 1 TB of RAM.

Storage

When considering the storage space for the hypervisor, you need to factor in the space required for the OS installation, SWAP, and virtual machines disk usage.

How much SWAP space is recommended?

Determining the ideal amount of SWAP space needed is a bit complicated. If you are not planning to do any memory overcommit, then you can use the following suggestion for an oVirt Node, which is a dedicated KVM hypervisor for running the VMs only:

- 2 GB of swap space for systems with 4 GB of RAM or less
- 4 GB of swap space for systems with 4 GB and 16 GB of RAM
- 8 GB of swap space for systems with 16 GB and 64 GB of RAM
- 16 GB of swap space for systems with 64 GB and 256 GB of RAM

If you are planning to do a memory overcommit, you will need to add additional swap space. If the overcommit ratio is .5 (that is, 50% more than the available physical RAM), then you need to use the following formula to determine the SWAP space:

(RAM x 0.5) + SWAP for OS = SWAP space required for overcommitting

For example, if your system has 32 GB RAM and you are planning to use a .5 overcommit ratio, then the SWAP space required is *(32 * .5) + 8 = 24 GB*.

A virtual disk can be stored as a file in the local file system storage (ext3, ext4, xfs, and so on) or in a shared file storage (NFS, GlusterFS, and so on). A virtual disk can also be created from block devices, such as LVM, a locally partitioned disk, iSCSI disk, Fibre Channel, FCoE, and so on. In short, you should be able to attach any block device that the hypervisor sees to a VM. As you have guessed by now, the space is decided by how much disk space VMs will require or the applications installed in it. In storage, you can also do overcommitting similar to what we explained for CPU and memory, but it is not recommended for virtual machines that do heavy I/O operations. An overcommitted virtual disk is called a thin provisioned disk.

Further explanation about CPU, memory, and storage overcommitting will be given in the later chapters that cover virtual machines performance tuning.

Network

One NIC with a bandwidth of at least 1 GBps is recommended for smooth network operation, but again, it totally depends on how you configure your virtual network infrastructure and how the network requirement varies according to various scenarios.

It is suggested to bind multiple network interfaces together into a single channel using Linux bonding technology and build virtual machine network infrastructure on top of it. It will help in increasing the bandwidth and providing redundancy.

> There are several bonding modes but not all are supported for building virtual network infrastructure. Mode 1 (active-backup), Mode 2 (balance-xor), Mode 4 (802.3ad/LACP), and Mode 5 (balance-tlb) are the only supported bonding modes; the remaining bonding modes are not suitable. In Mode 1 and Mode 4 are highly recommended and stable.

Setting up the environment

This section guides you through the process of installing virtualization packages, starting with the libvirt service and validating that the system is ready to host virtual machines using KVM virtualization technology.

> We assume that you have a Fedora 21 system ready with a graphical user interface loaded and Internet connectivity to access the default Fedora yum repository through which the required KVM virtualization packages can be downloaded. We also assume that the **Virtualization Technology (VT)** feature is enabled in your server's BIOS.

To verify whether the default yum repository is enabled or not on your system, use the yum repolist command. This command lists the yum repositories defined on the system:

```
[root@kvmHOST ~]# yum repolist
Loaded plugins: langpacks
repo id                       repo name                              status
fedora/21/x86_64              Fedora 21 - x86_64                     42,816
updates/21/x86_64             Fedora 21 - x86_64 - Updates           16,716
repolist: 59,532
[root@kvmHOST ~]#
```

Look for a repository named `Fedora 21 - X86-64` in the output. It is where you will find an access to all the KVM virtualization packages.

Installing virtualization packages

This is the first step to converting your Fedora 21 server or workstation system into a virtualization host. Actually, this is a very easy thing to do. As root, you just have to execute the `yum install <packages>` command, where `<packages>` is a space-separated list of package names.

The minimum required packages for setting up a virtualization environment on the Fedora 21 system are `libvirt`, `qemu-kvm`, and `virt-manager`.

So you should use the following `yum` command:

```
# yum install qemu-kvm libvirt virt-install virt-manager virt-install -y
```

There are many dependent packages which are installed along with the preceding packages but you do not need to worry what those are or remember their names, the `yum` command will automatically detect the dependency and resolve it for you.

The `yum groupinstall` method can also be used to install the necessary and optional packages required for setting up the KVM virtualization environment:

```
#yum groupinstall "virtualization" -y
```

It will install the `guestfs-browser`, `libguestfs-tools`, `python-libguestfs`, `virt-top` packages along with the core components, such as libvirt and qemu-kvm.

Here is the output of `yum groupinfo "virtualization"` for your reference:

```
#yum groupinfo "virtualization"
Group: Virtualization
 Group-Id: virtualization
 Description: These packages provide a virtualization environment.
 Mandatory Packages:
   +virt-install
 Default Packages:
```

```
libvirt-daemon-config-network
libvirt-daemon-kvm
qemu-kvm
  +virt-manager
  +virt-viewer
Optional Packages:
  guestfs-browser
  libguestfs-tools
  python-libguestfs
  virt-top
```

For the time being, we would suggest that you install just the core packages using the `yum install` command to avoid any confusion. In later chapters, the optional utilities available for KVM virtualization are thoroughly explained with examples and installation steps.

Starting the libvirt service

After installing the KVM virtualization packages, the first thing that you should do is start a libvirt service. As soon as you start the libvirt service, it will expose a rich **Application Programmable Interface (API)** to interact with `qemu-kvm` binary. Clients such as `virsh` and `virt-manager`, among others, use this API to talk with `qemu-kvm` for virtual machine life cycle management. To enable and start the service, run the following command:

```
# systemctl enable libvirtd && systemctl start libvirtd
```

 Use `libvirtd --version` command to find out the libvirt version in use.

Validate and understand your system's virt capabilities

Before creating virtual machines, it's very important to validate the system and make sure that it meets all the prerequisites to be a KVM virtualization host, and understand what are its virt capabilities.

Knowing this information will help you to plan the number of virtual machines and their configuration that can be hosted on the system. There are two important commands that help in validating a system configuration for KVM. Let's start with `virt-host-validate`:

- `virt-host-validate`: Executing this command as root user will perform sanity checks on KVM capabilities to validate that the host is configured in a suitable way to run the libvirt hypervisor drivers using KVM virtualization.

  For example: `TestSys1` has all the necessary packages required for KVM virtualization but lacks hardware virtualization support. In this case, it will print out the following:

  ```
  root@'TestSys1 ~]#virt-host-validate
  QEMU: Checking for hardware virtualization          :
  WARN (Only emulated CPUs are available, performance will be
  significantly limited)
  QEMU: Checking for device /dev/vhost-net            : PASS
  QEMU: Checking for device /dev/net/tun              : PASS
  LXC: Checking for Linux >= 2.6.26                   : PASS
  ```

- This output clearly shows that hardware virtualization is not enabled on the system and only "qemu" support is present, which is very slow as compared to qemu-kvm.

It's the hardware virtualization support which helps the KVM (qemu-kvm) virtual machines to have direct access to the physical CPU and helps it reach nearly native performance. Hardware support is not present in a standalone qemu.

Now, let's see what other parameters are checked by the `virt-host-validate` command when it's executed to validate a system for KVM virtualization:

- `/dev/kvm`: The KVM drivers create a `/dev/kvm` character device on the host to facilitate direct hardware access for virtual machines. Not having this device means that the VMs won't be able to access physical hardware, although it's enabled in the BIOS and this will reduce the VMs, performance significantly.

- `/dev/vhost-net`: The `vhost-net` driver creates a `/dev/vhost-net` character device on the host. This character device serves as the interface to configure the vhost-net instance. Not having this device significantly reduces the virtual machine's network performance.

- `/dev/net/tun`: This is another character special device used for creating tun/tap devices to facilitate network connectivity for a virtual machine. The tun/tap device will be explained in detail in future chapters. For now, just understand that having a character device is important for KVM virtualization to work properly.

Always ensure that `virt-host-validate` passes all the sanity checks before creating the virtual machine on the system. You will see the following output on the system where it validates all the parameters:

```
[root@kvmHOST ~]# virt-host-validate
  QEMU: Checking for hardware virtualization              : PASS
  QEMU: Checking for device /dev/kvm                      : PASS
  QEMU: Checking for device /dev/vhost-net                : PASS
  QEMU: Checking for device /dev/net/tun                  : PASS
   LXC: Checking for Linux >= 2.6.26                       : PASS
[root@kvmHOST ~]#
```

The second command is `virsh`. `virsh` (virtualization shell) is a command-line interface for managing the VM and the hypervisor on a Linux system. It uses the libvirt management API and operates as an alternative to the graphical virt-manager and a Web-based kimchi-project. The `virsh` commands are segregated under various classifications. The following are some important classifications of `virsh` commands:

- Guest management commands (for example `start`, `stop`)
- Guest monitoring commands (for example `memstat`, `cpustat`)
- Host and hypervisors commands (for example `capabilities`, `nodeinfo`)
- Virtual networking commands (for example `net-list`, `net-define`)
- Storage management commands (for example `pool-list`, `pool-define`)
- Snapshot commands (`create-snapshot-as`)

 To learn more about `virsh`, we recommend that you read the main page of virsh. virsh is a very well-documented command. `#man virsh` to access man pages of virsh command.

The reason why we introduced the `virsh` command in this chapter is because virsh can display a lot of information about the host's capabilities, such as, the host CPU topology, memory available for virtual machines, and so on. Let's take a look at the output of the `virsh nodeinfo` command, which will give us the physical node's system resource information:

`#virsh nodeinfo`

```
CPU model:          x86_64
CPU(s):             4
CPU frequency:      2534 MHz
CPU socket(s):      1
Core(s) per socket: 2
Thread(s) per core: 2
NUMA cell(s):       1
Memory size:        7967796 KiB
```

 You must be the root to run `virsh` commands.

In the `virsh nodeinfo` output, you can see the system hardware architecture, CPU topology, memory size, and so on. Obviously, the same information can also be gathered using the standard Linux commands, but you will have to run multiple commands. You can use this information to decide whether or not this is a suitable host to create your virtual machine suitable, in the sense of hardware resources.

Another important command is `#virsh domcapabilities`. The `virsh domcapabilities` command displays an XML document describing the capabilities of qemu-kvm with respect to the host and libvirt version. Knowing the emulator's capabilities is very useful. It will help you determine the type of virtual disks you can use with the virtual machines, the maximum number of vCPUs that can be assigned, and so on.

Hardware configuration examples

Let us take a look at some common hardware configurations; the `domcapabilities`
options of virsh commands will show you the host capabilities. You can parse the
output to find the exact supported value of a particular hardware configuration
which you can present to a virtual machine. The following is the maximum `vcpu`
that you can present to a VM:

```
[root@kvmHOST ~]# virsh domcapabilities  | grep -i max
  <vcpu max='255'/>
[root@kvmHOST ~]#
```

As per the output, on this host a maximum of 255 vcpus can be defined for a
virtual machine:

```
[root@kvmHOST ~]# virsh domcapabilities  | grep diskDevice -A 5
    <enum name='diskDevice'>
      <value>disk</value>
      <value>cdrom</value>
      <value>floppy</value>
      <value>lun</value>
    </enum>
[root@kvmHOST ~]#
```

As per the output, `disk`, `cdrom`, `floppy`, and `lun` type devices can be used with the
virtual machine on this host.

A lot of the physical node's hypervisor capabilities are exposed by this command.
Explaining all of these capabilities is beyond the scope of this book, so you may
want to try running this command in your own environment to see what it reports.
Alternatively, it might be good to link it to a definitive online resource. Hence,
we suggest that you run the command on your system and learn its capabilities.

Along with `libvirt` and the `qemu-kvm` packages, we also installed the virt-manager package on the system. As stated earlier, the virt-manager is a GUI tool for managing either a local or a remote hypervisor. For now, before finishing this chapter we just want to show you how to start a virt-manager and connect it to a local KVM hypervisor:

1. First, ensure that the libvirtd service is in a running state and the `virt-host-validate` command passes all its checks.

2. Then, navigate to the application from **Menu | System tools |** and click on **Virtual Machine Manager**.

3. After clicking on the virt-manager, a **Virtual Machine Manager** graphical tool connected to the local hypervisor (qemu-kvm) should be opened as shown in the following screenshot:

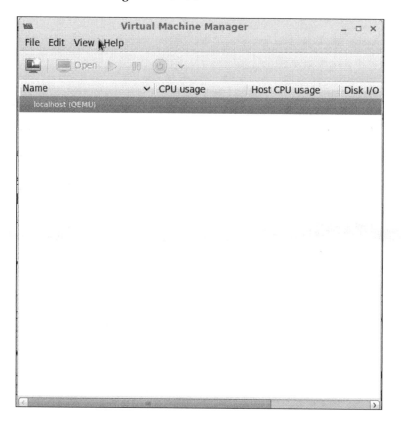

4. In case it could not search the local hypervisor and connect to it, click on the **File** menu and open the **Add Connection** dialogue box and fill in the connection details:

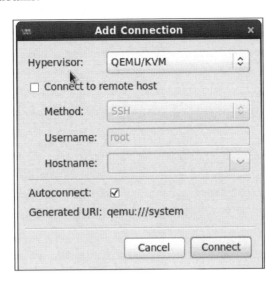

The preceding hypervisor item should be set to QEMU/KVM from the dropdown list and then you can click on **Connect**. That's it; it will connect the virt-manager to the local qemu-kvm hypervisor through the libvirt. If you want to connect to the remote hypervisor, check **Connect to remote host** and fill in the details.

If your virt-manager has successfully connected to the local KVM hypervisor, you are ready to create virtual machines. If the connection fails, check the /user-home/. cache/virt-manager/virt-manager.log log file.

Summary

In this chapter, we learned about KVM virtualization, along with libvirt management tools. We also learned about the various tools associated with KVM and libvirt, along with sample hardware configurations that will make your system run smoothly.

In the next chapter, you will learn more about the virsh command and its syntax through examples. You will also learn how to use virt-manager to create virtual machines using it. It will also explain the virt-manager and virsh command in more detail, with examples of how to create virtual machines.

4

Getting Started with libvirt and Creating Your First Virtual Machines

In *Chapter 3, Setting Up Standalone KVM Virtualization,* you installed and started the libvirtd services. You were also introduced to the libvirt tools `virt-manager` and `virsh`, which help you manage virtual machines.

New users always prefer the GUI rather than text-based commands. Hence we are starting with virt-manager. We also think understanding virt-manager will fast-forward the learning process of managing virtual machines using libvirt and later with `virsh`. Whenever possible we will present you with the equivalent `virsh` command so that you can try and learn both virt-manager and `virsh`.

In this chapter, we will cover the following topics:

- All about virt-manager
- Default virtual storage and network configurations
- Various guest installations methods (PXE/ISO/NETWORK/IMPORT)
- Using the `virt-builder` and `oz` utilities to rapidly create multiple VMs

Introducing virt-manager

The virt-manager application is a Python-based desktop user interface for managing virtual machines through libvirt. It primarily targets KVM VMs, but also manages Xen and **LXC** (Linux containers) among others. virt-manager displays a summary view of running VMs, supplying their performance and resource utilization statistics. Using the virt-manager graphical interface, one can easily create new VMs, monitor them, and make configuration changes when required. An embedded VNC and SPICE client viewer presents a full graphical console to the VM.

As we mentioned in *Chapter 3, Setting Up Standalone KVM Virtualization,* virtual machines need CPU, memory, storage, and networking resources from the host. In this chapter we will explain the basic configuration of the KVM host and creating virtual machines using virt-manager.

Let's start the **Virtual Machine Manager** by executing the `virt-manager` command or by pressing *Alt + F2* and it will then display the dialog box of `virt-manager`.

If you are not the root user, you will be prompted for the root password before continuing. Here the password authentication is handled by the polkit framework. polkit is an authorization API intended to be used by privileged programs (for example, system daemons) offering services to unprivileged programs.

If you wish to allow certain groups or users to access virt-manager without providing root credentials, a polkit rule needs to be created. The rule file has to be created in the `/etc/polkit-1/rules.d` directory.

For example, if you want all the users in the `wheel` group to have direct access to virt-manager without entering root password, create the `/etc/polkit-1/rules.d/70-libvirtd.rules` file and then write:

```
polkit.addRule(function(action, subject) {
  if (action.id == "org.libvirt.unix.manage" && subject.local &&
subject.active && subject.isInGroup("wheel")) {
  return polkit.Result.YES;
  }
});
```

Save and close the file. The libvirtd daemon monitors polikit's `rules.d` directory for changed content and automatically reloads the rules if changes are detected, so you don't need to reload the process with `systemctl`. If you've done it right, you should see that you can now launch virt-manager as the users in the wheel group without entering the password. To add users in the wheel group run:

```
# usermod -G wheel <username>
```

If you examine the polkit rule carefully you will notice that it checks to see if the user is in the wheel group, is on a local, and has an active session. If so then the result on the `org.libvirt.unix.manage` action is a *YES* to allow the action. This could also be configured as:

- NO: Reject the access request (`return polkit.Result.No;`)

- AUTH_SELF: Request the user's own password (`return polkit.Result.AUTH_SELF;`)

- AUTH_ADMIN: Request the password for an admin on the system (`return polkit.Result.AUTH_ADMIN`

Once virt-manager is opened, go to **Edit | Connection Details** to access the options to configure network and storage:

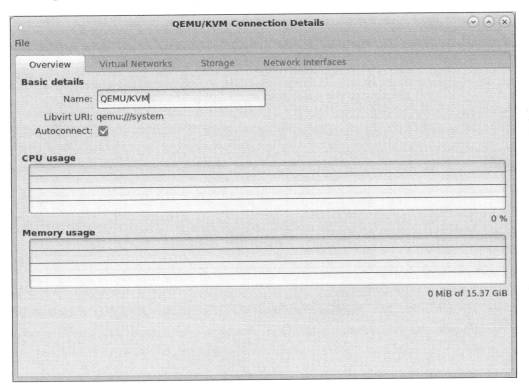

The **Overview** tab will give basic information on the libvirt connection URI, CPU, and memory usage pattern of the host system. **Virtual Networks** and **Storage** will present the details of the network and storage pools that can be used by the virtual machines. The **Network Interfaces** tab will give details of the host network and will offer options to configure them. We will cover this in more detail in *Chapter 5, Network and Storage*.

The Virtual Networks tab

The **Virtual Networks** tab allows us to configure various types of virtual network and monitor their status:

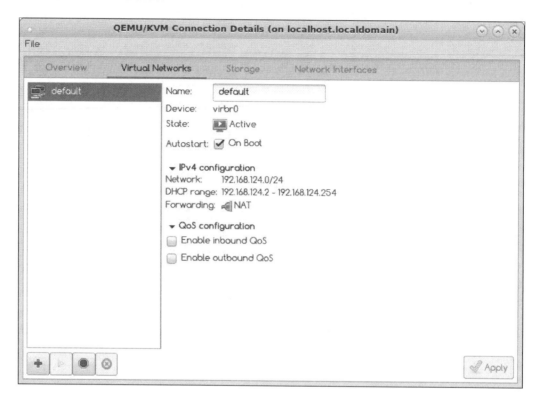

Using the **Virtual Networks** tab you will be able to configure the following types of virtual network:

- NATed
- Routed
- Isolated

NATed virtual network

A NAT-based virtual network provides outbound network connectivity to the virtual machines. That means the VMs can communicate with the outside network based on the network connectivity available on the host but none of the outside entities will be able to communicate with the VMs. In this setup, the virtual machines and host should be able to communicate with each other through the bridge interface configured on the host.

Routed virtual network

A routed virtual network allows the connection of virtual machines directly to the physical network. Here VMs will send out packets to the outside network based on the routing rules set on the hypervisor.

Isolated virtual network

As the name implies, this provides a private network between the hypervisor and the virtual machines.

We will cover each network configuration in detail in the next chapter (as well as other network implementations used in production environments) with practical examples. In this chapter, we will be concentrating on the `default` virtual network, which uses NAT. Once you understand how default networks work, it is very easy to understand other network topologies.

Use `virsh net list --all` to list the virtual networks. `--all` is used to list both active and inactive virtual networks. If `--all` is not specified only active virtual networks will be listed:

```
# virsh net-list --all
 Name              State      Autostart    Persistent
----------------------------------------------------------
 default           active     yes          yes
```

Default network

As mentioned earlier, the default network is a NAT-based virtual network. It allows virtual machines to communicate with the outside networks irrespective of the active network interface (Ethernet, wireless, VPN, and so on) available on the hypervisor. It also provides a private network with IP and a DHCP server so that the VMs will get their IP addresses automatically.

Check the details provided about the `default` network in the previous screenshot:

- `default` is the **Name** of the virtual network. This is provided when you create a virtual network.

- **Device** represents the name of bridge created on the host. The bridge interface is the main component for creating virtual networks. We will cover bridges in greater depth in a later chapter.

- **State** represents the state of the virtual network. It can be active or inactive.

- **Autostart** shows whether the virtual network should be started when you activate the libvirtd service.

- **IPv4 Configuration** provides the details of the private network, the DHCP range that will be provided to the VMs, and the forwarding mode. The forwarding mode can be NAT or isolated.

You can stop the `default` network using the red "stop sign" button and start again using the **PLAY** button. The **+** button is used for creating new virtual networks, which we will cover in the next chapter. The **x** button is used for deleting virtual networks.

You can see the same details using the `virsh` command:

```
# virsh net-info default
Name:          default
UUID:          ba551355-0556-4d32-87b4-653f4a74e09f
Active:        yes
Persistent:    yes
Autostart:     yes
Bridge:        virbr0


-----
```

```
# virsh net-dumpxml default
<network>
  <name>default</name>
  <uuid>ba551355-0556-4d32-87b4-653f4a74e09f</uuid>
  <forward mode='nat'>
    <nat>
      <port start='1024' end='65535'/>
    </nat>
  </forward>
  <bridge name='virbr0' stp='on' delay='0'/>
  <mac address='52:54:00:d1:56:2e'/>
  <ip address='192.168.124.1' netmask='255.255.255.0'>
    <dhcp>
      <range start='192.168.124.2' end='192.168.124.254'/>
    </dhcp>
  </ip>
</network>
```

Some of the basic commands that will get you started with the default network are as follows:

- Virtual network configuration files are stored in /etc/libvirt/qemu/ networks/ as XML files. For the default network it is /etc/libvirt/qemu/ networks/default.xml.

- This virsh command net-destroy will stop a virtual network and net-start will start a virtual network. Do not issue these commands when virtual machines are active using the virtual network. It will break the network connectivity for the virtual machine.

- # virsh net-destroy default: The default network is destroyed.

- # virsh net-start default: The default network is started.

Storage tab

This tab allows you to configure various types of storage pool and monitor their status. The following screenshot shows the **Storage** tab:

The **Storage** tab provides details of the storage pools available. A storage pool is just a store for saved virtual machine disk images.

At the time of writing, libvirt supports creating storage pools from the different types of source shown in the following screenshot; directory and LVM are the most commonly used. We will look into this in greater detail in the next chapter:

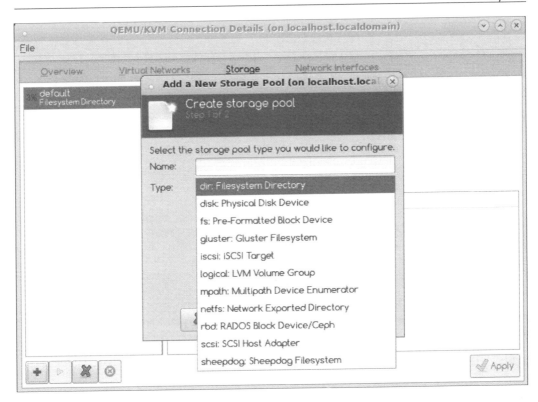

Default storage pool: Default is the name of file-based storage pool that libvirt created to store its virtual machine image file. The location of this storage pool is in /var/lib/libvirt/images.

Creating virtual machines using the Virtual Machine Manager

The following methods are available with virt-manager for Guest OS installation:

- Local installation media (ISO Image or CD-ROM)
- Network installation (HTTP, FTP, or NFS)
- Network boot (PXE)
- Importing existing disk images

In this section, we will create new virtual machines running different operating systems, each using one of the aforementioned installation methods, so that by the end of this chapter you will be familiar with all the available methods for creating virtual machines and will thoroughly understand the **Create a new virtual machine** wizard.

We will create the following Guest OS:

- Windows 7
- CentOS 6

To create the VM using a graphical interface, start the **Virtual Machine Manager** by executing the `virt-manager` command or open it from the **Applications | System Tools** menu.

Creating a new virtual machine wizard

From **Virtual Machine Manager**, click on the **Create a new virtual machine** button on the toolbar or select **File | New Virtual Machine** to open the wizard, which allows creating new virtual machines from virt-manager.

The wizard breaks down the virtual machine creation process into five steps:

1. Choosing the installation method.
2. Configuring the installation media.
3. Memory and CPU configuration.
4. Virtual machine storage configuration.
5. Naming the guest OS and networking configuration.

Let's create a virtual machine and install the CentOS 6.5 operating system using the Local Install media (ISO Image or CD-ROM) method.

This installation method requires the operating system installation media to be inserted into the system's CD-ROM tray, available in ISO form locally, or available over the network. The ideal location to keep the ISO file is `/var/lib/libvirt/images`, which acts as the default storage pool for virt-manager with all the SELinux and other permissions set properly. If the ISO file is stored somewhere else on the system, ensure that virt-manager can access it before you continue.

1. Once you have ensured that virt-manager has access to the installation media, the wizard will ask you to choose how you would like to install the operating system. Select **Local install media (ISO Image or CDROM)** and click on the **Forward** button:

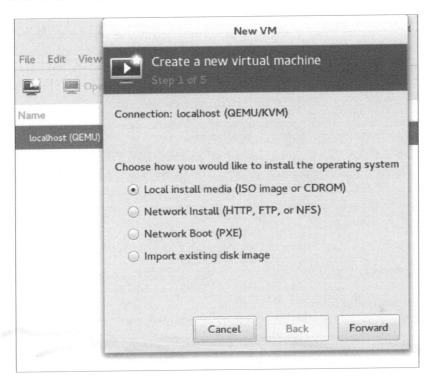

2. Clicking on the **Forward** button will take you to **Step 2** where you have to specify the ISO image location. If you are using a physical DVD or CD, select that:

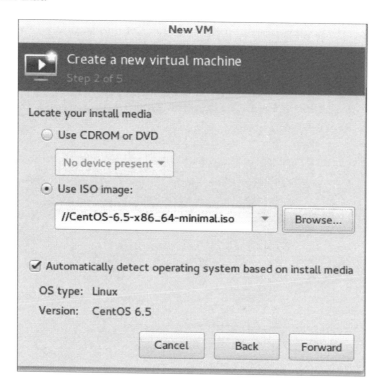

virt-manager automatically detects the operating system based on the install media. It uses the OS information database provided by `libosinfo`. At the time of writing, the `libosinfo` database contains information on nearly 302 operating systems, including Windows, Linux, Unix, and all of the most important Linux distributions. You can extract the operating system list from the `libosinfo` database by running the `sinfo-query os` command.

 It's important to select the correct operating system name because the emulated hardware selection for the virtual machine is closely mapped to the operating system type set. For example, by default for windows OS, the virtual disk format is selected as IDE whereas for Linux operating system it's the `virtio` disk.

3. On the next screen, specify the memory and CPU that you want allocate for the virtual machine:

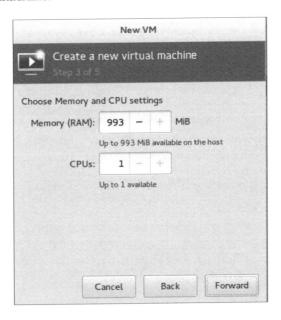

4. The wizard shows the maximum amount of CPUs and memory you can allocate. Configure these settings and click **Forward** to configure storage for the virtual machine:

5. Make sure you assign sufficient space for your virtual machine. By default, it creates a virtual disk at the `/var/lib/libvirt/qemu` location, which is the default pool. If there are any other custom storage pools defined on the system, select **Managed or other existing storage** and either directly enter the path of the disk or click on the **Browse** button, which will open the **Locate or create storage volume** dialog box where you can select an existing volume or create a new one from the defined storage pool, if any available. You will learn about storage pools and how to create them in the next chapter.

 There is also a radio button, **Allocate entire disk now**, to choose a disk allocation method; deselecting this button will result in a thin-provisioned disk and selecting it will result in a thick-provisioned disk (also called a pre-allocated disk).

6. The next and final step is naming the guest and networking configuration. The default machine name is based on the selected OS (for example, `centos6.5` for a CentOS 6.5 VM). You can change it to whatever name you want to give but note that only underscores (_), periods (.), and hyphens (-) are supported:

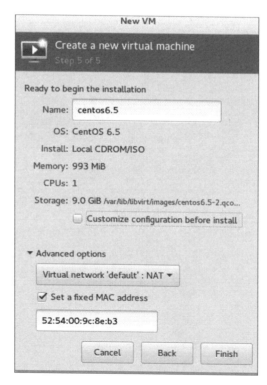

Expanding **Advanced options** will bring up the virtual network configuration setting. By default, KVM provides NAT-like bridged networking. The virtual machines connected to this NAT do not appear on the network as their own devices, but will have network access through the host operating system settings. If you're planning to run server software or a webserver on your virtual machine and want it accessible from other devices on the network, you'll have to use other virtual networking configurations such as Linux bridge or macvtap.

Set a fixed MAC Address allows you to define a custom MAC address for your virtual machine. The default MAC address range used by libvirt is `52:54:00`.

7. If you prefer to further configure the virtual machine's hardware first, check the **Customize configuration before install** box first before clicking **Finish**. Doing so will open another wizard that will allow you to add, remove, and configure the virtual machine's hardware settings.

8. If everything goes well, a virtual console for the newly created VM appears. The new domain name appears in the domain list in the **Virtual Machine Manager** window. The installation starts with the **boot:** prompt just as an installation would start on native hardware:

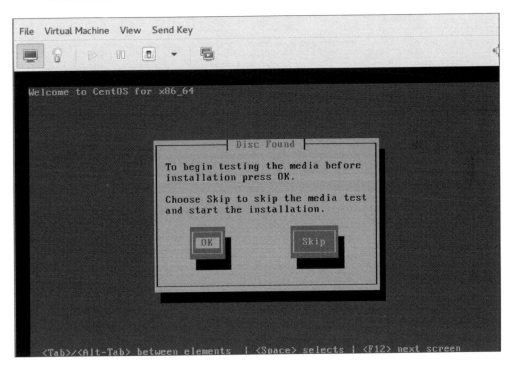

9. The last step in the installation wizard is clicking the **Reboot** button to reboot the system and complete the installation. After the VM reboots you will see the operating system login screen.

The Network installation (HTTP, FTP, or NFS) method

This method involves the use of a mirrored Red Hat Enterprise Linux, CentOS, or Fedora installation tree to install a guest. Virtual Machine creation and supported guest operating system installation using this method also involves five steps, starting with the installation method section and moving on to naming the guest and networking configuration.

The steps are the same as the ISO installation procedure except for step 2 (configuring the installation media). Instead of an ISO image, here we need to pass the URL of the RHEL/CentOS installation tree:

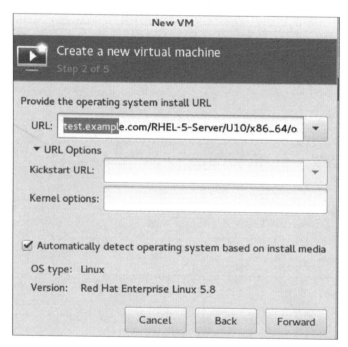

Optionally, you can also use **Kickstart URL** to point to your kickstart file for unattended guest installation, and **Kernel options** to pass a custom kernel boot parameter if required.

Network Boot (PXE)

This method uses a **Preboot eXecution Environment** (**PXE**) server to install the guest virtual machine. PXE Guest installation requires a PXE server running on the same subnet where you wish to create the virtual machine and the host system must have network connectivity to the PXE server.

The default NATed network created by virt-manager is not compatible with PXE installation, because a virtual machine connected to the NAT does not appear on the network as its own device, and therefore the PXE server can't see it and can't send the required data to perform the installation. To use PXE Guest OS installation, you need either a software-network bridge or a macvtap-based network on the host system. Here, for example, we will use a macvtap-based network and initiate the installation.

1. Select **PXE** as the installation method in the **Create a New Virtual Machine** wizard and follow the rest of the steps to configure the ISO installation procedure except for step 5 where the network is configured:

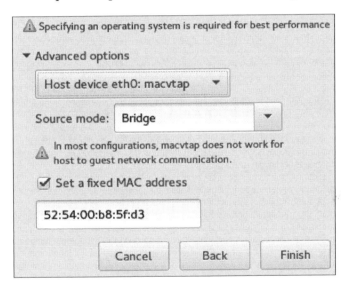

2. In **Advanced options** use **Host device eth0:macvtap** from the drop-down list and set **Source mode** to **Bridge**. Set a custom MAC address if you need to and click on the **Finish** button to begin the installation.

Importing an existing disk image

As the name suggests, this allows you to import a pre-installed and configured disk image instead of doing a manual installation. The disk image must contain a bootable operating system. This is commonly used for distributing pre-built appliance images and also for moving a virtual machine from one host to another in offline mode.

Importing a disk is much faster than other options for preparing a virtual machine. Many Linux distros are available as pre-configured bootable disk images.

 You can download a pre-configured disk Fedora 22 image here: `https://getfedora.org/en/cloud/download/`.

1. Launch the **Create a New Virtual Machine** wizard from the virt-manager GUI and select **Import existing disk image** as the OS installation method.

2. Provide the existing image path. Make sure it's stored in one of the defined storage pools or a place that is accessible by virt-manager. Click on the **Forward** button and follow the remaining steps, which are the same as the ISO installation procedure (except for the step that requires a virtual machine to be ready):

Introducing virt-install

`virt-install` is an interactive command-line tool that can be used to set up the guest and then start the installation process.

Execute the `virt-install` command as root to begin. There are many options available with `virt-install` that can be passed as arguments to configure the installation to meet your virtual machine creation requirements. `virt-install` is a scripting-friendly command. It can be easily embedded in scripts to automate virtual machine creation.

Installing a Windows 7 Guest using the virt-install command

Before starting the operating system installation using the `virt-install` command, it is necessary to have a virtual disk created. To create a virtual disk, use the `qemu-img` command:

1. Create a virtual disk of the desired size. Here for example, we will create a 20 GB disk with the `raw` disk format:

   ```
   qemu-img create -f raw -o size=10G /var/lib/libvirt/qemu/win7.img
   ```

2. Then start `virt-install` by running the following command:

   ```
   virt-install \
   --name Win7 \
   --ram 1024 \
   --disk path=./var/lib/libvirt/qemu/win7.img \
   --vcpus 1 \
   --os-type Windows \
   --os-variant Windows7 \
   --network bridge=virbr0 \
   --graphics vnc,port=5999 \
   --console pty,target_type=serial \
   --cdrom ./win7.iso \
   ```

   Similarly, you can use the `virt-install -promot` command for interactive installation. It will ask you to enter the above information sequentially and interactively.

3. Just like with the **Virtual Machine Manager**, after creating the virtual machine you have to take the console of the VM and proceed with actual guest installation. To take the virtual machine console, use the `virt-viewer` utility:

```
virt-viewer <virtual machine > name
```

Automated virtual machine deployment

Virtual machine creation and guest operating system installation are two different tasks. Creating a VM is like provisioning new PC hardware, but you need to install the OS separately

As you have seen with virt-manager or virt-install, a VM is first configured with the desired hardware resources, then you use one of the support installation methods to install the OS. Installing the actual operating system (also known as the Guest in virtualization terminology) is done in exactly same manner as on a physical system; the operating system's installer asks for configuration details and configures the system accordingly.

What if both of these tasks are combined and a virtual machine is created (along with a full operating system installation) in one go? It would clearly help to deploy the virtual machines much more rapidly and in a more automated way.

Tools such as virt-builder and oz can be used to combine these two tasks and accelerate the installation of new VM images by eliminating the need to manually install an OS. Let's first see what virt-builder is and how it works, with an example.

Introducing virt-builder

virt-builder is a command-line tool that creates disk images using cleanly prepared, digitally signed OS templates and customizes them to quickly build new virtual machines. virt-builder can build images for Fedora, Ubuntu, CentOS, Debian, and a few others.

This utility is provided by the `libguestfs-tools-c` package and can be installed by running the `yum install libguestfs-tools-c -y` command.

Please note that virt-builder by default downloads OS templates from the `http://libguestfs.org/download/builder/` repository; to access this repository Internet connectivity is mandatory. Without this, the tool will not work unless there is a local repository available. virt-builder's local repository creation is beyond the scope of this book. However, the procedure is well documented in the virt-builder man page.

For instance, if you want to create a CentOS 7.1 Guest with a 50 GB disk, using virt-builder this is as easy as running the following command:

```
# cd /var/lib/libvirt/qemu/ ; /usr/bin/virt-builder centos-7.1 --format
raw --size 50G
```

```
[    1.0] Downloading: http://libguestfs.org/download/builder/centos-
7.1.xz
[    2.0] Planning how to build this image
[    2.0] Uncompressing
[   14.0] Resizing (using virt-resize) to expand the disk to 50.0G
[  149.0] Opening the new disk
[  179.0] Setting a random seed
[  180.0] Setting passwords
virt-builder: Setting random password of root to Arw83LnDi66eMcmh
[  198.0] Finishing off
                   Output file: centos-7.1.img
                   Output size: 50.0G
                 Output format: raw
           Total usable space: 48.1G
                    Free space: 47.3G (98%)
```

Now enter the second command:

```
#virt-install --name centos --ram 1028 --vcpus=2 --disk path=/var/lib/
libvirt/qemu/centos-7.1.img  --import
```

As you can see, it first downloaded the template, uncompressed it, resized the disk image to fit the given size, seeded data from the template to the image, customized it (set a random root password), and then finished. The resulting VM has no user accounts, has a random root password, and only uses the minimum amount of disk space required by the OS itself, but will grow up to 50 GB if needed.

The image is stored in the `/var/lib/libvirt/qemu/` directory with `centos-7.1.img` as the name.

The second command—`virt-install`—just imported the image and created a virtual machine out of it.

Running `virsh list --all` will list the newly created virtual machine and `#virsh start <vmname>` will start it. To log in as the root user use the random root password displayed in the output; your virtual machine is now ready.

In this example, `root password` is the only customization that is done but there are many other customizations that can be done—for example, installing software, setting the hostname, editing arbitrary files, creating users, and so on. To learn more about the possible customization that can be done for a guest, refer to the man page for `virt-builder` and `#virt-builder --note <guest >` as they list the kickstart and installation scripts used for that particular guest.

virt-builder caches the downloaded template in the current user's home directory. The location of the cache is `$XDG_CACHE_HOME/virt-builder/` or `$HOME/.cache/virt-builder`.

You can print out information about the cache directory, including which guests are currently cached, by running the `virt-builder --print-cache` command:

```
# virt-builder --print-cache
cache directory: /root/.cache/virt-builder
centos-6              x86_64     no
centos-7.0            x86_64     no
centos-7.1            x86_64     cached
cirros-0.3.1          x86_64     no
debian-6              x86_64     no
debian-7              x86_64     no
debian-8              x86_64     no
fedora-18             x86_64     no
fedora-19             x86_64     no
fedora-20             x86_64     no
fedora-21             x86_64     no
fedora-21             aarch64    no
fedora-21             armv7l     no
fedora-21             ppc64      no
```

fedora-21	ppc64le	no
fedora-22	x86_64	no
fedora-22	aarch64	no
fedora-22	armv7l	no
scientificlinux-6	x86_64	no
ubuntu-10.04	x86_64	no
ubuntu-12.04	x86_64	no
ubuntu-14.04	x86_64	no

Here you can see that the `centos-7.1` template is cached. The next time you create a centos-7.1 guest it will use the cached template and create the virtual machine even faster.

The cache can be deleted by running the following command to free up space:

```
#virt-builder --delete-cache
```

You can even download all (current) templates to the local cache by executing the `virt-builder --cache-all-templates` command.

 Use the `--verbose` switch if you encounter any problems with `virt-builder` to produce verbose output.

While virt-builder is very fast, it only works with Linux guests. However, this utility is limited for Linux guests only and lacks Windows guest support; this is where the oz utility comes into the picture. If you want something more flexible, use oz.

Introducing oz

oz is another utility for creating **Just Enough Operating System (JEOS)** guests. It facilitates the automatic installation of operating systems with only minimal up-front input from the end user. The input for oz is a template (TDL format) which describes the instructions for creating the image:

- The ISO or URI on which the image will be based
- Disk size
- The extra packages to install
- The commands to execute after the image is created
- The files to inject after the image is created

...omatically install a wide variety of OSes, including Windows. Under the ... uses a set of predefined kickstart files for Red Hat-based systems, preseed ... for Debian-based systems, and XML files that allow unattended Windows ...stalls to automate the installation.

Currently, it supports the i386 and x86_64 architectures. The following is a list of OSes that it supports:

- Debian: 5, 6, 7
- Fedora Core: 1, 2, 3, 4, 5, 6
- Fedora: 7, 8, 9, 10, 11, 12, 13, 14, 15, 16, 17, 18, 19, 20, 21
- FreeBSD: 10
- Mageia: 4
- Mandrake: 8.2, 9.1, 9.2, 10.0, 10.1
- Mandriva: 2005, 2006.0, 2007.0, 2008.0
- OpenSUSE: 10.3, 11.0, 11.1, 11.2, 11.3, 11.4, 12.1, 12.2, 12.3, 13.1
- RHEL 2.1: GOLD, U2, U3, U4, U5, U6
- RHEL 7: Beta, 0
- RHEL/CentOS 3: GOLD, U1, U2, U3, U4, U5, U6, U7, U8, U9
- RHEL/CentOS/Scientific Linux 4: GOLD, U1, U2, U3, U4, U5, U6, U7, U8, U9
- RHEL/OL/CentOS/Scientific Linux{,CERN} 5: GOLD, U1, U2, U3, U4, U5, U6, U7, U8, U9, U10, U11
- RHEL/OL/CentOS/Scientific Linux{,CERN} 6: 0, 1, 2, 3, 4, 5
- RHL: 7.0, 7.1, 7.2, 7.3, 8, 9
- Ubuntu: 5.04, 5.10, 6.06[.1,.2], 6.10, 7.04, 7.10, 8.04[.1,.2,.3,.4], 8.10, 9.04, 9.10, 10.04[.1,.2,.3], 10.10, 11.04, 11.10, 12.04[.1,.2,.3,.4,.5], 12.10, 13.04, 13.10, 14.04[.1], 14.10
- Windows: 2000, XP, 2003, 7, 2008, 2012, 8, 8.1

The procedure for creating a virtual machine using oz is as follows:

1. Install the `oz` and `libguestfs-tools` packages using the following command:

   ```
   #yum install -y oz libguestfs-tools
   ```

2. Get the ISO media of the desired operating system that you wish to install using oz. For Linux guests, a network-based installation tree exposed over HTTP can also be used. For example:

   - For Fedora 22: `http://dl.fedoraproject.org/pub/fedora/linux/releases/22/Server/x86_64/os/`

   - For CentOS 7: `http://mirrors.dcarsat.com.ar/centos/7/os/x86_64/`

3. Create a simple **TDL (Template Definition Language)** file. All the supported attributes for a TDL file can be found here: `https://github.com/clalancette/oz/wiki/Oz-template-description-language`

4. Run the `oz-install` command to build an image:

   ```
   #oz-install -u -d3 TDL_FILE_PATH
   ```

Syntax:

- u: After installation, perform the customization
- d: Turn up the logging level. The levels are:
  - 0: Errors only (this is the default)
  - 1: Errors and warnings
  - 2: Errors, warnings, and information
  - 3: All messages
  - 4: All messages, prepended with the level and classname

This will result in a libvirt XML file (containing the image path and other parameters), which you can use to immediately boot the guest:

```
virsh define  <xml_fike>
virsh start <vm_name>
```

The oz configuration file

`/etc/oz/oz.cfg` is the oz file for VM configuration. It's in the standard INI format with four sections: `paths`, `libvirt`, `cache`, and `icicle`. Let's look at the content of the file:

```
------------
[paths]
output_dir = /var/lib/libvirt/images
data_dir = /var/lib/oz
screenshot_dir = /var/lib/oz/screenshots
# sshprivkey = /etc/oz/id_rsa-icicle-gen

[libvirt]
uri = qemu:///system
image_type = raw
# type = kvm
# bridge_name = virbr0
# cpus = 1
# memory = 1024

[cache]
original_media = yes
modified_media = no
jeos = no

[icicle]
safe_generation = no
```

The following are some important configuration directives of which you should be aware:

- `output_dir`: This describes the location in which to store images after they are built. The default location is `/var/lib/libvirt/images/`. If you wish to storage the resultant image in some other location, you can change it here.

- `bridge_name`: The bridge to which the VM should be connected. By default it uses `virbr0`.

- `memory`: Using the configuration directive you can define how much memory should be used inside the virtual machine.

- `cpus`: This defines how many CPUs should be used for the virtual machine.

All other configuration directive usage is documented at `https://github.com/clalancette/oz/wiki/oz-customize`.

Creating a virtual machine using oz

For demonstration purposes, let's create a Windows 7 virtual machine with the following configuration:

- The resultant virtual machine should have 2048 memory assigned to it
- The bridge to which the virtual machine is connected should be vswitch
- The disk size should be 50G
- The install media should be an ISO file stored locally on the system

To create a virtual machine with preceding configuration using oz tool, perform the following steps:

1. First edit the /etc/oz/oz.cfg file, set the memory and bridge configuration directives accordingly, and then save the file and exit:

    ```
    memory = 2048
    bridge_name = vswitch
    ```

2. Create a TDL file named win7.tdl containing the following element and save it at the /root/ location (you can use vi or any other editor of your choice):

    ```
    <template>
    <name>win7jeos</name>
    <os>
    <name>Windows</name>
    <version>7</version>
    <arch>i386</arch>
    <install type='iso'>
    <iso>file:///path/to/isos/win2k.iso</iso>
    </install>
    <key>MY_KEY_HERE</key>
    </os>
    <disk>
    <size>50</size>
    </disk>
    <description>Minimal Windows7 </description>
    </template>
    ```

    - Replace file:///path/to/isos/win2k.iso with the actual path of the ISO file
    - Replace MY_KEY_HERE with a valid key

Windows requires a key, so oz will fail if the `<key>` element is missing.

3. Now run `oz-install`:

```
#oz-install -u -d3 /root/win7.tdl
```

4. Completion of a successful `oz-install` should look like this:

```
[. . .]
INFO:oz.Guest.windows7:Cleaning up after install
        Libvirt XML was written to win7jeos_feb_11-2016
```

5. Define the virtual machine using `virsh` command and start it:

```
#virsh define win7jeos_feb_11-2016
#virsh start win7jeos
```

Summary

In this chapter you first learned about the default network and storage configuration set by libvirt to facilitate the required infrastructure for virtual machine creation and then learned the different guest installation methods, which include PXE, Network, ISO, and importing a pre-configured bootable OS image. We also have seen how `virt-builder` and `oz` help in rapidly creating virtual machines.

In the next chapter, we will provide more detailed information about virtual storage and networks.

5
Network and Storage

In the world of virtualization, networking and storage can be put into two categories:

- **Physical**: A network and storage infrastructure that is built with the help of a host system to provide networking and storage needs for the virtual machines. In the case of networking, this includes layer 3 and 2 components of the network, software bridge, iptables rules, and so on. In the case of storage, this includes storage devices to provide storage to hypervisor (SAN, ISCSI, and so on), LVM, different file systems, NFS, and so on.

- **Virtual**: A network and storage infrastructure, which is created with the help of virtualization software; it includes both emulated and paravirtualized network and storage devices created inside the VM and the virtual devices created on the host to provide network a connectivity and storage to the VMs.

When you imagine your virtualization infrastructure in these terms, it is easy to understand the whole setup. This approach is also good when you want to troubleshoot the environment.

In this chapter, we are going to discuss network and storage configuration for KVM virtualization. We will cover the following topics:

- Creation of Linux bridge
- What are TUN and TAP devices
- Various network connectivity options available for KVM VMs Virtual Storage Pools Creation

Virtual networking

Many people consider virtual networking in libvirt to be complicated. Perhaps it is the number of options available to provide networking to a virtual machine that makes the libvirt networking appear complicated.

The main component of libvirt networking is the virtual network switch, also known as the **bridge**. You can imagine a bridge as a physical switch. In a real switch, there are a limited number of physical ports to attach to your servers. Here, on the Linux bridge, there are unlimited numbers of virtual ports to which the interfaces to virtual machines are attached. Similar to a physical switch, bridge learns the MAC addresses from the packets it receives and stores those MAC addresses in the MAC table. The packet (frames) forwarding decisions are taken based on the MAC addresses that it learned and stored in the MAC table.

We mentioned about the interfaces attached to the ports of a bridge. These interfaces are special network devices called **TAP devices**. If you try to imagine this in physical network terms, consider TAP devices as the network cable that carries the Ethernet frames between your virtual machine and bridge. This TAP device is a part of TUN/TAP implementation available within the Linux kernel.

> TUN, which stands for "tunnel", simulates a network layer device and it operates at OSI reference model's layer 3 packets, such as IP packets. TAP (namely a network tap) simulates a link layer device and it operates at OSI reference model's layer 2 packets, such as Ethernet frames. TUN is used with routing, while TAP is used to create a network bridge.

Before moving to the next topic, we will create a bridge and then add a TAP device to it.

Make sure the bridge module is loaded into the kernel. If it is not loaded, use `modprobe bridge` to load the module:

```
# lsmod | grep bridge
bridge                 114688  1 ebtable_broute
```

Run the following command to create a bridge called `tester`:

```
# brctl addbr tester
```

> Note: The `brctl` command is provided by the package `bridge-utils`.

Let's see if the bridge is created:

```
# brctl show
bridge name     bridge id  STP enabled     interfaces
tester          8000.460a80dd627d       no
```

The # `brctl show` command will list all the available bridges on the server, along with some basic information, such as the ID of the bridge, **Spanning Tree Protocol (STP)** status, and the interfaces attached to it. Here the tester bridge does not have any interfaces attached to its virtual ports.

A Linux bridge will also be shown as a network device. To see the network details of the bridge tester, use the `ip` command:

```
# ip link show tester
6: tester: <BROADCAST,MULTICAST>mtu 1500 qdiscnoop state DOWN mode
DEFAULT group default link/ether 26:84:f2:f8:09:e0 brdff:ff:ff:ff:ff:ff
```

You can also use `ifconfig` to check and configure the network settings for a Linux bridge; `ifconfig` is relatively easy to read and understand but not as feature-rich as `ip` command:

```
# ifconfig tester
tester: flags=4098<BROADCAST,MULTICAST>mtu 1500
ether26:84:f2:f8:09:e0txqueuelen 1000   (Ethernet)
        RX packets 0  bytes 0 (0.0 B)
        RX errors 0  dropped 0  overruns 0   frame 0
        TX packets 0  bytes 0 (0.0 B)
        TX errors 0  dropped 0 overruns 0   carrier 0   collisions 0
```

The Linux bridge tester is now ready. Let's create and add a TAP device to it.

First check if the TUN/TAP device module is loaded into the kernel. If not, you already know the drill:

```
# lsmod | greptun
tun  28672  1
```

Run the following command to create a tap device named `vm-vnic`:

```
# ip tuntap add dev vm-vnic mode tap
# ip link show vm-vnic
 7: vm-vnic: <BROADCAST,MULTICAST>mtu 1500 qdiscnoop state DOWN
mode DEFAULT group default qlen 500 link/ether 46:0a:80:dd:62:7d
brdff:ff:ff:ff:ff:ff
```

We now have a bridge named `tester` and a tap device named `vm-vnic`. Let's add `vm-vnic` to tester.

```
# brctl addif tester vm-vnic
# brctl show
bridge name   bridge id       STP enabled   interfaces
tester        8000.460a80dd627d   no          vm-vnic
```

You can see that `vm-vnic` is an interface added to the bridge tester. Now `vm-vnic` can act as the interface between your virtual machine and the bridge tester, which in turn enables the virtual machine to communicate with other virtual machines added to this bridge:

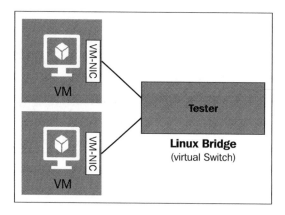

It is time to put on your thinking cap. See if you can answer the following questions; don't worry, we'll answer them later in this chapter. The questions are:

- Did you notice any difference in the MAC address of the bridge tester when you added the TAP device `vm-vnic`?
- Is it possible to assign an IP address to a bridge? If yes, why might you need to do that?
- Try to understand the details when you run, the `# brctlshowmacs tester` command?

We will now show you how to remove all the things that you just created. We will not need them for the rest of this chapter.

Remove the `vm-vnic` tap device from the `tester` bridge:

```
# brctl delif tester vm-vnic
# brctl show tester
bridge name   bridge id      STP enabled  interfaces
tester        8000.460a80dd627d   no
```

Once the `vm-vnic` is removed from the bridge, remove the tap device using the `ip` command:

```
# ip tuntap del dev vm-vnic mode tap
```

Finally, remove the `tester` bridge:

```
# brctl delbr tester; echo $?
0
```

If you want to see all the available options, then run `brctl -help`:

```
# brctl --help
 Usage: brctl [commands]
commands:
  addbr    <bridge>        add bridge
  delbr    <bridge>        delete bridge
  addif    <bridge><device>    add interface to bridge
  delif    <bridge><device>    delete interface from bridge
  hairpin       <bridge><port> {on|off}  turn hairpin on/off
  setageing  <bridge><time>     set ageing time
  setbridgeprio  <bridge><prio>     set bridge priority
  setfd  <bridge><time>     set bridge forward delay
  sethello  <bridge><time>     set hello time
  setmaxage  <bridge><time>     set max message age
  setpathcost  <bridge><port><cost>  set path cost
  setportprio  <bridge><port><prio>  set port priority
  show          [ <bridge> ]      show a list of bridges
  showmacs  <bridge>      show a list of mac addrs
  showstp  <bridge>      show bridge stp info
  stp  <bridge> {on|off}    turn stp on/off
```

These are the same steps that libvirt carried out in the backend while enabling or disabling networking for a virtual machine. We want you to understand this procedure thoroughly before moving ahead.

Virtual networking using libvirt

In the previous chapter, we introduced you to some of the available options of virtual networking in libvirt. In this chapter, we will revisit them again in detail.

The types of virtual networking available are as follows:

- Isolated virtual network
- Routed virtual network
- NATed virtual network
- Bridged network using a physical NIC, VLAN interface, bond interface, and bonded VLAN interface
- MacVTap
- PCI passthrough NPIV
- OVS

Additionally, we will cover the details of enabling DHCP and DNS for your virtual network and the *Default* virtual network that comes preconfigured with libvirt.

Before starting, let's go back to *Chapter 3, Setting Up Standalone KVM Virtualization*, and create one more Linux virtual machine. This is required to do the hands on.

Isolated virtual network

As the name suggests, we we are creating a closed network for the virtual machines. In this configuration, only the virtual machines which are added to this network can communicate with each other:

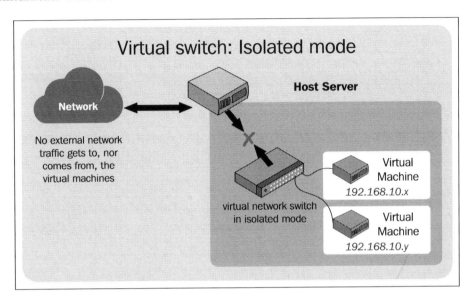

As you can see in the preceding image, even the host will be able to communicate with the virtual machines added to this virtual network.

To create an isolated virtual network using virt-manager, perform the following steps:

1. Navigate to **virt-manager** | **Edit** | **Connection details** | **Virtual Networks**. Click on the + sign.

2. Enter the name of the virtual network as `isolated`:

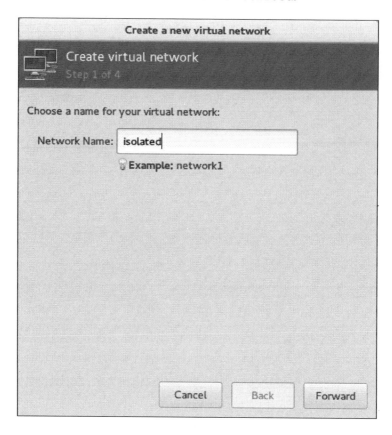

3. Skip the IPv4 address configuration:

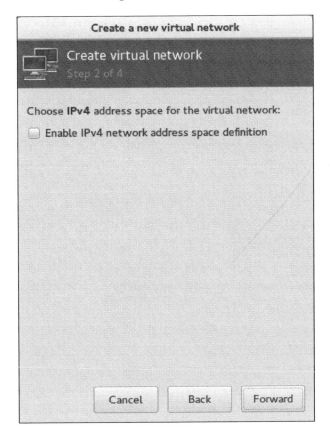

4. Disable the IPv6 address configuration:

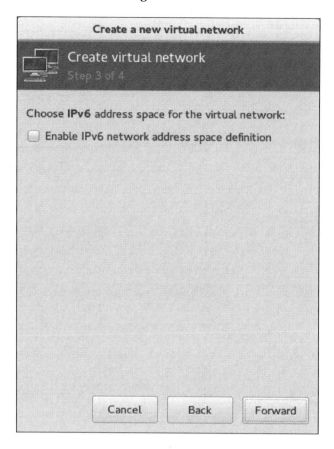

5. Select only **Isolated virtual network** and leave **DNS Domain Name** blank.
    Click on **Finish** to create the isolated virtual network:

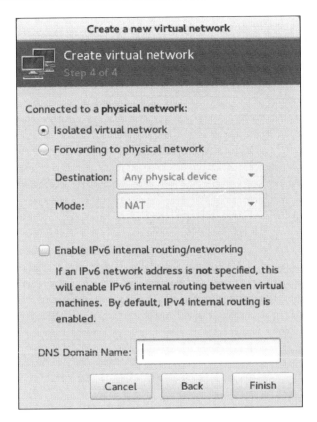

6. Check the details of the **isolated** virtual network:

We will now create the isolated network using the `virsh` command. For that, we need to create an XML file with the following contents and save it as `isolated.xml`:

```
# cat isolated.xml

<network> <name>isolated</name>

</network>
```

Here:

- `<network>`: This is used for defining the virtual network.
- `<name>`: This is used for defining the name of the virtual network. Here, it is isolated.

To define a network using the XML file created in the preceding section, use the `net-define` option of the `virsh` command followed by the path of the XML file:

```
# virsh net-define isolated.xml

 Network isolated defined from isolated.xml
```

Once the network is defined, you can list all the available networks using the `net-list` command:

```
# virsh net-list --all
Name              State        Autostart  Persistent
-------------------------------------------------------------
default           active       yes        yes
isolated          inactive     no         yes
```

In the preceding output, you can see that the Linux bridge named `isolated` is now defined (added/created). Let's see the XML file `libvirt` being created based on the configuration we provided through the `isolated.xml`. Use the `net-dumpxml` option, as shown in the following command, to get the details of the a Linux bridge:

```
# virsh net-dumpxml isolated
<network>
<name>isolated</name>
<uuid>84147b7d-a95f-4bc2-a4d9-80baab391a18</uuid>
<bridge name='virbr1' stp='on' delay='0'/>
<mac address='52:54:00:0e:c2:b5'/>
</network>
```

Here, you can see that libvirt added a few additional parameters. Each is explained in the following points:

- `<uuid>`: A unique ID of your bridge.
- `<bridge>`: Used for defining the bridge details. Here, the name of the bridge is `virbr1`, with STP ON and DELAY 0. These are the same parameters you can control using the `brctl` command. STP is set by `stp` and DELAY by `setfd`. Go back and check the `brctl` command options.
- `<mac>`: The MAC address of the bridge to be assigned at the time of the creation.

As you can see, libvirt added the rest of the required parameters; you can mention these in your XML file when required. Our recommendation is that you leave it to libvirt to avoid conflicts.

> `net-create` is similar to `net-define`. The difference is that it will not create a persistent virtual network. Once destroyed, it is removed and has to be created again using the `net-create` command.

Once you define a network using `net-define`, the configuration file will be stored in `/etc/libvirt/qemu/networks/` as an XML file with the same name as your virtual network:

```
# cat /etc/libvirt/qemu/networks/isolated.xml
<!--
WARNING: THIS IS AN AUTO-GENERATED FILE. CHANGES TO IT ARE LIKELY TO BE
OVERWRITTEN AND LOST. Changes to this xml configuration should be made
using:
virsh net-edit isolated
or other application using the libvirt API.
<network>
<name>isolated</name>
<uuid>84147b7d-a95f-4bc2-a4d9-80baab391a18</uuid>
<bridge name='virbr1' stp='on' delay='0'/>
<mac address='52:54:00:0e:c2:b5'/>
</network>
```

The isolated virtual network is now defined. Let's activate it. For virt-manger (fig 4-8), use the play and stop buttons after selecting the isolated virtual network. The button that shows a red circle with an x in the middle is used for un-defining the network. Un-defining a virtual network will remove it permanently:

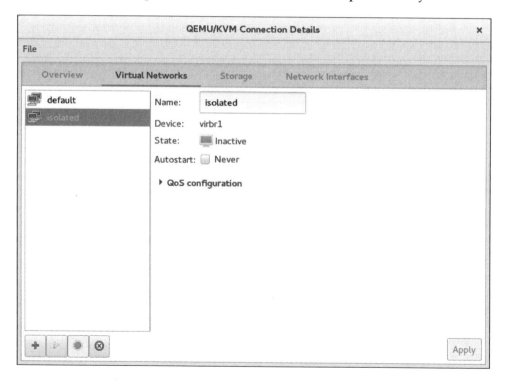

Use **Autostart** if you want to start the virtual network automatically when libvirt service is started. Using `virsh`, it is `virsh net-autostart isolated`.

Let's now activate an isolated virtual network using `virsh`. If the virtual network is activated using virt-manager, deactivate it using the stop button:

```
# virsh net-start isolated
Network isolated started
# virsh net-list --all
 Name              State        Autostart   Persistent
----------------------------------------------------------
 default           active       yes          yes
 isolated          active       no           yes
```

The state is changed from `inactive` to `active`. The virtual network (bridge) is now ready to use.

How do you add a virtual network interface card to a virtual machine?

In order to use the preceding virtual network, right-click on your virtual machine | **Open** | **Virtual Hardware details** (the bulb icon) | **Add Hardware** | **Network**. Select **Network source** as **isolated**; the MAC address will be generated by libvirt and **Device model** as **virtio**. Click on **Finish**. The other two device models, `e1000` (Intel) and `rtl1839` (Realtek), are not recommended for production workloads as they are emulated devices and do not give the best performance. They are mostly used while installing legacy operating systems that do not have support for virtio devices. For Linux, you need to use kernel version 2.6.25 or higher, as older kernels do not support virtio devices

For Windows, you have to install the virtio drivers separately. We will cover more on virtio in our virtualization optimization chapter:

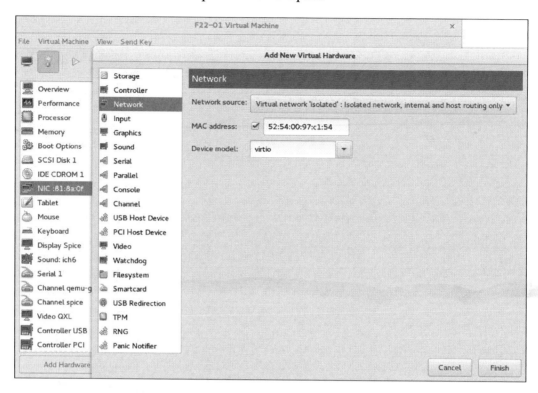

A virtio virtual NIC can be added while the virtual machine is running; it will be ready to use inside the virtual machine immediately.

Let's add a virtual NIC to the other virtual machine. In our environment, the name of the virtual machine is F22-02.

Before attaching a second NIC, we will get the details of the current virtual NIC attached to the virtual machine F22-02 using domiflist. The output of this command will help you define the parameters while attaching a second virtual NIC to the virtual machine:

```
# virsh domiflist F22-02
Interface   Type       Source     Model       MAC
---------------------------------------------------------------
vnet2       network    default    virtio      52:54:00:b0:50:98
Interface - Name of the tap interface attached to the bridge.
Type - Type of device
```

```
Source - Name of the virtual network.
Model - Virtual NIC model.
MAC - MAC address of the virtual NIC (not the MAC of vnet2).
```

Let's attach a new virtual interface to `F22-02`:

```
# virsh attach-interface --domain F22-02 --source isolated --type network
--model virtio --config --live
Interface attached successfully
# virsh domiflist F22-02
Interface  Type    Source    Model      MAC
-----------------------------------------------------------------
vnet2  network  default  virtio  52:54:00:b0:50:98
vnet3  network  isolated    virtio  52:54:00:2b:0d:0c
```

You have attached the virtual network interface of type `virtio`. The interface is using an isolated virtual network. There are two new options in this command, which is not self explanatory:

- `--config`: This will make the change persistent in the next startup of the VM.
- `--live`: This will inform libvirt that you are attaching the NIC to a live virtual machine. Remove `--live` if the virtual machine is not running.

 If you just wanted to attach a virtual network interface temporarily to a virtual machine, just use `--live` and ignore `--config`.

Another option that might be useful for some is `--mac`. This can be used to add a custom MAC address.

Let's now check how the bridge for the isolated virtual interface is created and the interfaces attached.

The bridge interface created by the virtual network is `virbr1`. How did we find it? Remember the `net-dumpxml` option.

Now you know the bridge name. Let's see the interfaces that are attached to the bridge:

```
# brctl show virbr1
bridge name    bridge id       STP enabled    interfaces
virbr1         8000.5254000ec2b5    yes       virbr1-nic
                    vnet1
                    vnet3
```

The `virbr1-nic` interface is created by libvirt when it starts `virbr1`. The purpose of this interface is to provide a consistent and reliable MAC address for the `virbr1` bridge. The bridge copies the MAC address of the first interface, which is added to it, and `virbr1-nic` is always the first interface added to it by libvirt and never being removed till the bridge is destroyed.

`vnet1` and `vnet3` are the virtual network interfaces added to the respective VMs.

You can now assign IPs to these newly added interfaces and see if you will be able to ping the virtual machines added to the isolated network. We are leaving that task to you. Will you be able to ping your virtual machines from the hypervisor?

Now, let's remove the new interface added to the virtual machine `F22-02` using `virsh`. In a production environment, be careful when you execute with the `--live` option. It can disrupt the existing network activity:

```
# virsh detach-interface --domain F22-02 --type network --mac
52:54:00:2b:0d:0c
```

```
--config --live
Interface detached successfully
```

Even if the topic is about isolated virtual networks, we have covered other operations on virtual network and virtual NIC. These operations are similar for all virtual networks.

Routed virtual network

In a routed mode, the virtual network is connected to the physical network using the IP routes specified on the hypervisor. These IP routes are used to route the traffic from the virtual machines to the network attached to the hypervisor. The key point that you need to remember with this configuration is that you need to set up the correct IP route on your router or gateway devices also so that the reply packet should reach the hypervisor back. If there are no routes defined, the reply packet will never reach the host. This mode is not commonly used, unless you have a special use case to create a network with this complexity. The following image shows how a routed network works in the real world:

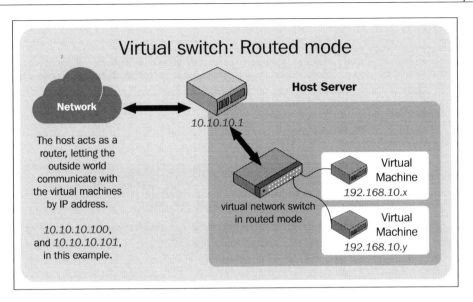

Let's first do the configuration using virt-manager. The name of the virtual network is routed, as shown in the following screenshot:

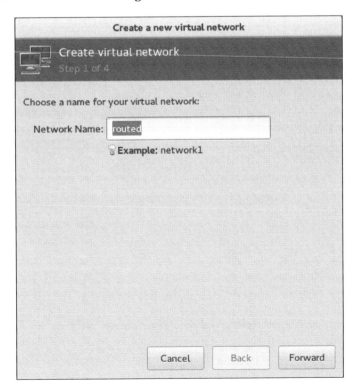

Enable IPv4 only. Disable **DHCP and Static Routes**. Here, we are using
`192.168.10.0/24` as our network. libvirt will automatically assign a gateway for
the network. Usually, it is going to be the first IP in the range, `192.168.10.1` and is
assigned to the bridge interface. In step 2 of the **Create virtual network** wizard, tick
Enable IPv4 network address space definition and **Enable DHCPv4**. The default
DHCP range is `192.168.100.128 – 192.168.100.254`; you are free to change it as
per your need:

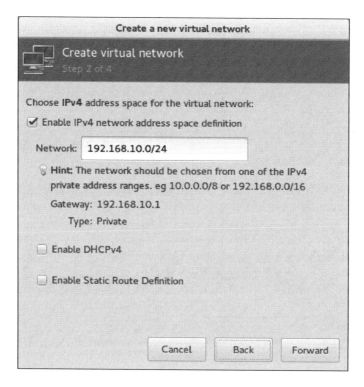

After specifying the DHCP range, click on the **Forward** button. In step 3, you can optionally enable IPv6 configuration:

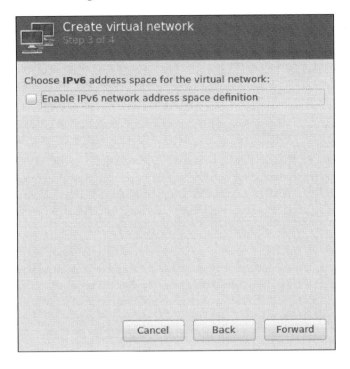

We are going to skip step 3, which is the IPv6 configuration. You can enable it later by editing the configuration file using the `virsh` command. We will provide a sample configuration for you to check. If required, you can enable it at this stage. We are leaving that to your choice.

In the final step, choose the host interface where you would like to forward the traffic (for us it is em1) from this virtual network and select the **Mode** as **Routed**. Click on **Finish** to create this virtual network:

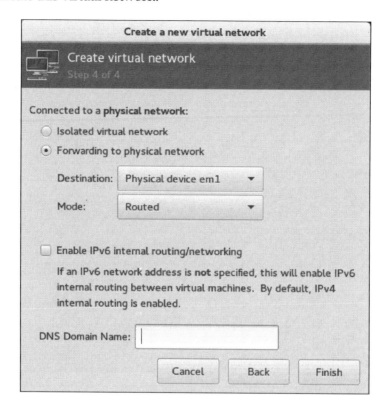

Let's now create the same configuration using virsh instead of the GUI tool. Delete the routed virtual network you have just created and open a terminal window.

Create an XML configuration file similar to the following example and save it as routed.xml. Once the configuration file is ready, you can start defining the network:

```
# cat routed.xml
<network>
<name>routed</name>
<forward dev='em1' mode='route'>
  <interface dev='em1'/>
</forward>
<ip address='192.168.10.1' netmask='255.255.255.0'>
</ip>
```

```
</network>
# virsh net-define routed.xml
```

Network routed defined from `routed.xml`:

```
# virsh net-start routed
Network routed started
# virsh auto-start routed
```

Network route marked as auto start:

```
# virsh net-info routed
Name:           routed
UUID:           9a1d8de7-5627-4f08-a3d1-836b7a5fe060
Active:         yes
Persistent:     yes
Autostart:      yes
Bridge:         virbr2
```

Editing a virtual network

Let's edit a routed virtual network and modify the routing configuration so that the packets from the virtual machines can be forwarded to any interface available on the host based on IP route rules specified on the host. The aim of this example is to show how to modify a virtual network once it is created with your configuration.

Before editing the virtual network, you need to stop the virtual network first:

```
# virsh net-destroy routed
Network routed destroyed
```

Edit the network using `net-edit`:

```
# virsh net edit routed
```

`net-edit` will make a temporary copy of the configuration file used by `routed` in `/tmp` and then open `vim` using that temp file. Here we are going to edit the `<forward>` tag.

Old configuration:

```
<forward dev='em1' mode='route'>
<interface dev='em1'/>
</forward>
```

New configuration:

```
<network>
  <name>routed</name>
  <uuid>9a1d8de7-5627-4f08-a3d1-836b7a5fe060</uuid>
  <forward mode='route'/>
  <bridge name='virbr2' stp='on' delay='0'/>
  <mac address='52:54:00:f1:cb:30'/>
  <ip address='192.168.10.1' netmask='255.255.255.0'>
  </ip>
</network>
```

After editing, save it using `:wq`. If you make a mistake, `virsh` will prompt you. Here, we removed < from `<forward>` and then tried to save the configuration:

```
error: (network_definition):6: Opening and ending tag mismatch: network line 1 and forward
  </forward>
-----------^
Failed. Try again? [y,n,f,?]:
Network routed XML configuration edited.
```

Even if you do not get a warning message, it is highly recommended that you verify the configuration change using the `net-dumpxml` command:

```
# virsh net-dumpxml routed

<network>

<name>routed</name>

<uuid>9a1d8de7-5627-4f08-a3d1-836b7a5fe060</uuid>

<forward mode='route'/>

<bridge name='virbr2' stp='on' delay='0'/>

<mac address='52:54:00:f1:cb:30'/>

<ip address='192.168.10.1' netmask='255.255.255.0'>

</ip>

</network>
```

To enable IPv6, you can add a similar to the preceding configuration. The IPv6 address provided is an example:

```
<ip family="ipv6" address="2001:db8:ca2:2::1" prefix="64" >
```

After verifying the configuration, start the virtual network using `net-start`, as shown in the following command:

```
# virsh net-start routed
Network "routed" started
```

NATed virtual network

NATed mode is the most commonly used virtual networking when you want to set up a test environment on your laptop or test machine. This mode allows the virtual machines to communicate with the outside network without using any additional configuration. This method also allows communication between the hypervisor and the virtual machines. The major drawback of this virtual network is that none of the systems outside the hypervisor can reach the virtual machines.

The NATed virtual network is created with the help of `iptables`, specifically using the masquerading option. Hence, stopping `iptables` when VMs are in use can cause network disruption inside the virtual machines:

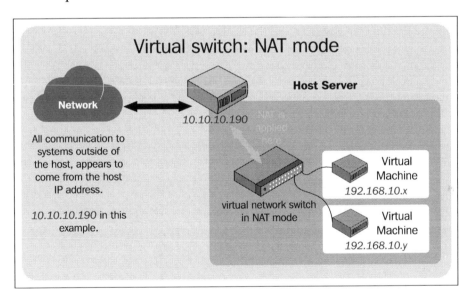

Let's create a virtual network in NATed mode using virt-manager. The steps are similar to a routed virtual network, but instead of choosing the routed method, you select NAT and click on the **Finish** button:

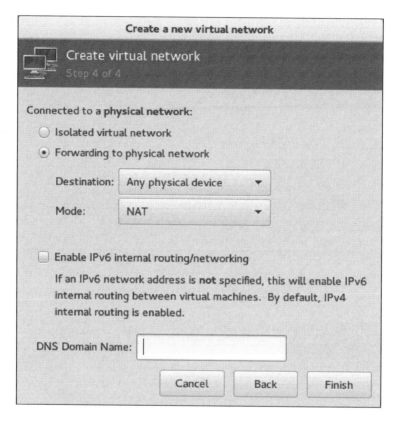

If you are not able reach or ping systems after configuring the NATed network, make sure that the value of `sysctl net.ipv4.ip_forward` is 1.

Bridged network using a physical NIC, VLAN interface, bond interface, and bonded VLAN interface (aka shared physical interface)

In most of the production environment, you will be using a bridge configuration that directly connects a physical NIC to the bridge. The primary reason for using this configuration is that your virtual machine will act as a system that is in the same network as the physical NIC. Unlike the NATed mode, virtual machines can be accessed directly using their IP address, which is essential when you host a service on your virtual machines.

In our test setup, we have three interfaces available: eth0, eth1, and eth2. eth0 has an IP assigned and is used as the management interface. Management interface is an interface used to access the host machine through SSH or similar method with an IP configured. Other two interfaces, eth1 and eth2, are dedicated for bridge configuration and do not have IPs configured.

The general workflow for creating a bridge with shared physical interface(s) is as follows:

1. Complete the physical interfaces' configuration with no IPs. This includes configuring VLAN, bonding, and and so on.

2. Once the physical interfaces are configured, add the final interface to the bridge. It could be a single interface (eth1), bonded interface (bond0), VLAN (eth1.121 or bond0.121), andand so on.

3. Optionally, you can assign an IP to the bridge, not to the physical interface. If you have the management interface, always create a bridge without an IP, unless there is a special requirement.

Your first task is to configure a bridge named br0 using eth0.

Fedora uses **Network Manager** for its network configuration and does not enable SysVinit based network service by default. In our setup, disable **Network Manager** and enable the network service. As this is a dedicated hypervisor, disable **Network Manager**.

Create (or modify) the files, ifcfg-eth1 and ifcfg-br0, so that it will look like the following. You can avoid the comments part:

```
# cd /etc/sysconfig/network-scripts
# cat ifcfg-eth1
DEVICE=eth1
TYPE=Ethernet
#Replace the following with your eth1 interface MAC address
HWADDR=52:54:00:32:56:aa
ONBOOT=yes
#Prevent Network Manager from managing this interface,eth1
NM_CONTROLLED=no
#Add this interface to bridge br0
BRIDGE=br0
# cat ifcfg-br0
DEVICE=br0
```

```
#Initiate bridge creation process for this interface br0
TYPE=Bridge
ONBOOT=yes
NM_CONTROLLED=no
#Set the bridge forward delay to 0.
DELAY=0
Enable the network service and start it.
# systemctl enable network
# systemctl disable NetworkManager
# ifup br0; ifup eth1
# brctl show
```

The br0 bridge is created with the eth1 interface. You can now start using br0 while creating VM's network interfaces. We assume that you have more than one NICs on the host to create virtual networks. If there is only one interface make sure you assign an IP address in the bridge configuration file to access the host over the network. We will now create a bond (bond0) using eth1 and eth2 and add it to br0:

```
# ifdown br0; ifdown eth1
# cat ifcfg-eth1
DEVICE=eth1
TYPE=Ethernet
HWADDR=52:54:00:32:56:aa
ONBOOT=yes
NM_CONTROLLED=no
SLAVE=yes
MASTER=bond0
# cat ifcfg-eth2
DEVICE=eth2
TYPE=Ethernet
HWADDR=52:54:00:a6:02:51
ONBOOT=yes
NM_CONTROLLED=no
SLAVE=yes
MASTER=bond0
# cat ifcfg-bond0
DEVICE=bond0
ONBOOT=yes
# Here we are using bonding mode 1 (active-backup)
```

```
BONDING_OPTS='mode=1 miimon=100'

BRIDGE=br0

NM_CONTROLLED=no

# ifup bond0

# brctl show
```

The `br0` bridge is now created with the `bond0` bond interface. The following diagram will explain the current configuration::

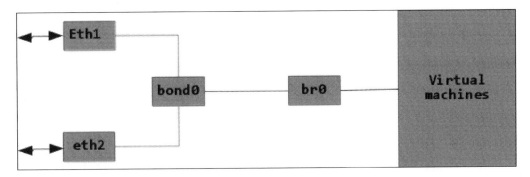

 Using bonding modes one (*active-backup*) and four (*802.3ad*) are considered stable when used with the bridge.

We will now modify `ifcfg-bond0` so that it will create a tagged VLAN named `bond0.123` and will be added to the `br0` bridge:

```
# ifdown bond0; ifdown br0

# cp ifcfg-bond0 ifcfg-bond0.123

# cat ifcfg-bond0.123

DEVICE=bond0.123

ONBOOT=yes

BONDING_OPTS='mode=1 miimon=100'

BRIDGE=br0

NM_CONTROLLED=no

VLAN=yes
```

Now edit `ifcfg-bond0` and comment out `BRIDGE=bro` (`#BRIDGE=br0`):

```
# ifup bond0.123
```

If you would like to configure custom MTU, add MTU to all configuration files, including the bridge. The same MTU should also be added inside a virtual machine's interface configuration.

MacVTap

MacVTap is used when you do not want to create a normal bridge, but want the users in local network to access your virtual machine. This connection type is not used in production systems and is mostly used on workstation systems.

Navigate to **Add Hardware | Network** to add a virtual NIC as the MacVTap interface using virt-manager. At **Network source**, select the physical NIC interface on the host where you want to enable MacVTap:

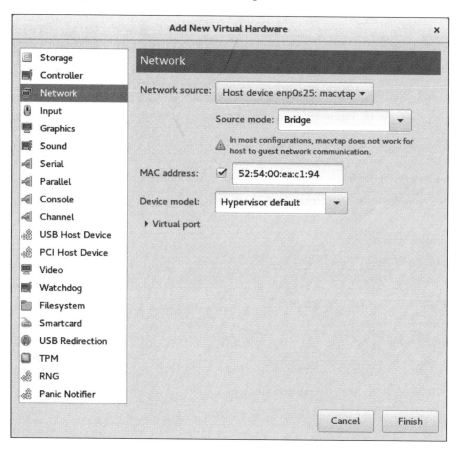

The following is the corresponding configuration from the VM:

```
<interface type='direct'>
<mac address='52:54:00:7b:4b:8c'/>
<source dev='enp0s25' mode='bridge'/>
<model type='virtio'/>
```

PCI passthrough

PCI passthrough is used to pass through PCI devices on the host to a virtual machine. This is primarily used to directly pass network interfaces on the host to a virtual machine for increased performance.

To enable PCI passthrough, you have to use the following steps:

1. Enable Intel VT-d or AMD IOMMU in the BIOS and kernel:

   ```
   # vi /etc/sysconfig/grub
   ```

2. Modify GRUB_CMDLINE_LINUX= to append intel_iommu=on or amd_iommu=on:

```
GRUB_CMDLINE_LINUX="                                         rd.lvm.lv=fedora/swap rhgb quiet intel_iommu=on
```

3. Rebuild the grub2 configuration file as follows and then reboot the hypervisor:

   ```
   # grub2-mkconfig -o /boot/grub2/grub.cfg
   ```

4. Navigate to **Hardware | PCI Host Device** and select the PCI device to pass through:

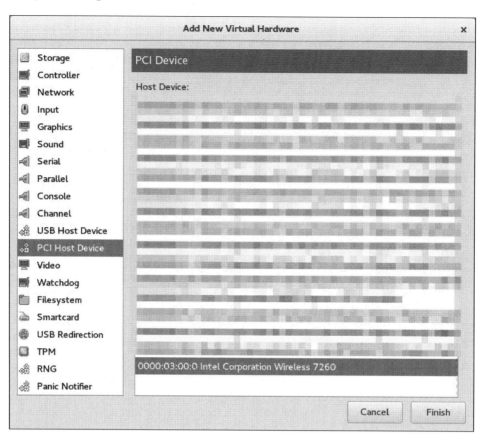

It's all about storage!

Similar to virtual network infrastructure, we need a storage backend to create and save the virtual disks. There is an option to choose a wide variety of storage solution is as backend for virtual machines, from normal file-based storage to logical volume managed storage, gluster container, and many more. Storage backend is created and managed using the libvirt storage API and is called a "storage pool".

In this section, you will learn how to work with unmanaged and managed storage. You will also see how to create storage pools and volumes, including some of the newer options, such as ceph block storage, which allows us to create really large sized virtual disks and attach them to a virtual machine. You will also learn how to attach multiple disks to a single VM.

Working with unmanaged storage

Storage, which is not directly controlled and monitored by libvirt, is s~
with virtual machines and is called unmanaged storage. This means th~
straightforwardly use any file or block a device that is available/visible ~
system as a virtual disk, provided the appropriate permissions are set. Th~
the quickest way to have storage available for virtual machines. This appro~
particularly useful in adding a secondary disk to a virtual machine.

You can attach network shared disks to your virtual machine and take a backup.
let's take an example where you noticed that the root partition (LVM) of your vir~
machine has become full and the guest operating system is alarming loudly. It's
going to crash if the root filesystem is not expanded.

This is an urgent situation; to save the guest operating system from crashing,
you either have to free up some space or expand the root filesystem by adding a
secondary disk to the virtual machine; however, you notice that there is no space left
in the default storage pool to create a secondary disk. However, there is free space
available on the host machine.

You can use that free space available on the host machine to create a disk image and
then attach that image as vDisk to the virtual machine to perform a resize on the root
filesystem of the VM. This should save the virtual machine from crashing.

Creating a disk image and attaching it to a guest

Disk images are standard files stored on the host's filesystem. They are large and act
as virtualized hard drives for guests. You can create such files using the dd command
as shown:

```
# dd if=/dev/zero of=/vms/dbvm_disk2.img bs=1G count=10
```

Here is the translation of this command for you:

Duplicate data (dd) from the input file (if) of /dev/zero (virtual limitless supply of
0s) into the output file (of) of /vms/dbvm_disk2.img (disk image) using blocks of 1G
size (bs = block size) and repeat this (count) just once (10).

> dd is known to be a resource-hungry command, It may cause I/O
> problems on the host system, so it's good to first check available free
> memory and I/O state of the host system, and then only, run it. If the
> system is already loaded, lower the block size to MB and increase the
> count to match the size of file you wanted (use bs=1M, count=10000
> instead of bs=1G count=10).

_disk2.img is the result of the preceding command. The image now has ...eallocated and ready to use with guests either as boot disk or second disk. ...arly, you can also create thin-provisioned disk images. Preallocated and thin-...ovisioned (sparse) are disk allocation methods or you may also call it as format. Each comes with its own advantages and disadvantages. If you are looking for I/O performance, go for preallocated format but if you have some non-IO intensive load, choose thin-provisioned.

- **Preallocated**: Preallocated virtual disk allocates the space right away at the time of creation. A virtual disk with a preallocated format has significantly faster write speeds than a virtual disk with a thin provisioning.

- **Thin-Provisioned**: In this method, space will be allocated for the volume as needed. For example, if you create a 10G virtual disk (disk image) with sparse allocation. Initially, it would just take a couple of MB of space from your storage and grow as it receives write from the virtual machine up to 10G size. This allows storage over commitment under the assumption that the given disk space. To create a thin-provisioned disk, use the seek option with the dd command, as shown in the following command:

```
# dd if=/dev/zero of=/vms/dbvm_disk2_seek.imgbs=1G seek=10 count=0
```

Now, you might be wondering how one can identify what disk allocation method a certain virtual disk uses. There is a good utility for finding out, qemu-img. This command allows you to read the metadata of a virtual image. It also supports creating a new disk and performing low level format conversion.

Getting image information

The info parameter of the qemu-img command displays information about a disk image, including the absolute path of image, file format, and virtual and disk size. By looking at the virtual and disk size of the disk, one can easily identify what disk allocation policy is in use. As an example, let's look at two of the disk images we created:

```
# qemu-img info /vms/dbvm_disk2.img
image: /vms/dbvm_disk2.img
file format: raw
virtual size: 10G (10737418240 bytes)
disk size: 10G
#qemu-img info /vms/dbvm_disk2_seek.img
image: /vms/dbvm_disk2_seek.img
file format: raw
virtual size: 10G (10737418240 bytes)
disk size: 10M
```

See the disk size line of both the disks. It's showing `10G` for `/vms/dbvm_disk2.img`, whereas for `/vms/dbvm_disk2_seek.img`, it's `10M` MiB. This difference is because the second disk uses a thin-provisioning format. `virtual size` is what guests see and `disk size` is what space the disk reserved on the host. If both the sizes are the same, it means the disk is preallocated. A difference means that the disk uses the thin-provisioning format.

Now let's attach the disk image to a virtual machine; you can attach it using virt-manager or CLI alternative `virsh`.

Attach a disk using virt-manager

Start virt-manager from the host system's graphical desktop environment. It can also be started remotely using SSH, as demonstrated in the following command:

```
ssh -X host's address
        [remotehost]# virt-manager
```

1. In the **Virtual Machine Manager** main window, select the virtual machine to which you want to add the secondary disk.

2. Go to the virtual hardware details window and click on the **Add Hardware** button located at the bottom-left side of the dialog box.

3. In **Add New Virtual Hardware**, select **Storage** component amount other storage: addnewvirtualhardware:

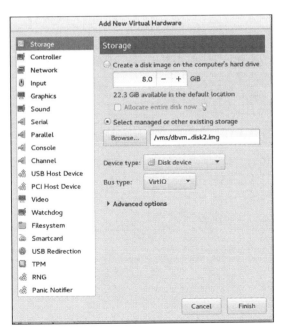

4. Choose **Select Managed or other existing storage** and either browse and point to the `dbvm_disk2.img` file from the `/vms` directory or directly enter the path of the file and click **Finish**.

> Here, we used disk image, but you are free to use any storage device that is present on the host system, such as a LUN, entire physical disk (`/dev/sdb`) or disk partition (`/dev/sdb1`), or LVM logical volume.

5. Clicking on the **Finish** button will attach the selected disk image (file) as a second disk to the virtual machine using the default configuration. The same operation can be quickly performed using the `virsh` command.

Attach a disk using virsh

`virsh` is a very powerful command-line alternative for virt-manager. You can perform an action in a second that would take minutes to perform through a graphical interface such as virt-manager. It provides an `attach-disk` option to attach a new disk device to a virtual machine. There are lots of switches provided with `attach-disk`:

```
attach-disk domain source target [[[--live] [--config] | [--current]] |
[--persistent]] [--targetbusbus] [--driver driver] [--subdriversubdriver]
[--iothreadiothread] [--cache cache] [--type type] [--mode mode]
[--sourcetypesourcetype] [--serial serial] [--wwnwwn] [--rawio]
[--address address] [--multifunction] [--print-xml]
```

But in a normal scenario, the following are sufficient to perform hot-add disk attachment to a virtual machine:

```
#virsh attach-disk F22-01 /vms/dbvm_disk2.img vdb --live --config
```

Here, `F22-01` is the virtual machine to which a disk attachment is executed. Then there is the path of disk image. `vdb` is the target disk name that would be visible inside the guest operating system. `--live` means performing the action while the virtual machine is running, and `--config` means attaching it persistently across reboot. Not adding a `--config` switch will keep the disk attached only till reboot.

HotPluggingSupport: "acpiphp" kernel module should be loaded in a Linux guest operating system in order to recognize a hot-added disk; "acpiphp" provides legacy hotplugging support, whereas "pciehp" provides native hotplugging support . "pciehp" is dependent on "acpiphp". Loading "acpiphp" will automatically load "pciehp" as a dependency.

You can use `virsh domblklist <vm_name>` command to quickly identify how many vDisks are attached to a virtual machine. Here is an example:

```
# virsh domblklist F22-01 --details
Type    Device   Target      Source
-------------------------------------------------
file   disk     vda         /var/lib/libvirt/images/fedora21.qcow2
file   disk     vdb         /vms/dbvm_disk2_seek.img
```

It clearly indicates that the two vDisks connected to the virtual machine are both file images. They are visible to the guest OS as vda and vdb respectively, and in the last column of the disk images path on the host system.

Working with managed storage

libvirt supports the following storage pool types:

- `-dir`: Uses the filesystem directory to store virtual disks
- `-disk`: Uses physical hard disks to create virtual disks
- `-fs`: Uses pre-formatted partitions to store virtual disks
- `-netfs`: Uses network-shared storage like NFS to store virtual disks
- `-gluster`: Allows using the gluster filesystem to store virtual disks
- `-iscsi`: Uses network-shared ISCSI storage to store virtual disks
- `-scsi`: Uses local SCSI storage to store virtual disks
- `-lvm`: Depends on LVM volume groups to store virtual disks
- `-rbd`: Allows connecting ceph storage for virtual disks

Covering all these storage pool types in details is not possible in this chapter, and is not required, as the steps to create a storage pool are almost identical; you just need to have a basic understanding of your chosen storage backend. These are some of the important and widely used storage pools that we are going to cover in this chapter:

- Filesystem Directory (local)
- LVM Volume Group (local)
- NFS Storage Pool
- iSCSI backend (shared)

The storage that is controlled and monitored by libvirt in terms of storage pools and storage volumes is called as managed storage here. A pool is a generic container for various storage objects. There are several types of storage pools. Starting from a simple local directory to advance network shares like ceph storage volumes are part of storage pool and they are actually the virtual disks used by virtual machines.

Storage management console

Virtual Machine Manager (virt-manager) provides a very sophisticated yet easy to use interface for configuring and managing storage pools. To access this console:

1. Open the virt-manager graphical interface.
2. Then go to the **Edit** menu and select **Connection Details**. Click on the **Storage** tab of the **Connection Details** window, virt-manager | Click **Edit** | **Connection Details** | **Storage**:

All the storage pools are listed in the left column and in the right pane; you will get the overview of the selected pool that includes the following information:

- **Name**: The name of storage pool
- **Size**: This tells us how much free space is available and how much is utilized
- **Location**: The path of the storage backend where actual vDisk data will be stored
- **State**: State tells us the pool status; whether it's active and in use or suspended
- **Autostart**: If checked, the storage pool will be started upon system boot otherwise it will require manual interaction to start the pool
- **Volumes**: This lists all the virtual disks (volumes) that exist in the pool, including their name, size, and it facilitates creating new volumes. There are three buttons. Buttons with a "plus" symbol denote adding new volume, a button with a "half round arrow" symbol denotes refresh, and the last one is for delete, which is represented by a "red circle".

By default, libvirt creates a directory backend storage pool with the name
`default`. You can also use the `virsh` command to list the storage pools
available on the system:

```
[root@Fedora22]# virsh pool-list
Name                 State     Autostart
-------------------------------------------
default              active    yes
```

To get more information about a specific storage domain use:

```
[root@Fedora22 ~]# virsh pool-info default
Name:          default
UUID:          3efb9c2b-2fa8-41cd-9e9e-de2eafa3b4a5
State:         running
Persistent:    yes
Autostart:     yes
Capacity:      26.00 GiB
Allocation:    4.00 GiB
Available:     23.00 GiB
```

The last three parameters actually indicate the usage of the storage pool. You can
see that out of a total 26 GiB capacity, 4 GiB has been used (allocated) and 23 GiB is
available for use.

Creating storage pools

Storage pools can be created with `virt-manager` or through its CLI alternative,
`virsh`. First we will see how to create different types of storage pools using the
Storage Management console and then using `virsh`. The XML definition file of each
storage pool is stored in `/etc/libvirt/storage`. Make sure that it does not get
modified manually or deleted.

File system directory backed storage pool

Directory backend storage is more commonly known as file-based storage.
In file-based storage and VM, diskshare is stored and managed within a
standard directory created on the host machine (or node). In simple terms,
you create a directory on the host system and designate it as a controlled
place to store virtual disks.

The files created under this directory act as virtual disks, and they can be fully allocated raw files, sparsely allocated raw files or qcow2, which is a special disk format.

To create a pool, open the Virtual Machine Manager graphical interface and follow the following steps:

1. Go to the **Storage** tab in the **Connection Details** window of virt-manager.

2. Start the **Add a New Storage Pool** wizard by clicking on the **+** button (located on the bottom-left side).

3. Enter a name and set the type as `dir:Filesystem Directory`, and then click on the **Forward** button.

4. The next step has different configuration parameters depending on the storage type selected. For filesystem directories, just input the **Target Path** and you're done. In the **Target Path** input box, enter the directory path where you wish to store virtual disks and hit the **Finish** button, and your directory based storage pool is ready:

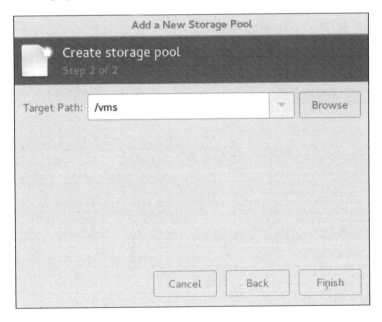

Directory permissions should be owned by a root user with the permission set to `700`. If SELinux is in enforcing mode. The following context needs to be set:

```
# semanage fcontext -a -t virt_image_t "/vms(/.*)?"
```

Directory-based storage pools may take up all available disk space where they are located. You should store the directory on its own partition so you don't fill up the host's main partition.

virsh makes life even easier; after running just three commands, the storage pool will get ready for use. The commands are:

```
#virsh pool-define-as dedicated_storagedir dir - - - -  "/vms"
#virsh pool-build dedicated_storage
#virsh pool-start dedicated_storage
```

The first command just defines the storage domain. It creates an XML definition file from the input located in the /etc/libvirt/storage/ directory, and the second command (pool-build) is what actually builds the storage pool. It creates the directory if it doesn't exist and sets the correct SELinux context. To verify the creation of storage pool run the following:

```
#virsh pool-list --all
Name              State     Autostart
-----------------------------------------
dedicated_storage  inactive   no
default   active    yes
```

Notice that the storage pool is created but is in an inactive state. To activate it and set it to automatically start, run the following:

```
#virsh pool-start dedicated_storage
#virsh pool-autostart dedicated_storage
#virsh pool-list
Name              State     Autostart
-----------------------------------------
dedicated_storage  active    yes
default    active    yes
```

LVM Volume Group backed storage pool

Logical Volume Manager is the most flexible and widely used storage technology on Linux. You can use LVM logical volumes as virtual disks. Just enter the pre-defined LVM volume group name (path), or build a new volume group using the **Add a New Storage Pool** wizard:

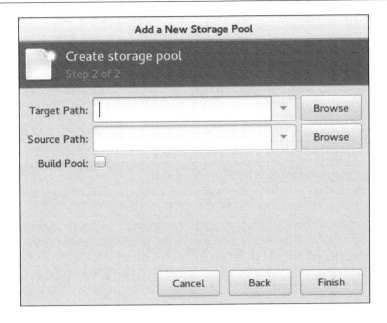

- **Target Path** is the location of the existing LVM volume group
- **Source Path** is the optional device to build a new LVM volume group

For example, let's assume that you have `sdb` and `sdc` disks attached to your host machine; you want to convert them into a single physical volume and create a volume group out of them in order to provide space for all of your virtual machine disks.

For this requirement, you will not need to go through the regular `pvcreate`, `vgcreate` way instead. Just open the **Add a New Storage Pool** wizard, provide `sdb`, and `sdc` as source devices, tick the **Build Pool** checkbox, and hit the **Finish** button.

The **Build Pool** checkbox instructs virt-manager to create a new LVM volume group. It will convert sdb and sdc devices into a physical volume and create a new LVM volume group on top of them and use it as storage pool.

To create an LVM backend storage pool using `virsh`, use the same `pool-define-as` and `pool-build` options:

```
virsh pool-define-as lvmpool logical - - /dev/sdb2 vg1 /dev/vg1
virsh pool-build lvmpool
virsh pool-start lvmpool ; virsh pool-autostart dedicated_storage
```

Here:

- `lvmpool` is the name of the storage pool
- `/dev/vdb1` is used as a physical volume to build to the vg
- `vg1` is the name of the LVM volume group

iSCSI backed storage pool

Internet Small Computer System Interface (iSCSI) is a network protocol for sharing storage devices. For iSCSI communication, iSCSI Initiator and iSCSI Target components talk with each other and construct a Storage Area Network, similar to the Fiber channel.

Unlike an LVM volume group, iSCSI volumes cannot be created via the libvirt API. Volumes must be preallocated on the iSCSI server (the iSCSI target). Once you have a iSCSI volumes created and ready for use, go to the **Add a New Storage Pool** wizard and select the type as **iscsi:ISCSI Target** and press **Forward**, which will bring the following window (step 2):

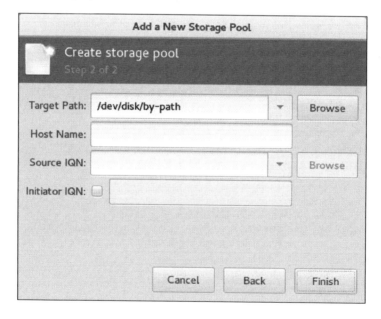

Enter the following information and click **Finish** to get your iSCSI-based storage domain ready:

- **Target Path**: Root location for identifying new storage volume
- **Host Name**: Name of the host sharing the storage (iscsi target)
- **Source IQN**: Path on the host that is being shared (IscsiLuns IQN)
- **Initiator IQN**: Your host system's iSCSI initiator qualified name

Creating an ISO image library

Although a guest operating system on the virtual machine can be installed from physical media doing passthrough host's CD/DVD drive to the virtual machine, it's not the most efficient way. Reading from a DVD drive is slow when compared to read ISO from a hard disk, so the better way is to store ISO files (or logical CDs) used to install operating systems and applications for the virtual machines in a file based storage pool and create an ISO image library.

To create an ISO image library, you can either use a virt-manager or a `virsh` command. Let's see how to create an ISO image library using the `virsh` command:

1. First, create a directory on the host system to store `.iso` images:

    `#mkdir /iso_lib`

2. Set correct permissions. It should be owned by a root user with permission set to 700. If SELinux is in enforcing mode, the following context needs to be set:

    `#chmod 700 /iso_lib`

    `# semanage fcontext -a -t virt_image_t "/iso_lib(/.*)?"`

3. Define the ISO image library using the `virsh` command, as shown in the following:

    `#virsh pool-define-as iso_librarydir - - - - "/iso_lib"`

    `#virsh pool-build iso_library`

    `#virsh pool-start iso_library`

 In the preceding example, I used the name `iso_library` to demonstrate how to create a storage pool that will hold ISO images, but you are free to use any name you wish.

4. Verify that the pool (ISO image library) got created:

```
#virsh pool-info iso_library
Name:              iso_library
UUID:              959309c8-846d-41dd-80db-7a6e204f320e
State:             running
Persistent:        yes
Autostart:         no
Capacity:          49.09 GiB
Allocation:        8.45 GiB
Available:         40.64 GiB
```

5. Now you can copy or move the .iso images to /iso_lib directory.

6. Upon copying the .iso files in /iso_lib directory, refresh the pool and then check its contents:

```
# virsh pool-refresh iso_library
Pool iso_library refreshed


# virsh vol-list iso_library
Name                    Path
------------------------------------------------------------------
-----------
centos6.iso             /iso_lib/centos6.iso
Fedora21.iso            /iso_lib/Fedora21.iso
Fedora22.iso            /iso_lib/Fedora22.iso
Win7.iso                /iso_lib/Win7.iso
```

7. It will list all the ISO images stored in the directory, along with their path. These ISO images can now be used directly with a virtual machine for guest operating system installation, software installation, or upgrades.

Deleting a storage pool

Deleting a storage pool is fairly easy. Please note that deleting a storage domain will not remove any file/block device. It just disconnects the storage from the virt-manager. The file/block device has to be removed manually.

Deleting storage pool using virt-manager

First, stop the storage pool. To do this, select the storage pool you want to stop and click on the red X icon at the bottom of the **Storage** window:

Clicking on the red X icon will make the storage domain *inactive*. Clicking the trash can icon will remove the storage domain.

Deleting storage pool using virsh

The sequence is the same; you first need to stop the pool by running: `virsh pool-destroy <pool-name>`, and then undefine it using `virsh pool-undefine<pool-name>`.

Creating storage volumes

Storage volumes are created on top of storage pools and attached as virtual disks to virtual machines. In order to create a storage volume, start the "Storage Management console", navigate to **virt-manager** | Click **Edit** | **connection Details** | **Storage** and select the storage pool where you want to create a new volume; click on the **Create New Volume** button (+):

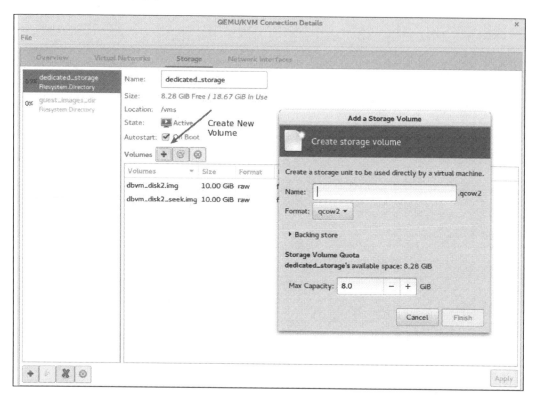

Next, provide the name of the new volume, choose the disk allocation format for it, and click on the **Finish** button to build the volume and get it ready to attach to a VM. You can attach it using the usual virt-manager or the `virsh` command.

There are several disk formats that are supported by libvirt (`raw`, `cow`, `qcow`, `qcow2`, `qed`, `vmdk`). Use the disk format that suits your environment and set the proper size in **Max Capacity** and **Allocation** fields to decide whether you wish to go with preallocated disk allocation or thin-provisioned. If you keep the disk size the same in **Max Capacity** and **Allocation**, it will be preallocated rather than thin-provisioned. Note that the `qcow2` format does not support the thick disk allocation method.

In *Chapter 7, Templates and Snapshots*, all the disk formats are explained in detail. For now, just understand that qcow2 is a specially designed disk format for KVM virtualization. It supports the advanced features needed for creating internal snapshots.

Creating volume using virsh command

The syntax to create a volume using `virsh` command is as follows:

```
# virsh vol-create-as dedicated_storage vm_vol1 10G
```

Here, `dedicated_storage` is the storage pool, `vm_vol1` is the volume name, and 10 GB is the size:

```
# virsh vol-info --pool dedicated_storage vm_vol1
Name:        vm_vol1
Type:        file
Capacity:    1.00 GiB
Allocation:  1.00 GiB
```

> The `virsh` command and arguments to create a storage volume are almost same regardless of the type of storage pool it is created on. Just enter the appropriate input for a `--pool` switch.

Deleting a volume using the virsh command

The syntax to delete a volume using `virsh` command is as follows:

```
#virsh vol-delete  dedicated_storage vm_vol2
```

Executing this command will remove the `vm_vol2` volume from the `dedicated_storage` storage pool.

> The `virsh` command and arguments to create a storage volume are almost the same, regardless of the type of storage pool it is created on. Just enter the appropriate input for `--pool` option.

Summary

In this chapter, we covered various virtual network and storage configurations for KVM virtualization. We also looked into various aspects of storage management. In the next chapter, we will see the lifecycle management of a virtual machine.

6
Virtual Machine Lifecycle Management

In the previous chapters, we have covered some of the main operations on a virtual machine. You have learned the steps to create a virtual machine. In this chapter, we are going to cover the major tasks associated with a system administrator to manage a virtual machine, including offline and live migration of a virtual machine. You might see some commands revisited or repeated from the previous chapters. You need a Fedora 22 virtual machine ready to follow the examples in this chapter. You can download fedora from the following link:

```
https://getfedora.org/en/workstation/download/
```

We will start this chapter by describing the state of a virtual machine during its lifecycle:

- **Undefined**: This is a state where the virtual machine is neither created nor defined in libvirt.

- **Defined/Shutoff**: In this state, libvirt is aware of the virtual machine. The configuration file to define and start a virtual machine is available in `/etc/libvirt/qemu`. We can also call this state as stopped or shut down.

- **Running**: This state is self explanatory. The virtual machine is started by libvirt.

- **Shutdown**: The virtual machine's OS has been notified about the shutdown and it is stopping its processes for a graceful shutdown.

- **Paused**: The virtual machine has been moved from a running state to a suspended state. The memory image has been stored temporarily. The virtual machine can be resumed without the guest OS being aware.

- **Saved**: In this state, the virtual machine is in a permanent suspend mode. The memory state has been dumped to a file stored in a persistent storage. The virtual machine can be resumed to the original running state from this saved state file.

- **Idle**: This state means that a virtual machine is waiting on I/O, or has gone to sleep as it has no job to perform.

- **Crashed**: The virtual machine has crashed. It could be a QEMU process killed or core dumped.

- **Dying**: The virtual machine has neither shut down nor crashed. It could be due to a failure in the shutdown process also.

- **Pmsuspended**: The virtual machine has been suspended by the guest OS's power management.

The current status of a virtual machine is displayed on the opening screen of the virt-manager. When you right-click on a virtual machine, virt-manager will present options to change the status of a virtual machine:

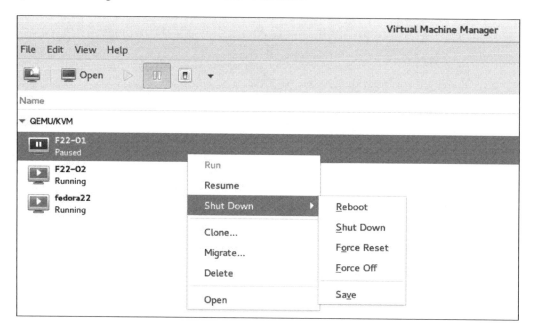

Let us now check the options available in `virsh`.

To check the status of all virtual machines defined and running on the hypervisor, execute the following command:

```
# virsh list --all
Domain F22-01 is being shutdown
 Id     Name                               State
----------------------------------------------------------
 12     F22-02                             paused
 13     fedora22                           running
 14     F22-01                             in shutdown
```

The `virsh list` command has a couple of options to filter the output displayed, based on the status of the virtual machines. These filter options are very useful when you have to automate the actions based on a virtual machine's status using custom scripts:

- `inactive`: This lists the inactive domains
- `all`: This lists the inactive & active domains
- `transient`: This lists the transient domains
- `-persistent`: This lists the persistent domains
- `with-snapshot`: This lists the domains with an existing snapshot
- `without-snapshot`: This lists the domains without a snapshot
- `state-running`: This lists the domains in running state
- `state-paused`: This lists the domains in paused state
- `state-shutoff`: This lists the domains in shutoff state
- `state-other`: This lists the domains in other states
- `autostart`: This lists the domains with autostart enabled
- `no-autostart`: This lists the domains with autostart disabled
- `with-managed-save`: This lists the domains with managed save state
- `without-managed-save`: This lists the domains without managed save
- `uuid`: This lists the uuid's only
- `name`: This lists the domain names only
- `table`: This lists the table (default)
- `managed-save`: This marks the inactive domains with managed save state
- `title`: shows domain title

To get help on `virsh` use `virsh help`. An example of the command is `virsh help list`.

Let's now play with some `virsh` commands that are used to change the status of a virtual machine. In most cases, the command itself answers its purpose.

`start`: Start a (previously defined) inactive domain. Previously defined means you should be able to list the domain using `virsh list --inactive`:

- `shutdown`: Gracefully shuts down a domain
- `reboot`: Reboots a domain

When you issue `virsh shutdown vm_name` or `virsh reboot vm_name` and the VM is not responding to the commands, then you need to check if the ACPI service is active in VM OS:

- `reset`: This resets a domain. Imagine this command to be a power cycle operation.
- `destroy`: This destroys (stops) a domain. This is like you pulling a power cable from the server. libvirt will just kill the associated QEMU process for the VM in the hypervisor. You need to use destroy if the VM is not responding to any of the `virsh` commands, and if you cannot access its console, the VM has either crashed or the status shown is incorrect.

Before going to the next option, try out the preceding commands yourself and understand the results.

Let's take a look at a set of `virsh` commands, which will help you to create/define a virtual machine:

- `create`: This creates a domain from an XML file. Using this option, you can start a virtual machine using its XML file. This virtual machine is not defined in libvirt. Once stopped, it disappears from libvirt till you start using it again `virsh create /location/vm_name.xml`.
- `define`: This defines (but doesn't start) a domain from an XML file. Here you add the virtual machine to libvirt.
- `undefine`: This undefines a domain. `undefine` will remove a virtual machine from libvirt.

Let's try those commands with a real world example. The following step is also one of the backup strategies, which we are going to describe in the next chapter.

1. First dump a defined VM's configuration file. In this example, the name of the VM is F22-03:

   ```
   # virsh dumpxml F22-03 > /root/F22-03.xml
   ```

2. We have now saved the configuration file of F22-03 as an XML file. Just open the file and try to understand the tags.

3. Remove the virtual machine from libvirt. Executing undefine alone will not remove the underlying storage:

   ```
   # virsh undefine F22-03


   # virsh list --all
    Id  Name                        State
   ----------------------------------------------------


   # virsh create F22-03.xml
   Domain F22-03 created from F22-03.xml


   # virsh list
    Id  Name                        State
   ----------------------------------------------------
    18  F22-03                      running


   # virsh destroy F22-03
   Domain F22-03 destroyed


   # virsh list --all
    Id  Name                        State
   ----------------------------------------------------


   # virsh define F22-03.xml --validate
   Domain F22-03 defined from F22-03.xml


   # virsh list --all
    Id  Name                        State
   ----------------------------------------------------
    -   F22-03                      shut off
   ```

You can now start the VM as usual. Once it starts try the following commands yourself and observe the state changes:

- `suspend`: Suspend a domain
- `resume`: Resume a domain

An advanced level of suspend and resume is `save` and `restore`. Here you are saving the machine state to a file and then restoring it later. This feature comes in handy for system administrators when they want to make an unscheduled restart of the virtual environment and one of the domains has an application that needs a complex starting process:

```
# virsh save F22-03 /root/F22-03_before_host_reboot
```

libvirt will stop the virtual machine after saving the state to a file.

```
# virsh restore /root/F22-03_before_host_reboot
```

There are some interesting add-on commands once the image is saved:

- `save-image-define`: Redefines the XML for a domain's saved state file
- `save-image-dumpxml`: Saves state domain information in XML
- `save-image-edit`: Edits XML for a domain's saved state file

Once the VM is saved, it is not mandatory to restore it from the saved image file. You can always start the VM as usual.

There is one more option, called `managedsave`. This will save the state file automatically in `/var/lib/libvirt/qemu/save`. When the VM starts next time, libvirt will try to restore it from the state file saved there. If the VM fails to start, do not panic, just delete the file using `managedsave-remove` and start the VM again. Our recommendation is to always use save instead of `managedsave`. Try to run `virsh managedsave vm_name` and `virsh start vm_name`.

QEMU guest agent

libvirt uses the QEMU guest agent which runs inside a Guest OS as a service. It acts as a communication channel between the hypervisor and the guest. Hypervisor uses this channel to fetch information of the Guest OS or issue commands to the Guest OS. The communication protocol used to issue commands to the Guest OS is **Qemu Machine Protocol (QMP)**. For example, libvirt uses a guest agent to fetch network and filesystem details from the guest. The communication between the guest agent and hypervisor happens through a virtio-serial, or through an isa-serial channel named `org.qemu.guest_agent.0`. On the hypervisor side, a corresponding Linux socket file will also be created in `/var/lib/libvirt/qemu/channel/target/`.

For Fedora 22 it is as follows:

```
# file /var/lib/libvirt/qemu/channel/target/fedora22.org.qemu.guest_
agent.0
/var/lib/libvirt/qemu/channel/target/fedora22.org.qemu.guest_agent.0:
socket
```

The same socket file will be shared by multiple Fedora 22 instances. This means that you will not see socket files created for every VM you start on the hypervisor.

Now you can install the guest agent on Fedora. On other distributions, the package name should be the same.

```
# dnf install qemu-guest-agent
```

Stop and start the VM. Once started, check if the service is started:

```
# systemctl status qemu-guest-agent
```

Now from the hypervisor, check if the guest agent is working:

```
# virsh qemu-agent-command F22-01 '{"execute": "guest-info"}' --pretty
{
    "return": {
        "version": "2.3.0",
        "supported_commands": [
            {
                "enabled": true,
                "name": "guest-get-memory-block-info",
                "success-response": true
            },
<truncated>
```

Remember that the agent uses QMP and QMP uses JSON formatting. The output of the preceding command shows all the supported guest agent commands. Try to find some interesting commands and execute them yourself; for example, `guest-get-fsinfo`, `guest-network-get-interfaces`, and so on. How do you find the IP address assigned to your VM or filesystem details without logging into it?

QEMU provides a guest agent for Microsoft Windows. But we will cover that in the next chapter. For the adventurous and those who can't wait, we are giving the link to get the agent and drivers for Windows: `https://fedoraproject.org/wiki/Windows_Virtio_Drivers`. We recommend installing the guest agent after creating a new VM.

Virtual video cards and graphics

In order to make the graphics work on virtual machines, QEMU needs to provide two components to its virtual machines: a virtual video card and a method or protocol to access the graphics from the client.

Virtual video card

The purpose of the graphics card is to provide graphics output to a display device. A virtual graphics card can also perform the same function. QEMU supports emulation of multiple graphics cards, and you can use libvirt to add those emulated graphic cards to the virtual machines. The emulated graphic cards options are:

- **Cirrus** (Default in libvirt): Cirrus Logic GD5446 Video card. All Windows versions starting from Windows 95 should recognize and use this graphic card. For optimal performance, use 16-bit color depth in the guest and the host OS.

- **VGA**: Standard VGA card with Bochs VBE extensions. If your guest OS supports the VESA 2.0 VBE extensions (e.g. Windows XP) and if you want to use high resolution modes (>= *1280x1024x16*), then you should use this option.

- **VMVGA**: VMWare SVGA-II compatible adapter. Use it if you have a sufficiently recent XFree86/XOrg server or a Windows guest with a driver for this card.

- **QXL**: The QXL paravirtual graphic card. It is VGA-compatible (including VESA 2.0 VBE support), although it works best with installed QXL guest drivers. This is the recommended choice when using the spice protocol.

There is also a Xen video card option available, which is used when you use Xen virtualization and it is not compatible with KVM.

When you install a virtual machine, libvirt will automatically choose an appropriate card based on the VM OS you select at the time of the installation. For latest OS versions, such as Fedora 18, and later the card will be QXL, but for Windows or older Linux distros, it will be Cirrus.

Adding or removing a virtual graphics card model is easy using a virt-manager. The following screenshot tells how you can add a new **Video Device** to a virtual machine. For changing the existing **Video Device** associated with the virtual machine. Open virt-manager, take the virtual machine's console, and click on **Video < Model >** under **Show Hardware Settings details**. This setting can be edited only when the virtual machine is in the "off" state:

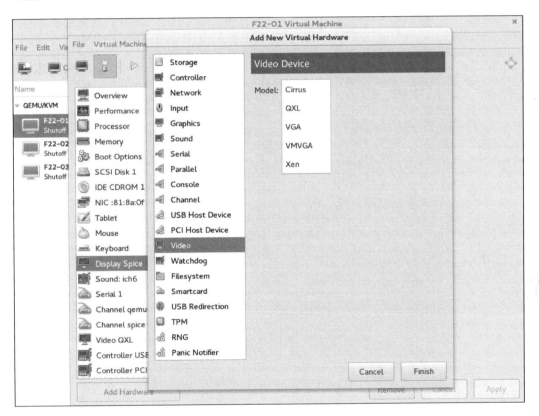

Graphics

You have now configured your virtual video card. Now you need a method to access the graphics. In a physical system, it is done through a monitor. But in the case of virtual machines, it is done through graphic servers; Spice, and VNC are two graphic servers that KVM virtualization supports currently. Why do we call them graphics servers? Because when you start a virtual machine, based on the graphics you have chosen, QEMU will start Spice or VNC network servers, which are attached to the virtual machine's virtual graphics card. When you access your virtual machines through a console using a client, you are basically connecting to these network ports and accessing the graphics from the virtual machines.

VNC graphics server

When the VNC graphics server is enabled through libvirt, QEMU will redirect the graphics output to its inbuilt VNC Server implementation. The VNC Server will listen to a network port where the VNC clients can connect.

The following screenshot shows how to add a VNC graphics server:

When adding VNC graphics, you will be presented with the options shown in preceding figure:

- **Type**: The type of the graphics server. Here, it is VNC
- **Address**: VNC Server listening address. It can be all, localhost, or an IP address. By default, it is localhost only.
- **Port**: VNC Server listening port. You can either choose auto, where libvirt defines the port based on the availability, or you can define one yourself. Make sure it does not create a conflict.
- **Password**: Password protecting the VNC access.
- **Keymap**: If you want to use a specific keyboard layout instead of an auto detected one.

You can do the same using the command-line tool `virt-xml`.

Add VNC graphics f22-01 and then modify its VNC listening IP to 192.168.122.1:

```
# virt-xml f22-01 --add-device --graphics type=vnc
# virt-xml f22-01 --edit --graphics listen=192.168.122.1
```

This is how it looks in the f22-01 XML configuration file:

```
<graphics type='vnc' port='-1' autoport='yes' listen='192.168.122.1'>
  <listen type='address' address='192.168.122.1'/>
</graphics>
```

You can also use `virsh edit f22-01` and change the parameters individually.

Why VNC?

You can use VNC when you access VMs on LAN or you access the VMs directly from the console. It is not a good idea to expose VMs over a public network using VNC, as the connection is not encrypted. VNC is a good option if the VMs are servers with no GUI installed. Another point which is in favor of VNC is the availability of clients. You can access VM from any OS platform, as there will be a VNC viewer available for that platform.

SPICE graphics server

Like KVM, a **Simple Protocol for Independent Computing Environments (SPICE)** is one of the best innovations that came into open source virtualization technologies. It propelled the open source virtualization to a large virtual desktop infrastructure (VDI) implementation.

Note: Qumranet originally developed SPICE as a closed source codebase in 2007. Red Hat, Inc acquired Qumranet in 2008, and in December 2009, decided to release the code under an open-source license and treat the protocol as an open standard.

Source: `https://en.wikipedia.org/wiki/SPICE_(protocol)`. Difference between SPICE and VNC.

SPICE is the only open source solution available on Linux, that gives a two-way audio. It has high quality 2D rendering capabilities which can make use of a client system's video card capabilities. SPICE also supports encryption, compression, and USB passthrough over the network. For a complete list of features, you can visit `http://www.spice-space.org/features.html`. If you are a developer and want to know about the internals of SPICE, visit `http://www.spice-space.org/documentation.html`. If you are planning for VDI or installing VMs that needs GUI, SPICE is the best option for you.

SPICE may not be compatible with some older VMs, as they do not have support for QXL. In those cases, you can use SPICE along with other video generic virtual video cards.

Adding SPICE graphics server

Libvirt now selects SPICE as the default graphics server for most VM installations. You have to use the same procedures that we mentioned earlier for VNC to add the SPICE graphics server. Just change the VNC to SPICE in the dropdown. Here you will get an additional option to select a TLS port, as SPICE supports encryption:

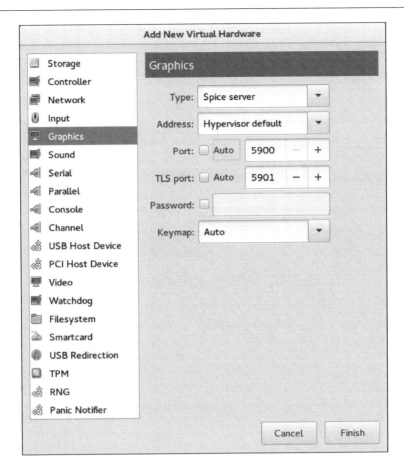

Methods to access a virtual machine console

There are multiple ways to connect to a VM console. If your environment has a full GUI access, then the easiest method is to use the `virt-manager` console itself.

`virt-viewer` is another tool that can give access to your virtual machine console. This tool is very helpful if you are trying to access a VM console from a remote location. In the following example, we are going to make a connection to a remote hypervisor that has an IP `192.168.122.1`. The connection is tunneled through an SSH session and is secure.

The first step is to set up an authentication system without a password between your client system and the hypervisor.

On the client machine:

```
$ ssh-keygen
$ ssh-copy-id root@192.168.122.1
$ virt-viewer -c qemu+ssh://root@192.168.122.1/system
```

You will be presented with a list of VMs available on the hypervisor. Select the one you have to access, as shown:

To connect to a VM's console directly, use the following:

```
$ virt-viewer -c qemu+ssh://root@192.168.122.1/system F22-01
```

If your environment is restricted to only a text console, then you have to rely on your favorite `virsh`. To be more specific, `virsh console vm_name`. This needs some additional configuration inside the VM OS.

If your Linux distro is using GRUB (not GRUB2), append the following line to your existing boot Kernel line in `/boot/grub/grub.conf` and shutdown the virtual machine.

```
console=tty0 console=ttyS0,115200
```

If your Linux distro is using GRUB2, then steps become a little complicated. Note that the following command has been tested on a Fedora 22 VM. For other distros, the steps to configure GRUB2 might be different though the changes required on GRUB configuration file should remain the same:

```
# cat /etc/default/grub (only relevant variables are shown)
GRUB_TERMINAL_OUTPUT="console"
GRUB_CMDLINE_LINUX="rd.lvm.lv=fedora/swap rd.lvm.lv=fedora/root rhgb
quiet"
```

The changed configuration is as follows:

```
# cat /etc/default/grub (only relevant variables are shown)
GRUB_TERMINAL_OUTPUT="serial console"
GRUB_CMDLINE_LINUX="rd.lvm.lv=fedora/swap rd.lvm.lv=fedora/root
console=tty0 console=ttyS0"
# grub2-mkconfig -o /boot/grub2/grub.cfg
```

Now shut down the virtual machine. Start it using `virsh`:

```
# virsh start F22-01 --console
```

To connect to a virtual machine console that has already started:

```
# virsh console F22-01
```

Or from a remote client:

```
$ virsh -c qemu+ssh://root@192.168.122.1/system console F22-01
```

Connected to domain F22-01:

```
Escape character is ^]
Fedora release 22 (Twenty Two)
Kernel 4.0.4-301.fc22.x86_64 on an x86_64 (ttyS0)
localhost login:
```

In some cases, we have seen a console command stuck at ^]. To work around it, press the enter key multiple times to see the login prompt. Sometimes configuring a text console is very useful when you want to capture the boot messages for troubleshooting purposes.

Use *ctrl +]* to exit from the console.

VM migration

Virtualization is all about flexibility. Migration is one of the features in virtualization that showcase its flexibility. What is migration then? In simple terms, it enables you to move your virtual machine from one physical machine to another physical machine with a very minimal downtime or no downtime.

There are two types of migration: offline and online migration.

Offline migration

As the name suggests, during offline migration, the state of the VM will be either shut down or suspended. The VM will be then resumed or started at the destination host.

Live or online migration

In this type of migration, the VM is migrated to the destination host while it's running on the source host. The process is invisible to the users who are using the virtual machines. They will never know that the virtual machine they are using has been transferred to another host while they are working on it. Live migration is one of the main features that made virtualization so popular.

Migration implementation in KVM is unique. It does not need any support from the virtual machine. It means that you can live migrate any virtual machines irrespective of the OS they are using. Another unique feature of KVM live migration is that it is almost hardware independent. You should ideally be able to live migrate a virtual machine running on a hypervisor that has an AMD processor to an Intel-based hypervisor.

Benefits of VM migration

The most important benefit of VM live migration is *increased uptime* and *reduced downtime*. A carefully designed virtualized environment will give you the maximum uptime for your application. The second most important benefit is saving energy and going green. You can easily consolidate your virtual machines based on the load and usage to a smaller number of hypervisors during off hours. Once the virtual machines are migrated, you can power off the unused hypervisors.

Other benefits include easy hardware/software upgrade process by moving your VM between different hypervisors. Once you have the capability to move your virtual machines freely between different physical servers the benefits are countless. VM migration needs proper planning in place. There are some basic requirements the migration looks for. Let's see them one by one. The migration requirements for production environments

VM should be using a storage pool, which is created on a shared storage. The name of the storage pool and the virtual disks path should remain the same on both hypervisors (source and destination hypervisors). Check *Chapter 5, Network and Storage* to know the steps on how to create a storage pool using a shared storage:

- It is possible to do live storage migration using a storage pool that is created on a non-shared storage. You only need to maintain the same storage pool name and file location. But shared storage is still recommended on a production environment.

- If there is an unmanaged virtual disk attached to a VM which uses an FC, an ISCSI, LVM, and so on. The same storage should be available on both hypervisors.

- The virtual networks used by the VMs should be available on both hypervisors.

- Bridge, which is configured for a networking communication, should be available on both the hypervisors.

- Migration may fail if the major versions of libvirt and qemu-kvm on the hypervisors are different. But you should be able to migrate the VMs running on a hypervisor that has a lower version of libvirt or qemu-kvm to a hypervisor that has higher versions of those packages without any issues.

- The time on both the source and destination hypervisors should be synced. It is highly recommended that you sync the hypervisors using the same NTP or **Precision Time Protocol (PTP)** servers.

- It is important that the systems use a DNS server for name resolution. Adding the host details on /etc/hosts will not work. You should be able to resolve the hostnames using the host command.

Setting up the environment

Let's build the environment to do VM migration—both offline and live migrations. The following diagram depicts two standard KVM virtualization hosts running VMs with a shared storage:

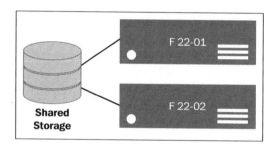

Shared storage

We start this by setting up a shared storage. In this example, we are using NFS as the shared storage. We use NFS because it is simple to set up, thus helping you to follow the migration examples easily. In actual production, it is recommended to use ISCSI-based or FC-based storage pools. NFS is not a good choice when the files are large and the VM performs heavy I/O operations. Gluster is a good alternative to NFS and we would say that you should try it. Gluster is well integrated in LIbvirt. You can re-visit *Chapter 5, Network and Storage,* to know how to create a storage pool using ISCSI or FC.

We created the following NFS share on a Fedora 22 server. The name of the server is nfs-01.

Exporting directory /testvms from nfs-01:

```
# echo '/testvms *(rw,sync,no_root_squash)' >> /etc/export
```

Allow the NFS service in firewall:

```
# firewall-cmd --get-active-zones
FedoraServer
  interfaces: eth0
# firewall-cmd --zone=FedoraServer --add-service=nfs
# firewall-cmd --zone=FedoraServer --list-all
```

Start NFS service:

```
# systemctl start rpcbind nfs-server
# systemctl enable rpcbind nfs-server
# showmount -e
```

Confirm that the share is accessible from your KVM hypervisors. In our case it is f22-01.example.local and f22-02.example.local:

```
# mount 192.168.122.1:/testvms /mnt
```

If mounting fails, disable the firewall on the NFS server and recheck the mount.

Unmount the volume once you have verified the NFS mount point from both hypervisors:

```
# umount /mnt
```

On f22-01 and f22-02, create a storage pool named testvms:

```
# mkdir -p /var/lib/libvirt/images/testvms/
# virsh pool-define-as \
--name testvms \
--type netfs \
--source-host 192.168.122.1 \
--source-path /testvms \
--target /var/lib/libvirt/images/testvms/
# virsh pool-start testvms
# virsh pool-autostart testvms
```

Storage pool testvms is now created and started on two hypervisors.

Network: In this example, we are going to isolate the migration and virtual machine traffic. It is highly recommended that you do this isolation in your production. There are two main reasons for this:

- **Network performance**: Migration of VM uses the full bandwidth of the network. If you use the same network for VM traffic network and migration (live), it will choke that network, thus affecting the servicing capability of VMs. You can control the migration bandwidth, but it will increase the migration time. Here is how we create the isolation:

```
f22-01 -- eth0 (192.168.0.5) <--switch------> eth0 (192.168.0.6) -- f22-02

          eth1 -> br1         <-----switch------> eth1  -> br1
```

  eth0 interfaces on f22-01 and f22-02 are used for migration as well as administrative tasks. They have an IP assigned and connected to a network switch. Bridge br1 is created using eth1 on both f22-01 and f22-02. br1 does not have an IP address assigned and is used exclusively for VM traffic. It is also connected to a network switch.

- **Security**: It is always recommended that you keep your management network and virtual network isolated. You don't want your users to mess with your management network where you access your hypervisors and do the administration.

Offline migration

Let's start with offline migration. In this migration, libvirt will just copy VM's XML configuration file from the source to the destination. It also assumes that you have the same shared storage pool created and ready to use at the destination.

As the first step in the migration process, you need to set up a two way password-less SSH authentication on the participating hypervisors. In our example, they are f22-01 and f22-02.

For the following exercises, disable SELinux temporarily.

In /etc/sysconfig/selinux, change SELINUX=enforcing to SELINUX=permissive.

On `f22-01.example.local`:

```
# ssh-keygen
# ssh-copy-id root@f22-02.example.local
On f22-02.example.local
# ssh-keygen
# ssh-copy-id root@f22-01.example.local
```

You should now be able to log in to the hypervisors without typing a password.

Let's do an offline migration of `vm1`, which is already installed, from `f22-01` to `f22-02`. The general format of migration command looks similar to the following:

```
# virsh migrate migration-type options name-of-the-vm destination-uri
On f22-01
f22-01]# virsh migrate --offline --verbose --persistent vm1 qemu+ssh://
f22-02.example.local/system
Migration: [100 %]
On f22-02
f22-02]# virsh list --all
# virsh list --all
 Id    Name                          State
----------------------------------------------------
 -     vm1                           shut off
f22-02]# virsh start vm1
Domain vm1 started
```

You can do an offline migration even if the VM is running.

What if I start the VM accidently on both the hypervisors?

Accidently starting the VM on both the hypervisors can be a sysadmin's nightmare. It can lead to filesystem corruption especially when the filesystem inside the VM is not cluster aware. Developers of libvirt thought about this and came up with a locking mechanism. In fact, they came up with two locking mechanisms. When enabled, will prevent the VMs from starting at the same time on two hypervisors.

The two locking mechanisms are:

- `lockd`: `lockd` makes use of POSIX `fcntl()` advisory locking capability. It was started by `virtlockd` daemon. It requires a shared file system (preferably NFS), accessible to all the hosts which share the same storage pool.

- `sanlock`: This is used by oVirt projects. It uses a disk paxos algorithm for maintaining continuously renewed leases.

For libvirt only implementations, we prefer `lockd` over `sanlock`. It is best to use `sanlock` for oVirt.

Enabling lockd

For image-based storage pools which are POSIX compliant, you can enable it easily by uncommenting `lock_manager = "lockd"` in `/etc/libvirt/qemu.conf` or on both hypervisors:

Now, enable and start the `virtlockd` service on both the hypervisors. Also, restart `libvirtd` on both the hypervisors.

```
# systemctl enable virtlockd; systemctl start virtlockd
# systemctl restart libvirtd
# systemctl status virtlockd
```

Starting vm1 on f22-02:

```
[root@f22-02]# virsh start vm1
Domain vm1 started
```

Starting the same vm1 on f22-01:

```
[root@f22-01]# virsh start vm1
error: Failed to start domain vm1
error: resource busy: Lockspace resource '/var/lib/libvirt/images/
testvms/vm1.qcow2' is locked
```

Another method to enable `lockd` is to use a hash of the disk's file path. Locks are saved in a shared directory that is exported through the NFS, or similar sharing, to the hypervisors. This is very useful when you have virtual disks, which are created and attached using multipath LUN. `fcntl()` cannot be used in these cases. We recommend that you use the following method to enable the locking.

On the NFS server:

```
# echo /flockd *(rw,no_root_squash) >> /etc/exports
# service nfs reload
# showmount -e
Export list for :
/flockd   *
/testvms *
```

Add the following to both the hypervisors in /etc/fstab:

```
# echo "192.168.122.1:/flockd  /flockd  nfs  rsize=8192,wsize=8192,timeo=
14,intr,sync" >> /etc/fstab
# mkdir -p /var/lib/libvirt/lockd/flockd
# mount -a
# echo 'file_lockspace_dir = "/var/lib/libvirt/lockd/flockd"' >> /etc/
libvirt/qemu-lockd.conf
# reboot both hypervisors
```

Once rebooted, verify that the libvirtd and virtlockd started correctly on both the hypervisors:

```
[root@f22-01 ~]# virsh start vm1
Domain vm1 started
[root@f22-02 flockd]# ls
36b8377a5b0cc272a5b4e50929623191c027543c4facb1c6f3c35bacaa7455ef
51e3ed692fdf92ad54c6f234f742bb00d4787912a8a674fb5550b1b826343dd6
```

vm1 has two virtual disks. One created from an NFS storage pool and the other created directly from a multipath LUN.

vm1 fails to start on f22-02.

```
[root@f22-02 ~]# virsh start vm1
error: Failed to start domain vm1
error: resource busy: Lockspace resource
'51e3ed692fdf92ad54c6f234f742bb00d4787912a8a674fb5550b1b826343dd6' is
locked
```

When using LVM volumes that can be visible across multiple host systems, it is desirable to do the locking based on the unique UUID associated with each volume, instead of their paths. Setting this path causes libvirt to do UUID based locking for LVM.

```
lvm_lockspace_dir = "/var/lib/libvirt/lockd/lvmvolumes"
```

When using SCSI volumes that can be visible across multiple host systems, it is desirable to do locking based on the unique UUID associated with each volume, instead of their paths. Setting this path causes libvirt to do UUID-based locking for SCSI.

```
scsi_lockspace_dir = "/var/lib/libvirt/lockd/scsivolumes"
```

Like `file_lockspace_dir`, the preceding directories should also be shared with the hypervisors.

> Note: If you are not able to start VMs due to locking errors, just make sure that they are not running anywhere and then delete the lock files. Start the VM again.

We deviated a little from migration for the lockd topic. Let's get back to migration.

Live or online migration

This is where the migration gets interesting, and it is one of the most useful features of virtualization.

Before we start the process, let's go a little deeper to understand what happens under the hood. When we do a live migration, we are moving a live VM while users are accessing it. This means that the users shouldn't feel any disruption in VM availability when you do a live migration.

Live migration is a five stage, complex process, even though none of these processes are exposed to the sysadmins. libvirt will do the necessary work once the VM migration action is issued. The stages through which a VM migration goes are explained in the following:

- **Stage 1: Preparing the destination**

  When you initiate live migration, the source libvirt (SLibvirt) will contact the destination libvirt (DLibvirt) with the details of VM, which is going to be transferred live. DLibvirt will pass this information to the underlying QEMU with relevant options to enable live migration. QEMU will start the actual live migration process by starting the VM in pause mode, and start listening on a TCP port for VM data. Once the destination is ready DLibvirt will inform SLibvirt with the details of QEMU. By this time, QEMU, at the source, is ready to transfer the VM and connects to destination TCP port.

- **Stage 2: Transfer the VM**

  When we say transferring the VM; we are not transferring the whole VM, only the parts that are missing at the destination are transferred; for example, the memory and state of the virtual devices (VM State). Other than the memory and VM state, all other stuffs (virtual network, virtual disks and virtual devices) are available at the destination itself. Here is how QEMU moves the memory to destination.

  The VM will continue running at the source and the same VM is started in pause mode at the destination.

  In one go, we will transfer all the memory used by the VM to the destination. The speed of transfer depends upon the network bandwidth. Suppose VM is using 10 GiB, it will take the same time to transfer 10 GiB of data using SCP to destination. In default mode, it will make use of the full bandwidth. That is the reason we are separating the administration network from the VM traffic network.

  Once the whole memory is at the destination, QEMU starts transferring the dirty pages (pages which are not yet written to the disk). If it is a busy VM, the number of dirty pages will be high and it takes time to move them. Remember dirty pages will always be there and there is no state of zero dirty pages on a running VM. Hence QEMU will stop transferring the dirty pages when it reaches a low threshold (50 or fewer pages). It will also consider other factors, such as iterations, amount of dirty pages generated, and so on. This can also be determined by `migrate-setmaxdowntime` which is in milliseconds.

- **Stage 3: Stop the VM at the source**

  Once the amount of dirty pages reaches the said threshold, QEMU will stop the VM on destination. It will also sync the virtual disks.

- **Stage 4: Transfer VM state**

  In this stage, QEMU will transfer the state of the VM's virtual devices and remaining dirty pages to destination as fast as possible. We cannot limit the bandwidth at this stage.

- **Stage 5: VM continuation**

  At the destination, the VM will be resumed from the paused state. Virtual NICs become active and the bridge will send out gratuitous ARPs to announce the change. After receiving the announcement from the bridge, the network switches will update their respective ARP cache and start forwarding the data for the VM to the new hypervisors.

Note that stages 3, 4, and 5 will be completed in milliseconds. If some errors happen, QEMU will abort the migration and the VM will continue running on the source hypervisor. In all through the migration process, libvirt from both participating hypervisors will be monitoring the migration process.

Our VM, vm1 is now running on f22-01 safely with lockd enabled. We are going to live migrate vm1 to f22-02.

Open the TCP ports used for migration. You only need to do that at the destination server. You end up migrating VMs from both servers. Open the ports on all the participating hypervisors:

```
# firewall-cmd --zone=FedoraServer --add-port=49152-49216/tcp --permanent
```

Check the name resolution on both the servers:

```
[root@f22-01 ~]# host f22-01.example.local
f22-01.example.local has address 192.168.122.5
[root@f22-01 ~]# host f22-02.example.local
f22-02.example.local has address 192.168.122.6
[root@f22-02 ~]# host f22-01.example.local
f22-01.example.local has address 192.168.122.5
[root@f22-02 ~]# host f22-02.example.local
f22-02.example.local has address 192.168.122.6
```

Check and verify all the virtual disks attached are available at the destination, on the same path with the same storage pool name. This is applicable to attached unmanaged (ISCSI and FC LUNS, and so on) virtual disks also:

Check and verify all the network bridges and virtual networks used by the VM available at the destination.

Now initiate the migration:

```
# virsh migrate --live vm1 qemu+ssh://f22-02.example.local/system
--verbose --persistent
Migration: [100 %]
```

Our VM is using only 512 MB. All the five stages completed in a second. `--persistant` is optional but we recommend adding that.

This is the output of ping during the migration process: 0% packet-less.

```
# ping 192.168.122.24
PING 192.168.122.24 (192.168.122.24) 56(84) bytes of data.
64 bytes from 192.168.122.24: icmp_seq=12 ttl=64 time=0.338 ms
64 bytes from 192.168.122.24: icmp_seq=13 ttl=64 time=3.10 ms
64 bytes from 192.168.122.24: icmp_seq=14 ttl=64 time=0.574 ms
64 bytes from 192.168.122.24: icmp_seq=15 ttl=64 time=2.73 ms
64 bytes from 192.168.122.24: icmp_seq=16 ttl=64 time=0.612 ms
--- 192.168.122.24 ping statistics ---
17 packets transmitted, 17 received, 0% packet loss, time 16003ms
rtt min/avg/max/mdev = 0.338/0.828/3.101/0.777 ms
```

If you get the following error message, change cache to none on the virtual disk attached:

```
# virsh migrate --live vm1 qemu+ssh://f22-02.example.local/system
--verbose
error: Unsafe migration: Migration may lead to data corruption if disks
use cache != none
# virt-xml vm1 --edit --disk target=vda,cache=none
```

`target` is the disk to change cache. You can find the target name by running `virsh dumpxml vm1`.

You can try a few more options while performing a live migration:

- `--unndefinesource`: Undefines the domain on the source host
- `--suspend`: Leaves the domain paused on the destination host.
- `--compressed`: Activates compression of memory pages that have to be transferred repeatedly during live migration
- `--abort-on-error`: Cancels the migration if a soft error (for example I/O error) happens during the migration
- `--unsafe`: Forces a migration when libvirt suspects a data corruption

Now let's move to another type of migration, where you transfer the underlying virtual disks of a running VM along with its memory. It is also known as live storage migration. Here, virtual disks are saved on a non-shared storage. When you initiate this migration, the image file is copied first and then the memory:

```
[root@f22-02 ~]# ls /var/lib/libvirt/images/testvm.qcow2

ls: cannot access /var/lib/libvirt/images/testvm.qcow2: No such file or
directory

[root@f22-01 ~]# virsh migrate --live --persistent --verbose --copy-
storage-all testvm qemu+ssh://f22-02.example.local/system

Migration: [100 %]

[root@f22-02 ~]# ls /var/lib/libvirt/images/testvm.qcow2

/var/lib/libvirt/images/testvm.qcow2
```

`--copy-storage-inc` will only transfer the changes:

```
[root@f22-01 ~]# virsh migrate --live  --verbose --copy-storage-inc
testvm qemu+ssh://f22-02.example.local/system

Migration: [100 %]
```

Live storage migration is a good option to have, but it is not something you can use regularly like a normal live migration. This consumes a lot of bandwidth based on the disk size. In a production environment, use a shared storage for migration activities.

Additionally, libvirt `virsh` also supports the following options:

- `virsh migrate-setmaxdowntime domain`: This will set a maximum possible downtime for a domain that is being live-migrated to another host. The specified downtime is in milliseconds. The downtime is calculated based on the dirty pages to be transferred.

- `virsh migrate-compcache domain [--size bytes]`: Sets and/or gets the size of the cache (in bytes) used for compressing repeatedly transferred memory pages during live migration. When called without size, the command just prints the current size of the compression cache. When the size is specified, the hypervisor is asked to change the compression cache to size bytes and then the current size is printed (the result may differ from the requested size due to rounding done by the hypervisor). The size option is supposed to be used while the domain is being live-migrated as a reaction to the migration process and increasing number of compression cache misses obtained from domjobinfo.

- `virsh migrate-setspeed domain bandwidth`: Sets the maximum migration bandwidth (in MiB/s) for a domain, which is being migrated to another host. Bandwidth is interpreted as an unsigned long value. Specifying a negative value results in an essentially unlimited value being provided to the hypervisor. The hypervisor can choose whether to reject the value or convert it to the maximum value allowed.

- `virsh migrate-getspeed domain`: Get the maximum migration bandwidth (in MiB/s) for a domain.

- `virsh migrate-setspeed domain bandwidth`: Sets the migration bandwidth in MiB/sec for the specified domain, which is being migrated to another host.

- `virsh migrate-getspeed domain`: Gets the maximum migration bandwidth that is available in MiB/sec for the specified domain.

Future of migration

Currently, the KVM is using precopy migration, that is, the VM is started when memory is in destination; remember Stage 2. The plan is to implement postcopy, so that the VM will be started at the destination instantly, and then move the memory based on the request from the VM. Risk is that if the source is lost all VM is gone. The advantage is that there is less downtime.

Summary

In this chapter, we covered various states of virtual machines, setting virtual hardware that includes display protocols, and how to enhance graphical performance by installing QEMU guest agent. Then we covered VM migration in detail and live and offline VM migration. In the next chapter, we will explore Kimchi.

7

Templates and Snapshots

Virtualization is not just about server consolidation, it also provides agility benefits such as faster provisioning, snapshots, and uncomplicated yet viable backup and recovery options that aren't easily available within the physical world.

You have already learned how efficiently a physical server can be turned into multiple virtual servers using the virtualization technologies provided in Linux. In this chapter, you'll learn how to keep those virtual machines up and running using snapshots, do rapid VM provisioning using templates, and take backups to react appropriately to disaster situations.

Introducing virtual machine templates

A virtual machine template (more commonly referred to as simply a template) is a pre-configured operating system image that can used to quickly deploy virtual machines. Using templates, you can avoid many repetitive installation and configuration tasks. The result is a fully installed, ready to operate (virtual) server in less time than manual installation would take.

Consider this example; suppose you wish to create four Apache web servers to host your web applications. Normally, with the traditional manual installation method, you would first have to create four virtual machines with specific hardware configurations, install an operating system on each of them one by one, and then download and install the required apache packages using yum or some other software installation method. This is a time-consuming job as you will be mostly doing repetitive work but with a template approach. However, it can be done in considerably less time. How? Because you will bypass operating system installation and other configuration tasks and directly spawn virtual machines from a template that consists of a pre-configured operating system image containing all the required web servers packages ready for use.

The following screenshot shows the steps involved in the manual installation method. You can clearly see that steps 2-5 are just repetitive tasks performed across all four virtual machines and they would have taken up most of the time required to get your apache web servers ready:

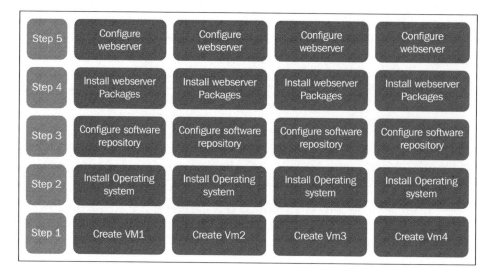

Now see how the number of steps is drastically reduced by simply following Steps 1-5 once, creating a template, and then using it to deploy four identical VMs. This will save you a lot of time:

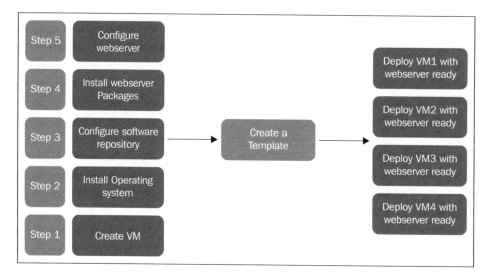

Working with templates

In this section, you will learn how to create templates of Windows and Linux virtual machines using the `virt-clone` option available in virt-manager. Although the `virt-clone` utility was not originally intended for creating templates, when used with `virt-sysprep` and other operating system sealing utilities it serves that purpose. Be aware that a clone is just a single copy of a virtual machine, whereas a template is a master copy of the virtual machine that can be used to create many clones.

You will also learn how to create and manage templates with the help of the `virsh` and `qemu-img` commands and deploy virtual machines from a template using the thin and clone methods:

- **Thin method**: A virtual machine deployed using the thin cloning mechanism uses the template image as a base image in read-only mode and links an additional "copy on write image" to store newly generated data. It requires less disk space but cannot run without access to the base template image.

- **Clone method**: A virtual machine deployed using the full cloning mechanism creates a complete copy of the virtual machine that is fully independent of the original VM or VM template. But it requires the same disk space as the original.

Creating templates

Templates are created by converting a virtual machine into a template. This is actually a three-step procedure that includes:

1. Installing and customizing the virtual machine, with all the desired software, which will become the template or base image.

2. Removing all system-specific properties to ensure that machine-specific settings are not propagated through the template such as SSH host keys, persistent network configuration, the MAC address, and user accounts.

3. Mark the virtual machine as a template by renaming it with `template` as a prefix.

To understand the actual procedure let's create two templates and deploy a virtual machine from them.

Example 1 – preparing a CentOS 7 template with a complete LAMP stack

1. Create a virtual machine and install CentOS 7.0 on it using the installation method that your prefer. Keep it minimal as this virtual machine will be used as the base for the template that is being created for this example.

2. SSH into or take control of the virtual machine and install the LAMP stack. I assume you are aware of the procedure to install the LAMP stack on CentOS.

> If you need to recap LAMP stack installation, the following article by Mitchell explains LAMP stack installation on RHEL7 in a very simple way:
>
> ```
> https://www.digitalocean.com/community/
> tutorials/how-to-install-linux-apache-mysql-php-
> lamp-stack-on-centos-7
> ```

3. Once the required LAMP settings are configured the way you want them, `shutdown` the virtual machine and run the `virt-sysprep` command to seal it:

```
KVMHOST# virsh shutdown CentOS ; sleep 10 ; virsh list --all
    Domain CentOS is being shutdown
        Id   Name                        State
        ----------------------------------------
        -    CentOS                      shut off
```

What is virt-sysprep?

This is a command-line utility provided by `libguestfs-tools-c packages` to ease the sealing and generalizing procedure of Linux virtual machine. It prepares a Linux virtual machine to become a template or clone by removing system-specific information automatically so that clones can be made from it. `virt-sysprep` can also customize a virtual machine, for instance by adding SSH keys, users, or logos.

There are two ways to invoke `virt-sysprep` against a Linux virtual machine, using the `-d` or `-a` options. The first option points to the intended guest using its name or UUID and the second one points to a particular disk image. This gives the flexibility to use the `virt-sysprep` command even if the guest is not defined in libvirt.

Once the `virt-sysprep` command is executed, it performs a bunch of `sysprep` operations that make the virtual machine image clean by removing system-specific information from it. Add the `--verbose` option to the command if you are interested in knowing how this command works in the background:

```
KVMHOST#  virt-sysprep -d CentOS
[    0.0] Examining the guest ...
[  19.4] Performing "abrt-data" ...
[  19.4] Performing "bash-history" …
[  20.0] Performing "udev-persistent-net" ...
[  20.0] Performing "utmp" ...
[  20.0] Performing "yum-uuid" ...
[  20.1] Performing "customize" ...
[  20.1] Setting a random seed
[  20.5] Performing "lvm-uuids" ...
```

 This is actually truncated output; by default it performs 32 operations.

You can also choose which specific `sysprep` operations you want to use. To get a list of all the available operations, run the `virt-sysprep --list-operation` command. The default operations are marked with an asterisk. You can change the default operations using the `--operations` switch followed by a comma-separated list of operations that you want to use. See the following example:

```
virt-sysprep  --operations ssh-hostkeys,udev-persistent-net -d CentOS
[    0.0] Examining the guest ...
[  19.6] Performing "ssh-hostkeys" ...
   19.6] Performing "udev-persistent-net" ...
```

Notice that this time it only performed the `ssh-hostkeys` and `udev-persistent-net` operations instead of the typical 32 operations. It's up to you how much cleaning you would like to undertake in the template.

Now we can mark this virtual machine as a template by adding the word `template` as a prefix in its name. You can even undefine the virtual machine from libvirt after taking a backup of its XML file.

Warning: Make sure that from now on this virtual machine is never started; otherwise, it will lose all `sysprep` operation and can even cause problems with virtual machines deployed using the thin method.

In order to rename a virtual machine, use virt-manager and, to take a backup of the XML configuration of the virtual machine, run:

```
#virsh dumpxml Template_CentOS /root/Template_CentOS.xml
 virsh list --all
 Id  Name                       State
---------------------------------------------
 24  Fed21                      running
 -   Template_CentOS            shut off
 -   Win7_01                    shut off
```

`Template_CentOS`, our template, is ready and visible in the `virsh list` command.

Example 2 – preparing a Windows 7 template with a MySQL database

Currently `virt-sysprep` does not work for Windows guests and there is little chance support will be added anytime soon. So in order to generalize a Windows machine would have to access the Windows system and directly run Sysprep.

The **System Preparation (Sysprep)** tool is a native Windows utility to remove system-specific data from Windows images. To know more about this utility, refer to this article:

https://technet.microsoft.com/en-us/library/cc721940%28v=ws.10%29.aspx

1. Create a virtual machine and install the Windows 7 operating system on it.
2. Install MySQL software and, once it's configured the way you want, restart it and follow the following steps to generalize it:
    1. Log on as the administrator user, type `regedit` into the **Run** box, and press *Enter* to launch the registry editor.
    2. On the left pane, expand the **HKEY_LOCAL_MACHINE** branch and navigate to **SYSTEM | SETUP**.

3. On the main pane, right click to add a new string value using **New | String Value** and name it `UnattendFile`.

4. Right-click on the newly created `UnattendFile` string and select **Modify**, type `a:\sysprep.inf` in the value data field and press **OK**. At the end it should display as:

   `Value name: UnattendFile    Value data: a:\sysprep.inf`

5. Now launch the `sysprep` application. The `.exe` file of `sysprep` is present in `C:\Windows\System32\sysprep\`. Navigate there by entering `sysprep` in the run box and double-click on `sysprep.exe`.

6. Under **System Cleanup Action**, select **Enter System Out-of-Box-Experience (OOBE)** and tick the **Generalize** checkbox if you need to change the computer's system identification number (SID).

7. Under **Shutdown** options, select **Shutdown** and click on the **OK** button. The virtual machine will now go through the sealing process and shut down automatically.

3. This time, instead of renaming the virtual machine name with the prefix `template`, we will undefine it from libvirt after taking a backup of its XML file. In order to do this, run:

```
#virsh dumpxml Win7_01 > /root/Win7.xml
```

This will create a `/root/Win7_01.xml` file. Here I choose `/root` as the location to back up the file but you may use any different location. Note down the attached disk image path of the virtual machine by running:

```
KVMHOST#virsh domblklist Win7

Target    Source
------------------------
hda       /vms/win7.qcow2
```

In this `Win7` virtual machine, `/vms/win7.qcow2` is the disk image and it's detected as `hda` inside the guest operating system. Now undefine the virtual machine:

```
KVMHOST#virsh undefine Win7

Domain Win7 has been undefined
```

Once the virtual machine is undefined it will not appear in the `virt-manager` or `virsh list --all` command output.

Deploying virtual machines from a template

In the previous section, we created two template images; the first template image is still defined in libvirt as vm and named `Template_CentOS` but the second is undefined from libvirt after saving its XML file at `/root/win7.xml` and the sealed image at `/vms/win7.qcow2`.

Deploying VMs using the clone provisioning method

Perform the following steps to deploy the VM using clone provisioning:

1. Open the Virtual Machine Manager (virt-manager), then select the **Template_CentOS** virtual machine. Right-click on it and select the **Clone** option, which will open the **Clone Virtual Machine** window:

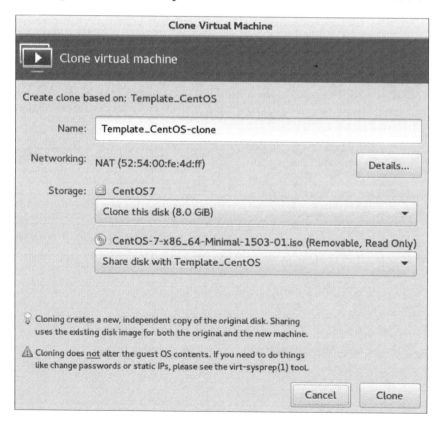

2. Provide a name for the resulting virtual machine and click on the **Clone** button to start the deployment. Wait till the cloning operation finishes.

3. Once it's finished, your newly deployed virtual machine is ready to use and you can start using it:

```
KVMHOST# virsh list  --all
 Id  Name                       State
--------------------------------------------
 24  Fed21                      running
  -  CentOS_LAMP1               shut off
  -  CentOS_LAMP2               shut off
  -  Template_CentOS            shut off
```

CentOS_LAMP1 and CentOS_LAMP2 are two virtual machines deployed from Template_CentOS but as we used clone provisioning they are independent; even if you remove Template_CentOS they will operate just fine.

Deploying VMs using the thin provisioning method

Perform the following steps to get started with VM deployment using the thin provisioning method:

1. Create two new qcow2 images using /vms/win7.raw as the backing file:

```
# qemu-img create -b /vms/win7.img -f qcow2 /vms/vm1.qcow2
#qemu-img create -b /vms/win7.img -f qcow2 /vms/vm2.qcow2
```

2. Verify that the backing file attribute for newly created qcow2 images is pointing correctly to the image /vms/win7.raw, using the qemu-img command:

```
qemu-img info /vms/vm2.qcow2
image: /vms/vm2.qcow2
file format: qcow2
virtual size: 10G (10737418240 bytes)
disk size: 196K
cluster_size: 65536
backing file: /vms/win7.img
Format specific information:
```

```
compat: 1.1

lazy refcounts: false

refcount bits: 16

corrupt: false
```

3. Now deploy the virtual machines named `Windows1` and `Windows2` using the `virt-clone` command:

```
virt-clone --original-xml=/root/small.xml -f /vms/vm1.qcow2 -n
Windows7-01 --preserve-data

virt-clone --original-xml=/root/large.xml -f /vms/vm2.qcow2 -n
Windows7-02 --preserve-data
```

4. Use the `virsh` command to verify if they are defined:

```
virsh list --all
 Id   Name                        State
 --------------------------------------------
 24   Fed21                       running
 -    CentOS_LAMP1                shut off
 -    Template_CentOS             shut off
 -    Windows7-01                 shut off
 -    Windows7-02                 shut off
```

5. Start the virtual machines and download something on to them; you will notice that the guest disk image size is just the size of your download:

```
du -sh /vms/vm1.qcow2
196K    /vms/vm1.qcow2
```

Snapshots

A VM snapshot is a file-based representation of the system state at a particular point in time. The snapshot includes configuration and disk data. With a snapshot, you can revert a VM to a point in time, which means by taking a snapshot of a virtual machine you preserve its state and can easily revert to it in the future if needed. Snapshots have many use cases, such as saving a VM's state before a potentially destructive operation.

For example, suppose you want to make some changes on your existing web server virtual machine, which is running fine at the moment, but you are not certain if the changes you are planning to make are going to work or break something. In that case you can take a snapshot of the virtual machine before doing the intended configuration changes and if something goes wrong, you can easily revert to the previous working state of the virtual machine by restoring the snapshot.

libvirt supports taking live snapshots. You can take a snapshot of a virtual machine while the guest is running. However, if there are any I/O-intensive applications running on the VM, it is recommended to shutdown or suspend the guest first to guarantee a clean snapshot.

There are mainly two classes of snapshots for libvirt guests: internal and external; each has its own benefits and limitations:

- **Internal snapshot:** Internal snapshots are contained completely within a qcow2 file. Before snapshot and after snapshot bits are stored in a single disk, allowing for greater flexibility. virt-manager provides a graphical management utility to manage internal snapshots. The following are the limitations of an internal snapshot:
    - Supported only with the qcow2 format
    - VM is paused while taking the snapshot
    - Doesn't work with LVM storage pools

- **External snapshot**: External snapshots are based on a copy-on-write concept. When a snapshot is taken, the original disk image becomes read-only and a new overlay disk image is created to accommodate guest writes:

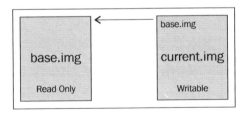

The overlay disk image is initially created as zero bytes in length and it can grow to the size of the original disk. The overlay disk image is always qcow2. However, external snapshots work with any base disk image. You can take external snapshot of raw disk images, qcow2, or any other libvirt-supported disk image format. However, there is no GUI support available yet for external snapshots so they are more expensive to manage as compared to internal snapshots.

VM disk image formats

We have already learned that internal snapshots require the virtual disk to be in the qcow2 format. Before we go further with some examples on how to create snapshots and manage them, let's talk about disk formats. libvirt supports several types of virtual disk format:

- raw: An exact byte-for-byte copy of the original disk without any other metadata

- bochs: Bochs disk image format

- cloop: Compressed loopback disk image format

- cow: User mode Linux disk image format

- dmg: Mac disk image format

- iso: CDROM disk image format

- qcow: QEMU v1 disk image format

- qcow2: QEMU v2 disk image format

- qed: QEMU Enhanced disk image format

- vmdk: VMware disk image format

- vpc: VirtualPC disk image format

As you can see, proprietary disk formats are supported, along with KVM, native qcow2, and other open source formats, so you can download a VM exported in .vpc format and import it into libvirt to create a new virtual machine without needing disk image conversion or additional software. While libvirt can work with all of these disk formats, not all of them are ideal for regular use in a KVM environment.

It is always recommended to convert disk images to either raw or qcow2 in order to achieve good performance. So raw and qcow2 are the most important formats? No. They are definitely not the most important. There happen to be some good reasons in this case to use them; let's understand the raw format first.

raw: This is a direct representation of a disk's structure. It has no additional metadata or structure and thus has very little overhead and therefore a performance advantage. However it lacks features such as snapshots (internal), compression, and so on. If you want to run any highly I/O-intensive application on virtual machines this format is recommended as it gives near-native performance.

qcow2: This format is designed for virtualization with cloud-like use cases in mind. It supports a range of special features including read-only backing files, snapshots (internal and external), compression, and encryption. It supports pre-allocation as well as the on-demand allocation of blocks and is the most recommended format to use.

You can use one of two methods to identify what format a VM disk image is in:

- The `file` command:

  qcow2 format:

  ```
  # file disk1
  disk1: QEMU QCOW Image (v3), 1073741824 bytes
  ```

  Raw format:

  ```
  # file disk2
  diskd: data
  ```

The `file` command is a standard Linux utility to classify filesystem objects, for example file, directory, and link. It uses a *magic number* embedded in files to determine the file format. In the preceding examples, `disk1` and `disk2` are the name of the disk image files on the host. `disk1` is the QEMU QCOW image, and `disk2` is raw data file:

- The `qemu-img` command:

  ```
  # qemu-img info disk1
  image: disk1
  file format: qcow2
  virtual size: 1.0G (1073741824 bytes)
  disk size: 196K
  cluster_size: 65536
  Format specific information:
      compat: 1.1
      lazy refcounts: false
      refcount bits: 16
      corrupt: false
  ```

The `info` option of the `qemu-img` command provides detailed information about the disk image formats supported by KVM virtualization.

Converting a VM disk format

Although it sounds a big task, converting a disk image from one format to another is relatively straightforward. The qemu-img convert command can do conversion between multiple formats:

- RAW to QCOW2:

  ```
  $ qemu-img convert -f raw -O qcow2 vm_disk1.img vm_disk1.qcow2
  ```

- QCOW2 to RAW:

  ```
  $ qemu-img convert -f qcow2 -O ram vm_disk2.qcow2 vm_disk2.img
  ```

Working with internal snapshots

In this section, you'll learn how to create, delete, and restore internal snapshots (offline/online) for a virtual machine. You'll also learn how to use virt-manager to manage internal snapshots.

Internal snapshots work only with qcow2 disk images so first make sure that the virtual machine for which you want to take a snapshot uses the qcow2 format for the base disk image. If not, convert it to qcow2 using the qemu-img command. An internal snapshot is a combination of disk snapshots and the VM memory state, It's a kind of checkpoint to which you can revert easily when needed.

I am using a CentOS_01 virtual machine here as an example to demonstrate internal snapshots. The CentOS_01 VM is residing on a directory filesystem-backed storage pool and has a qcow2 image acting as a virtual disk.

The following command lists the snapshot associated with a virtual machine:

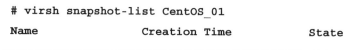

```
# virsh snapshot-list CentOS_01
Name                    Creation Time           State
-------------------------------------------------
```

As can be seen, currently there are no existing snapshots associated with the virtual machine; the CentOS_01, virsh snapshot-list command lists all of the available snapshots for the given virtual machine. The default information includes the snapshot name, creation time, and domain state. There is a lot of other snapshot-related information that can be listed by passing additional options to the snapshot-list command.

Creating the first internal snapshot

The easiest and preferred way to create internal snapshots for a virtual machine on KVM host is through `virsh` command. `virsh` has a series of options listed in the following to create and manage snapshots:

- `snapshot-create`: Create a snapshot from XML
- `snapshot-create-as`: Create a snapshot from a set of arguments
- `snapshot-current`: Get or set the current snapshot
- `snapshot-delete`: Delete a domain snapshot
- `snapshot-dumpxml`: Dump XML for a domain snapshot
- `snapshot-edit`: Edit XML for a snapshot
- `snapshot-info`: Get snapshot information
- `snapshot-list`: List snapshots for a domain
- `snapshot-parent`: Get the name of the parent of a snapshot
- `snapshot-revert`: Revert a domain to a snapshot

The following is a simple example of creating a snapshot. Running the following command will create an internal snapshot for virtual machine `CentOS_01`:

```
#virsh snapshot-create CentOS_01
    Domain snapshot 1439949985 created
```

By default, a newly created snapshot gets a unique number as its name. To create a snapshot with a custom name and description, use the `snapshot-create-as` command. The difference between these two commands is that the latter one allows passing configuration parameters as an argument whereas the earlier does not. It only accepts XML files as the input. We are using `snapshot-create-as` in this chapter as it's more convenient and easy to use.

Creating an internal snapshot with a custom name and description

To create an internal snapshot for the `CentOS_01` VM with the name `Snapshot 1` and the description `First snapshot`, type the following command:

```
#virsh snapshot-create-as CentOS_01 --name "Snapshot 1"
--description"First snapshot" --atomic
```

With the `--atomic` option specified, libvirt will guarantee that the snapshot either succeeds or fails with no changes. It's always recommended to use the `--atomic` option to avoid any corruption while taking the snapshot. Now check the `snapshot-list` output:

```
#  virsh snapshot-list CentOS_01
 Name                  Creation Time            State

 ------------------------------------------------------

 snapshot1             2015-08-19 08:41:23 +0530 running
```

Our first snapshot is ready to use and we can now use it to revert the VM's state if something goes wrong in the future. This snapshot was taken while the virtual machine was in a running state. The time to complete snapshot creation depends on how much memory the virtual machine has and how actively the guest is modifying that memory at the time.

> Note that the virtual machine goes into `paused` while snapshot creation is in progress; therefore it is always recommended you take the snapshot while the VM is not running. Taking a snapshot from a guest that is shut down ensures data integrity.

Creating multiple snapshots

We can keep creating more snapshots as required. For example, if we create two more snapshots, so that we have a total of three, the output of `snapshot-list` will look like this:

```
#virsh snapshot-list CentOS_01 --parent
 Name                  Creation Time              State        Parent

 ---------------------------------------------------------------------

 Snapshot1             2015-08-19 09:00:13 +0530 running        (null)
 Snapshot2             2015-08-19 09:00:43 +0530 running        Snapshot1
 Snapshot3             2015-08-19 09:01:00 +0530 shutoff        Snapshot2
```

Here, I used `-parent` switch, which prints the parent-children relation of snapshots. The first snapshot's parent is `(null)`, which means it was created directly on the disk image, and `snapshot1` is the parent of `snapshot2` and `snapshot2` is the parent of `snapshot3`. This helps us know the sequence of snapshots. A tree-like view of snapshots can also be obtained using the `--tree` option:

```
#virsh snapshot-list CentOS_01 --tree
Snapshot1
```

```
        |
    +- Snapshot2
        |
        +- Snapshot3
```

Now check the `state` column, which tells whether the particular snapshot is live or offline. In the preceding example, the first and second snapshots were taken while the VM was running whereas the third was taken when the VM was shut down. Restoring to a shutoff state snapshot will cause the VM to shutdown:

You can also, use the `qemu-img` command utility to get more information about internal snapshots—for example, the snapshot size, snapshot tag, and so on. In below example output you can see that the disk named as `vmdisk1.qcow2` three snapshot with different tags. This also show you when was particular snapshot was take, its date and time:

```
#qemu-img info /var/lib/libvirt/qemu/vmdisk1.qcow2

image: /var/lib/libvirt/qemu/vmdisk1.qcow2

file format: qcow2

virtual size: 8.0G (8589934592 bytes)

disk size: 1.6G

cluster_size: 65536

Snapshot list:
ID      TAG              VM SIZE           DATE       VM CLOCK
1       1439951249        220M 2015-08-19 07:57:29    00:09:36.885
2       Snapshot1         204M 2015-08-19 09:00:13    00:01:21.284
3       Snapshot2         204M 2015-08-19 09:00:43    00:01:47.308
4       Snapshot3           0 2015-08-19 09:01:00     00:00:00.000
Format specific information:
```

It can also be used to check the integrity of the qcow2 image using the `check` switch:

```
#qemu-img check /var/lib/libvirt/qemu/vmdisk1.qcow2
No errors were found on the image.
```

If any corruption occurred in the image, the preceding command will throw an error. One should immediately take a backup from the virtual machine as soon as an error is detected in the qcow2 image.

Reverting to internal snapshots

The main purpose of taking snapshots is to revert to a clean/working state of the VM when needed. Let's take an example. Suppose, after taking Snapshot3 of your virtual machine, you installed an application that messed up the whole configuration of the system. In such a situation, the VM can easily reverted to the state it was in when Snapshot3 was created. To revert to a snapshot, use the snapshot-revert command:

```
#virsh snapshot-revert <vm-name> --snapshotname "Snapshot1"
```

If you are reverting to a shutdown snapshot, then you will have to start the VM manually. Use the '--running' switch with virsh snapshot-revert to get it started automatically.

Deleting internal snapshots

Once you are certain that you no longer need a snapshot, you can and should delete it to save space. To delete a snapshot of a VM, use the snapshot-delete command. From our previous example, let's remove the second snapshot:

```
#virsh snapshot-list CentOS_01
Name                 Creation Time              State

-----------------------------------------------------

 Snapshot1           2015-08-19 09:00:13 +0530 running
 Snapshot2           2015-08-19 09:00:43 +0530 running
 Snapshot3           2015-08-19 09:01:00 +0530 shutoff
 snapshot4           2015-08-19 10:17:00 +0530 shutoff
# virsh snapshot-delete CentOS_01 Snapshot2
Domain snapshot Snapshot2 deleted
# virsh snapshot-list CentOS_01
Name                 Creation Time              State

-----------------------------------------------------

 Snapshot1           2015-08-19 09:00:13 +0530 running
 Snapshot3           2015-08-19 09:00:43 +0530 running
 snapshot4           2015-08-19 10:17:00 +0530 shutoff
```

Managing snapshots using virt-manager

Recently, virt-manager was given a user-interface for creating and managing VM snapshots. At present, it works only with qcow2 images but soon there will be support for raw as well. Taking a snapshot with virt-manager is actually very easy; to get started, open virt-manager (Virtual Machine Manager) and click on the virtual machine for which you would like to take a snapshot.

The snapshot UI button is present on the toolbar; this button gets activated only when the VM uses a qcow2 disk:

This is how its main screen looks:

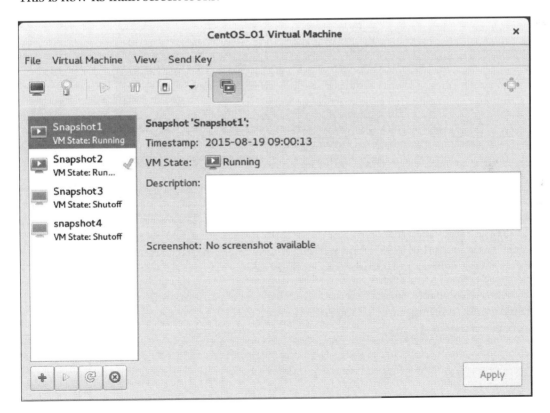

The **Manage** VM snapshot UI is actually pretty straightforward. It is divided into two panes. The left side pane lists all the snapshots and the right side displays information about the selected snapshot, including the snapshot name, timestamp, VM state, description, and a screenshot:

To create a new snapshot, click on the **+** button located at the bottom left. The **Create snapshot** dialog box will open. Enter the snapshot name, add an informative description, and hit the **Finish** button. Your snapshot is ready.

To remove or revert a snapshot, use the **Run Selected Snapshot** ▷ and **Delete Selected Snapshot** ⊗ buttons respectively. The **Refresh** button reloads snapshot changes.

Working with external disk snapshots

You learned about internal snapshots in the previous section. Internal snapshots are pretty simple to create and manage. Now let us explore external snapshots. External snapshotting is all about `overlay_image` and `backing_file`. Basically, it turns `backing_file` into the read-only state and starts writing on the `overlay_image`.

 `backing_file`: The original disk image of a virtual machine (read-only)

`overlay_image`: The snapshot image (writable)

If something goes wrong, you can simply discard the `overlay_image` and you are back to the original state.

With external disk snapshots, the `backing_file` can be any disk image (raw, qcow, even vmdk) unlike internal snapshots, which only support the `qcow2` image format.

Creating an external disk snapshot

I am using a `Win7_01` virtual machine here as an example to demonstrate external snapshots. This VM resided in a filesystem storage pool named `vmstore1` and has a `raw` image acting as a virtual disk:

```
# virsh domblklist Win7_01 --details
Type      Device   Target   Source
------------------------------------------------
file      disk     vda      /vmstore1/win7_01.img
```

1. Checking the virtual machine you want to take a snapshot of is running:

   ```
   # virsh list
    Id  Name                 State
   -----------------------------------------
    4   Win7_01              running
   ```

   You can take an external snapshot while a virtual machine is running or when it is shut down. Both live and offline snapshot methods are supported.

2. Create a snapshot (disk-only) of the guest this way:

   ```
   # virsh snapshot-create-as Win7_01  snapshot1 "My First Snapshot"
   --disk-only --atomic
   ```

Some details of the flags used:

The `--disk-only` parameter takes a snapshot of just the disk. The `atomic` parameter ensures that the snapshot either runs completely or fails without making any changes. This is used for integrity and to avoid any possible corruption.

3.   Now check the `snapshot-list` output:

```
# virsh snapshot-list Win7_01
 Name                 Creation Time              State
------------------------------------------------------------
 snapshot1            2015-08-21 10:21:38 +0530 disk-snapshot
```

4.   Now the snapshot has been taken, but it is only a snapshot of the disk's state; the contents of memory have not been stored:

```
# virsh snapshot-info Win7_01 snapshot1
Name:         snapshot1
Domain:       Win7_01
Current:      no
State:        disk-snapshot
Location:     external <<
Parent:       -
Children:     1
Descendants:  1
Metadata:     yes
```

5.   Now list all the block devices associated with the virtual machine once again:

```
#virsh domblklist Win7_01
Target    Source
-------------------------------------
vda       /vmstore1/win7_01.snapshot1
```

Notice that the source got changed after taking the snapshot. Let us gather some more information about this new image /vmstore1/win7_01. snapshot1:

```
#qemu-img info /vmstore1/win7_01.snapshot1
image: /vmstore1/win7_01.snapshot1
file format: qcow2
```

```
virtual size: 19G (20401094656 bytes)

disk size: 1.6M

cluster_size: 65536

backing file: /vmstore1/win7_01.img

backing file format: raw
```

Note that the `backing file` field is pointing to /vmstore1/win7_01.img.

6. This indicates that the new image /vmstore1/win7_01.snapshot1 is now a read/write snapshot of the original image /vmstore1/win7_01.img; any changes made to win7_01.snapshot1 will not be reflected in win7_01.img:

```
/vmstore1/win7_01.img = is backing file (original disk )

/vmstore1/win7_01.snapshot1 = is newly created overlay image where
now all the writes are happening
```

7. Now let's create one more snapshot. This time we will save it to a different place on the host system. By default the snapshot is created in the same storage pool where the original virtual machine disk resides:

```
#virsh snapshot-create-as Win7_01 snapshot2 "Second Snapshot"
--disk-only --diskspec vda,snapshot=external,file=/snapshot_store/
win7_01.snapshot2 --atomic

Domain snapshot snapshot2 created

# virsh domblklist Win7_01 --details

Type    Device  Target  Source

--------------------------------------------------

file    disk    vda     /snapshot_store/win7_01.snapshot2
```

Here we used the `--diskspec` option to create a snapshot in the desired location. The option needs to be formatted in exactly this way: `disk[,snapshot=type]` `[,driver=type][,file=name]` format.

- Disk: The target disk shown in `virsh domblklist <vm_name>`.

- Snapshot: Internal or external.

- Driver: libvirt.

- File: The path of the location where you want to create the resulting snapshot disk. You can use any location; just make sure the appropriate permissions have been set.

Let's create one more snapshot:

```
# virsh snapshot-create-as Win7_01 snapshot3 "Third Snapshot" --disk-only
--quiesce

        Domain snapshot snapshot3 created
```

Notice that this time I added one more option: `--quiesce`. Let's discuss this in the next section.

What is quiesce?

Quiesce is a file system freeze (fsfreeze/fsthaw) mechanism. This puts the guest file systems into a consistent state. If this step is not taken, anything waiting to be written to disk will not be included in the snapshot. Also, any changes made during the snapshot process may corrupt the image. To work around this, the `qemu-guest` agent needs to be installed on, and running inside, the guest. Snapshot creation will fail with an error:

```
error: Guest agent is not responding: Guest agent not available for now
```

Always use this option to be on the safe side while taking a snapshot. Guest tool installation is covered in *Chapter 5, Network and Storage*; you might want to revisit this and install the guest agent in your virtual machine if it's not already installed.

We have created three snapshots so far. Let us see how they are connected with each other to understand how an external snapshot chain is formed:

1. List all the snapshots associated with the virtual machine:

   ```
   # virsh snapshot-list Win7_01
   
   Name                Creation Time              State
   
   ------------------------------------------------------------
   
   snapshot1           2015-08-21 10:21:38 +0530 disk-snapshot
   snapshot2           2015-08-21 11:51:04 +0530 disk-snapshot
   snapshot3           2015-08-21 11:55:23 +0530 disk-snapshot
   ```

2. Check which is the current active (read/write) disk/snapshot for the virtual machine:

   ```
   # virsh domblklist Win7_01
   
   Target    Source
   
   ---------------------------------------------------------
   
   vda       /snapshot_store/win7_01.snapshot3
   ```

3. You can enumerate the backing file chain of the current active (read/write) snapshot using the `--backing-chain` option provided with qemu-img.

`--backing-chain` will enumerate information about backing files in a disk image chain. Refer to the following for a further description:

```
# qemu-img info --backing-chain /snapshot_store/win7_01.
snapshot3|grep backing

backing file: /snapshot_store/win7_01.snapshot2

backing file format: qcow2

backing file: /vmstore1/win7_01.snapshot1

backing file format: qcow2

backing file: /vmstore1/win7_01.img

backing file format: raw
```

From the preceding details we can see the chain is formed in the following manner:

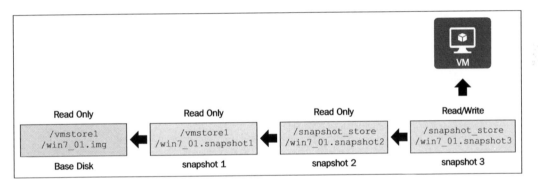

So it has to be read as: snapshot3 has snapshot2 as its backing file, snapshot2 has snapshot1 as its backing file, and snapshot1 has the base image as its backing file. Currently snapshot3 is the current active snapshot, where live guest writes happen.

Reverting to external snapshots

External snapshot support in libvirt is still incomplete. Snapshots can be created online or offline but there is no built-in feature to revert to or delete snapshots. If you try to revert an external snapshot using `virsh`, it will throw an error:

```
# virsh snapshot-revert Win7_01 --snapshotname "snapshot3"

error: unsupported configuration: revert to external snapshot not
supported yet
```

Does that mean that, once an external disk snapshot is taken for a virtual machine, there is no way to revert to that snapshot? No it's not like that; you can definitely revert to a snapshot but there is no libvirt support to accomplish this. You will have to revert manually by manipulating the domain XML file.

Take as an example a `Win7_01` VM that has three snapshots associated with it:

```
virsh snapshot-list Win7_01
 Name                 Creation Time                State
--------------------------------------------------------------
 snapshot1            2015-08-21 10:21:38 +0530 disk-snapshot
 snapshot2            2015-08-21 11:51:04 +0530 disk-snapshot
 snapshot3            2015-08-21 11:55:23 +0530 disk-snapshot
```

Suppose you want to revert to `snapshot2`. The solution is to shutdown the virtual machine (yes, a shutdown/power off is mandatory) and edit its XML file to point to the `snapshot2` disk image as the boot image:

1. Locate the disk image associated with `snapshot2`. We need the absolute path of the image. One can simply look into the storage pool and get the path but the best option is to check the snapshot XML file. How? Get help from your friend `virsh`:

    ```
    # virsh snapshot-dumpxml  Win7_01 --snapshotname snapshot2 | grep
    'source file' | head -1

      <source file='/snapshot_store/win7_01.snapshot2'/>
    ```

2. `/snapshot_store/win7_01.snapshot2` is the file associated with `snapshot2`. Verify that it's intact and properly connected to the `backing_file`:

    ```
    #qemu-img check /snapshot_store/win7_01.snapshot2

    No errors were found on the image.

    46/311296 = 0.01% allocated, 32.61% fragmented, 0.00% compressed
    clusters

    Image end offset: 3670016
    ```

If checking against the image produces no errors, this means `backing_file` is correctly pointing to the `snapshot1` disk. All good. If an error is detected in the qcow2 image, use the `-r leaks/all` parameter. It may help repair the inconsistencies but this isn't guaranteed:

Excerpt from qemu-img manpage:

The `-r` switch with `qemu-img` tries to repair any inconsistencies that are found during the check. `-r leaks` repairs only cluster leaks, whereas `-r all` fixes all kinds of errors, with a higher risk of choosing the wrong fix or hiding corruption that has already occurred:

```
# qemu-img info /snapshot_store/win7_01.snapshot2 | grep
backing
backing file: /vmstore1/win7_01.snapshot1
backing file format: qcow2
```

3. It is time to manipulate the XML file. You can remove the currently attached disk from the VM and add /snapshot_store/win7_01.snapshot2. Alternatively, edit the virtual machine's XML file by hand and modify the disk path. One of the better options is to use the `virt-xml` command:

```
#virt-xml Win7_01  --remove-device --disk target=vda

#virt-xml --add-device --disk /snapshot_store/win7_01.snapshot2,fo
rmat=qcow2,bus=virtio
```

This should add `win7_01.snapshot2` as the boot disk for the virtual machine; you can verify that by executing:

```
#virsh domblklist  Win7_01

Target    Source
----------------------------------------------

vda       /snapshot_store/win7_01.snapshot2
```

There are many options to manipulate a VM XML file in the `virt-xml` command. Refer to its man page to get acquainted with it. It can also be used in scripts.

4. Start the virtual machine and you are back to the state when `snapshot2` was taken. Similarly, you can revert to `snapshot1` or the base image when required.

Deleting external disk snapshots

Deleting external snapshots is somewhat tricky. An external snapshot cannot be deleted directly, unlike an internal snapshot. It first needs to be manually merged with the base layer or towards the active layer; only then can you remove it. There are two live block operations available for merging online snapshots:

- `blockcommit`: Merges data with the base layer. Using this merging mechanism you can merge overlay images into backing files. This is the fastest method of snapshot merging because overlay images are likely to be smaller than backing images.

- `blockpull`: Merges data towards the active layer. Using this merging mechanism you can merge data from `backing_file` to overlay images. The resulting file will always be `qcow2`.

Merging external snapshots using blockcommit

The `VM1` virtual machine has a base image (`raw`) called `vm1.img` with a chain of four external snapshots. `/vmstore1/vm1.snap4` is the active snapshot image where live writes happen; the rest are in read-only mode. Our target is to remove all the snapshots associated with this virtual machine:

1. List the current active disk image in use:

    ```
    #virsh domblklist VM1

    Target    Source

    ---------------------------

    hda       /vmstore1/vm1.snap4
    ```

    Here we can verify that the `/vmstore1/vm1.snap4` image is the currently active image on which all writes are occurring.

2. Now enumerate the backing file chain of `/vmstore1/vm1.snap4`:

    ```
    #qemu-img info --backing-chain /vmstore1/vm1.snap4 | grep  backing
    backing file: /vmstore1/vm1.snap3
    backing file format: qcow2
    backing file: /vmstore1/vm1.snap2
    backing file format: qcow2
    backing file: /vmstore1/vm1.snap1
    backing file format: qcow2
    backing file: /vmstore1/vm1.img
    backing file format: raw
    ```

3. Time to merge all the snapshot images into the base image:

```
# virsh blockcommit VM1 hda --verbose --pivot --active
Block Commit: [100 %]
Successfully pivoted
```

4. Now, check the current active block device in use:

```
# virsh domblklist VM1
Target    Source
-------------------------
hda       /vmstore1/vm1.img
```

Notice that now the current active block device is the base image and all writes are switched to it, which means we successfully merged the snapshot images into the base image. But the snapshot-list output shows that there are still snapshots associated with the virtual machine:

```
# virsh snapshot-list VM1
Name              Creation Time              State
-------------------------------------------------------
 snap1            2015-08-22 09:10:56 +0530  shutoff
 snap2            2015-08-22 09:11:03 +0530  shutoff
 snap3            2015-08-22 09:11:09 +0530  shutoff
 snap4            2015-08-22 09:11:17 +0530  shutoff
```

If you want to get rid of this, you will need to remove the appropriate metadata and delete the snapshot images. As mentioned earlier, libvirt does not have complete support for external snapshots. Currently, it can just merge the images but no support is available for automatically removing snapshot metadata and overlaying image files. It has to be done manually:

To remove snapshot metadata, run:

```
#virsh snapshot-delete VM1 snap1 --children  --metadata
#virsh snapshot-list VM1
Name              Creation Time          State
-----------------------------------------------------------
```

Merging external snapshots using blockpull

The VM2 virtual machine has a base image (raw) called vm1.img with only one external snapshot. The snapshot disk is the active image where live writes happen and the base image is in read-only mode. Our target is to remove snapshots associated with this virtual machine:

1. List the current active disk image in use:

   ```
   #virsh domblklist VM2

   Target    Source
   ----------------------------
   hda       /vmstore1/vm2.snap1
   ```

   Here we can verify that the /vmstore1/vm2.snap1 image is the currently active image on which all writes are occurring.

2. Now enumerate the backing file chain of /vmstore1/vm1.snap4:

   ```
   #qemu-img info --backing-chain /vmstore1/vm2.snap1 | grep  backing
   backing file: /vmstore1/vm1.img
   backing file format: raw
   ```

3. Merge the base image into the snapshot image (base to overlay image merging):

   ```
   #virsh blockpull VM2 --path /vmstore1/vm2.snap1 --wait --verbose
   Block Pull: [100 %]
   Pull complete
   ```

   Now check the size of /vmstore1/vm2.snap1. It got considerably larger because we pulled the base_image and merged it into the snapshot image to get a single file.

4. Now you can remove the base_image and snapshot metadata:

   ```
   #virsh snapshot-delete VM1 snap1  --metadata
   ```

We ran the merge and snapshot deletion tasks while the virtual machine is in the running state, without any downtime. blockcommit and blockpull can also be used to remove a specific snapshot from the snapshot chain. See the man page for virsh to get more information and try it yourself. You may refer to the following URL:

http://wiki.qemu.org/Features/Snapshots

This link will provide you with a lot more information about how snapshots work.

Best practices for dealing with snapshots

- When you take a VM snapshot, you are creating new delta copy of the virtual machine disk, qemu2, or a raw file and then you are writing to that delta. So the more data you write, the longer it's going to take to commit and consolidate it back into the parent. Yes, you will eventually need to commit snapshots, but it is not recommended you go into production with a snapshot attached to the virtual machine.

- Snapshots are not backups; they are just a picture of a state, taken at a specific point in time, to which you can revert when required. Therefore, do not rely on it as a direct backup process.

- Don't keep a VM with a snapshot associated with it for long time. As soon as you verify that reverting to the state at the time a snapshot was taken is no longer required, merge and delete the snapshot immediately.

- Use external snapshots whenever possible. The chances of corruption are much lower in external snapshots when compared to internal snapshots.

- Limit the snapshot count. Taking several snapshots in a row without any cleanup can hit virtual machine and host performance as qemu will have to trawl through each image in the snapshot chain to read a new file from base_image.

- Have Guest Agent installed in the virtual machine before taking snapshots, Certain operations in the snapshot process can be improved through support from within the guest.

- Always use the --quiesce and --atomic options while taking snapshots.

Summary

In this chapter, you learned how to create Windows and Linux templates for rapid VM provisioning. We also saw how to create external and internal snapshots and when to use each. Snapshot management including merge and deletion is also covered, together with snapshot best practices.

8
Kimchi – An HTML5-Based Management Tool for KVM/libvirt

This chapter explains how to manage the KVM virtualization infrastructure remotely using libvirt-based web management tools. You will learn how to create new virtual machines, adjust an existing VM's resource configuration settings remotely, implement user access controls, and so on, through a browser using Kimchi Web-based UI. It also introduces VM-King, an Android application which helps you manage KVM virtual machines remotely from your Android mobile or tablet.

The following topics will be covered in this chapter:

- Libvirt APIs
- Introduction to the Kimchi project
- Setting up a Kimchi server
- Managing KVM virtualization infrastructure using Kimchi WebUI
- Creating virtual machines through Kimchi Web-based UI
- Managing virtual machine remotely using the vm_king android application

Libvirt Web API

In *Chapter 2, KVM Internals*, you learned about libvirt. It provides a set of stable APIs to manage virtualization infrastructure on a host machine. This includes storage, networks, network interface, host devices, hypervisor, and virtual machines. It basically acts as an intermediary between hypervisor (qemu-kvm) and user-space applications.

The libvirt API supports C and C++ directly and has bindings for other languages, such as C#, Java, Python, OCaml, PHP, and Ruby.

The virt-manager, is a de facto GUI tool that manages KVM virtualization and uses a Python binding, whereas the `virsh` command is written in the C-programming language. The virt-manager application logic is written in Python, while the UI is constructed with the help of Glade and GTK+.

Similarly, a WebUI can also be constructed using a libvirt Python binding so that you can access libvirt (virtual machines) directly from your Web application written in Python, with no need to have the virt-manager or libvirt-based CLI/GUI tools installed.

The biggest and most obvious advantage of accessing libvirt through Web applications is flexibility. A Web application can be accessed from any computer, no matter what operating system it uses. This means that you can easily access and manage your virtual machines from Intranet or, Internet through a browser.

Detailed information about how to use libvirt-API bindings with various languages is documented at `http://libvirt.org/bindings.html`.

You can create your own Web application or simply start using one on of the pre-created web-based management tools available for libvirt. There are several tools, some are commercial, but most are free. The list is available at `http://www.linux-kvm.org/page/Management_Tools`.

Introduction to the Kimchi project

Kimchi is an HTML5-based management tool for KVM. Among the various tools listed on `http://www.linux-kvm.org/page/Management_Tools`, to manage KVM infrastructure, Kimchi is simple to configure and use. The management console provided by Kimchi is feature-rich and cross browser and platform. It is also a perfect tool for any small organization that wants to create its own private cloud without investing considerable resources and money.

 The Kimchi project was started by Adam Litke and Anthony Liguori in 2012. The first community version (v0.1) was released in 2013. The current version is 1.5.0.

Kimchi is a lightweight and easy to install tool that gives you a great Web-based graphical interface for your KVM VMs very quickly, thus allowing you to control their life cycle (power on/off/resume) and access the display console over browser with no additional software installed. You can also create templates and use ISO images to create new virtual machines. Here are some important features of Kimchi:

- Cross browser and platform: It works on any client that has a modern Web browser.

- Supports PAM and LDAP based user authentication.

- Supports user access control. You can control which user see which VMs.

- I18n support; currently it supports English, Portuguese, and Chinese.

- Allows host software management. You can upgrade the packages on the host system through Kimchi WebUI.

- Federation feature: You can register Kimchi server on openSLP and discover peers in the same network.

- noVNC/Websocket and Spice HTML5 for the in-browser VM console.

- Host management using the Ginger admin plugin.

- Provides RestAPI, allowing integration with external systems to manage KVM infrastructure.

Kimchi architecture

Kimchi uses Python binding to communicate with libvirt. It comprise four main modules written in Python to facilitate interaction with libvirt, and Ngnix is used as a Web application server to serve the UI that is developed in HTML5 + JavaScript + CSS:

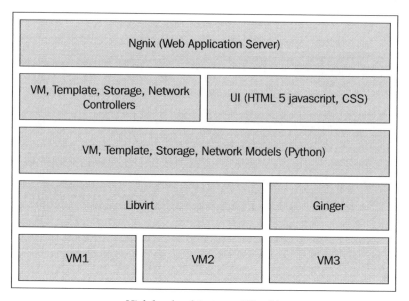

High-level architecture of Kimchi

Setting up Kimchi server

Kimchi is now available in Fedora 22 stable repository; so to install it, as root, you just have to execute the # dnf install kimchi command and this will install Kimchi and all of its dependencies. You can always use sudo if you don't want to login as a root user but still execute the command with root privileges.

 Although Kimchi is now available in Fedora 22 stable repository, the version is not the latest. If you want to use the latest version head to Kimchi's community website at http://kimchi-project.github.io/kimchi/.

They provide the latest version packages for Fedora, openSUSE, Ubuntu, and RHEL. You can download the rpm from `http://kimchi-project.github.io/kimchi/downloads/` and then install it using the following commands:

`$yum localinstall <local rpm path> or`

`$yum localinstall http://kimchi-project.github.io/kimchi/downloads/kimchi-1.5.0-0.fc22.noarch.rpm`

If you wish to use Ginger, an open source host management plug-in for Kimchi, it needs to be complied from the source. As of now, there are no `rpm` packages available for a Ginger plug-in.

1. Download the latest version of Ginger from GitHub:

   `#cd /opt ; git clone https://github.com/kimchi-project/ginger.git.`

2. Build Ginger using the following command:

   `##./autogen.sh --system`

3. Install ginger using the following command:

   `# make`

   `sudo make install`

This will install the Ginger plugin; you can verify whether the installation succeeded or failed by looking at the `/usr/local/share/kimchi/plugins` directory. If a directory with the name `ginger` is created there, it means that the installation was successful:

`# ls /usr/local/share/kimchi/plugins/`

`ginger`

Starting kimchid service

After installing the Kimchi package, the first thing you need to do is start its service to get it up:

`# systemctl restart kimchid.service`

Once the service is started, you can access Kimchi using a Web browser, `https://localhost:8001`. By default, it uses port number `8001` for HTTPS and `8000` for HTTP redirector.

To access Kimchi from Internet or intranet, use the `https://IPADDRESS:8001/` URL, where `IPADDRESS` is the IP address that you configured for the server during installation. For example, if its `10.65.209.103`, the URL is `https://10.65.209.103:8001/` or `https:kimchi.example.com:8001` provided that `10.65.209.103` resolves to `kimchi.example.com`.

```
# netstat -ntlp | grep nginx:
tcp      0     0 0.0.0.0:8000          0.0.0.0:*
         LISTEN    8356/nginx: master
tcp      0     0 0.0.0.0:8001          0.0.0.0:*
         LISTEN    8356/nginx: master
```

You can change the access ports to whatever ports you want by editing its main configuration file `/etc/kimchi/kimchi.conf`. After changing the ports, make sure you add appropriate iptable rules to allow access.

The main configuration file of Kimchi is divided into four sections; server, logging, display, and authentication. Let's see what configurative directives there are in each of these sections:

- The **Server** section consists of various settings to control the access of Kimchi WebUI. The following are some important configuration parameters:

```
[server]
# Hostname or IP address to listen on
#host = 0.0.0.0
```

By default, Kimchi listens on all networks. If you want to restrict a access to particular subnet or IP address, uncomment the "host" directive and specify the network subnet or a comma separated list of IP addresses:

```
# Port to listen on
#port = 8000
# If present, start an SSL-enabled server on the given port
#ssl_port = 8001
```

Default access ports are `8000` (HTTP) and `8001` (HTTPS), the application actually works only on the HTTPS, `8000` HTTP is just a redirector. Pointing your browser to `http:localhost:8000` will automatically redirect you to `https:localhost:8001`. You can change these default ports by editing the preceding two directives. These two directives are directly reflected with the listen directives in the `/etc/nginx/conf.d/kimchi.conf` Nginx Web server configuration file.

- The **Logging** section consists of only two settings, which are:

```
# Log directory
#log_dir = /var/log/kimchi
# Logging level: debug, info, warning, error or critical
#log_level = debug
```

  It is recommended to keep it to default logging setting, but keep in mind that the debug logging can consume a lot of disk space. Moreover, right now there are no `logrotate` scripts available for these log files and it is not managed by `rsyslog` daemon to send logs to the centralized log server.

- The **Display** section is there for just one directive. That is, a port for websocket proxy to listen on. A websocket is used to for noVNC and HTML5 spice console.

- The **Authentication** section consists of settings to manage authentication for the WebUI. The default method is via **Pluggable Authentication Module (PAM)**. However, it can also be configured with enterprise directory servers, such as Microsoft Active Directory or FreeIPA using the ldap protocol.

  I have configured it with a FreeIPA server so that all the users in my directory server can access the Kimchi WebUI and take console of the virtual machines:

```
# If specified method to ldap, following fields need to be
specified.
# ldap server domain name used to authenticate.
ldap_server = "kvm.example.com"
# Search tree base in ldap
ldap_search_base = "ou=People, dc=kvm,dc=example, dc=com"
# User id filter
ldap_search_filter = "uid=%(username)s"
# User IDs regarded as kimchi admin
ldap_admin_id = "admin@kvm.example.com"
# systemctl restart kimchid.service
```

> Configuration changes made in /etc/kimchi/kimchi.conf can be effective only when the kimchid service is restarted. So make sure that you restart the service upon making changes in the configuration file.

Managing KVM virtualization infrastructure using kimchi WebUI

To access the Kimchi WebUI, open your Web browser and type `https://<IP/FQDN of your host>:8001`.

Proceed past any SSL warnings and continue to the interface. You should see something similar to the following screenshot:

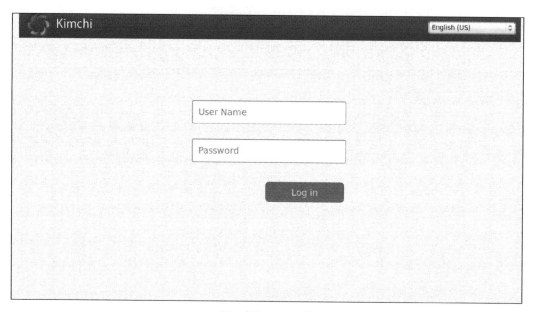

Kimchi login panel

By default, Kimchi uses PAM for authenticating users, so you can log in with the credentials of the root user. You can also login as other local users available on the system, but they will not see any virtual machines unless required permissions are granted.

Once you are logged in as a root user, you should be able to see a screen like the following screenshot, listing all guest virtual machines defined on the host. It displays resource utilization for the running virtual machines, you have buttons to perform shutdown, restart, and connect to console by clicking on action:

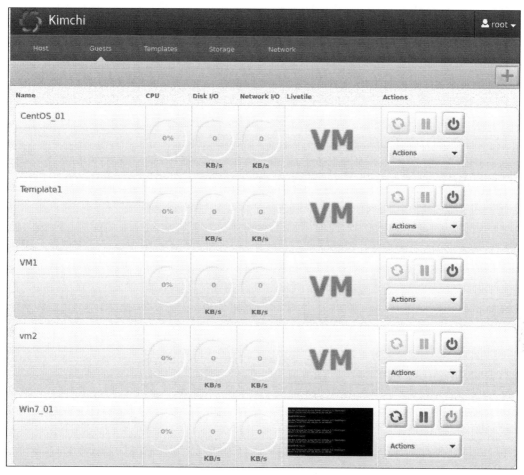

Guests tab in Kimchi WebUI

The small button located at the right-hand corner, with the power icon, indicates a virtual machine's state; green means that it's running and red means shutdown/power off.

Creating virtual machines through Kimchi WebUI

Kimchi uses the concepts of templates that can be re-used to create similar guests. Its a two step task to create a virtual machine:

1. Create a template from an ISO or a pre-installed guest OS image file.

2. Deploy the VM from the template; Kimchi automatically allocates a new disk and gets emulated hardware configuration according to the template chosen.

   To create a new guest, click on the **Guests** menu item, and then click on the green **+** icon. Simply give your virtual machine a name, select a template to build it from, and click on **Create**. That's all.

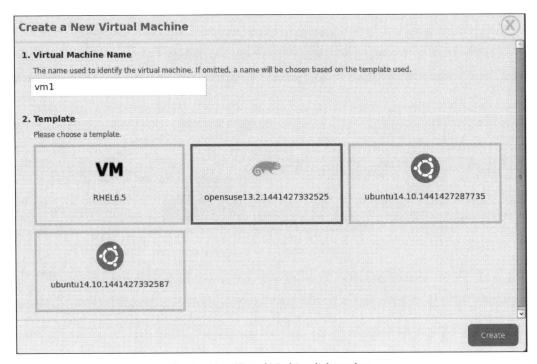

Create a New Virtual Machine dialogue box

Your virtual machine is ready. Memory, CPU, vDisk size, and other configurations options are inherited from the template to the virtual machine. If your template is ISO backed, you will have to manually install the operating system on the newly created virtual machine, but if it's image backed, the manual guest operating system installation is not required. The template configuration includes the following information:

- The local or remote ISO for the OS
- Number of CPUs
- Amount of memory
- Disk size
- Storage pool to allocate disk from
- Networks to be used

You can view or modify templates by clicking on the **Templates** menu item in the top navigation bar:

Template tab

Templates with an earth icon indicate that its source image is located on the Internet, whereas a template with a disk icon indicates that source images are located locally on the host systems's file system.

To create a new template, click on the **+** sign in the right-hand corner. You can create a template using an ISO image or a local image file, as well as remote ISO images:

 The local `.iso` or image files should be stored in `/var/lib/kimchi/isos` so that the template and guest creation dialogs can see them automatically.

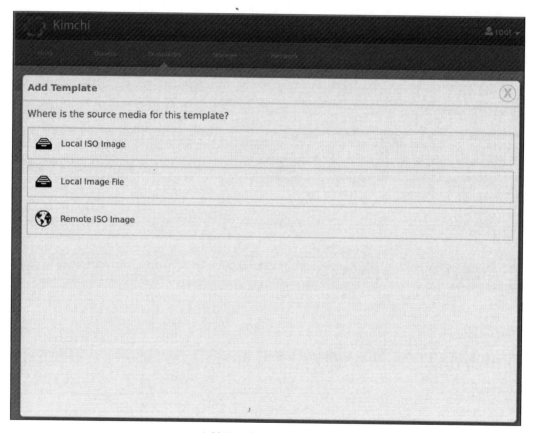

Add Template dialogue box

The remote ISO option looks for ISO images on the respective vendor's website; by default, Kimchi configures remote ISO access from the following Linux distribution files:

```
# ls /etc/kimchi/distros.d/
debian.json  fedora.json  gentoo.json  opensuse.json  ubuntu.json
```

You can also configure your own JSON file with a path to your local ISO library or vault similar to what I defined for Windows 7:

```
Win7.json
[
  {
      "name": "Win7_Professional",
      "os_distro": "Windows",
      "os_arch": "x86_64",
      "path": "http://vault.server.example.com/win7.iso"
  }
```

Save the file and it will appear in the Remote ISO Image window.

For local ISO images, you can directly specify the path of the .iso image present on the host system or click on the **Search ISOs** button:

Search ISOs will find out all the .iso images on the host system and give you a list. You can the required image and make a template out of it.

Similarly, you can manage the storage pool by going to the storage menu and then creating a new storage by clicking on the + sign. It supports NFS, iSCSI, and Fiber Channel-backed storage pool creation:

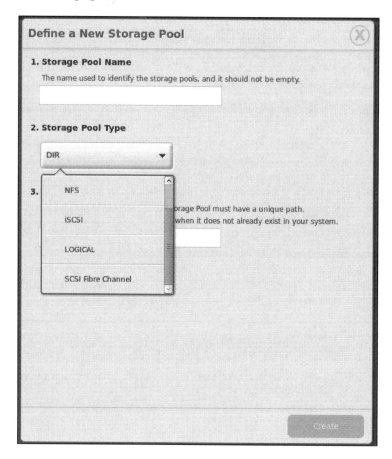

The following screenshot shows the **Storage** tab where the storage pool can be listed and managed. You can list volumes in a pool by clicking on the down-arrow button in the right-hand corner of the pool. Each thumbnail of the vDisk contains informative details, such as the type, format, allocation statistics, and so on:

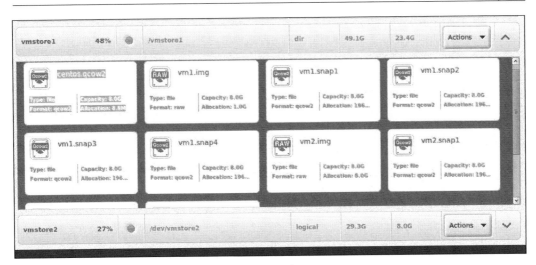

Storage tab

Network can also be managed by clicking on the **network** menu; you can create a new network with a Private Virtual Network (Isolated), Masqueraded Virtual Network (Outside-reach), or Aggregated Public Network (In-outside Reach):

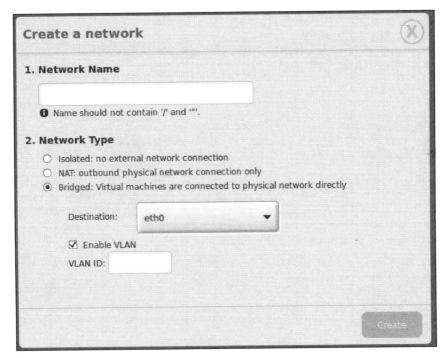

Create a network dialogue box

The following screenshot shows the **Network** tab in Kimchi. You can see the default NAT network and the three custom networks, named **Net1**, **Net2**, and **Net3**. To create a new network, click on the + button located in the upper-left corner of the page:

Network tab

Starting and stopping guests

To start a guest, click on **Actions** to **activate** the menu and then click on **Start**.

To stop a guest, click on **Actions** and then click on **Stop**.

Editing a virtual machine's resource allocation

To change the resource allocation of a virtual machine, for example, to change the memory and CPU allocation, select the VM and click on the **Action** button. It will show you the list of actions that can be performed against the virtual machine. For now, forget about other options and simply click on **Edit**; this will open an **Edit Guest** dialogue box through which you can change the resource allocations, such as memory size, vCPUs numbers, and so on:

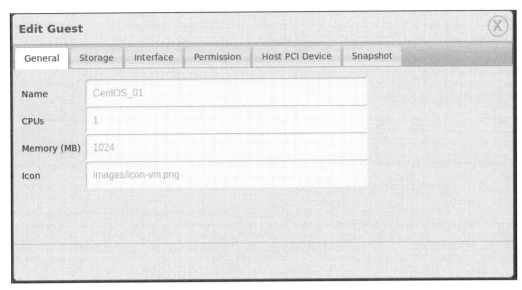

Edit Guest dialogue box

Accessing a virtual machine's graphical console

Kimchi provides noVNC or Spice HTML5 console access options for virtual machines.

You can define which option to use at the template level. To access a console, click on the preview image on the **Guests** tab, or click on **Actions** and then click on **Connect**.

This opens a new browser tab containing a graphical interface, using which, the user can interact with the guest machine.

 Your browser should allow pop-up windows to get a noVNC/Spice window. If your browser blocks pop-ups, you will not be able to see the graphical console.

Permissions and user access control

By default, only the root user can see all the virtual machines; other local or ldap users would be able to login, but will see a **No guests found** message when they click on the **Guests** tab. This is because of the user access control capability of Kimchi.

You (administrator) can decide which user can see and operate which virtual machines. To set access permission on a virtual machine, log in as a root user and perform the following steps:

1. Select an existing VM and navigate to **Actions | Edit**.

2. This will open the **Edit Guest** dialogue box. There is a **Permission** tab, just besides the **Interface** tab. Click on it.

3. The following screenshot shows the **Permission** tab, through which you can set the permission. On the left, there is a list of local system users and group. You can select the desired user/group and move it to the right-hand side box to give that user access to the virtual machine:

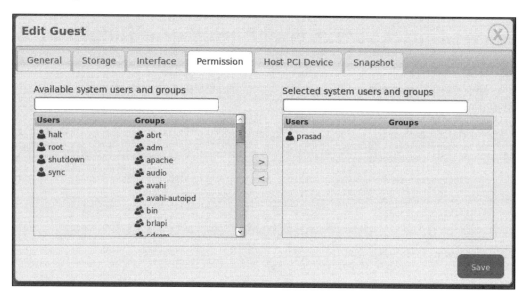

Here, for example, user `prasad` is added to the access list of the virtual machine named **RHEL6_Prasad** by the root (administrator). Now, when the user prasad logs in to Kimchi WebUI, only one virtual machine will be visible to him despite the fact that there are many virtual machine defined on the same host machine:

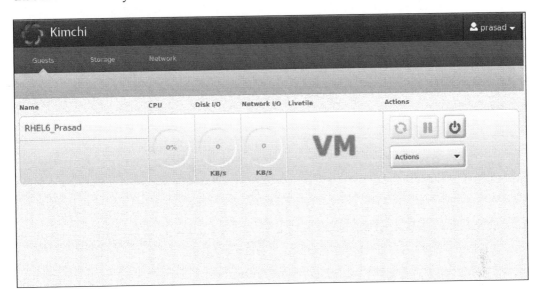

Monitoring and managing a host system with the Kimchi WebUI

You can monitor the performance of your host system by clicking on the **Host** menu item. There are **Shut down** and **Restart** buttons to manage the lifecycle of the host. It also allows you to connect the console of the host, but this functionality is currently limited to the **IBM Power System** only.

The first section gives the basic information about the host system, that includes, **OS Distro, OS Version**, Number of CPU, and **Memory** size, and the second section displays host performance statistics, including **CPU, Memory, Network IO**, and **Disk IO**:

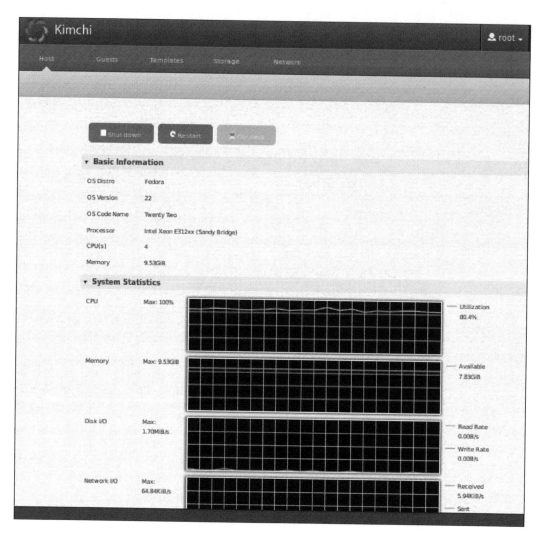

 The **Host** menu item in the Kimchi WebUI is only visible to a root user. Normal users will not be able to access it because this menu item is disabled for them.

It also facilitates updating the rpm packages and yum repository configuration. The packages that require updates are listed in the **Software Updates** dialog box:

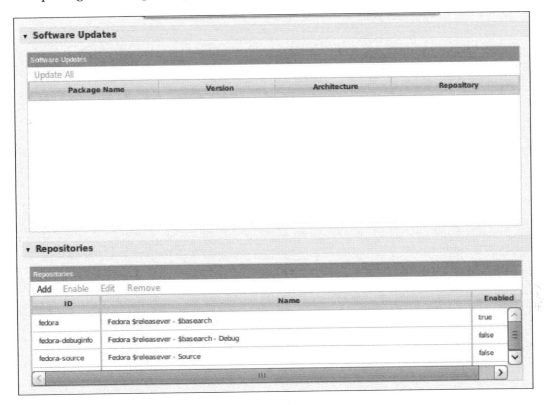

It actually uses the `#yum check-update` command in the background to get a list of the packages those had updates that needed to be applied. You can update a package individually, or perform the **Update All** function. It also allows you to manage the yum repositories on the host. You can add a new repository, or delete or edit an existing yum repository. This makes the RPM package management easier and more configurable.

Host system management using the Kimchi-Ginger plugin

Ginger is an open source host management plugin for Kimchi. With the Ginger plugin installed, you get extended management options for the host system.

The current features include:

- Retrieving system health (sensors) stats
- User login account management
- Network interface configuration
- Configuration backup
- + Power (ppc) firmware update
- + Power policy management

 The Kimchi-Ginger plugin is at present tightly integrated with the IBM Power system. For the IBM Power system, it provides the following additional functionalities.

There are many use cases for Kimchi. Using this simple yet powerful tool, you can even start your own **virtual private server (VPS)** offering service. It's a community project backed by many open source contributors, thus making it more stable and feature-rich. The following are some of the features that are planned for future development of Kimchi:

- OVS bridges
- Logical Storage Pool extension
- OVA support
- Support creation of non-sparse disk
- VM/Template Hooks
- oVirt node integration

If you would like to learn more about Kimchi and get involved, subscribe to `https://groups.google.com/forum/#!forum/project-kimchi`.

Managing virtual machine through android phones

Nowadays, there are many free and commercial applications available for the Android mobile operating system, which allow you to manage your virtual machines remotely from your mobile or tablet. The following are some free apps that work great with libvirt:

Application name: **VM-king**

Download URL: http://bit.ly/216SW1e

The supported functions are:

- Start/pause/managedSave/stop/destroy VM
- Restore and delete Snapshots
- Getting a screenshot of the running VMs
- Getting the remote display (VNC/Spice) connection information
- Encrypted storage of your SSH connection credentials
- Supports SSH password and RSA key authentication

Application name: **VM Manager**

Download URL: http://bit.ly/1SfOY6a

The supported functions are:

- start/pause/managedsave/stop/destroy VM
- Changing a VM's emulated hardware configuration

Application name: **aSPICE: Secure SPICE Client**

Download URL: bit.ly/1VOYlIP

The supported functions are:

- Control any SPICE-enabled qemu virtual machine with ANY guest OS
- Multi-factor (two-factor) SSH authentication in the Pro version
- Multi-touch control over the remote mouse. One finger taps left-clicks, two-finger taps right-clicks, and three-finger taps middle-clicks
- Sound support pinch-zooming
- Dynamic resolution changes that allow you to reconfigure your desktop while connected and control the other virtual machines from BIOS to OS
- Full rotation support. Use the central lock rotation on your device to disable rotation
- Full desktop visibility even with soft keyboard extended
- UI casing for different screen sizes (for tablets and smartphones)

Summary

In this chapter, you learned how to install Kimchi and use it to manage your standalone KVM host and virtual machines remotely through a modern Web-browser. You also learned how to implement role-based access control for virtual machines, monitor performance of the host system through Kimchi HTML5 WebUI, and got an idea about android applications available to manage KVM virtual machines remotely.

9
Software-Defined Networking for KVM Virtualization

Everyone is talking about **Software-Defined Networking** (SDN) these days. It is often referred to as a technology revolution that was much needed for computer networks, especially in the cloud and virtualization world which tends to have a rapid provisioning of network services for virtual machines, multi tenancy support, and improved network visibility. The core concept of SDN is to decouple the control plane from the forwarding plane and enable innovation through network programmability. In this chapter we will be covering the SDN approach in KVM virtualization using the Open vSwitch and supporting tools that includes OpenDaylight SDN controller. You will learn about:

- OpenvSwitch installation and setup
- Creating VLANs for KVM virtual machines
- Applying granular traffic and policy control to KVM VMs
- Creating overlay networks
- Port mirroring and SPAN
- Managing OpenvSwitch using the OpenDaylight SDN Controller

Introducing Software Defined Networking

Let us start with a formal definition of **SDN**, The following definition cited comes from the **Open Networking Foundation** (**ONF**) (www.opennetworking.org),which is a user-driven nonprofit organization dedicated to the promotion and adoption of SDN through open standards development.

SDN is an emerging architecture that is dynamic, manageable, cost-effective, and adaptable, making it ideal for the high-bandwidth, dynamic nature of today's applications. This architecture decouples network control and forwarding functions, enabling network control to become directly programmable and the underlying infrastructure to be abstracted for applications and network services. The OpenFlow® protocol is a foundational element for building SDN solutions.

The key themes of the ONF definition are:

- Separation of the control from the forwarding plane
- Software programmability for network elements
- Centralized network control and management

What do we mean by the decoupling of forwarding from the control plane? What are the forwarding plane and data plane exactly? These are probably the questions in your mind now, right?

They are conceptual terms in the networking world. To get a fair understanding of what the control plane and data plane, also known as forwarding plane are, let us go back in time and recap how an Ethernet Hub device used to work.

Ethernet Hub: No Intelligence addressing or knowledge. It acts as a repeater and simply forwards data to every other port it has (kind of "broadcasting"). You can think of hub forwarding decisions as, "Oh! I see bits! Let's forward them to everyone." This is the simplest way to create a network:

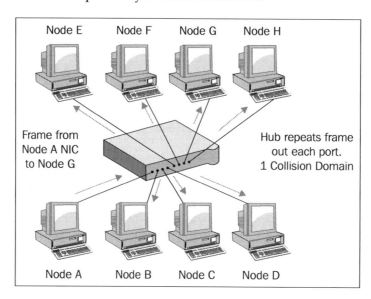

But this simplest of approaches to creating networks had various disadvantages, such as broadcast storms, the inefficient use of bandwidth, and looping. The primary reason for an Ethernet hub device to fail was not having software intelligence in it. A hub device used to do just forwarding work, transferring the bits (packets) received at one port to all its connected ports. The only thing it knew was how to send a packet to a port. This bit to bit packet transferring is referred to as the **Data Plane/ Forwarding Plane**. There was no control plane (software intelligence) for Ethernet hubs as they were intended for small networks with very little traffic.

Due to its dumb approach of managing network traffic, Ethernet hub technology soon got replaced by the new-world L2 network device referred to as a network switch (also called a switching hub, bridging hub, and officially a MAC bridge). If you compare a Network Switch with an Ethernet hub, from the hardware (physical) appearance point of view both will look pretty much identical but there is a major distinction between both and that is software intelligence:

- A Network switch has inbuilt software intelligence. This software intelligent logic orchestrates the dumb forwarding plane to send received packets on the correct interfaces. This intelligent logic is called routing and, together with some other sophisticated features, such as QoS and rate limiting, is what is called the control plane. In a nutshell: the control plane is where forwarding and routing decisions are made (software logic).

- The data plane is where the data forwarding action takes place (instructions to carry traffic over the hardware).

The following diagram shows the functioning of a network device. Network devices have a control plane that provides information used to build a forwarding table with the data plane that consults the forwarding table. The forwarding table is used by the network device to make a decision on where to send frames or packets entering the device. Both of these planes exist directly on the networking device:

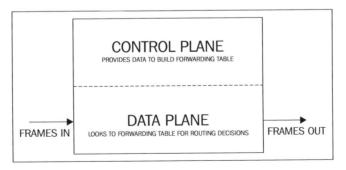

I repeat here, in traditional networking both control and data planes reside directly on the networking device, whether a network switch or router.

The SDN architecture decouples the network control and forwarding functions, enabling the network control to become directly programmable and the underlying infrastructure to be abstracted for the applications and network service. You can see how SDN differs from traditional networking in the following screenshot:

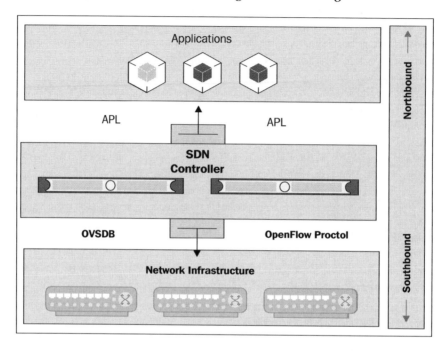

Notice how control and data planes are separated and how this separation helps applications to directly control the network, opening new doors for innovation. Let us examine the component illustrated in the screenshot in detail to gain more knowledge of SDN concepts:

- **Network infrastructure**: This consists of network devices such as routers and switches, both physical as well as virtual.

- **Controller**: This encompasses software based on a centralized controller, which could be on a server that talks to all the devices in the network using open API's, such as OpenFlow or OVMDB.

> A centralized controller does not mean a single controller; it can logically be a centralized controller that exists in multiple datacenters with all the redundancy needed for critical servers.

- **Applications**: This encompasses the variety of applications for which the network exists. This includes voice, video, enterprise applications, and security appliances such as intrusion detection. These applications can talk to the controller using open API's to give them what they want. For example, Voice traffic may ask the controller to be treated with the least latency while an enterprise backup server may tell the controller to give it bandwidth whenever it is available.

 Note: The conversation between the controller and applications is referred to as **northbound** and conversation between the controller and switches is referred to as **southbound**.

This was just a brief overview. There are many more use cases and benefits of SDN. For more details on SDN I recommend reading this IEEE paper, "Software-Defined Networking: A Comprehensive Survey" available here for download: http://arxiv.org/abs/1406.0440.

Limitations of Linux bridges

Guest (VM) networking in KVM has traditionally been done using Linux bridging, which performs well. It is simple to configure and manage but was not originally designed for virtual networking and therefore poses integration and management challenges. It does not support tunneling protocols and is apparently not an OpenFlow-compatible device, limiting the scope of innovation and scaling problems, so there was need of a more intelligent virtual switching device. That place has been taken by Open vSwitch in the Linux world. The following table shows how Open vSwitch is superior to Linux bridge when it comes to virtual networking.

Introducing Open vSwitch

Open vSwitch is an open source OpenFlow-capable virtual switch. If you're familiar with VMware, think of it as an open source distributed virtual switch. To give you a fair idea of how great **Open vSwitch (OVS)** is, here is a brief feature list, as of version 2.3:

- Visibility into inter VM communication via NetFlow and sFlow
- Standard 802.1q VLAN model via trunking
- Per VM interface traffic policing
- NIC bonding

- OpenFlow protocol support

- Multiple tunneling protocols such as GRE, VxLAN, IPSec, and GRE over IPSEC

- Mobility of states

See the full feature list here: `http://Openvswitch.org/features/`.

Comparison between Linux bridge and Open vSwitch

Before we go further and learn more about Open vSwitch including its architecture, let us quickly see how Open vSwitch is more feature-rich and powerful by comparing it with Linux bridge in terms of the operational functionalities provided:

Open vSwitch	Linux bridge
• Designed for virtual and cloud networking	• Originally not designed for virtual networking.
• Full L2-L4 matching capability	• Just L2 device
• Decision in UserSpace	• Scaling is limited
• ACLs, QoS, Bonding	• Simple forwarding
• Mobility of state	• Not suitable for cloud environment
• OpenFlow controller	• No tunneling support
• Distributed vSwitches	
• netflow and sflow support	

Open vSwitch architecture

The implementation of Open vSwitch is broken down into two parts, the Open vSwitch kernel module (Data Plane) and user space tools (Control Plane).

Since the incoming data packets have to be processed as fast as possible, the data plane of Open vSwitch was pushed to the kernel space:

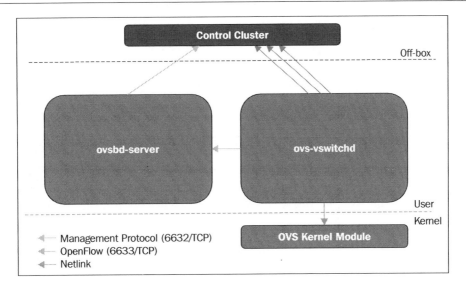

The data path (OVS kernel module) uses the netlink socket to interact with the vswitchd daemon that implements and manages any number of OVS switches on the local system. The SDN Controller interacts with vswitchd using the OpenFlow protocol. The ovsdb-server maintains the switch table database and external clients can talk to the ovsdb-server using json rpc; JSON is the data format. The ovsdb database currently contains around 13 tables and this database is persistent across restarts.

Open vSwitch works in two modes, normal and flow mode. This chapter will primarily concentrate on how to bring up a KVM VM connected to Open vSwitch's bridge in standalone/normal mode and will a give brief introduction to flow mode using the OpenDaylight controller:

- Normal Mode: As the name suggests, in this mode the Open vSwitch bridge handles all the switching/forwarding functionality by itself. In this mode OVS acts as a l2 learning switch. This mode is specifically useful when configuring several overlay networks is what your target rather than manipulating switch's flow.

- Flow Mode: In flow mode, the Open vSwitch bridge flow table is used to decide on which port the receiving packets should be forwarded to. The flow table is managed by a remote SDN controller. You can install or remove control flows using the SDN controller connected to the bridge or using the of ctl command. This mode allows a greater level of abstraction and automation; the SDN controller exposes the REST API. The applications can make use of this API to directly manipulate the bridge's flows to meet network needs.

Open vSwitch installation and setup

Starting with Fedora 16 the Open vSwitch user space tools and the required kernel modules are included in the Fedora distribution. There is no need to do any source compilation; the Kernel module (forwarding plane) is already there in the Fedora kernel. To get user space tools, just install the packages named `openvswitch`. This package is present in the official fedora DNF repository:

```
# dnf install openvswitch
```

The Open vSwitch package contains all the required user space tools including the ovsdb and a series of command-line utilities to configure, monitor, and manage Open vSwitch instances. The following are the important configuration files in Open vSwitch:

```
#rpm -qc openvswitch
/etc/logrotate.d/openvswitch
/etc/openvswitch/conf.db
/etc/openvswitch/system-id.conf
/etc/sysconfig/openvswitch
```

- `/etc/logrotate.d/openvswitch` controls log rotation for all the Open vSwitch logs `/var/log/openvswitch/*.log`. By default the logs are compressed and then rotated daily.

- `/etc/openvswitch/conf.db` is not actually a configuration file but it is the database used by Open vSwitch to store and retrieve configurations.

- `/etc/openvswitch/system-id.conf` is created by the Open vSwitch startup script using `uuidgen` and it is used by controllers to distinguish between multiple machines.

- `/etc/sysconfig/openvswitch` is a configuration-cum-environment file for Open vSwitch. The configuration parameters set in this file act as environmental variables for Open vSwitch daemons.

Starting openvswitch.service

On completing the installation of the Open vSwitch packages, the first step towards using Open vSwitch capabilities and features with KVM virtual networking is starting `openvswitch.service` and marking it as starting automatically on boot.

The `openvswitch.service` comprises two daemons. One is a database and another is the switch itself.

To start `openvswitch.service`, simply run:

`#/bin/systemctl start  openvswitch.service`

Running this command will start the service in runtime. You can check the status of the service by running:

```
# systemctl status openvswitch.service
 openvswitch.service - Open vSwitch
   Loaded: loaded (/usr/lib/systemd/system/openvswitch.service; enabled;
vendor preset: disabled)
   Active: active (exited) since Fri 2015-11-06 11:52:54 IST; 44min ago
  Process: 4029 ExecStop=/bin/true (code=exited, status=0/SUCCESS)
  Process: 4099 ExecStart=/bin/true (code=exited, status=0/SUCCESS)
 Main PID: 4099 (code=exited, status=0/SUCCESS)
   CGroup: /system.slice/openvswitch.service
```

`Active: active` in the earlier output highlights the status. As soon as the service is started, it loads the required Open vSwitch kernel module and performs initialization startup routines such as creating your Open vSwitch database and running daemons. The database is created using the schema available here: `/usr/share/openvswitch/vswitch.ovsschema`.

 Note: In the event of a failure in the service startup, the first thing you should do is look at the logs and find out what error caused the failure in starting the service.

To access `openvswitch` service logs, run the following command:

`#journalctl -u openvswitch`

The log files of both `ovsdb-server` and `ovs-vswitchd` are stored in the `/var/log/openvswitch` directory.

In order to enable the service on boot, run the following command:

`#systemctl enable openvswitch.service'`

Open vSwitch kernel module

When you start `openvswitch.service`, the first thing it does is load the kernel module required for switching the datapath. The OVS kernel module is named `openvswitch` in Fedora. You can also load it manually by running the following command as root:

`#modprobe openvswitch`

To get more information about the `openvswitch` kernel module, use the `modinfo` command as shown in the following:

```
#modinfo openvswitch
filename:    /lib/modules/4.1.6-200.fc22.x86_64/kernel/net/openvswitch/
openvswitch.ko.xz
license:     GPL
description:Open vSwitch switching datapath
depends:     libcrc32c
intree:      Y
vermagic:    4.1.6-200.fc22.x86_64 SMP mod_unload
signer:      Fedora kernel signing key
sig_key:     95:D8:8B:1A:62:3B:BF:DF:EF:E2:58:6B:05:ED:0A:C5:C2:88:C1:3A
```

Getting started with the Open vSwitch command-line interface

This section gives a quick overview of various command-line interfaces available for managing different aspects of virtual networking infrastructure, either locally or remotely.

`OVS-<functionality>` is the naming convention used for Open vSwitch commands. To get the list of all the OVS commands available on your system, just type `ovs` in your terminal and press the *Tab* key twice. The following are the important commands for configuration and troubleshooting Open vSwitch:

`#ovs-vsctl`: This command is used to set up, maintain, and inspect various OVS switch configurations. It provides a high-level interface for Open vSwitch Database to query and apply changes on runtime.

There are many different options you can carry out with this command-line tool. Here are some of the most commonly used options with the `ovs-vsctl` commands:

- `ovs-vsctl show`: A very handy and frequently used command. It gives the current running configuration of the switch. Detailed information on how to read its output is explained in the next section.
- `#ovs-vsctl list-br`: Shows the names of all the configured bridges. The output is sorted in ascending order.
- `#ovs-vsctl list-ports <bridge>`: Shows the names of all the ports on BRIDGE.
- `#ovs-vsctl list interface <bridge>`: show the names of all the interfaces on BRIDGE
- `#ovs-vsctl add-br <bridge>`: Creates a bridge in the switch database.
- `#ovs-vsctl add-port <bridge> : <interface>`: Binds an interface (physical or virtual) to the Open vSwitch bridge.
- `#ovs-ofctl` and `ovs-dpctl`: These two commands are used for administering and monitoring flow entries. You learned that OVS manages two kinds of flow:
  - OpenFlows: The flows managed at the control plane
  - Datapath: A kernel flow. A kind of cached version of OpenFlow
  - `#ovs-ofctl` speaks to OpenFlow module, whereas `ovs-dpctl` speaks to the Kernel module.

The following two are the most used options for each of these commands:

- `#ovs-ofctl show <BRIDGE>`: Shows brief information about the switch, including the port number to port name mapping.
- `#ovs-ofctl dump-flows <Bridge>`: Examines OpenFlow tables.
- `#ovs-dpctl show`: Prints basic info about all the logical datapaths, referred to as "bridges," present on the switch.
- `#ovs-dpctl dump-flows`: It shows the flow cached in datapath.
- `ovs-appctl`: This command offers a way to send commands to a running Open vSwitch and gathers information that is not directly exposed to the `ovs-ofctl` command. This is the Swiss Army knife of OpenFlow troubleshooting.
- `#ovs-appctl bridge/dumpflows <br>`: Examines flow tables and offers direct connectivity for VMs on the same hosts.
- `#ovs-appctl fdb/show <br>`: Lists mac/vlan pairs learned.

The Man pages of each of the preceding commands contain detailed information in easy-to-understand language. Don't forget that there is extensive help by following any command with a `--help` option.

Setting up your first Open vSwitch bridge

Open vSwitch bridge setup can be done in multiple ways. `OVS-vsctl` is the primary command to create, remove, and administer Open vSwitch. Operations performed using `OVS-vsctl` are persistent across system reboot. However, the IP address assigned to the bridge interface will not be persistent unless a matching `ifcfg` file is created manually. Another method of creating an Open vSwitch bridge is using network scripts in the same way that a Linux bridge is generally created, The benefit of the latter option is a greater level of integration with the operating system.

We will first see how to create an OVS bridge manually using `ovs-vsctl` and then using a network script with an example. I am using my two KVM hypervisors to demonstrate the procedure. They are named KVMHOST1 and KVMHOST2.

> Note: Open vSwitch is not compatible with NetworkManager yet. Before creating an OVS bridge, make sure that NetworkManager is disabled and the classic networking service is enabled instead:
>
> - Disable NetworkManager service:
>   ```
>   $ systemctl disable NetworkManager.service
>   ```
> - Enable classic networking:
>   ```
>   $ systemctl enable network.service
>   ```

Configuring an Open vSwitch bridge manually using the ovs-vsctl command

The following steps demonstrate how to configure an isolated OVS bridge. Isolated bridges will not have connectivity to the physical network of the host system. Isolated networks are useful for testing and development environments.

Before you run the command to configure the OVS bridge, make sure all the Open vSwitch services are up and running. Once confirmed, run the following commands to create a vSwitch-based bridge named `vswitch001` and display the current state of Open vSwitch database contents:

```
[root@kvmHOST1 ~]# ovs-vsctl add-br vswitch001
[root@kvmHOST1 ~]# ovs-vsctl show
```

```
[root@kvmHOST1 ~]# ovs-vsctl show
e9c72657-5021-4db6-8cda-52adec50a53d
Bridge "vswitch001"
Port "vswitch001"
"vswitch001"
type: internal
ovs_version: "2.4.0"
```

Note that, on creating a bridge, the system creates an internal interface whose name corresponds to the name of the bridge; you can check it using the `ifcomfig` command:

```
[root@kvmHOST1 ~]# ifconfig vswitch001
vswitch001: flags=4098<BROADCAST,MULTICAST>  mtu 1500
ether 12:ff:be:9b:24:4d  txqueuelen 0  (Ethernet)
```

What is type internal? It indicates a simulated network device that sends and receives traffic. An internal interface whose name is the same as its bridge's name is called the "local interface." Optionally, an IP address can be assigned to the interface. This will help the host system communicate with the virtual machine, useful in many ways.

A quick note on the output of the `ovs-vsctlshow` command:

- uuid: The uuid in the first line is a unique identification of the vSwitch. This uuid is generated at the time of initializing the Open vSwitch instance. At the moment we just have one bridge named `vswitch1`.

- Port: The ports attached to the bridge.

- Interface: The interface that logically corresponds to a port.

Configuring an Open vSwitch bridge using network scripts

To get the OVS bridge and its configuration a little more permanent with an IP address assignment, the preferred approach is to use a network script. The following steps demonstrate how to configure an OVS bridge named vswitch002 and connect physical interface eth0 as UPLINK. The UPLINK is used to get virtual machines on the physical network:

1. Make sure eth0 does not have an IP Address assigned to it. If you have only one Ethernet card attached the system, you will have to get its console access because this bridge configuration will move the IP Address from eth0 to the vswitch002 interface.

2. Once that is verified, create a configuration file for the Open vSwitch bridge. Name the file ifcfg-vmswitch002 and save it to the /etc/sysconfig/ network-scripts directory. The most important part is at the bottom of the script; we are telling the system that the type of bridge is OVSBridge and our device type is ovs. This way the Open vSwitch kernel module will be used:

   ```
   [root@kvmHOST2]cat /etc/sysconfig/network-scripts/

   DEVICE="vswitch002"

   BOOTPROTO="dhcp"

   DEFROUTE="yes"

   IPV4_FAILURE_FATAL="yes"

   IPV6INIT=no

   ONBOOT="yes"

   TYPE="OVSBridge"

   DEVICETYPE="ovs"

   "OVSBridge", parameter configure and set an OVS bridge named
   <name>.

   "DEVICETYPE" Always set to "ovs".
   ```

 In this example, I am using DHCP lease to get the IP address. If you don't have a DHCP server in your environment, use the standard IFCFG script parameters to configure a static IP address.

3. Now configure the `/etc/sysconfig/network-scripts/ifcfg-eth0` file to get this interface added to the `vswitch002` OVS bridge.

```
DEVICE="eth0"
ONBOOT="yes"
HWADDR="XX:XX:XX:XX:XX:XX"
TYPE="OVSPort"
DEVICETYPE="ovs"
OVS_BRIDGE="vswitch002"
TYPE="OVSPort" =  Treat this device as OVSPort.
OVS_BRIDGE="vswitch002"  = is the parameter that tell to connect
this device to "vswitch002" OVS bridge as port.
```

4. Restart the network service to get the bridge ready.

5. Check the Open vSwitch bridge configuration with the `ovs-vsctl show` command as shown next:

```
[root@kvmHOST2 ~]# ovs-vsctl show
429d7f42-5f52-4b65-a856-41bd0ae5be88
Bridge "vswitch002"
Port "vswitch002"
Interface "vswitch001"
type: internal
Port "eth0"
Interface "eth0"
ovs_version: "2.4.0"
```

6. Check by pinging the gateway. You will be able to ping it but notice that the IP address is now set on the `vswitch002` interface and `eth0` is working as an uplink. It is also possible to create a bond interface and attach it to the bridge using the same approach.

There are many other options for OVS bridge configurations. It is strongly recommended you go through this README file to know more about Open vSwitch integration with Red Hat's network scripts: `/usr/share/doc/Open vSwitch/` README.RHEL.

Integrating KVM VMs and OVS

You learned how to create an OVS bridge and were introduced to various Open vSwitch command-line tools. Now it's time to start using Open vSwitch as a virtual networking infrastructure for the KVM virtual machines and experience the features and all the great benefits it provides.

For existing virtual machines, it is good to attach the virtual machine directly to the Open vSwitch bridge by modifying its XML file. Let us take the example of the virtual machine VM001. This VM is currently attached to a regular Linux bridge named br0 on the same host on which we created the vswitch001 OVS bridge. The following procedure demonstrates the steps to migrate VMs from the Linux bridge to the smarter Open vSwitch bridge:

1. Check the network configuration of the virtual machine. virsh will be handy in performing this task. The dumpxml option prints VM configuration information in XML:

   ```
   [root@kvmHOST1 ~]# virsh dumpxml vm001 | grep -i 'interface type' -A 5
   <interface type='bridge'>
   <mac address='52:54:00:ce:51:53'/>
   <source bridge='br0'/>
   <target dev='vnet0'/>
   <model type='rtl8139'/>
   <alias name='net0'/>
   ```

   source bridge and target dev are particularly important elements in identifying to which bridge a virtual machine is attached.

   Note: vnet* is a naming convention used by KVM hypervisor for automatically generated TUN devices. It can optionally set to **Custom name** . Looking at these two elements in a VM's XML file we can quickly identify that the vm001 is currently attached to the Linux bridge named br0 with the vnet0 TUP device.

   Another method to get this info is to use the domiflist option with the virsh command. This option prints a table showing brief information about all virtual interfaces associated with the VM:

   ```
   #virsh domiflist vm001
   Interface  Type   Source Model   MAC
   --------------------------------------------------------
   ```

```
vnet0   bridge br0     rtl8139 52:54:00:ce:51:53
```

```
'brctl shows' command confirms that br0 is a Linux bridge
```

```
#brctl show
bridge namebridge id    STP enabledinterfaces
br0     8000.fe54006cd757no        vnet0
vnet1
```

2. To migrate this virtual machine from the `vswitch001` Linux bridge to the `vswitch001` OVS bridge and name its port in the OVS bridge `vm001_vp01`, shut down the VM and edit its XML configuration for the Ethernet interface:

```
#virsh edit vm_02
```

```
<interface type='bridge'>

<mac address='52:54:00:ce:51:53''/>

<source bridge=vswitch001/><- name of your OVS bridge

<virtualport type='openvswitch'/>< - This is important option to
add/

<target dev=<vm001_vp01><- set up name of port IN OVS bridge (i.e
'vswitch001')

<model type='virtio'/>

</interface>
```

The `virtualport` line marks the interface of an Open vSwitch port. The port name is optional, but very useful when you perform diagnostic procedures.

> Note: I strongly recommend setting the target device name. This is the name of the network interface seen on Open vSwitch. I always start the name with `veth`. The number following is the interface number on the guest and I add the name of the VM. So `veth0-vmtest` corresponds to `eth0` on the guest `vmtest`. If you do not set the interface name, you will get `vnet<some number>`. If you have to troubleshoot something on the virtual network, predefined interface names help a lot.

3. Now start the virtual machine:

```
#virsh start vm001
```

4. Check the `ovs-vsctl` configuration to verify that the VM is now using:

```
openvswitch bridge "vswitch001" for network connectivity.
[root@kvmHOST1 ~]#ovs-vsctl show
e9c72657-5021-4db6-8cda-52adec50a53d
    Bridge "vswitch001"
    Port "vswitch001"
    Interface "vswitch001"
    type: internal
    Port "vm001_vp01"
    Interface "vm001_vp01"
    ovs_version: "2.4.0"
[root@kvmHOST1 ~]#
```

5. Port "vm001_vp01" in above output belongs to the "vm001" virtual machine. Double verify this by running virsh domiflist vm001:

```
[root@nkvmHOST1 ~]# virsh domiflist vm001
Interface  Type      Source    Model     MAC
-------------------------------------------------------
vm001_vp01 bridge    vswitch001 rtl8139   52:54:00:ce:51:53
```

This is a lengthy procedure; imagine how boring and time-consuming it would be if you have many virtual machines and wished to migrate them to Open vSwitch bridge. Is there quicker way to accomplish this? Yes, you can do it just by running a single-line command. Awesome but which command, and how?

Remember the `virt-xml` command? The same command can be used here to make this migration task a single command job:

```
#virt-xml vm_01 --edit --network virtualport_type='openvswitch',source=vswitch001,target=vm001_vp01
```

Even better, `virt-xml` is scripting-friendly; you can use the `for` loop and other bash scripting features for automation purposes, for example, to update the network configuration of all the VMs defined on the host:

```
#for i in $(virsh list --all --name ) ; do virt-xml $i --edit --network source=NewNetwork ; done
```

For new virtual machines, the easiest and most practical way is to create a libvirt network that points to the OVS bridge. The following steps demonstrate how to create a libvirt network:

1. libvirt configurations are in XML files so the first step is to create a network xml file. See the following example:

    ```
    #cat ovs-network.xml

    <network>

    <name>NewNetwork</name>

    <forward mode='bridge'/>

    <bridge name='vswitch1'/>

    <virtualport type='openvswitch'/>

    </network>
    ```

2. Make sure that the name attribute of the bridge element exactly matches the vSwitch bridge name and the type attribute of the `virtualport` element matches Open vSwitch.

3. Once the XML file is ready, define the libvirt network, autostart it on host boot, and start it:

    ```
    #virsh net-define ovs-network.xml
    Network vswitch-net defined from ovs-network.xml


    # virsh net-start vswitch-net
    Network vswitch-net started


    # virsh net-autostart vswitch-net
    Network vswitch-net marked as autostarted
    ```

4. This will create a virtual network named `NewNetwork` that is Open vSwitch-compatible. You can verify its status and other information by running the following:

    ```
    virsh net-info NewNetwork
    Name:        NewNetwork
    UUID:        ee50a6f9-b298-4a72-89e4-47b411402fce
    Active:      yes
    Persistent:  yes
    Autostart:   yes
    Bridge:      vswitch01
    ```

5. With this libvirt network in an active state, you can directly attach new virtual machines to this network (or remove one). When you start the VM attached to this virtual network, it will pass the necessary parameters to OVS to apply the configuration automatically.

6. Select **New Network** in the new **Network Selection** of the virtual machine creation wizard of virt-manager to get the VM directly connected to Open vSwitch bridge. This is shown in the following screenshot:

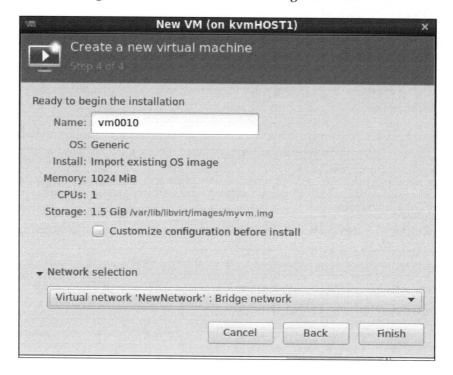

VLANs with Open vSwitch

Open vSwitch supports **VLANS (Virtual LANs)**. You can create tagged as well as native VLANS on an OVS bridge to segment the network into different broadcast domains so that packets are only switched between ports that are designated for the same VLAN. The following are a few advantages of VLANs:

- Increased bandwidth usage: less broadcast traffic on segments
- Security enhanced: different VLANs cannot communicate directly
- Isolated environments for specialized network applications

Configuring VLANs for KVM virtual machines

Let's consider a scenario. In a single Open vSwitch bridge, add two different VLANs and connect four guests to it. Two in VLAN1 with tag 10 and the others in VLAN2 with tag 20. As a result, VMS can communicate in the same VLAN, whereas, between different VLANs, they cannot:

1. This walkthrough assumes you already have four virtual machines defined on the host and they are connected to an OVS bridge.

2. I am using an OVS bridge named `vswitch001` and four fedora 21 VMs — `Fed1`, `Fed2`, `Fed3`, and `Fed4` — to demonstrate the procedure:

```
[root@KVMHOST1 ~]# virsh list

 IdName                  State
-----------------------------------
 15Fed1                  running
 16Fed2                  running
 17Fed3                  running
 18Fed4                  running
```

```
[root@kvmHOST1 ~]ovs-vsctl show
e9c72657-5021-4db6-8cda-52adec50a53d
Bridge "vswitch001"
Port "fed4"
Interface "fed4"
  Port "vswitch001"
Interface "vswitch001"
   type: internal
   Port "fed1"
Interface "fed1"
  Port "fed3"
Interface "fed3"
Port "fed2"
Interface "fed2"
ovs_version: "2.4.0"
```

Presently, all these four virtual machines are in a single network subnet. All the virtual machines can communicate with each other.

 Note: `virsh domifnet <vmname>` comes in handy if custom target names are not set to the VM's network interface. This command will help you to identify which VNET mapped to which VMs.

3. Add `Fed1` and `Fed2` VMs as an "access port" on `vlan10`:

    VLan1 :

    ```
    [root@kvmHOST1 ~]# ovs-vsctl set port fed1 tag=10
    [root@kvmHOST1 ~]# ovs-vsctl set port fed2 tag=10
    ```

    vLan2:

4. Add `Fed3` and `Fed4` VMs as an "access port" on `vlan20`:

    ```
    [root@kvmHOST1 ~]# ovs-vsctl set port fed3 tag=20
    [root@kvmHOST1 ~]# ovs-vsctl set port fed4 tag=20
    ```

5. Verify the changes by checking the `ovs-vswitch` output:

    ```
    [root@kvmHOST1 ~]# ovs-vsctl show
    e9c72657-5021-4db6-8cda-52adec50a53d
    Bridge "vswitch001"
    Port "fed4"
    tag: 20
    Interface "fed4"
    Port "vswitch001"
    Interface "vswitch001"
    type: internal
    Port "fed1"
    tag: 10
    Interface "fed1"
    Port "fed3"
    tag: 20
    Interface "fed3"
    Port "fed2"
    ```

```
tag: 10
Interface "fed2"
ovs_version: "2.4.0"
```

Notice the tag field in the port section of the earlier command. The default
VLAN_mode used is "access", the native mechanism of the VLAN. A VLAN tag is
added when packets enter an access port, and stripped off when leaving an access
port. Other VLAN_modes are native-tagged, native-untagged, and trunk.

With this setting, pinging from `Fed1` to `Fed4` fails, As these two VMs are on two
different VLANs although on the same OVS bridge, pinging from `Fed3` to `Fed4`
succeeds, as these two VMs are on the same VLAN. This is true with `Fed1` to `Fed2`;
these two VMs can communicate with each other.

Let's consider scenario two: four virtual machines with three VLANs to isolate traffic
from different applications running on them. All four virtual machines should be
accessible to each other over three different network subnets.

This walkthrough assumes you already have four virtual machines defined on the
host and they are connected to an OVS bridge.

I am using an OVS bridge named `vswitch001` and four fedora 21 VMs—Fed1, Fed2,
`Fed3`, and `Fed4`—to demonstrate the procedure:

1. Current Configuration, No VLAN configuration. All four virtual machines
   can communicate with each other on a single subnet:

```
[root@kvmHOST1 ~]ovs-vsctl show
e9c72657-5021-4db6-8cda-52adec50a53d
Bridge "vswitch001"
Port "fed4"
Interface "fed4"
Port "vswitch001"
Interface "vswitch001"
type: internal
Port "fed1"
Interface "fed1"
Port "fed3"
Interface "fed3"
Port "fed2"
Interface "fed2"
ovs_version: "2.4.0"
```

2. Modify the OVS ports of the four virtual machines.

```
ovs-vsctl set port fed1 trunks=20,30,40
ovs-vsctl set port fed2 trunks=20,30,40
ovs-vsctl set port fed3 trunks=20,30,40
ovs-vsctl set port fed4 trunks=20,30,40
```

3. Verify the changes by checking the `ovs-vsctl show` command output as shown next:

```
# ovs-vsctl show
e9c72657-5021-4db6-8cda-52adec50a53d
Bridge "vswitch001"
Port "fed4"
trunks: [20, 30, 40]
Interface "fed4"
Port "vswitch001"
Interface "vswitch001"
  type: internal
Port "fed1"
trunks: [20, 30, 40]
Interface "fed1"
Port "fed3"
trunks: [20, 30, 40]
Interface "fed3"
Port "fed2"
trunks: [20, 30, 40]
Interface "fed2"
ovs_version: "2.4.0"
```

Notice the `trunks` field in the port section of the earlier command. VLAN_mode trunks allow passing traffic from multiple VLANs through a port. Here, the allowed list is VLAN 20,30,40. This is the tagged implementation of VLAN.

Another quick way to check the OVS port configuration is to use the `ovsdb-client Monitor` command:

```
[root@kvmHOST1 ~]# ovsdb-client monitor Port name,trunks --detach
row                               action  name       trunks
--------------------------------- ------- ---------- --------
---
bcabc803-8da7-41da-9172-7806965401ff initial "fed1" [20, 30, 40]
9e12eb7d-f31f-481c-bbdb-3a8a4cdfff31 initial "vswitch001" []
```

```
f4e6c670-b441-4383-9acd-e95eb97ce45b initial "fed2"[20, 30, 40]
36c7e644-771c-494a-8b70-fa6f7a3effe1 initial "fed4"[20, 30, 40]
ec6a6272-f944-4f02-ab8f-45f984cfced9 initial "fed3"[20, 30, 40]
[root@kvmHOST1 ~]#
```

4. Take the console of the virtual machines and configure a VLAN-tagged interface in the guest operating system:

```
[root@Fed1]#vconfig add eth0 20 ; ifconfig eth0.20 192.168.20.1
[root@Fed1]#vconfig add eth0 30 ; ifconfig eth0.20 192.168.30.1
[root@Fed1]#vconfig add eth0 40 ; ifconfig eth0.20 192.168.40.1
```

Repeat these steps on the other three VMs. Make sure you use a different IP address, You may also want to create IFCFG scripts to make the setting persistent across reboots. Use cat /proc/net/VLAN/config to verify the tagged interfaces status:

```
[root@Fed1]# cat /proc/net/vlan/config
VLAN Dev name    | VLAN ID
Name-Type: VLAN_NAME_TYPE_RAW_PLUS_VID_NO_PAD
eth0.20    | 20 | eth0
eth0.30    | 30 | eth0
eth0.40    | 40 | eth0
Result:
```

With this setting in place, all four VMs will be able to communicate with each other over three different subnets.

 Note that, if you want the virtual machines to receive untagged (native VLAN) traffic as well as tagged (trunked) traffic, set the vlan_mode to native-untagged:

```
#ovs-vsctl set port <port> vlan_mode=native-untagged
```

To verify which VLAN_mode is currently in use for a particular port or group of ports, use the ovsdb-client command as shown next:

```
# ovs-vsctl --format table --column=name,vlan_mode list port
name    vlan_mode
------------ ----------------
"fed4"trunk
"fed2"trunk
"vswitch001" []
"fed3"trunk
"fed1"native-untagged
```

Using libvirt integration

If you find this manual method of configuring OVS vLANs a bit hard to remember and lengthy, the portgroup feature of libvirt will make it much easier. portgroup provides a method of easily putting guest connections to the network into different classes, with each class potentially having a different level or type of service. We can create multiple portgroup classes specifying specific VLAN configurations and then use them while creating new virtual machines or by editing existing VM network configurations.

Let us see how to configure portgroups for our existing libvirt NewNetwork network and how to connect a virtual machine to the specific trunk or VLAN easily:

1. First check the libvirt network present on the system using the
   `virsh net-list` command:

```
#virsh net-list

Name                State   Autostart Persistent
-------------------------------------------------
default             active yes       yes
NewNetwork          active no        yes
```

2. Modify the desired libvirt network's XML definition to include the portgroup assignments as shown next, using `virsh net-edit` commands:

```
<portgroup name='novlan' default='yes'>
</portgroup>
<portgroup name='vlan-finance'>
<vlan>
<vlan-mode=native-tagged>
<tag id='10'/>
</vlan>
</portgroup>
<portgroup name='vlan-marketing'>
  <vlan trunk='yes'>
  <tag id='20'/>
  <tag id='30'/>
  <tag id='30'/>
  </vlan>
</portgroup>
```

3. Restart the libvirt network to select changes:

```
[root@kvmHOST1]# n=NewNetwork; virsh net-destroy $n ; virsh net-
start $n
Network NewNetwork destroyed
Network NewNetwork started
```

4. Dump the XML definition of the libvirt network to ensure the portgroup configuration has loaded:

```
[root@kvmHOST1 ~]# virsh net-dumpxml NewNetwork
<network>
<name>NewNetwork</name>
<uuid>03f36174-04cb-4446-87ba-729a4dee4dfd</uuid>
<forward mode='bridge'/>
<bridge name='vswitch001'/>
<virtualport type='openvswitch'/>
<portgroup name='novlan' default='yes'>
</portgroup>
<portgroup name='vlan-finance'>
  <vlan>
  <tag id='10'/>
  </vlan>
</portgroup>
<portgroup name='vlan-markating'>
  <vlan trunk='yes'>
  <tag id='20'/>
  <tag id='30'/>
  <tag id='30'/>
  </vlan>
</portgroup>
</network>
```

As you can see from the preceding, we modified the libvirt NewNetwork network and created three portgroups: noVLAN, VLAN-finance, and VLAN-marketing.

The noVLAN portgroup is the default portgroup and has noVLAN configurations defined. The VLAN-finance portgroup has tag 10 VLAN defined and the VLAN-marketing portgroup has a VLAN trunk defined for tag 10,20,30.

Now you can use these portgroups through virt-manager or virt-install to get your virtual machine connected to specific VLAN tags or trunks.

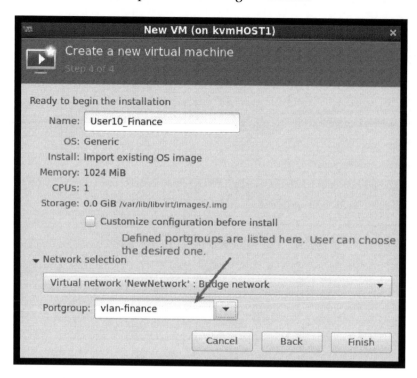

With this approach you can quickly attach VMs to desired VLAN or trunks.

Open vSwitch QoS – controlling KVM VM traffic

Open vSwitch is aimed at addressing shortcomings in using bridging in virtualized environments. One of the great features of Open vSwitch over Linux bridging is the ability to set very granular network traffic, shaping and policing rules on the virtual switch to implement network QoS. The network QoS (quality of service) refers to the ability of the network to handle traffic such that it meets the service needs of certain applications. It is often used as a synonym for traffic control. The following screenshot shows how QoS helps in managing traffic:

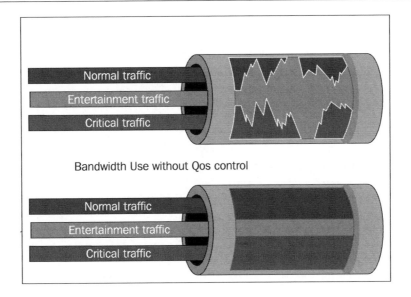

Bandwidth Use without Qos control

With proper QoS implementation in place, one can limit the input or output transmission rate of a class of traffic based on user-defined criteria. The previous screenshot shows how network shaping of entertainment traffic helped boost critical application performance by dedicating the required network bandwidth. The network QoS technique is widely used by IaaS providers to restrict bandwidth of the **VPS (Virtual Private Server)** depending on the hosting plan.

The terms input (inbound) and output (outbound) are more often referred to as ingress and egress in networking terminology when it comes to QoS. Ingress = packets entering your network, egress= packets exiting the network. Ingress policing is used for incoming traffic at the interface and QoS or Queue shaping is used for egressing (outgoing). Before we start with the actual implementation of QoS, it is important to understand what policing and shaping are:

- **Policing**: This network traffic controlling mechanism can be used to ingress or egress on an interface. It simply drops or remarks excess packets. There is no queuing or buffering. It controls the output rate by dropping packets.

- **Shaping**: This network traffic controlling mechanism is for ingress traffic only. It buffers and queues excess packets, meaning there is less chance of causing retransmissions due to dropped packets.

Controlling the inbound (ingress) traffic of VMs: In order to apply QoS on a VM to control its inbound traffic, modify its interface table to configure an ingress policing rule.

There are two rules to set:

- `ingress_policing_rate`: The maximum rate (in Kbps) that this VM should be allowed to send
- `ingress_policing_burst`: A parameter to the policing algorithm to indicate the maximum amount of data (in Kb) that this interface can send beyond the policing rate

Use Case: Virtual Machine (`Fed1`) is your file hosting server. Users connect to it to download files or images. You recently noticed that, due to very high download requests, this VM is eating your network bandwidth causing problems for other critical VMs. Rate limiting is an ideal solution for this.

Applying traffic rate limiting

Let us see how we can apply traffic rate limiting on an interface for designing Network QoS. The steps mentioned next will walk you through the procedure:

1. As a rate limiting policy is applied on the interface, find out the corresponding network interface name of the virtual machine. `virsh domiflist <vm-name>` is a handy command for this:

```
[root@kvmHOST1 ~]# virsh domiflist Fed1
Interface  Type      Source       Model     MAC

------------------------------------------------------------

fed1       bridge    NewNetwork   virtio    52:54:00:b3:40:
```

2. SSH to the virtual machine and check what the current ingress traffic bandwidth is. I am using the `iperf` command to determine it. There are many other utilities available such as `netperf`, check speed, and so on:

```
[root@Fed1 ~]# iperf -s

------------------------------------------------------------

Server listening on TCP port 5001

TCP window size: 85.3 KByte (default)

------------------------------------------------------------

[  4] local 10.0.0.1 port 5001 connected with 10.0.0.2 port 35322
[ ID] Interval      Transfer    Bandwidth
[  4]  0.0- 5.0 sec  3.81 GBytes  6.51 Gbits/sec
```

`iperf -s` start `iperf` in server mode. Notice that the bandwidth shows 6.51 Gbits/sec. Huge!

To rate-limit `Fed1` to 20 Mbps, use these commands:

```
ovs-vsctl set interface fed1 ingress_policing_rate=20000
ovs-vsctl set interface fed1 ingress_policing_burst=200
```

To see the current limits applied for the `fed1` network interface, run this command: #`ovs-vsctl list interface fed1` and look for values in the `ingress_policing_rate` and `ingress_policing_burst` columns or use this more fine-tuned method to fetch details from the ovsdb. #`ovsdb-client monitor Interface name,ingress_policing_burst,ingress_policing_rate --detach`

3. Now SSH the same system and run the `iperf` command again:

```
[root@Fed1 ~]#iperf -s
------------------------------------------------------------
Server listening on TCP port 5001
TCP window size: 85.3 KByte (default)
------------------------------------------------------------
------------------------------------------------------------
[  3] local 10.0.0.1 port 55922 connected with 10.0.0.2 port 5001
[ ID] Interval       Transfer     Bandwidth
[  3]  0.0- 6.0 sec  1.58 MBytes  2.23 Mbits/sec
```

Check the bandwidth, It reduced to 2.23 Mbits from 6.51 Gbits. You can change the bandwidth limit on the fly.

4. To remove the applied limits, set the value of the preceding two parameters to zero:

```
#ovs-vsctl set interface fed1 ingress_policing_rate=0
#ovs-vsctl set interface fed1 ingress_policing_burst=0
```

Zero (0) means none, no limit applied.

Controlling outbound (egress) traffic

Network traffic that begins inside a network and proceeds through its routers to a destination somewhere outside the network is egress traffic. It is applied at port level. You can create queues with different speeds, and put packets into those different queues depending on QoS policy.

One or more QoS policy can be assigned to a port. Each QoS policy consists of a class and a qdiscs. Classes and qdisc use the Linux kernel's `tc` implementation.

Use Case: You created 10 VMs and gave them to your students for their project work, Students found these systems (VMs) are connected to a high-speed network and the download speed is amazing so they could not resist it and started downloading huge files from the Internet. You can use network shaping features to prevent this and give just the required network bandwidth to your students. You may give a higher bandwidth to the student who is leading the project and a limited one to the members.

Applying traffic shaping

1. Create a queue (q0) with the required network bandwidth. Here in this example I am limiting the egress traffic bandwidth to 10 Mbps:

   ```
   #ovs-vsctl --id=@q0 create queue other-config:min-rate=10000000
   other-config:max-rate=10000000
   ```

   Here:

   - min-rate: Its minimum guaranteed bandwidth in bytes
   - max-rate: Its maximum allowed bandwidth, in bytes

   Setting both min-rate and max-rate to the same value will give the same speed permanently. You can also configure rate limiting policing here by setting the max-rate value higher than min-rate and applying the qos rate limiting mechanism,

2. List the currently available queues on the ovs switch:

   ```
   [root@kvmHOST1 ~]# ovs-vsctl list queue
   _uuid          : 05c73c42-3191-4025-96ce-cd6b86ab2775
   dscp           : []
   external_ids   : {}
   other_config   : {max-rate="10000000", min-rate="10000000"}
   ```

3. Create a qos (newqos) and connect a queue into the qos:

   ```
   #ovs-vsctl create qos type=linux-htb queues=0=05c73c42-3191-4025-
   96ce-cd6b86ab2775
   ```

4. List the currently available queues on the ovs switch:

   ```
   [root@kvmHOST1 ~]# ovs-vsctl list qos
   _uuid          : 09f5b3c4-35b7-4326-bae8-780b7ccadb3f
   external_ids   : {}
   other_config   : {}
   queues         : {0=05c73c42-3191-4025-96ce-cd6b86ab2775}
   type           : linux-htb
   ```

Note: The QoS can be enforced using **Linux HTB (Linux Hierarchical Token Bucket** – please read up on this) or **Linux HSFC (Linux Hierarchical Fair Service Curve** – please read up on this).

5. Apply this QoS to a virtual machine's port. Use `virsh domiflist <vm_name>` to find out the network port name of the VM:

```
[root@kvmHOST1 ~]# ovs-vsctl --column=name,qos list port fed1
name               : "fed1"
qos                : 09f5b3c4-35b7-4326-bae8-780b7ccadb3f
[root@kvmHOST1 ~]#
```

6. SSH to the virtual machine and check the inbound speed by downloading any file from the Internet. It should be limited to 10 Mbps. Test the result on the `Fed1` machine using `iperf`:

```
------------------------------------------------------------
Server listening on TCP port 5001
TCP window size: 85.3 KByte (default)
------------------------------------------------------------
[  4] local 10.0.0.1 port 5001 connected with 10.0.0.2 port 35325
[ ID] Interval       Transfer     Bandwidth
[  4]  0.0- 6.1 sec  7.00 MBytes  9.57 Mbits/sec
```

Bandwidth is now 9.57 Mbits. Before applying the network shaping it was 6.51 Gbits/sec.

It is also possible to create qos and queue together. An example is given next:

```
root@switch:~# ovs-vsctl set port eth1 qos=@newqos -- --id=@newqos
create qos type=linux-htb queues=0=@q0 -- --id=@q0 create queue
other-config:min-rate=2000000 other-config:max-rate=2000000
```

7. To deconfigure the QoS record from a port, run:

```
#ovs-vsctl clear Port eth1 qos
```

8. To remove qos and the | queue, run:

```
ovs-vsctl destroy qos (uuid)
ovs-vsctl destroy Queue (uuid)
or
"ovs-vsctl -- --all destroy Queue"
"ovs-vsctl -- --all destroy qos"
```

Overlay networks

Overlay networks are industry-standard techniques designed to achieve Network Virtualization. Network Overlays such as **Virtual eXtensible Local Area Network (VXLAN)** and **Generic Routing Encapsulation (GRE)** achieve network virtualization by overlaying layer-2 networks over physical layer-3 networks, which enables network scalability and the efficient use of current network infrastructure.

Open vSwitch supports multiple tunneling protocols (GRE, VXLAN, STT, and Geneve, with IPsec support), which allow scaling private networks over public networks. You can connect two or more Open vSwitches running on different hosts with each other and form a distributed switch.

Use Case of overlay networks: Suppose you have an application cluster (five VMs serving as nodes) on the KVM1-Mumbai-DC host, The cluster is architectured on a private network that is isolated to the host, The recent growth of your application requires more nodes on the cluster but you found there is no scope to create new VMs on the host as it is already over-utilized. As the cluster is on a private network there is no scope to live-migrate VMs and do the load balancing and so on.

Solution: Get a new host, perhaps `KVM2-Mumbai-DC`. Install Open vSwitch. Create an OVS bridge with the exact same name that you have on KVM1-Mumbai-DC. Connect these two switches to each other using a GRE or VxLan tunnel. Now, create VMs (nodes) on this new host and connect to your private network that is shared between two hosts using a VxLan tunnel.

Configuring Open vSwitch tunnels with VxLan

The following diagram represents two instances running on two separate hosts connected by a VxLan tunnel. Also illustrated are the required supporting physical and virtual components. VTEP interfaces allows us to create Layer 2 network over layer 2.

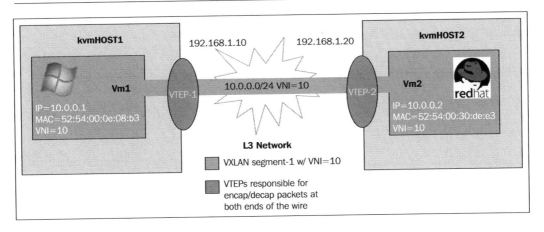

The example depicted earlier steps through the creation of a VXLaN tunnel between two OVS bridges running on two separate bare metal hosts named KVMhost1 and KVMhost2.

KvmHOST1 host side configuration

We have to first create a virtual tunnel endpoint and then connect it to the virtual tunnel endpoint created on a second host to form the tunnel. The following steps are involved in VTEP creation:

1. First verify to which OVS bridge the vm1 is connected:

```
#virsh domiflist vm1

Interface  Type       Source     Model       MAC
-----------------------------------------------------------

vnet0      bridge     vswitch_vlans_portgroup rtl8139
52:54:00:b7:d1:3a
```

2. Check the configuration of the ovs switch:

```
ovs-vsctl show
6e121fc0-2f05-42a3-b265-7e5ab958bb91
   Bridge vswitch
   Port "vnet0"
   Interface "vnet0"
   Port vswitch
   Interface vswitch
   type: internal
   ovs_version: "2.4.0"
```

3. Ensure the connectivity between kvmhost1 and kvmhost2 host over the layer 3 IP address. Check the ping result: $ping 192.168.1.20.

4. Run the ovs-vsctl command on kvmhost1 to create the tunnel and link it to the bridge on kvmhost2:

```
#ovs-vsctl add-port vswitch vxlan1 -- set interface vxlan1
type=vxlan options:remote_ip=192.168.1.20
```

5. Re-check the ovs switch configuration and ensure the interface with vxlan has been created:

```
   Bridge vswitch
Port "vxlan1"
Interface "vxlan1"
type: vxlan
options: {remote_ip="192.168.1.20"}
Port "vnet0"
Interface "vnet0"
Port vswitch
Interface vswitch
type: internal
ovs_version: "2.4.0"
```

kvmHOST2 host configuration

Repeat the same steps on KVMHOST2 that are performed on HOST1. Just ensure that the remote_ip option for the vxlan interface is set properly. The exact steps are documented next:

1. First check to which ovs bridge the vm2 is connected:

```
#virsh domiflist vm2
Interface  Type      Source Model    MAC
------------------------------------------------------------
vnet0  bridge vswitch_vlans_portgroup rtl8139   52:54:00:fa:e9:a3
```

2. Check the configuration of the ovs switch:

```
#ovs-vsctl show
0bc49c1e-71c6-4b80-8f14-d83ddf332eac
   Bridge vswitch
   Port vswitch
   Interface vswitch
```

```
type: internal
Port "vnet0"
Interface "vnet0"
ovs_version: "2.4.0"
```

3. Ensure connectivity between the `kvmhost2` and `kvmhost1` hosts over layer 3. Ping result. Check `$ping 192.168.1.10`.

4. Run the `ovs-vsctl` command on `kvmhost2` to create the tunnel and link it to the bridge on `kvmhost1`:

```
$ovs-vsctl add-port vswitch vxlan1 -- set interface vxlan2
type=vxlan options:remote_ip=192.168.1.10
```

5. Re-check the `ovs` switch configuration and ensure the interface with `vxlan` has been created:

```
Bridge vswitch
Port "vxlan1"
Interface "vxlan2"
type: vxlan
options: {remote_ip="192.168.1.10"}
Port "vnet0"
Interface "vnet0"
Port vswitch
Interface vswitch
type: internal
ovs_version: "2.4.0"
```

The preceding configuration example is for two hosts. In this example, the VXLAN tenant IP addresses are `10.0.0.0/24` and the hypervisor IP network that serves it is `192.168.1.10/24`. This example uses an OVS instance named `vswitch`. The OVS instance has the following interfaces attached:

A VXLAN port named `vxlan1` that uses UDP port 478 9 and vnid 11. A tap interface for the VM named VNET0.

With this configuration in place, `10.0.0.1` can communicate with `10.0.0.2` as if they have a direct L2 connection between them.

Ping results:

```
ping 10.0.0.1 -c 2
PING 10.0.0.1 (10.0.0.1): 56 data bytes
64 bytes from 10.0.0.1: seq=0 ttl=64 time=3.010 ms
64 bytes from 10.0.0.1: seq=1 ttl=64 time=3.639 ms


ping 10.0.0.2 -c 2
PING 10.0.0.2 (10.0.0.2): 56 data bytes
64 bytes from 10.0.0.2: seq=0 ttl=64 time=3.984 ms
64 bytes from 10.0.0.2: seq=1 ttl=64 time=3.694 ms


# "tcpdump -i vnet0" on hosts show Vxlan encapsulation

tcpdump: verbose output suppressed, use -v or -vv for full protocol
decode
listening on vnet0, link-type EN10MB (Ethernet), capture size 262144
bytes
01:32:47.601984 IP 192.168.1.10.55453 > 192.168.1.20.vxlan: VXLAN, flags
[I] (0x08), vni 11
```

Similarly, a GRE tunnel can be created; just change the interface type to `gre` and you have a GRE tunnel instead of a VxLan one.

```
Host1 : ovs-vsctl add-port br1 gre1 -- set interface gre1 type=gre
options:remote_ip=192.168.1.20


Host2 : ovs-vsctl add-port br1 gre1 -- set interface gre1 type=gre
options:remote_ip=192.168.1.10
```

Network port mirroring

Open vSwitch supports port mirroring features out-of-the-box. This feature is exactly similar to the port mirroring capability available on the new-generation physical switches. With port mirroring, network administrators can get an insight into what kind of traffic is flowing on the network and implement traffic analysis systems such as IDS/IPS. It is also helpful in troubleshooting network-related issues in the virtual infrastructure.

The basic purpose of port mirroring is to replicate layer 3 traffic flowing from one or more virtual ports to a designated port. It's easy to implement but take the following into consideration before you go ahead and configure it:

- A virtual machine with port mirroring enabled uses more host CPU and RAM as compared to other virtual ports.
- Port Mirroring may reduce the network latency if not implemented correctly.
- Be aware that enabling port mirroring reduces user privacy. Plain passwords will be clearly visible to analysis tools.

Configuring port mirroring

To implement port mirroring with Open vSwitch, the first thing to do is to create and add a mirror to the bridge:

```
#ovs-vsctl -- --id=@m create mirror name=M1 -- add bridge vswitch001
mirrors @m
```

Here we're actually running two ovs-vswitch commands at once; each command is introduced by --. The first command creates a mirror named M1 and, thanks to the --id=@m part, saves its UUID in the "variable" @m, which remains available for later commands and associates the newly created mirror with the <vswitch001> bridge,

The mirror information is stored in ovsdb immediately and you get a mirror visible on the OVS bridge. Initially, it's a blank mirror; it will not copy any packets:

```
#ovs-vsctl list mirror
```

```
_uuid            : bdfdc9e4-d6db-4a45-a3ac-6a11addccc95
external_ids     : {}
name             : M1
output_port      : []
output_vlan      : []
select_all       : false
select_dst_port  : []
select_src_port  : []
select_vlan      : []
statistics       : {}
```

In order to start the mirroring, you have to define a source or destination port (or both) and an output_port. The source and destination port terminology is a little confusing. At first it looks as if the source is where we want to capture the traffic from and the destination port is where to dump the captured traffic, but it's not like that. Let's get a clear understanding of the terminology used:

- select_dst_port: Ports on which incoming packets are selected for mirroring.

- select_src_port: Ports on which outgoing packets are selected for mirroring.

- select_all: This is Boolean. When set to true, every packet (incoming or outgoing) on any port connected to the bridge will be mirrored.

- output_port: Specifies to which port we want to send the mirrored traffic. So now we have the mirror associated with the OVS bridge. The next step is to configure its source ports and destination ports, for example, if you want to mirror all traffic going in and out of the fed1 port and we want to send it to the dummy01 bridge port.

The fed1 port belongs to the virtual machine named Fed1 and the dummy01 port is a dummy port created for testing purposes. You may choose any other port that is connected to the bridge. It could be your IDS VM port or the packet analysis system's port. The following are the steps:

1. First verify that fed1 does indeed belong to the Fed1 virtual machine.

   ```
   [root@kvmHOST1 ~]# virsh domiflist Fed1
   Interface  Type     Source      Model    MAC
   --------------------------------------------------------
   fed1       bridge   NewNetwork  virtio   52:54:00:6c:92:c7
   ```

2. Create a dummy01 port on the host and on the ovs bridge.

   ```
   #ip link add name dummy0 type dummy
   #ovs-vsctl add-port vswitch001 dummy0
   ```

3. Add the fed1 port in select_dst_port and select_src_port to start capturing its incoming and outgoing traffic:

   ```
   [root@kvmHOST1 ~]# ovs-vsctl -- --id=@fed1 get port fed1 -- set
   mirror M1 select_src_port=@fed1 select_dst_port=@fed1
   ```

4. Check the `ovs-vsctl` list `mirror` output to ensure that the `fed1` port is configured to capture incoming and outgoing packets. The mirror configuration of the bridge doesn't accept the name; it shows the uuid of the port. If you are not sure about the uuid of the port whose traffic you want to mirror, check the output of `ovs-vsctl list port <port-name>` command:

```
[root@kvmHOST1 ~]# ovs-vsctl list mirror
_uuid               : bdfdc9e4-d6db-4a45-a3ac-6a11addccc95
external_ids        : {}
name                : M1
output_port         : []
output_vlan         : []
select_all          : false
select_dst_port     : [a1df93f2-9e50-4c2e-9e71-7a8a6619e406]
select_src_port     : [a1df93f2-9e50-4c2e-9e71-7a8a6619e406]
select_vlan         : []
statistics          : {}
```

5. Now set the `output_port` attribute, specifying where to dump the capture packets. In our case, it's `dummy0`:

```
[root@kvmHOST1 ~]# ovs-vsctl --column=_uuid list port dummy0
_uuid               : a5add212-58ff-438f-bbf2-c8ca850a4e8a
[root@kvmHOST1 ~]#

#ovs-vsctl set mirror mymirror output-port=a5add212-58ff-438f-
bbf2-c8ca850a4e8a


root@kvmHOST1 ~]# ovs-vsctl list mirror
_uuid               : bdfdc9e4-d6db-4a45-a3ac-6a11addccc95
external_ids        : {}
name                : mymirror
output_port         : a5add212-58ff-438f-bbf2-c8ca850a4e8a <<
output_vlan         : []
select_all          : false
select_dst_port     : [a1df93f2-9e50-4c2e-9e71-7a8a6619e406]
select_src_port     : [a1df93f2-9e50-4c2e-9e71-7a8a6619e406]
select_vlan         : []
statistics          : {tx_bytes=0, tx_packets=0}
```

6. With this, OVS should do the port mirroring of any traffic that is flowing from the `fed1` port to `dummy0`. You can quickly verify that by using `tcpdump`. Start packet capturing:

on dummy0 :

```
[root@kvmHOST1 ~]# ip link set dummy0 up
[root@kvmHOST1 ~]# tcpdump -i dummy0
```

7. Now send or receive some traffic on the `Fed1` VM. A ping test should be adequate to verify this:

```
[root@kvmHOST1 ~]# tcpdump -i dummy0
15:46:01.239593 IP 10.0.0.1 > 10.0.0.2: ICMP echo request, id 917,
seq 3, length 64
15:46:01.240342 IP 10.0.0.2 > 10.0.0.1: ICMP echo reply, id 917,
seq 3, length 6
```

This HTTPD traffic:

```
15:46:55.318655 IP 10.0.0.2.37591 > 10.0.0.1.http: Flags [P.], seq 1:73,
ack 1, win 913, options [nop,nop,TS val 21775344 ecr 21777310], length
72: HTTP: GET / HTTP/1.1
```

Are you more interested in watching all traffic passing through the OVS bridge, instead of a single port? If so, the quickest way to mirror all traffic passing through the bridge to a given port is to use the `select_all` property of the mirror:

```
# ovs-vsctl -- --id=@dummy0 get port dummy0 -- set mirror mymirror
select_all=true output-port=@dummy0
```

How about VLANs? Yes, VLAN traffic can also be mirrored. Use `select-VLAN` and `output-VLAN` attributes to disable mirroring. Run:

```
#ovs-vsctl clear bridge vswitch001 mirrors
```

Managing Open vSwitch using the OpenDaylight SDN controller

Till now we have seen how Open vSwitch works in normal mode. In normal mode, Open vSwitch works just like a typical L2 learning switch with an option to manipulate the flow using the `ofctl` command. While this approach offers features such as tunneling, QoS, Overlay, and SPAN natively, the real value comes from being able to directly influence flow tables, creating a powerful L2-L4 service insertion in the Open vSwitch data plane to bring programmability to otherwise inflexible networks.

By connecting an Open vSwitch to an SDN controller, we get the level of abstraction and automation required to revolutionize networking. It essentially turns OVS into an access layer to the virtual environment, taking instructions from the centralized controller that pushes flows down to the vSwitch. The following diagram represents the high-level architecture of Open vSwitch integration with a SDN controller:

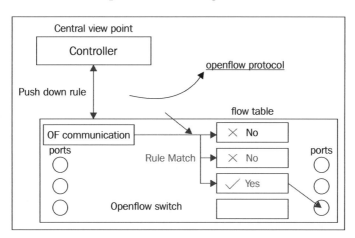

This diagram can be broken down into three parts: flow tables installed on switches, an SDN controller, and an OpenFlow protocol for the SDN controller to talk securely with switches.:

- The flow table is the network switch's intelligence that is referred by its data plane to decide how to transfer received packets.

- The OpenFlow protocol is the key enabler of Software Defined Networking. The SDN controller interacts with Open vSwitch, using OpenFlow protocol to manipulate and add fields in a frame of traffic (L2 to L4) to make decisions programmatically. This decision might be to modify some fields, or to encapsulate the frame inside something else, or simply forward out a port. OpenFlow is defined in RFC 7426.

- An SDN controller is an application in software-defined networking that manages the control plane of one or more switches via OpenFlow channels. It also provides a network-wide abstraction for applications through a rich set of REST APIs that add programmable capability for networks.

Today, there are many SDN Controllers on the market, Both proprietary and open source options are available. OpenDaylight is an open source SDN controller with the largest community support and is most often regarded as the industry's de facto standard. Hence, I have chosen this controller to demonstrate implementation of Open vSwitch in flow mode to manage KVM VMs networks. Fundamentally, any SDN controller that supports the OpenFlow protocol can be used with Open vSwitch.

I'll walk you through the process of installing and configuring OpenDaylight on a Fedora 22 System, connecting Open vSwitch to the controller, and basic flow management methods.

These steps assume that you've already configured OVS and it is being used to facilitate network connectivity for the KVM VMs. The following screenshot shows the basic topology of what we have going on here:

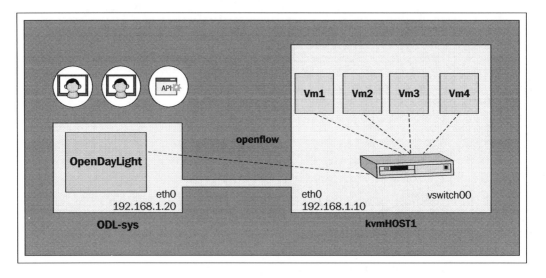

Two systems: `ODL-sys` is where the OpenDaylight application is installed and `KVMHOST1` is the KVM Hypervisor with four virtual machines connected to the `vswitch001` OVS bridge. The VM network is 10.0.0.0/24 and it's an isolated network. Both systems (`KVMHOST001` and `ODL-sys`) are connected over an interface network and are part of the 192.168.1.0/24 subnet.

Installing the OpenDaylight controller (ODL-sys)

You need Fedora 22 x86_64 system. The OpenDaylight Hydrogen release is available through the yum repository.

Hardware requirements

The minimum and recommended hardware requirements outlined here are based on a typical small- to medium-sized installation. You can also use a VM for the OpenDaylight controller system. It is also feasible to install the OpenDaylight controller on the same system where OVS is being used.

Minimum:

- A dual core CPU
- 4 GB of available system RAM if Data Warehouse is not installed and if memory is not being consumed by existing processes
- 25 GB of locally accessible, writable, disk space
- 1 Network Interface Card (NIC) with bandwidth of at least 1 Gbps

Installing and configuring ODL

Perform the following steps to get started:

1. Configure the OpenDaylight yum repository:

   ```
   #rpm -ivh https://nexus.opendaylight.org/content/repositories/
   opendaylight-yum-fedora-19-x86_64/rpm/opendaylight-
   release/0.1.0-2.fc19.noarch/opendaylight-release-0.1.0-2.fc19.
   noarch.rpm
   ```

2. Install the OpenDaylight server and its dependencies:

   ```
   #yum install opendaylight-serviceprovider
   ```

3. Start the OpenDaylight server and enable it on boot:

   ```
   # systemctl enable opendaylight-controller.service
   # systemctl disable opendaylight-controller.service
   # systemctl start opendaylight-controller.service
   ```

4. Now access the OpenDaylight dashboard from the following URL: `http://ip-address:8080`:

 Note: Configure the firewall to open ports `8080` and `8181`.

Default credentials: user: `admin` and password: `admin`

Adding an Open vSwitch (vswitch001) instance to the OpenDaylight controller on system (ODL-sys)

The following procedure outlines how to add an Open vSwitch (referred to as a node by ODL):

1. Make sure that that the ODL-sysnetwork-pingable port `6633` is open. The OpenDaylight controller listens on OpenFlow port `6633` to connect to its nodes.

2. Specify the ODL SDN controller address on the `vswitch001` bridge using the set-controller option for the `ovs-vsctl` command as follows `#ovs-vsctl set-controller` bridge target is the syntax. Target may use any of the following forms: `ssl:ip[:port]`, `tcp:ip[:port]`, `unix:file`, `pssl:[port][:ip]`. By default, the OpenDaylight controller uses `tcp:ip[port]` as the target form on the fedora 22 system:\

```
#ovs-vsctl set-controller vswitch001
192.168.1.20:6634
```

3. Execute `ovs-vsctl` show and verify that the switch is connected to the controller:

```
[root@kvmHOST1 ~]# ovs-vsctl show
e9c72657-5021-4db6-8cda-52adec50a53d
  Bridge "vswitch001"
  Controller "tcp:192.168.1.2:6633"
  is_connected: true
  Port "vswitch001"
  Interface "vswitch001"
  type: internal
```

Look at `Controller "tcp:192.168.1.2:6634"` and `is_connected: true`; this means that your Open vSwitch connects properly to the OpenFlow controller.

4. Now login to the OpenDaylight dashboard, You will see that the SDN controller has learned the node and its topology. OpenDaylight uses the Link Layer Discovery protocol to learn about ports connected to the switch:

5. Now ping the virtual machines connected to the OVS bridge and monitor the OF flow table of the switch:

```
"#ovs-ofctl ofctl dump-xml vswitch001"
```

6. You will notice that the first packet arriving on the switch's datapath goes to the SDN Controller (SlowPath). The controller maintains the MAC table of the switch; using this, it decides which port the packet needs to send on. It works as illustrated in the following diagram:

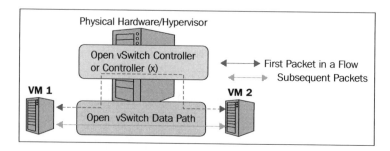

The first packet goes through the slowpath to learn the destination port and install the flow on the datapath; subsequent packets use the installed flow without requiring each packet to go to the controller, They directly use the fastpath (data path). However, note that each Flow Table entry has two timers:

*   `idle_timeout`: The seconds when there are no matching packets and after which the flow is removed (`zero` means never timeout)

*   `hard_timeout`: Seconds after which the flow is removed (`zero` mean never timeout)

If both `idle_timeout` and `hard_timeout` are set, then the flow is removed when the first of the two expires. Let us learn more about OpenFlow via the following example:

A simple example of OpenFlow:

```
cookie=0x0, duration=14.604s, table=0, n_packets=61, n_bytes=7418,
idle_timeout=10, hard_timeout=30,tcp, vlan_tci=0x0000, dl_
src=52:54:00:CE:51:52, dl_dst=52:54:00:CE:51:53, nw_src=10.0.0.1, nw_
dst=10.0.0.2, nw_tos=0, tp_src=22, tp_dst=554 actions=output:1
```

It's self-explanatory. If the traffic comes in from src MAC address `52:54:00:CE:51:52` destination mac address `52:54:00:CE:51:53`, traffic is TCP traffic, src `ip=10.0.0.1`, dest `ip=10.0.0.2`, TCP source port 22, TCP destination port 554 forward the packet to port 1 (`actions:1`).

Using OpenFlow allows us to create powerful L2-L4 service insertions. A flow contains entries that match the packets and apply actions that may include packet forwarding, packet modification, and others. The following diagram gives a basic idea about flow tables:

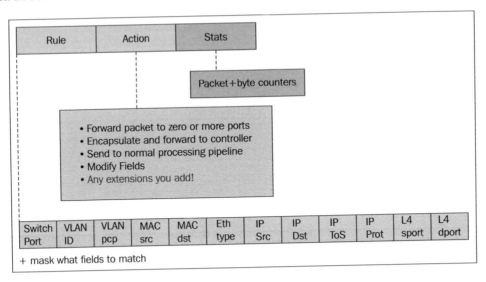

Basically, rules are used to create expressions. If expressions match, the defined action is applied. OpenFlow supports extensive flow matching capabilities that include:

- Meta – Tunnel ID, In Port, QoS priority, skb mark
- Layer 2 – MAC address, VLAN ID, Ethernet type
- Layer 3 – IPv4/IPv6 fields, ARP
- Layer 4 – TCP/UDP, ICMP, ND
- Chain of actions, output to ports (single, range, flood, and mirror)
- Discard, resubmit to another table
- Packet mangling (Push/Pop VLAN header, TOS...)
- Send to controller, learn
- Set tunnel ID

The *Software Defined Networking with OpenFlow* book authored by Siamak Azodolmolky has much more detail about OpenFlow protocol and flow. You are highly recommended to refer to this book to learn more about SDN. The book can be bought here:

```
https://www.packtpub.com/networking-and-servers/
software-defined-networking-openflow
```

Another highly recommended tool to learn OpenFlow protocols is FlowSim `https://flowsim.flowgrammable.org/`FlowSim is designed to simulate five different versions of the OpenFlow switch data plane, their documentation is clear and easy to understand, and the simulator really imparts a high-level knowledge of OpenFlow.

Installing flows on the OVS bridge using OpenDaylight Dashboard

Example 1: Block all inbound and outbound ICMP traffic from the switch. With this flow inserted, no ICMP traffic should be allowed to traverse through any port of the OVS bridge.

Perform the following steps:

1. Login to OpenDaylight Dashboard; `admin:admin` are the default credentials. Change the password ASAP.

2. Click the **Flows** tab and then the **Add Flow Entry** button located on the top left-hand side.

3. Complete the fields under **Add Flow Entry**. First name the flow and select the node (vSwitch).

4. Scroll down to the **Layers** section, In the **Protocol** section type `icmp` and select **Drop** as the action:

5. Click on the **Install Flow** button.

6. Try pinging between your virtual machines, It should not work.

7. Verify the installed flow on the switch using the `ovs-ofctl` command:

   "#OVS-ofctl dump-flows <bridge -name>" gives us information about the flows installed:

   ```
   [root@kvmHOST1 ~]# watch -n1 ovs-ofctl dump-flows vswitch001
   cookie=0x0, duration=168.943s, table=0, n_packets=0, n_bytes=0,
   idle_age=168, priority=500,icmp actions=drop
   ```

Example 2: If a TCP packet destined for port 8080 arrives on the OVS bridge, modify the port to `80`. The following are the installation steps:

1. Add flows with the following details:

2. Install the flow.

3. s

   "`#OVS-ofctl dump-flows <bridge -name>`" gives us information about the flows installed:

   ```
   [root@kvmHOST1 ~]# ovs-ofctl dump-flows vswitch001
   NXST_FLOW reply (xid=0x4):
    cookie=0x0, duration=2.427s, table=0, n_packets=0, n_bytes=0,
    idle_age=2, priority=500,tcp,tp_dst=8080 actions=mod_tp_dst:80
   ```

There are many more use cases. Modifying the network source and destination is useful in many scenarios. A typical scenario is a load-balancing application or redirecting to a Beta version. The user believes they "talk" with `10.0.0.2` but it's actually connected to `10.0.0.3` on another port.

The enqueuing action is very helpful in shaping network traffic, for example by giving the lowest speed to entertainment traffic and the highest to critical business applications.

Further, OpenDaylight exposes a RESTful API that makes it really easy for apps to control networks. The API accepts regular get/post/put/delete HTTP requests, passing JSON payloads.

Basic Open vSwitch troubleshooting

Open vSwitch is a rather complex system that consists of multiple components and protocols. In the event of problems, it may be very difficult to keep track of the specific level of the problem. However, Open vSwitch provides many tools and the database it uses (OVSDB) is very easy to read and understand. The objective of this section is to provide basic guidelines for diagnosing problems arising from the use of Open vSwitch:

- Log Files: Logs are the most important and vital source of information when it comes to troubleshooting or diagnosing problems. OpenvSwitch's core components record logs in the /var/log/openvswitch/ovs-vswitchd.log and /var/log/openvswitch/ovsdb-server.log files. If a problem occurs in starting up the Open vSwitch service, first review these logs.

- Built-in VLOG facility: Open vSwitch has a built-in logging mechanism called VLOG. The VLOG facility exposes deep internal information about various components. First, determine at what level your problem is occurring. Is it a bonding problem?

```
#ovs-appctl vlog/list
```

Run the earlier command and find out the Open vSwitch module corresponding to the bond and check what verbosity is set:

```
[root@kvmHOST1 openvswitch]# ovs-appctl vlog/list | grep -i bond
bond              OFF      ERR      INFO
```

Verbosity levels are emer, err, warn, info, or dbg); dbg is what we need while troubleshooting problems. To enable debug logging use the syntax of ovs-appctl to customize VLOG as follows.

```
#ovs-appctl vlog/set module[:facility[:level]]
```

For example, enabling debug logging for the bonding module:

```
#ovs-appctl vlog/set ANY:dbg:INFO
```

The man page of OVS-appctl explains other options available to tune and configure Open vSwitch logging.

Check the bridge or port configurations by querying OVSDB. ovsdb-client is an interface provided to interact with the ovsdb-server:

#ovsdb-client list-dbs: Prints databases present on the system.

ovsdb-client list-tables: Prints tables in the database. The following is a list of tables in the Open_vSwitch database:

- Controller
- Bridge
- Queue
- IPFIX
- NetFlow
- Open_vSwitch
- QoS
- Port
- sFlow
- SSL
- Flow_Sample_Collector_Set
- Mirror
- Flow_Table
- Interface
- AutoAttach
- Manager

"ovsdb-client list-columns <table_name>": Prints columns in a particular table. There are many columns in each table.

"#ovsdb-client monitor <table_name><cloumn_name> --detach": Prints the content of the columns. You can also get output in various formats, including table, list, HTML, CSV, and JSON.

ovsdb-tool showlog shows data inserted into ovsdb, its Open vSwitch configuration data; this can be very handy in understanding the configuration history of a vSwitch.

For OpenFlow-related issues,: `ovs-ofctl` speaks to the OpenFlow module and it comes with many debugging options:

```
#ovs-ofctl dump-flows <OVS bridge>
```

```
#ovs-ofctl snoop <OVS bridge>
```

See "hidden" flows (inband, failopen, and so on) using:

```
ovs-appctl bridge/dump-flows <OVS bridge>
```

For kernel datapath-related issues: `ovs-dpctl` speaks to the kernel module. To check datapaths and their attached interfaces use: `#ovs-dpctl show <OVS Bride >` and to exact match flows cached in the datapath use: `#ovs-dpctl dump-flows <OVS Bridge>` and to get Top like behavior for `OVS-dpctl dump-flows` use `OVS-dpctl-top` command.

When configuring a VLAN, make sure the `vlan_mode` set for the port is correct. Sometimes, users configure VLAN tagging with `vlan_mode` access and expect it to work with a tagged VLAN:

```
[root@kvmHOST1 openvswitch]# ovs-vsctl --format=table --column=name,vlan_
mode list port
```

```
name         vlan_mode
----------- ---------
"vswitch001" []
"vnet1"access
"vnet0"access
"vm001_vp01" trunk
```

`access`, `native-tagged`, `native-untagged`, and `trunk` are four `VLAN_modes` supported by Open vSwitch.

Reading an Open vSwitch bridge configuration by querying database or using command-line tools although gives us the required information, having an illustrated view of various network configurations including OVS will surely help in quickly getting a fair understanding of the OVS configuration.

Show My Network State is a good utility for graphically displaying the virtual and physical network topology inside a single host. The tool is available here for download: `https://sites.google.com/site/showmynetworkstate/`.

I find this utility extremely helpful while debugging Open vSwitch-related issues. The following screenshot shows how it looks:

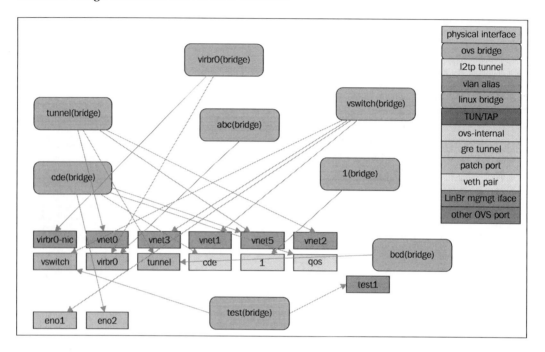

Summary

In this chapter, we covered the practical use of SDN with KVM virtualization. We installed Open vSwitch and configured it to facilitate virtual networking for VMs. We also implemented advanced networking features such as VLANs, overlay networks, port mirroring, and so on, and then learned about the open source SDN controllers on the OpenDaylight market. The last section of the chapter covered general troubleshooting steps for Open vSwitch.

In the next chapter, we will learn about the configuration of oVirt and familiarize ourselves with the advanced enterprise virtualization features it provides.

10
Installing and Configuring the Virtual Datacenter Using oVirt

Until now we have been trying to learn virtualization using a single system or two. What if your environment has grown big? Or if your management has decided to virtualize most of your physical systems, for efficiency and hence reduce costs?

You are now staring at hundreds of virtual machines scattered around multiple KVM hypervisors. Your head is filled with questions. How am I going to monitor and manage the vast pool of virtual machines? What about resource allocation? How will I make sure that high availability works for my clusters? What if a hypervisor goes down? Will I be able to manage everything using virsh, virt-manager, and kimchi? Then somebody says it is time introduce VM$. Only VM$ can manage virtual machines on a larger scale. But you are a fighter. You want open source in your environment where you are in control, not any proprietary solutions company. You opened your browser and searched for `open source virtual machine manager`. The first result points to a website named `http://www.ovirt.org/` and you started smiling. You found what you were looking for—a centralized enterprise class virtualization manager.

In this chapter, we will cover the following topics:

* The oVirt architecture
* The oVirt engine installation
* The oVirt node installation

Introducing oVirt

oVirt is a virtual data center manager. It manages virtual machines, hosts, storage, and virtualized networks. It provides a powerful web management interface. Virtual machines are managed using libvirt and vdsm (a host service that runs along with libvirt). The hypervisors use KVM to run the virtual machines.

Remember, just like KVM and SPICE, oVirt also came from Qumranet. It started as a closed source desktop virtualization manager developed on .NET and runs on Windows servers. When Red Hat acquired Qumranet, they open sourced the project and ported the code to Java and named the project as oVirt. oVirt is an upstream project for **Red Hat Enterprise Virtualization (RHEV)**.

 oVirt is a huge product with hundreds of features. Covering them all in two chapters is not possible. What we did is, we identified the core features in oVirt and explained the backend. This should provide you with a strong basis in oVirt which will help you explore oVirt in detail.

oVirt is all about scaling up the virtualization environment from a single hypervisor managed by virt-manager or virsh to a multi-hypervisor multiuser environment. We will start by understanding the oVirt architecture.

oVirt architecture

There is no better representation of an oVirt architecture than the following figure. This is taken from `http://www.ovirt.org/`:

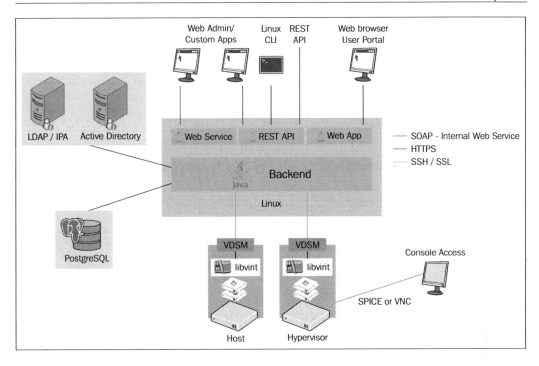

Lets try to understand the preceding figure. In the simplest form, consider oVirt as a remote management tool to manage multiple libvirt-based hypervisors that use KVM as the virtualization technology.

It has four major components:

- oVirt engine
- oVirt node
- Storage
- Networking

The oVirt engine

The oVirt engine is a JBoss-based Java application that runs as a web service. In the previous diagram, an oVirt engine is represented by the back end. It is the management component of the oVirt infrastructure and is installed on a dedicated Linux server. The oVirt engine uses PostgreSQL as its database. In our examples, we use Fedora as the Linux server. The main functions of the oVirt engine are the following:

- **VM lifecycle management**: These are operations to manage a virtual machine.

- **Authentication**: Uses LDAP/IPA (`http://www.freeipa.org/page/Main_Page`) and Active Directory.

- **Network management**: Manages network on both hypervisor nodes and virtual machines.

- **Storage management**: Manages shared storage used for creating virtual machines and virtual disks attached to virtual machines.

- **Monitoring**: Virtual machines, storage, network, and hypervisor nodes.

- **High Availability**: When an oVirt node fails, it restarts virtual machines on other nodes.

- **Live migration**: Live migration of virtual machines and storage.

- **System scheduler**: Continuously load balances virtual machines based on the cluster resource polices. This also includes aggregating virtual machines on fewer hosts for power saving.

- **Virtual machine image management**: Creates and removes virtual disks, templates, and snapshots.

- **Importing and exporting virtual machines**.

- **Communication**: The oVirt engine interacts with the oVirt nodes through a VDSM service that runs on each node. The VDSM service is also known as **host agent**.

The oVirt node

In simple terms, an oVirt node is a hypervisor that contains just enough packages to be part of the oVirt virtual data center and can run virtual machines. It only contains a minimal set of packages to run the OS and the virtualization management tools. An oVirt node is the workhorse in an oVirt data center. It is a dump host that performs the task delegated to it by an oVirt engine and gathers details of the infrastructure for an oVirt engine to act upon. The oVirt engine interacts with the oVirt node using the **Virtual Desktop and Server Manager (VDSM)**. The VDSM then interacts with the libvirt service, to check if those instructions need VM lifecycle management. VDSM is referred to as a host agent. Similar to libvirt, the VDSM is also developed in Python. The primary functions of the VDSM include storage management, network management, and VM lifecycle management with the help of libvirt.

An oVirt node has the following packages installed (other than the basic packages required for it to run):

- `qemu-kvm`: This provides QEMU.
- `qemu-kvm-tools`: This provides the `kvm_stat` command. It is a Python script that retrieves runtime statistics from the KVM kernel module and is used to diagnose the guest behavior visible to KVM.
- `vdsm` and related packages: This provides a VSDM service for managing the node from oVirt Engine.
- `vdsm-cli`: Its the command-line interface to VDSM service.
- `libvirt`: This provides the libvirt service.
- `spice-server`: This is used to provide remote connections for the virtual machines.

There are two ways to set up an oVirt node. Install a minimal Fedora or CentOS server, add it to oVirt Manager or use a

Storage

oVirt can make use of both local storage or shared storage to store virtual machine disks and snapshots. One exception is ISO files, which are used for installing virtual machines that need a shared storage (NFS). When you create and attach storage to an oVirt infrastructure, it is called a storage domain. Understanding the storage domain is very important when you work with oVirt infrastructure. This includes understanding the architecture of a storage domain and its types. We will discuss its architecture in the next chapter.

The storage domain in oVirt can be classified into two categories, based on the type of storage you use: a local storage domain or a shared storage domain.

 Storage domains are attached to hypervisor nodes only. They are not attached to an oVirt engine server.

A local storage domain is storage that is attached directly to an oVirt node that is not shared or accessed by any other nodes. Usually, it is created from the local disk itself. In production environments, it is very unlikely that you use local storage, the oVirt data center, created from a local storage domain due to its limitations. One major limitation is that you will not be able to migrate the virtual machines between nodes. It functions like a standalone libvirt host.

A shared storage domain, like a local storage domain, is also attached directly to the oVirt nodes. The difference is that it is shared on all the nodes that are part of the oVirt data center. The shared storage domains are created from a centralized storage system. oVirt supports the following centralized storage systems:

- **Network File System (NFS)** and **Parallel NFS (pNFS)**
- **Internet Small Computer System Interface (iSCSI)**
- **Fibre Channel Protocol (FCP)**
- **GlusterFS**

We classified the storage domains as local and shared them based on the type of storage you use. Now we will again classify a storage domain based on its purpose:

- **Data domain**: A data domain acts as the storage for everything related to virtual disks used by virtual machines. It is used for storing virtual disks, snapshot disks, metadata, and so on. oVirt uses a data domain for all the storage operations of its VMs.

Data domain cannot be shared among oVirt data centers.

- **Export domain**: As the name suggests, export domains are used for exporting and importing virtual machines. An export domain can be used to backup virtual machines or move virtual machines between two oVirt data centers.

An export domain can be created from an NFS share. oVirt allows only one export domain per data center.

- **ISO domain**: An ISO domain is used to store ISO files and is created from NFS share only. If your environment does not have network booting such as PXE you need ISOs to boot or install virtual machines.

An ISO domain is the only type of storage domain that can be shared across different data centers simultaneously.

Networking

The networking architecture in oVirt is not very complicated and makes use of the Linux bridge in the backend. It is similar to what you learned in libvirt networking in *Chapter 4, Getting Started with libvirt and Creating Your First Virtual Machines*. oVirt uses the term **Logical Network** when defining a new network, that is, you create a logical network and apply to all participating oVirt nodes. By default, all data centers in oVirt have a logical network named **oVirt**. You can perform advanced tasks, such as creating a vlan, a simple bond, and bonding over the vlan using the oVirt management interface. We will discuss logical networks more in the next chapter.

Now, you have an idea about oVirt and its architecture. Lets start setting up the environment by first installing the oVirt engine and then the oVirt nodes.

Installing the oVirt engine

Lets first take a look at the minimum system requirements to install oVirt 3.5 Manager:

- A dual core CPU
- 4 GB RAM
- 25 GB free space
- 1 GiB NIC
- Fedora 20

Now we will check the actual requirements for installing oVirt 3.5 Manager:

- A quad core or better CPU
- 16 GB of system RAM to start with, and an option to increase as per the need
- 50 GB free space, ideally on LVM
- 1 GiB NIC
- Fedora 20

We assume that you already have a Fedora 20 server installed. If you need help to install Fedora 20, follow the instructions at `https://docs.fedoraproject.org/en-US/Fedora/20/html/Installation_Guide/index.html`

It is also important that you dedicate this server, exclusively, to an oVirt engine. This will make the installation less complicated and error free.

Preparing the system for oVirt engine installation

Perform the following steps to prepare your system:

1. Set the hostname. This hostname should be resolvable using your DNS server. Name resolution is very important for an oVirt environment:

   ```
   [root@ovirt ~]# hostnamectl set-hostname ovirt.example.local
   [root@ovirt ~]# host ovirt.example.local
   ovirt.example.local has address 192.168.122.8
   ```

2. Update and reboot the system:

   ```
   [root@ovirt ~]# yum update -y
   [root@ovirt ~]# reboot
   ```

3. Install the oVirt engine repository and then install the oVirt-engine package:

```
# yum install http://plain.resources.ovirt.org/pub/yum-repo/ovirt-
release35.rpm

# yum -y install ovirt-engine
```

The installation will take some time, as it has to download and install a long list of packages.

4. Once the package installation is finished, start the oVirt installation:

```
[root@ovirt ~]# engine-setup  --generate-answer=/root/ovirt-
answer.txt
```

 We have removed some messages from the succeeding output.

```
Configure Engine on this host (Yes, No) [Yes]: Yes (This will
start the engine installation)
Websocket proxy?
Configure WebSocket Proxy on this host (Yes, No) [Yes]: Yes
```

Configuring a websocket proxy server will allow users to connect to virtual machines via the noVNC or HTML 5 consoles.

```
Do you want Setup to configure the firewall? (Yes, No) [Yes]: Yes
```

The host name should be resolvable using the host command:

```
Host fully qualified DNS name of this server [ovirt.example.local]:
ovirt.example.local

--== DATABASE CONFIGURATION ==--
```

Here, we are going with the local postgres DB:

```
Where is the Engine database located? (Local, Remote) [Local]: Local
Setup can configure the local postgresql server automatically for the
engine to run. This may conflict with existing applications.
Would you like Setup to automatically configure postgresql and create
Engine database, or prefer to perform that manually? (Automatic, Manual)
[Automatic]: Automatic

--== OVIRT ENGINE CONFIGURATION ==--
```

Enter the oVirt engine administrator password. Admin is the only user created in oVirt DB. To add more users, you have to join a directory server, such as Windows Active Directory or IPA (https://www.freeipa.org/page/Main_Page).

We are also enabling both Gluster and the virtualization manager GUI. oVirt can also be used to manage Gluster bricks, which is all together a different topic; however, it is recommended that you enable it while installing.

```
Engine admin password:
Confirm engine admin password:
Application mode (Virt, Gluster, Both) [Both]:
```

```
--== PKI CONFIGURATION ==--
```

This is used to create the certificate:

```
Organization name for certificate [example.local]:
```

```
--== APACHE CONFIGURATION ==--
```

Do not use the oVirt engine server to run any other web application.

```
Setup can configure the default page of the web server to present the
application home page. This may conflict with existing applications.
Do you wish to set the application as the default page of the web server?
(Yes, No) [Yes]:
Setup can configure apache to use SSL using a certificate issued from the
internal CA.
Do you wish Setup to configure that, or prefer to perform that manually?
(Automatic, Manual) [Automatic]:
```

```
--== SYSTEM CONFIGURATION ==--
```

In our setup, we are using the engine server as the ISO domain. In production, always create that use a dedicated NFS server for the purpose. We do not want the NFS network traffic to flood the oVirt engine server.

```
Configure an NFS share on this server to be used as an ISO Domain? (Yes,
No) [Yes]:
Local ISO domain path [/var/lib/exports/iso]:
Local ISO domain ACL - note that the default will restrict access to
ovirt.example.local only, for security reasons [ovirt.example.local(rw)]:
Local ISO domain name [ISO_DOMAIN]:
--== CONFIGURATION PREVIEW ==--
```

This is the summary of your configuration. If everything is fine, go ahead and finish the setup. Otherwise, type `cancel` and run the engine setup again.

```
Application mode      : both
Firewall manager      : firewalld
Update Firewall       : True
Host FQDN : ovirt.example.local
Engine database name: engine
Engine database secured connection      : False
Engine database host: localhost
Engine database user name      : engine
Engine database host name validation      : False
Engine database port: 5432
Engine installation : True
NFS setup : True
PKI organization      : example.local
NFS mount point       : /var/lib/exports/iso
NFS export ACL        : ovirt.example.local(rw)
Configure local Engine database      : True
Set application as default page      : True
Configure Apache SSL: True
Configure WebSocket Proxy      : True
Engine Host FQDN      : ovirt.example.local


Please confirm installation settings (OK, Cancel) [OK]:
[ INFO  ] Stage: Transaction setup
[ INFO  ] Stopping engine service
[ INFO  ] Stopping ovirt-fence-kdump-listener service
[ INFO  ] Stopping websocket-proxy service
[ INFO  ] Stage: Misc configuration
[ INFO  ] Stage: Package installation
[ INFO  ] Stage: Misc configuration
[ INFO  ] Initializing PostgreSQL
[ INFO  ] Creating PostgreSQL 'engine' database
[ INFO  ] Configuring PostgreSQL
[ INFO  ] Creating/refreshing Engine database schema
[ INFO  ] Upgrading CA
[ INFO  ] Creating CA
[ INFO  ] Configuring WebSocket Proxy
[ INFO  ] Generating post install configuration file '/etc/ovirt-engine-
setup.conf.d/20-setup-ovirt-post.conf'
[ INFO  ] Stage: Transaction commit
```

```
[ INFO  ] Stage: Closing up
[ INFO  ] Restarting nfs services


--== SUMMARY ==--

SSH fingerprint: A0:F7:96:9F:31:92:8A:10:9E:DE:9A:31:61:74:5C:C4
Internal CA 82:47:1C:7F:C0:09:CE:82:78:62:08:4E:0E:DF:84:23:F1:0E:71:A4
Web access is enabled at:
    http://ovirt.example.local:80/ovirt-engine
    https://ovirt.example.local:443/ovirt-engine
Please use the user "admin" and password specified in order to login

--== END OF SUMMARY ==--
[ INFO  ] Execution of setup completed successfully
```

Installation has finished and you can now log in to the oVirt manager using the URL mentioned in the summary. For us it is `http://ovirt.example.local/ovirt-engine`.

When you open the URL you will be greeted with a web page shown in the following screenshot that shows links to three types of portals:

Let's discuss the fields shown in the screenshot:

- **User Portal**: Used by non-administrator users to manage their virtual machines. This user interface provides very limited functions that are confined to virtual machine management.

- **Administration Portal**: Used by an oVirt administrator to manage the oVirt environment. We are focusing on **Administrator Portal**.

- **Reports Portal**: Used to generate reports regarding the environment. The reports are not in real time.

Click on **Administration Portal** and log in as user admin.

 We will cover **Administration Portal** in detail in *Chapter 11, Starting Your First Virtual Machine in oVirt.*

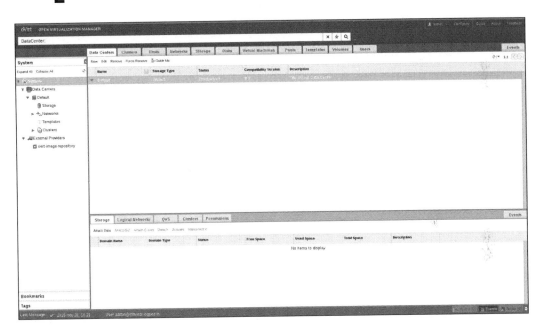

If something goes wrong, you can check the installation logs at `/var/log/ovirt-engine/setup/ovirt-engine-setup-XX.log`. When installing a production system it is a good idea to watch the logs in real time (`# tail ovirt-engine-setup-XX.log`) and monitor the progress of the installation. If you face some unrecoverable errors, then you need to start the installation again, by executing the following commands:

```
# engine-cleanup
# yum remove ovirt-engine
# yum install ovirt-engine
# engine-setup
```

Installing oVirt node

Perform the following steps to install an oVirt node:

1. Download the `ovirt-node-iso` rpm to oVirt Manager server.

   ```
   # wget http://resources.ovirt.org/pub/ovirt-3.5/rpm/el7/noarch/
   ovirt-node-iso-3.5-0.999.201504280931.el7.centos.noarch.rpm
   ```

   ```
   # yum localinstall ovirt-node-iso-3.5-0.999.201504280931.el7.
   centos.noarch.rpm
   ```

   ```
   # yum install livecd-tools
   ```

2. Locate the ISO file in `/usr/share/ovirt-node-iso/`:

   ```
   # livecd-iso-to-disk --format --reset-mbr /usr/share/ovirt-node-
   iso/ovirt-node-iso-3.5-0.999.201504280931.el7.centos.iso /dev/sdb
   ```

   `/dev/sdb` is the location of the USB disk.

   You can also initiate the installation from PXE as follows:

   ```
   # livecd-iso-to-pxeboot /usr/share/ovirt-node-iso/ovirt-node-
   iso-3.5-0.999.201504280931.el7.centos.iso
   ```

3. Use the automatically generated configuration file in your PXE server for PXE booting. Here, we are using the USB disk to boot and install the oVirt node.

4. Once booted, you will be greeted with the following screen. Select **Start Ovirt Node** to continue:

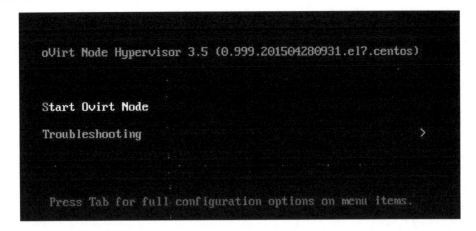

 Use the arrow keys to do the navigation and the *Tab* key to switch through the options.

5. Select **Install Hypervisor** and press *Enter*.

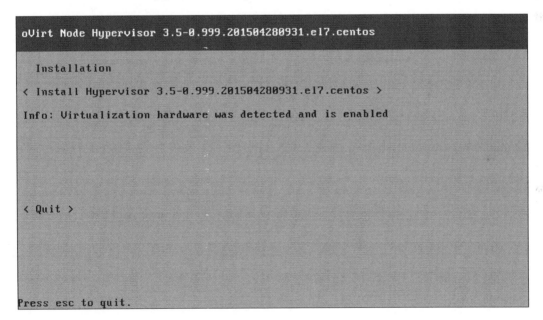

6. In the next screen, select the HDD to install the oVirt node.

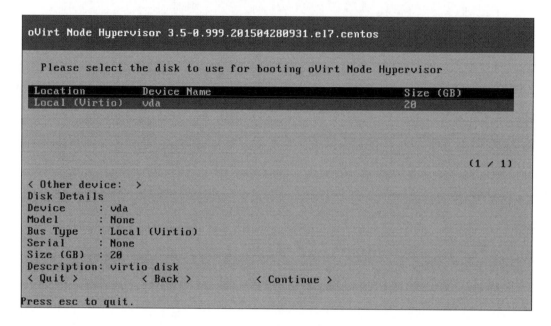

7. Use the default partitioning and continue.

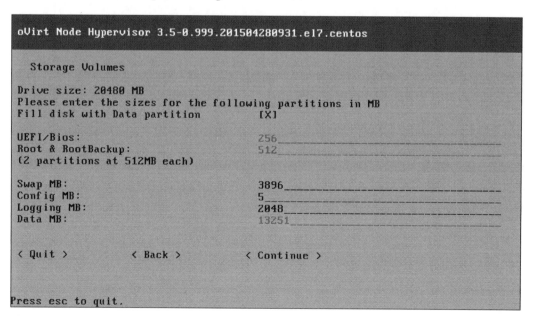

8. Confirm the details.

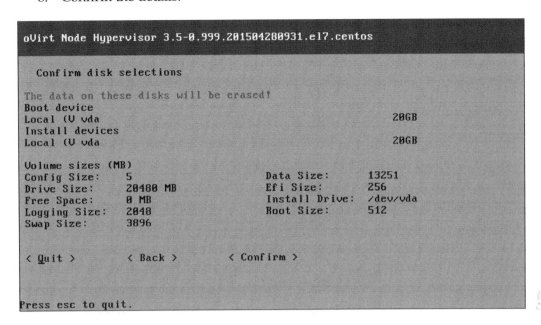

9. Set the password for the `admin` user and select **Install**.

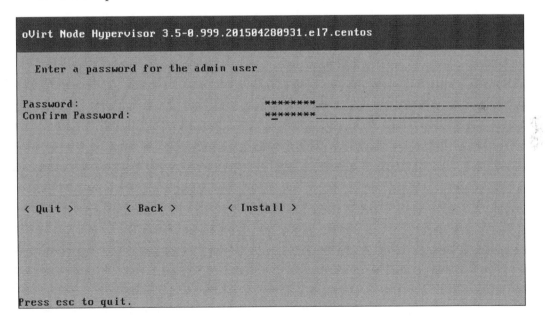

10. The installation will take few minutes to complete. Reboot.

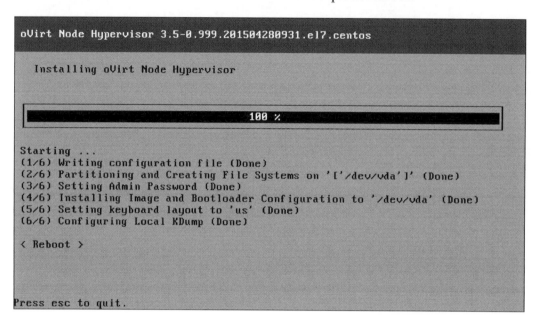

11. Once rebooted, log in as user `admin` and not `root`.

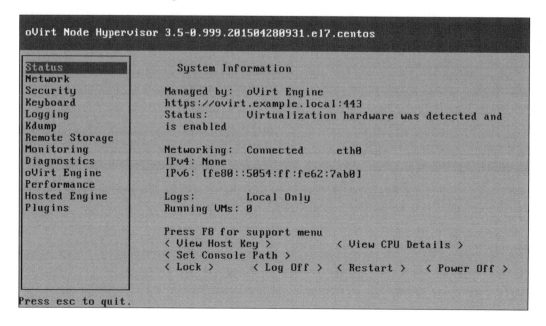

Summary

In this chapter, you got an introduction to oVirt, its architecture, and installation. In the next chapter, we will learn how to start your first virtual machine using oVirt.

11
Starting Your First Virtual Machine in oVirt

In *Chapter 10, Installing and Configuring the Virtual Datacenter Using oVirt*, you learned the architecture of oVirt and installed the oVirt engine and an oVirt node. In this chapter, you will learn how to initiate an oVirt data center in order to start your first virtual machine. This initialization process will walk you through the following topics:

- Creating a data center
- Adding a host to a data center
- Adding storage domains and its backend
- Configuring networking

Getting acquainted with oVirt data center and cluster

An oVirt data center is like a physical data center. It has multiple servers and various storage and network options. Every oVirt data center needs a cluster, a data storage domain, and a logical network named **ovirtmgmt**.

The purpose of an oVirt cluster is to group its hypervisor or oVirt nodes. A data center can have multiple clusters. In general, hypervisors in an oVirt cluster have same CPUs and the same network configurations. Another name for an oVirt cluster is migration domain, as you can only live migrate virtual machines within hypervisors in a cluster.

Every hypervisor in an oVirt data center should have access to the storage domain created for the data center. If you cannot give access for storage to any of the hypervisors, then you have to create a new data center and cluster for them.

Initiating an oVirt data center

Let's first create a data center by performing the following steps:

1. Go to the oVirt engine page and click on **Administration Portal**.

2. Once you are logged in as an admin user, you will be presented with a page as shown in *fig 8-3*. The installation procedure will automatically create a data center and a cluster named **Default**. In our exercise, we will not use the Default data center, instead we will create a new one named DevDC. Go to the **Data centers** tab and click on **new**.

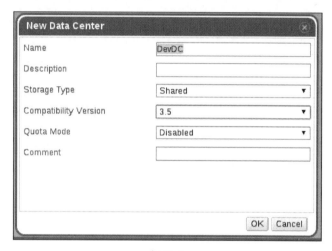

fig 11-1

Enter the name of the data center as DevDC. Storage type is **Shared**, as we are going to use a shared storage infrastructure. Compatibility version will remain **3.5** and Quota mode as **Disabled**. Quota is used to restrict the access of cluster resources, such as storage and network.

3. Click on **OK** to create the data center. Now, you will be presented with a screen that will give you an option to configure a cluster. Click on **configure cluster**.

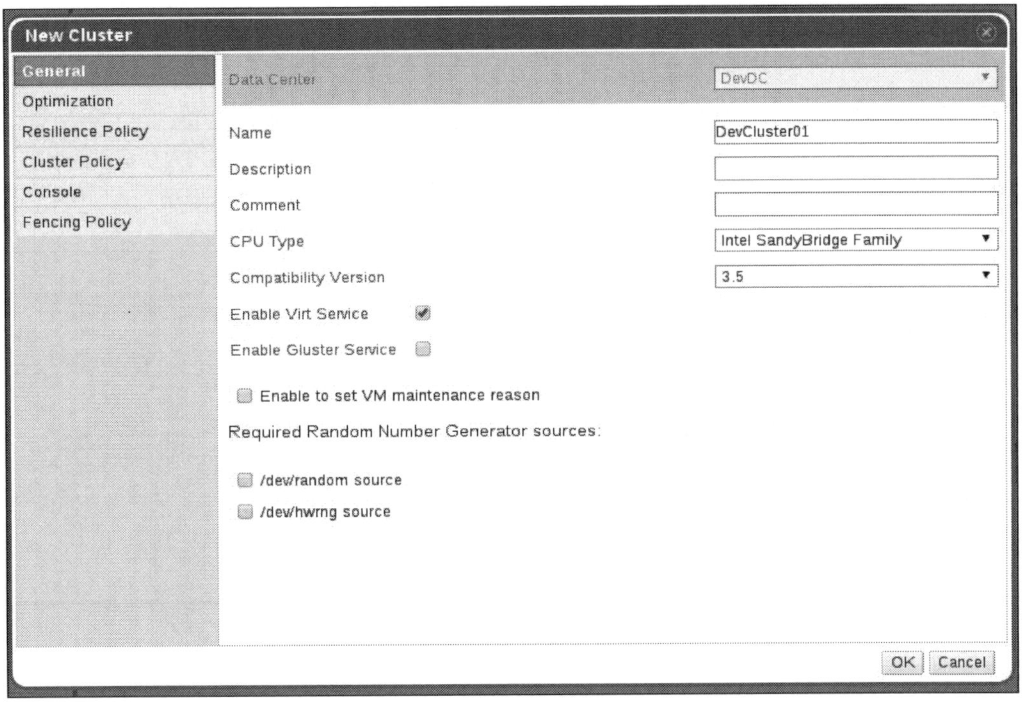

fig 11-2

Enter the name of the cluster as `DevCluster01` and select a CPU type based on your hypervisors, CPU type. We are leaving the other options as default. You can change these settings later, as required, by editing the cluster. Click on **OK** to create the cluster.

> The oVirt engine can be used to manage cluster nodes also, but here we are only using the oVirt service.

Now, you have created a data center named `DevDC` and a cluster under it named `DevCluster01`.

4. The next step is to add a hypervisor to the data center. Let's go back to the previously installed hypervisor in *Chapter 10, Installing and Configuring the Virtual Data Center Using oVirt* and configure networking.

5. On the hypervisor console, login as `admin` user and go to the **Network** tab (*fig 11-3*). Select the network interface you wish to configure and press *Enter*.

```
oVirt Node Hypervisor 3.5-0.999.201504280931.el7.centos

 Status                    System Identification
 Network
 Security            Hostname:                    localhost_____
 Keyboard
 Logging             DNS Server 1:                _____
 Kdump               DNS Server 2:                _____
 Remote Storage
 Monitoring          NTP Server 1:                0.centos.pool.ntp.org____
 Diagnostics         NTP Server 2:                1.centos.pool.ntp.org____
 oVirt Engine
 Performance         Available System NICs
 Hosted Engine       Device  Status     Model          MAC Address
 Plugins             eth0    Unconfigured Red Hat, Inc  52:54:00:62:7a:b0

                                                             (1 / 1)
                     < Ping >                  < Create Bond >

                     < Save >      < Reset >

Press esc to quit.
```

fig 11-3

This will take you to the next screen (*fig 11-4*), where you configure IPv4 or IPv6. In our example, we are only enabling IPv4.

6. Save to start the network configuration.

```
NIC Details: eth0
Driver:       virtio_net              Vendor:       Red Hat, Inc
Link Status: Connected                MAC Address: 52:54:00:62:7a:b0

IPv4 Settings
Bootprotocol:     ( ) Disabled     (X) DHCP            ( ) Static
IP Address:       _____    Netmask:         _____
Gateway:          _____

IPv6 Settings
Bootprotocol: (X) Disabled   ( ) Auto      ( ) DHCP      ( ) Static
IP Address:       _____  Prefix Length:       _____
Gateway:          _____

VLAN ID:          _____

< Flash Lights to Identify >

< Save >      < Close >
```

fig 11-4

7. Once the network configuration is done, go to security and enable SSH Login (*fig 11-5*). Save to start the SSH service.

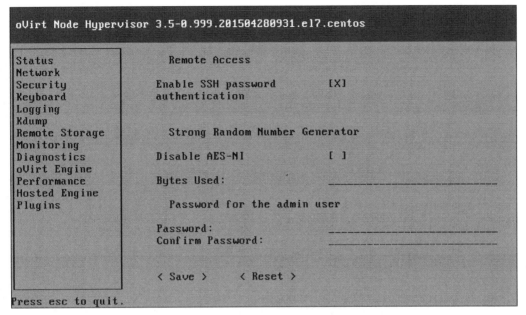

```
oVirt Node Hypervisor 3.5-0.999.201504280931.el7.centos

Status                    Remote Access
Network
Security        Enable SSH password          [X]
Keyboard        authentication
Logging
Kdump
Remote Storage      Strong Random Number Generator
Monitoring
Diagnostics     Disable AES-NI               [ ]
oVirt Engine
Performance     Bytes Used:                  _____
Hosted Engine
Plugins             Password for the admin user

                Password:                    _____
                Confirm Password:            _____


                < Save >        < Reset >

Press esc to quit.
```

fig 11-5

If you want to check the configuration manually, press the *F2* key. This will take you to the rescue shell with root access where you can issue commands to check the configuration. As direct root access is disabled, system admins usually SSH as admin user to an oVirt node and then press *F2* to get into the console to troubleshoot.

8. Now add this hypervisor to your data center DevDC by going to the **oVirt Engine** tab (*fig 11-6*) and add Management Server as the oVirt engine hostname. You can also enter the IP address of the oVirt engine server but using hostname is recommended. Now click on **Save & Register**. If you add a password, this will enable the SSH service on the oVirt node, which will help the administrator to initiate the hypervisor addition process from the oVirt engine. In this case, you do not need to add the management server details.

```
 oVirt Node Hypervisor 3.5-0.999.201504280931.el7.centos

┌──────────────────┐         oVirt Engine Configuration
│Status            │
│Network           │    Management Server:        ovirt.example.local_____
│Security          │    Management Server Port:   443_____
│Keyboard          │
│Logging           │
│Kdump             │    Certificate Status: N/A
│Remote Storage    │
│Monitoring        │    Optional password for adding Node through oVirt Engine
│Diagnostics       │    Note: Setting password will enable SSH daemon
│oVirt Engine      │    Password:             _____
│Performance       │    Confirm Password:     _____
│Hosted Engine     │
│Plugins           │
│                  │
│                  │        < Save & Register >
│                  │
│                  │
└──────────────────┘
 Press esc to quit.
```

fig 11-6

On successful completion you will see your host under the **Hosts** tab waiting for approval (*fig 11-7*).

9. Select the host and click on **Approve**.

10. You will be asked to configure power management, which is an optional step to enable fencing of Host, thus ensuring high availability of VMs. Leave it unconfigured for now. However, if you plan to use the host in a production environment, then configuring the power management is important. While approving the hypervisor, make sure that you have selected the right data center and cluster. You can change it later by going to **Edit** properties after putting the host into the **Maintenance** mode.

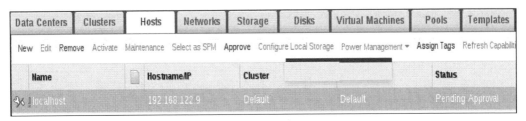

fig 11-7

During the approval process, the oVirt engine will configure the host's vdsm service so that it can have a secure connection over SSL with the vdsm service. The libvirt service will also be reconfigured. This process will also add and configure the *ovirtmgmt* logical network on the host, which is nothing but a bridge name, *ovirtmgmt*. Once approved, your host's status will change to **Up** (*fig 11-8*).

fig 11-8

The output of the `brctl show` command is captured from the `node01.example. local` host after the approval process. Here you can see that the `ovirtmgmt` bridge has been:

```
node01 # brctl show
bridge    name  bridge    id  STP enabled   interfaces
ovirtmgmt       8000.525400627ab0  no      eth0
```

In some cases, your host will not be activated due to the wrong CPU type selected for the cluster. To know the correct CPU type, after selecting the Host, go to the **Hardware Information** tab at the bottom of the admin portal and then modify the cluster's CPU type accordingly.

At this stage, you can install one more hypervisor and add it to your data center by following the steps laid out in the preceding section.

Creating storage domains

To create storage domains, we will use an ISCSI storage which is already configured. You can proceed with the following steps:

1. Go to the **Storage** tab and click on **New Domain**. You'll get a screen similar to the following screenshot:

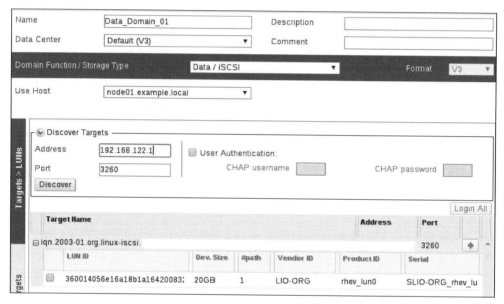

fig 11-9

2. Choose a **Name** for your storage domain, select **Storage Type** as **Data ISCSI**, expand **Discover Targets** to enter the target address, and click on **Discover**. The discover process will find the target.

3. Use **Login All** to get LUNs. Select the LUNs you want to use to create the data domain and click on **OK**.

    During the initiation process, the domain status will remain locked and then automatically change the status to UP. In this way, we can add an NFS data domain as well as an ISO Domain.

4. When you create an NFS share to use with the oVirt engine, make sure you change the owner and group ID of that directory to 36 before exporting it (`# chown 36:36 </NFS/export>`). The reason for this is that all operations initiated by vdsm service used `uid 36`. The following `id` command output will show the details of the user and the group used by `uid 36`:

```
node01 # id 36

uid=36(vdsm) gid=36(kvm) groups=36(kvm),179(sanlock),107(qemu)
```

Domain Name		Domain Type	Storage Type	Format	Cross Data Center Status	Total Space	Free Space
Data_Domain_01		Data	iSCSI	V3	Active	19 GB	15 GB
ISO_Domain		ISO	NFS	V1	Active	167 GB	104 GB
StorageOne		Data (Master)	NFS	V3	Active	49 GB	32 GB

fig 11-10

5. Now, you can go back to **Hosts** and check the status of the host. You can see that it has now become a **Storage Pool Manager (SPM)** host:

fig 11-11

The SPM host is responsible for all storage-related operations. For example, if you add a virtual disk, that operation will be initiated and carried out by the SPM host. No other host will do a write operation on the storage other than the SPM host.

If there is no SPM host, the data center will become unusable until a new host takes over the SPM role. This is one of the primary reasons why you configure power management for your hosts. When power management is configured, oVirt can automatically initiate a fence on the current SPM host when it becomes nonfunctional or not reachable from the oVirt engine server. Fencing the faulty SPM host will make sure that it is not doing any storage operations on the storage domains, thus avoiding data corruption. If no fencing is configured, you have to manually reboot the faulty SPM host and then right-click on the faulty SPM host and use the *confirm host has been rebooted* option to choose another host as the SPM.

We will now check what happened in the backend when you created your storage domains:

- If the shared storage is a block device (ISCSI, FC, and so on), oVirt will make use of the multipath to group the LUNs together and then create a logical volume group using the multipath device as the physical volume. *fig 11-12* shows the output of the `multipath -ll` command, where `3600**1c` is the multipath device created from the ISCSI LUN we added:

```
360014056e16a18b1a164200832935b1c dm-0 LIO-ORG,rhev_lun0
size=20G features='0' hwhandler='0' wp=rw
`-+- policy='round-robin 0' prio=1 status=active
  `- 2:0:0:0 sda 8:0    active ready running
```

fig 11-12

- In *fig 11-13*, you will see the output of the pvs command, which shows the details of the VG created on top of `3600**1c`. oVirt will generate a random UUID using uuidgen to create the VG name. Once created, the details will be added to its database:

```
PV                                            VG                                    Fmt  Attr PSize  PFree
/dev/mapper/360014056e16a18b1a164200832935b1c 4343e974-1359-4b86-bf1f-508dd436504b lvm2 a--  19.62g 15.75g
```

fig 11-13

- How will you know which UUID is used to create your data domain? In the case of VGs, the oVirt uses VG tags to store its metadata. To find your VG, use `vgs -o name,tags | grep <data_domain_name> --color`. In our case, the name of the data domain is `Data_Domain_01`:

```
4343e974-1359-4b86-bf1f-508dd436504b MDT_CLASS=Data,MDT_DESCRIPTION=Data_Domain_01,
```

fig 11-14

- A less nerdy method is to use the `vdsClient` command, which is used to interact with the vdsm service:

```
node01 # vdsClient -s 0 getStorageDomainInfo 4343e974-1359-4b86-bf1f-508dd436504b
        uuid = 4343e974-1359-4b86-bf1f-508dd436504b
        vguuid = dmQ82i-vLkh-q0jZ-jWxQ-tL2w-Au9e-vGawgu
        state = OK
        version = 3
        role = Regular
        type = ISCSI
        class = Data
        pool = ['00000002-0002-0002-0002-0000000001e9']
        name = Data_Domain_01
```

fig 11-15

 `vdsClient --help` will show the complete list of supported vdsm commands.

- oVirt also creates the following LVs for its storage operations (*fig 11-16*):

```
node01 # lvs -o name,vg_name
  LV                                    VG
  1efa67e7-d943-4806-8f28-05680dce584a  4343e974-1359-4b86-bf1f-508dd436504b
  58306bf8-418b-40a8-9522-a4d19de7f144  4343e974-1359-4b86-bf1f-508dd436504b
  ids                                   4343e974-1359-4b86-bf1f-508dd436504b
  inbox                                 4343e974-1359-4b86-bf1f-508dd436504b
  leases                                4343e974-1359-4b86-bf1f-508dd436504b
  master                                4343e974-1359-4b86-bf1f-508dd436504b
  metadata                              4343e974-1359-4b86-bf1f-508dd436504b
  outbox                                4343e974-1359-4b86-bf1f-508dd436504b
```

fig 11-16

In the case of file-based storage, instead of VGs and LVs, oVirt will be creating corresponding directories. Use the `mount` command on the oVirt node to find the NFS mount points used to mount the NFS shares and then issue the `tree /mount/point` command to see the storage domain structure.

Creating logical networks

As explained earlier, logical networks are nothing but the bridges configured on the oVirt nodes. They are created in order to segregate the traffic. For example, if you use the ovirtmgmt logical network for every purpose, including the VM traffic, which includes live migration traffic, display traffic, and so on, it can choke the bandwidth. Therefore, we create multiple logical networks using different NICs based on the VM traffic and purpose. To create a logical network, follow these steps:

1. Go to the **Network** tab and click on **New Logical Network**.

2. Select your **Data Center** and enter a name for the logical network. Here, it is `vmdata`.

3. Make sure that the **VM network** option is enabled and click on **OK**, otherwise it will create a non-bridge interface, which can only be used for VM live migration or to display network traffic.

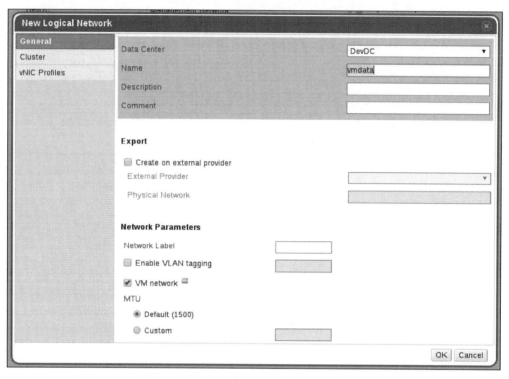

fig 11-17

Once the logical network is created, you have to apply that logical network to each host. If this step is not done, your host status will change from **UP** to **NON OPERATIONAL**. Non-operational status means that cluster resources (storage and network) are missing from the hosts.

To apply the newly created logical network: navigate to the **Hosts** tab, click on the host, (here, it is **node01**). Under host the **Network Interfaces** (fig 11-18), click **Setup Host Networks**.

fig 11-18

Drag and drop **vmdata** to a free interface and click on **OK** to save the configuration. In our case, the free interface is **eth1**.

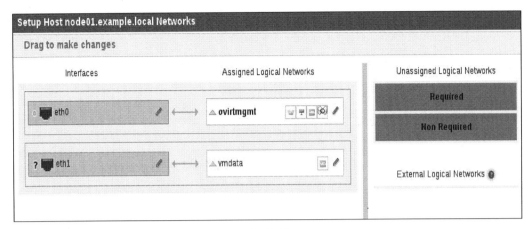

fig 11-19

Now let's check on `node01`. You can see a bridge named `vmdata` created and attached to `eth1`. Repeat the same procedure for other nodes.

```
node01 # brctl show
bridge   name bridge idSTP enabled interfaces ovirtmgmt 8000.525400627
ab0no eth0 vmdata                   8000.525400e5a57c   no      eth1
```

Creating and starting a virtual machine

Now we have all the infrastructure support (storage, network, and hosts) for creating a virtual machine. Before creating, we need to do one more task to upload an ISO image to the ISO storage domain. To upload, go to the RHEV Manager server and run the following set of commands.

- List the ISO Domains:

  ```
  # engine-iso-uploader list (enter the admin user password when
  prompted)
  ```

- Upload the ISO image `centos7.iso`:

  ```
  # engine-iso-uploader upload -i ISO_Domain centos7.iso (enter the
  admin user password when prompted)
  ```

Now, there is one more method where you copy the image directly to the NFS share. If you have exported the directory /isos/, then use the following steps to copy the ISO image:

- On the NFS Server, type the following command:

```
# cp /location/image.iso  /isos/*/
images/11111111-1111-1111-1111-111111111111
```

```
# chown 36.36 /isos/*/images/11111111-1111-1111-1111-111111111111/
image.iso
```

Let's create a virtual machine in oVirt now:

1. Go to **Virtual Machines | New VM** and select **Cluster** as **DevDC/DevCluster01**.

2. Choose the OS type and then add a **Name** for the VM. Press **OK** to continue.

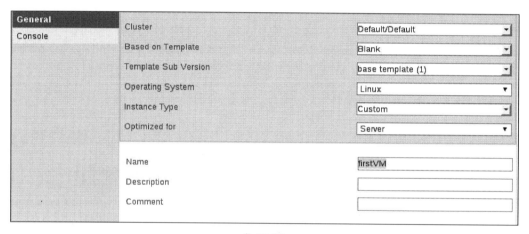

fig 11-20

3. In the next screen you will be asked to configure the virtual disk for the VM. Choose the size and storage domain you need to create the virtual disk. Click on **OK**.

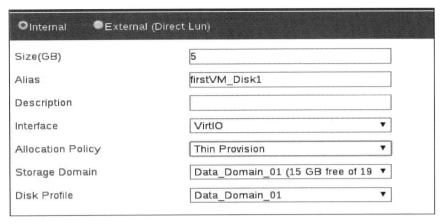

fig 11-21

Your virtual machine is now ready to start.

4. If you simply start the virtual machine, it does not have any OS to boot, so you need to attach the uploaded ISO image and then start the virtual machine. For this, select and right-click on the virtual machine you just created and choose the option **Run Once**.

5. Clicking on **Run Once** will open a window. In that window, check the **Attach CD** option, select the ISO you wish to use for booting, and click on **OK** (*fig 11-22*).

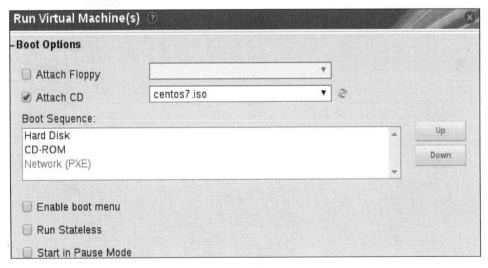

fig 11-22

VM will start now. In order to access the VM console, use the green TV icon at the top panel.

Once the installation is finished, you can stop the virtual machine and start it normally. When you start the virtual machine, the engine will send the details for starting a VM to the VDSM service. VDSM will then pass that to libvirt and libvirt will start the virtual machine. Here, the VDSM service is the bridge between the oVirt engine and libvirt:

```
node01 # virsh -r list
 Id     Name                              State
- - - - - - - - - - - - - - - - - - - - - - - - - - - - - - -
 1      firstVM                           running
```

fig 11-23

We will now check some of the common oVirt engine commands used:

- `engine-config`: This command is used for changing the default options of the oVirt engine. The changes will be written directly to the database. Since the database is modified, you have to restart the `ovirt-engine` service to apply newly set parameters. To get a list of configurable parameters, run `engine-config --list`. The command can then be used to reset the admin password as shown:

  ```
  # engine-config -s AdminPassword=interactive

  # systemctl restart ovirt-engine
  ```

- `engine-manage-domains`: This command is used to integrate oVirt with directory services.

- `engine-backup`: This command is used to backup and restore the oVirt engine. To backup, run the following command:

  ```
  # engine-backup --mode=backup --scope=all --file=backup.bz2
  --log=backup.log
  ```

  Restore is not as straightforward as the backup. It needs some additional configuration and changes. You can find those details at http://www.ovirt.org/develop/release-management/features/engine/engine-backup.

- `ovirt-shell`: This is an interesting tool. It can be used as a direct replacement for GUI. System administrators love this tool a lot, as it allows them to do a lot of automation work. To use `ovirt-shell`, install `ovirt-engine-cli`. It can be installed on any Fedora system and is independent of the oVirt engine server.

```
# yum install ovirt-engine-cli
```

Now, download the certificate file and save it in your home directory:

```
# wget http://ovirt.example.local/ca.crt
# ovirt-shell -l https://ovirt.example.local/api -u admin@internal -A
ca.crt
```

Once you are in the shell, try the following commands. Use the *Tab* key to navigate and find commands. Try the following commands:

```
[oVirt shell (connected)]# list vms
[oVirt shell (connected)]# show vm <VM_Name>
[oVirt shell (connected)]# action vm <VM_Name> start
```

What next?

oVirt has so many operations that it, in itself, needs a book to cover everything. Our intent was to get you started with oVirt with some details of the backend operations. oVirt supports quota, QOS, snapshot, templating, desktop pools, storage live migration, advanced network configurations including vlan and bonding, vdsm hooks, and so on. It also supports a powerful reporting tool and API support.

We recommend you visit the following websites to learn more on the topic:

- `http://www.ovirt.org/documentation/admin-guide/administration-guide/`
- `https://www.packtpub.com/virtualization-and-cloud/getting-started-ovirt-33`
- `https://www.packtpub.com/virtualization-and-cloud/getting-started-red-hat-enterprise-virtualization`
- `http://www.ovirt.org/develop/api/rest-api/rest-api/`
- `http://www.ovirt.org/documentation/how-to/reports/reports/`

Summary

In this chapter, you learned about creating your first virtual machine using oVirt. During the process you have learned to configure a data center, cluster, storage domain, and logical network. You also learned about some common commands used by oVirt engine.

In the next chapter, you will learn about the OpenStack platform, which is used to create public and private cloud environments.

12
Deploying OpenStack Private Cloud backed by KVM Virtualization

OpenStack is and has been one of the hottest projects in cloud computing for 5 years running. OpenStack provides an open source software platform for creating and managing public and private **Infrastructure As A Service** for new scale out-based workload. There are various independent components/projects in OpenStack that work together to build highly scalable cloud infrastructures.

OpenStack Compute (Nova) is one of the core components of OpenStack and provides computing power to run cloud workloads. Nova itself is not virtualization software but it is a framework that supports multiple hypervisors including those from VMware, Citrix, and Microsoft, to name a few. To date, however, OpenStack's strength lies in KVM. Various surveys (such as OpenStack Superuser [1]) clearly show that the majority of OpenStack deployments, at nearly 90 percent, are based on KVM and this book's aim is to touch on all the aspects of KVM virtualization and its usage.We have included this short chapter covering how KVM powers OpenStack Cloud, along with brief information on how to debug the virtualization layer of OpenStack and best practices for building and managing the OpenStack environment.

[1]:`http://superuser.OpenStack.org/articles/OpenStack-users-share-how-their-deployments-stack-up`

OpenStack architecture

Let us begin with understanding the OpenStack architecture. At first glance, the OpenStack architecture looks complex because of its modular design. OpenStack is not a single piece of software, it is an umbrella over multiple independent projects (components), each managing a dedicated resource of the infrastructure independently while working together with each other. The following screenshot shows the core components in the OpenStack Kilo version, a collection of interacting components that control compute, storage, and networking resources.

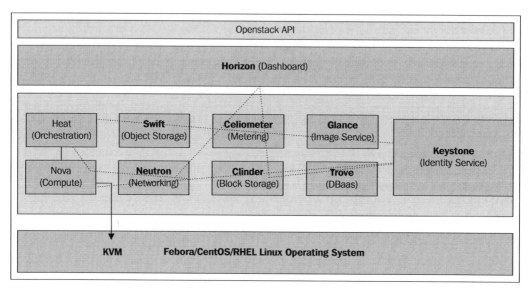

Overview of OpenStack

Administrators use a Web-based interface to control, provision, and automate OpenStack resources. Additionally, programmatic access to the OpenStack infrastructure is facilitated through an extensive REST API, which enables a rich set of add-on capabilities.

Core OpenStack components

The preceding screenshot shows the core components of OpenStack and how they work together. Each component has a well-defined API, except for Horizon, the Web GUI.

For internal communication within each component, OpenStack uses **Advanced Message Queuing Protocol (AMQP)**. AMQP is a Protocol for enterprise messaging. The official specification of AMQP is available here: `http://www.amqp.org/`. Each OpenStack component requires a separate database. The database can be MySQL, MariaDB, or PostgreSQL; the default is MariaDB. The following is a brief introduction to each component.

- Compute service (Nova): Provisions and manages virtual machines, creating a redundant and horizontally scalable cloud computing platform. It is both hardware- and hypervisor-agnostic and has a distributed and asynchronous architecture that provides high availability and tenant-based isolation.

- Block storage (Cinder): Provides persistent block storage for virtual machine instances. The ephemeral storage of deployed instances is non-persistent, hence any data generated by the instance is destroyed once the instance is terminated. Cinder uses persistent volumes that are attached to instances for data longevity, and it is possible for instances to boot from a Cinder volume rather than from a local image.

- Virtual network (Neutron): OpenStack virtual networking is a pluggable "networking as a service" framework for managing networks and IP addresses. This framework supports several flexible network models, including **Dynamic Host Configuration Protocol (DHCP)** and VLAN.

- Image management (Glance): Provides discovery, registration, and delivery services for virtual disk images. The images can be stored on multiple back-end storage units and are cached locally to reduce image staging time

- Authentication (Keystone): Provides a central and unified authorization mechanism for all OpenStack users and services across all projects. It supports integration with existing authentication services such as **Lightweight Directory Access Protocol (LDAP)**.

- Telemetry (Ceilometer): Provides the infrastructure to collect measurements within OpenStack. Delivers a unique point of contact for billing systems to acquire all of the measurements needed to establish customer billing across all current OpenStack core components. An administrator can configure the type of data collected to meet operating requirements.

- Dashboard (Horizon): An extensible, web-based application that runs as a Hypertext Transfer Protocol (HTTP) service, enabling cloud administrators and users to control and provision compute, storage, and networking resources.

- Object Storage (Swift): Cloud storage software that is built for scale and optimized for durability, availability, and concurrency across the entire data set. It can store and retrieve lots of data with a simple API, and is ideal for storing unstructured data that can grow without bounds. (Ceph is used in this reference architecture, instead of Swift, to provide object storage service.)

- Orchestration (Heat): An orchestration engine to launch multiple composite cloud applications based on templates in the form of text files. It is able to launch other existing templates such as AWS CloudFormation.

The previous components are core components of OpenStack. Many optional components (more commonly known as OpenStack projects) are also available. A list of OpenStack components is available here: `https://www.OpenStack.org/software/project-navigator`.

We encourage you to browse OpenStack Project Navigator to learn more about the various projects.

OpenStack deployment

OpenStack in on the same path as Linux. In the Linux world, there are many Linux distributions to choose from. Similarly there are now many OpenStack distributions; some are community supported and freely available while most are commercial. Head to the OpenStack Marketplace, `https://www.OpenStack.org/marketplace/distros/`, for a list of all the tested OpenStack distributions. In this chapter, we will be using the RDO OpenStack distribution.

RDO OpenStack

This freely-available, community-supported distribution of OpenStack runs on Red Hat Enterprise Linux, CentOS, Fedora, and their derivatives. RDO is easy to install, contains the latest OpenStack bits and is supported by a large community that is always there when you need help. RDO is facilitated by Red Hat and available at `https://www.rdoproject.org/` for download and use.

RDO OpenStack deployments methods

Deploying RDO OpenStack requires you to install all of the services that are part of the distribution. There are three ways to install and configure RDO OpenStack:

- Install and configure each service manually. This requires a lot of time and effort from an administrative point of view. Details of how each OpenStack service can be installed and configured manually are provided in the following documentation: `http://docs.OpenStack.org/kilo/install-guide/install/yum/content/`.

- Use **RDO-Manager**: RDO-Manager is an OpenStack deployment and management tool for RDO. It is based on the OpenStack TripleO project and its philosophy is inspired by the SpinalStack project. More information about this deployment method is available here: `https://www.rdoproject.org/rdo-manager/`.

- Use **Packstack** to install and configure RDO: Packstack can be run interactively by prompting users for required details to install each service, you can perform an all-in-one installation, or it can read the required details from an "answer file" configured up-front, by using a command such as `packstack --gen-answer-file=GEN_ANSWER_FILE`.

Installing Packstack

Packstack installation is a quick and easy process. RDO OpenStack deployment using Packstack is broken down into three simple steps and it takes around 20 minutes to complete the installation.

Prerequisites

- **Software**: Fedora 21 and later 64-bit or any other RHEL-based Linux distributions such as CentOS and Scientific Linux.

- **Hardware**: A machine with at least 4 GB RAM, multi-processors with hardware virtualization extensions, and at least one network adapter.

- **Other requirements**:
  - ○ The system must have Internet connectivity or access to locally created RDO package repositories.
  - ○ The Network Manager service must be disabled on the system as OpenStack networking currently does not properly work on any system that has the Network Manager service enabled. To disable Network Manager, run the following code:

    ```
    #systemctl stop NetworkManager.Service
    #systemctl disable NetworkManager.Service
    ```

  - ○ The time on the system must be synchronized with a time server.

Installing the Packstack installer

Install the required packages for the Packstack installation. To do this, start by configuring the RDO software repository on the system by running the following command:

```
#rpm -ivh https://repos.fedorapeople.org/repos/OpenStack/OpenStack-kilo/
rdo-release-kilo-1.noarch.rpm
```

Next, run the following command:

```
#yum install -y OpenStack-packstack
```

Several other packages will be installed as well as the Packstack software.

Running Packstack to install OpenStack

Once the required packages have been installed, the OpenStack deployment can begin.

To do this, run the following command:

```
#packstack --allinone
```

The installation will take about 15-20 minutes to complete and it will install and automatically configure all the core OpenStack services on your system. Once the process is complete, it will summarize the installation as follows:

```
**** Installation completed successfully ******
Additional information:
 * A new answer file was created in: /root/packstack-
answers-20151207-132535.txt
```

```
 * File /root/keystonerc_admin has been created on OpenStack client host
192.168.1.10. To use the command line tools you need to source the file.

 * To access the OpenStack Dashboard browse to http://192.168.1.10/
dashboard .

Please, find your login credentials stored in the keystonerc_admin in
your home directory.

 * To use Nagios, browse to http://192.168.1.10/nagios username:
nagiosadmin, password: e32fe7ed5fa54d6d

 * The installation log file is available at: /var/tmp/
packstack/20151207-132534-8roLyQ/OpenStack-setup.log

 * The generated manifests are available at: /var/tmp/packstack/20151207-
132534-8roLyQ/manifests
```

Now you can log in to the OpenStack web interface "Horizon" by going to
`http://$YOURIP/dashboard`. The username is `admin`. The password can be
found in the `keystonerc_admin` file in the `/root/` directory.

Launching First Instance

The OpenStack dashboard is really easy to use. Log in to the dashboard, then switch
to the **Instances** page using the switcher on the left-hand pane. The Instances page
displays all running instances and there is a **Launch Instance** button on the top
toolbar. Clicking on **Launch Instance** will bring up the **Launch Instance** dialog.
Input an instance name, select the flavor, boot source, and network, then select
Launch, and it will create the instance, which you can access over a VNC connection.

An instance can also be launched from the command line. The following is the
typical procedure to launch the instance:

1. First make sure all OpenStack services are running properly by executing
    the `#OpenStack-status` command. This command shows an overview
    of installed OpenStack services and basic information managed by
    those services.

2. After verifying all the services are running properly, source the
    `keystonerc_admin` file present at the `/root/` directory. This file contains
    the keystone API endpoint and credentials. This is the entry point from
    which to access OpenStack. When you source this file, the OpenStack access
    details are exported in the environment and made available to various
    OpenStack client utilities on the cloud:

    ```
    #source keystonerc_admin
    ```

3. Before launching an instance, we need an operating system image in the image repository: Glance project. Packstack deployment downloads and adds the CirrOS image in the repository by default. CirrOS is a tiny Linux operating system specially meant for OpenStack testing.

   `#glance image-list` will list the images currently available in the Glance repository.

```
[root@dhcp210-192 ~(keystone_admin)]# openstack image list
+--------------------------------------+--------+
| ID                                   | Name   |
+--------------------------------------+--------+
| a106fe87-0201-4d6d-aca3-85bc42b20de7 | cirros |
```

To import any other pre-made images, use the `glance create-image` command. Fedora cloud images are available here to download and they can be used with OpenStack: `https://getfedora.org/cloud/download/`.

Example: Uploading the Fedora22 image

In the following example, I downloaded the Fedora image locally on my OpenStack AIO system and uploaded it to the Glance image repository by running the following command:

```
#glance image-create --name "Fedora22" --container-format --disk-format
qcow2 --file Fedora-Cloud-Base-22.x86_64.qcow2
```

The output of the previous command is as follows:

```
[root@openstack ~(keystone_admin)]# glance image-list
+--------------------------------------+----------+
| ID                                   | Name     |
+--------------------------------------+----------+
| a106fe87-0201-4d6d-aca3-85bc42b20de7 | cirros   |
| 78a959eb-7d2e-4eb3-90fd-9234a33fd09a | Fedora22 |
+--------------------------------------+----------+
```

Now we check the available flavor. Flavors are virtual hardware templates in OpenStack, defining the memory size, disk, vCPUs, and so on. To list the available flavors, run the #nova flavor-list command. The output of the command is as follows:

```
[root@openstack ~(keystone_admin)]# nova flavor-list
+----+-----------+-----------+------+-----------+------+-------+-------------+-----------+
| ID | Name      | Memory_MB | Disk | Ephemeral | Swap | VCPUs | RXTX_Factor | Is_Public |
+----+-----------+-----------+------+-----------+------+-------+-------------+-----------+
| 1  | m1.tiny   | 512       | 1    | 0         |      | 1     | 1.0         | True      |
| 2  | m1.small  | 2048      | 20   | 0         |      | 1     | 1.0         | True      |
| 3  | m1.medium | 4096      | 40   | 0         |      | 2     | 1.0         | True      |
| 4  | m1.large  | 8192      | 80   | 0         |      | 4     | 1.0         | True      |
| 5  | m1.xlarge | 16384     | 160  | 0         |      | 8     | 1.0         | True      |
+----+-----------+-----------+------+-----------+------+-------+-------------+-----------+
```

There are two other things that are needed to launch an instance: **keypairs** and **security groups**.

Keypairs are used for a password-less login to the instance created on OpenStack. Each keypair has two parts: the **public key** and the **private key**. The public key is what is injected into instances. The private key is what you save in a .pem file on your local machine. You use your private key to SSH into your instance.

1. Run the following command to create a new keypair:

   #nova keypair-add key-NAME

2. Once the keypair has been created, it will output PRIVATE KEY on the console. Copy it and store it somewhere with the .pem extension.

   #nova keypair-list will list the keys present in your tenant.

```
[root@openstack ~(keystone_admin)]# nova keypair-list
+------+-------------------------------------------------+
| Name | Fingerprint                                     |
+------+-------------------------------------------------+
| Tom  | 13:2f:c5:fa:ba:29:50:5d:04:18:92:a1:5a:9a:db:e5 |
| John | 12:13:7f:a0:3d:88:d6:fa:d1:7c:4d:00:17:0c:45:b4 |
+------+-------------------------------------------------+
```

3. Security groups are sets of IP filter rules that are attached to an instance's networking. They are used to filter packets even before they reach the instance. They are the gatekeeper for your instances. From the command line, you can get a list of security groups for the project you're acting by using the nova command:

```
root@openstack ~(keystone_admin)]# nova secgroup-list
+--------------------------------------+---------+------------------------+
| Id                                   | Name    | Description            |
+--------------------------------------+---------+------------------------+
| 6ca34486-a20b-4da9-8123-185b95d0e5fb | default | Default security group |
+--------------------------------------+---------+------------------------+
```

○ To create a new security group, use the nova secgroup-create command as shown next:

```
[root@openstack ~(keystone_admin)]# nova secgroup-create global_web "allow web traffic from the Internet"
+--------------------------------------+------------+--------------------------------------+
| Id                                   | Name       | Description                          |
+--------------------------------------+------------+--------------------------------------+
| c8c63605-7452-42bf-b2be-3630b81adcba | global_web | allow web traffic from the Internet  |
+--------------------------------------+------------+--------------------------------------+
```

○ This creates the empty security group. To add IP filter rules, use the following syntax:

```
#nova secgroup-add-rule <secgroup> <ip-proto> <from-port>
<to-port> <cidr>
```

```
[root@openstack ~(keystone_admin)]# nova secgroup-add-rule global_web tcp 80 80 0.0.0.0/0
+-------------+-----------+---------+-----------+--------------+
| IP Protocol | From Port | To Port | IP Range  | Source Group |
+-------------+-----------+---------+-----------+--------------+
| tcp         | 80        | 80      | 0.0.0.0/0 |              |
+-------------+-----------+---------+-----------+--------------+
```

○ To list all the IP filter rules in a security group, run the following syntax as shown in the screenshot:

```
[root@dhcp210-192 ~(keystone_admin)]# nova secgroup-list-rules global_web
+-------------+-----------+---------+-----------+--------------+
| IP Protocol | From Port | To Port | IP Range  | Source Group |
+-------------+-----------+---------+-----------+--------------+
| tcp         | 80        | 80      | 0.0.0.0/0 |              |
| tcp         | 8080      | 8080    | 0.0.0.0/0 |              |
+-------------+-----------+---------+-----------+--------------+
```

- ○ Check what networks are available for instances. `#neutron net-list` lists the logical network defined. To create a new logical network, use `#neutron net-create`:

```
+--------------------------------------+---------+------------------------------------------------------+
| id                                   | name    | subnets                                               |
+--------------------------------------+---------+------------------------------------------------------+
| ef405cc4-dc2a-453e-9df2-e28be91eebe4 | public  | 91be090d-c0d7-423e-8202-0fb29e228b51 172.24.4.224/28 |
| 90905851-38c7-41d4-a331-515c725075ec | private | 63ca5500-0d05-4286-bb7e-d5ab82a499a8 10.0.0.0/24     |
+--------------------------------------+---------+------------------------------------------------------+
```

4. Now you can spawn an instance. Have the following details handy before you fire the command that will spawn an instance:

    - ○ Instance name
    - ○ Glance image name
    - ○ Flavor name
    - ○ Network ID
    - ○ Security Group name

5. Boot an instance:

```
root@(keystone_admin)]# nova boot --flavor=m1.tiny --image
Fedora22 --nic net-id=90905851-38c7-41d4-a331-515c725075ec
--security-groups default --key-name john FirstInstance
```

This will create an instance named `FirstInstance` using the `Fedora22` image, connected to the private logical network with virtual hardware configuration defined in `m1.tiny` flavor and the public key injected for password-less login.

6. You can access it using the IP address assigned it from your logical network. To discover the IP address of the instance, run the following:

```
(keystone_admin)]# nova show FirstInstance | grep -i network
| private network                      | 10.0.0.3
```

Troubleshooting the virtualization layer of OpenStack

KVM is the de facto hypervisor choice for OpenStack compute as service. There are plenty of native KVM debugging mechanisms that you can use for troubleshooting issues that occur while launching an instance on your OpenStack environment. Alternatively, if something unusual suddenly happened with a critical instance, libvirt and QEMU provide a rich set of debugging controls that allow us to query (or modify) the state of virtual machines in distress.

The following log files play a very important role in troubleshooting compute layer issues. Please note these files are on the nova compute hosts nodes:

/var/log/nova/nova-api.log

/var/log/nova/nova-compute.log

/etc/libvirt/qemu/*.xml

/var/lib/nova/instances/*

/var/lib/libvirt/qemu/

/var/lib/libvirt/qemu/ is the directory where QEMU creates a log file for each instance or VM that was started on the node. If there is an I/O problem faced by the instance, or storage performance is degraded, QEMU quickly detects that and records this in the <vm_name>.log file. Here, <vm_name> is the libvirt vm that gets created in the background when you run an instance. You can correlate the instance name and vm name using the UUID:

```
# nova list --minimal

+----------------------------------------+----------------+
| ID                                     | Name           |
+----------------------------------------+----------------+
| 442db95c-4a01-40e1-8560-a6ab2d6c5908   | FirstInstance  |
| 6a5b77ac-f57d-45e7-ae99-a56469e9eddd   | SeccondInstance|
+----------------------------------------+----------------+
```

Here, on this host, two instances are running named FirstInstance and SecondInstance. If you run virsh list or grep kvm in the ps aux command, you will see two virtual machines with different names:

```
[root@dhcp210-192 ~(keystone_admin)]# virsh list

 Id   Name                       State
----------------------------------------------
 2    instance-00000002          running
 3    instance-00000003          running
```

To match the running VMs with the nova ID names, run the following command:

```
[root@dhcp210-192 ~(keystone_admin)]# virsh list --uuid
442db95c-4a01-40e1-8560-a6ab2d6c5908
6a5b77ac-f57d-45e7-ae99-a56469e9eddd
```

Match the UUID displayed in the virsh command output with the ID of the nova instance.

Accessing the instance configuration database

All the instance configurations are stored in the nova database. Sometimes accessing the database gives good information for troubleshooting purposes. For example, Instance creation fails with an error. Identifying on which compute-node the particular instance was scheduled to run will give us a starting point for troubleshooting. The instance table in the nova database holds all the information, including the host details. To access the nova database, follow the following steps:

1. SSH into the your OpenStack AIO system and run the `mysql` command to get into the database:

```
# mysql
Welcome to the MariaDB monitor.  Commands end with ; or \g.
Your MariaDB connection id is 559251
Server version: 5.5.42-MariaDB-wsrep MariaDB Server, wsrep_25.11.
r4026
        Copyright (c) 2000, 2015, Oracle, MariaDB Corporation Ab and
others.
        Type 'help;' or '\h' for help. Type '\c' to clear the
current input statement.
        MariaDB [(none)]>
```

2. At the MariaDB prompt, you can use the SHOW DATABASES command to list all the databases configured on the system. See the following output:

```
MariaDB [(none)]> SHOW DATABASES;
+--------------------+
| Database           |
+--------------------+
| information_schema |
| cinder             |
| glance             |
| keystone           |
| mysql              |
| neutron            |
| nova               |
| performance_schema |
| test               |
+--------------------+
9 rows in set (0.00 sec)
```

3. To connect a database, execute the USE MySQL query followed by the database name, as shown next. Here, we are connecting to the nova database:

```
MariaDB [(none)]> USE NOVA

Reading table information for completion of table and column names
You can turn off this feature to get a quicker startup with -A
        Database changed
```

4. The SHOW TABLES query displays all the tables present in the database.

5. A table named instance in the nova database holds all the configuration-related information about the instances. You can query this table to fetch required diagnostic information.

The following example will return all the records from the instance table for which instance status is stopped.

```
MariaDB [nova]> SELECT display_name,host,vcpus,memory_mb FROM instances WHERE vm_state='stopped';
+--------------+--------------+-------+-----------+
| display_name | host         | vcpus | memory_mb |
+--------------+--------------+-------+-----------+
| instance033  | compute-node1 |    1 |       512 |
| instance033  | compute-node1 |    1 |       512 |
+--------------+--------------+-------+-----------+
2 rows in set (0.00 sec)
```

Similarly you can query the VMs that are in the error state: just change vm_state to error. You can make use of the SQL query language and collect all the required information from the database for an issue investigation.

QEMU Monitor Protocol

QEMU Monitor Protocol (QMP) is a JSON-based protocol that allows applications to communicate with a QEMU instance. The qemu-monitor-command provided by the virsh shell allows users to interact with the QEMU monitor from the command line.

To enumerate all available QMP commands for a particular virtual machine, run the following:

```
#virsh qemu-monitor-command

<vm_name> --pretty '{"execute":"query-commands"}'
```

There are many query commands that can expose a lot of internal information that is not exposed to OpenStack and is vital for effective root cause analysis. For example, `query-block` returns detailed information about block devices being used by the virtual machine.

```
#virsh qemu-monitor-command instance-00000002 --pretty
'{"execute":"query-block"}
{
    "return": [
        {
            "io-status": "ok",
            "device": "drive-virtio-disk0",
            "locked": false,
            "removable": false,
            "inserted": {
                "iops_rd": 0,
                "image": {
                    "backing-image": {
                        "virtual-size": 41126400,
                        "filename": "/var/lib/nova/instances/_base/
d5068b90842c6b574b2e5319279d970447627085",
                        "format": "raw",
                        "actual-size": 18173952
                    },
                    "virtual-size": 1073741824,
                    "filename": "/var/lib/nova/instances/442db95c-4a01-
40e1-8560-a6ab2d6c5908/disk",
                    "cluster-size": 65536,
                    "format": "qcow2",
                    "actual-size": 1904640,
                    "format-specific": {
                        "type": "qcow2",
                        "data": {
```

```
                "compat": "1.1",
                "lazy-refcounts": false
            }
        },
        "backing-filename": "/var/lib/nova/instances/_base/
d5068b90842c6b574b2e5319279d970447627085",
        "dirty-flag": false
    },
    "iops_wr": 0,
    "ro": false,
    "backing_file_depth": 1,
    "drv": "qcow2",
    "iops": 0,
    "bps_wr": 0,
    "backing_file": "/var/lib/nova/instances/_base/
d5068b90842c6b574b2e5319279d970447627085",
    "encrypted": false,
    "bps": 0,
    "bps_rd": 0,
    "file": "/var/lib/nova/instances/442db95c-4a01-40e1-8560-
a6ab2d6c5908/disk",
    "encryption_key_missing": false
    },
    "type": "unknown"
}
```

libvirt debug logs:

libvirt plays very a important role in the OpenStack nova component: it handles all management and interaction with QEMU. The default logging level set for libvirt is a warning message only; enabling more verbose logging helps in tracing orchestration-level issues more efficiently. To enable debug logging for the libvirt daemon, perform the following steps:

1. Uncomment the `log_level` option and set the option that you would like to use:

   ```
   0 - None
   1 - debug
   2 - Information
   3 - Warnings
   4 - Errors
   ```

2. The following is an example:

```
# vi /etc/libvirt/libvirtd.conf
  log_level = 1


# vi /etc/libvirt/libvirtd.conf
  log_outputs="1:file:/var/log/libvirt/libvirtd.log"
```

3. Restart libvirt daemon:

```
#systemctl restart libvirtd.service
```

Collecting vmcore from instances

When you need to investigate and debug complex guest performance problems, such as the guest going unresponsive, the instance's memory state can be dumped into a file and analyzed to get a detailed insight into what exactly is happening with the instance.

The `virsh dump` command is used to collect a vmcore from a virtual machine from the hypervisor.

The command's syntax is as follows:

```
virsh dump <domain> /target/save/path/<virtual_machine>.vmcore <opts>
```

The options are as follows:

- `---bypass-cache`: Will not collect the file system cache.
- `--live`: The domain continues to run until the core dump is complete, rather than immediately pausing.
- `--crash`: The domain is halted with a crashed status, rather than left in a paused state.
- `--reset`: The domain is reset after a successful dump.
- `--verbose`: Increases the verbosity of the command output.
- `--memory-only`: The file is an elf file, and will only include domain memory and CPU common register values. It is very useful if the domain uses host devices directly.

Summary

In this chapter, you learned a very high level overview of OpenStack, how to deploy RDO OpenStack, and how to use various KVM debugging mechanisms to troubleshoot issues that may occur at the OpenStack compute layer. For further information on OpenStack, refer to *OpenStack Essentials* and *Mastering OpenStack* by *Packt Publishing*.

The next chapter covers debugging and performance-tuning in detail.

13
Performance Tuning and Best Practices in KVM

In this chapter, we will see how performance tuning can be done on a KVM setup. We will also discuss the best practices that can be applied in a KVM setup to improve performance. We have included steps to tune different components such as CPUs, memory, networking, blocks and time keeping.

Performance tuning is a trial-and-error process. Virtual machines host different type of applications and hence the type of tuning required varies with virtual machines. In most cases default configuration is enough to get a decent performance. Before performance tuning we should understand all the components involved, the options available and the subsystems. Then we can start implementing the options, gather the results, and finally come to a conclusion. It is not possible to grab and fix in the performance world. It has to be done by a trial-and-error method. Either your setup is bare-metal or virtualized. One common way to improve performance is to run the software on a supported hardware configuration and always make sure the minimal/recommended configuration is met to run the environment. If these prerequisites are not met, it can affect the performance a lot. One other way is to allocate the required resources instead of wasting lots of them. There should be proper planning, because the environments may scale in future.

Before diving into the virtualization or performance-tuning of VMs, I would like to recall or reiterate the KVM fundamentals. As we discussed in earlier chapters, guest systems or VMs are simple Linux processes in the host system. vCPUs are Linux POSIX threads. So obviously, the scheduling subsystem of Linux or the Linux scheduler will take care of these threads/processes. Don't get confused about the term "threads"; threads are lightweight processes in Linux. As discussed in *Chapter 2, KVM Internals* Linux Kernel features are by default inherited by KVM; thus NUMA, memory support such as *hugepages* are available for KVM, because in short, KVM turns Linux systems into a hypervisor.

This chapter gives some insights into best practices and performance-tuning options available with KVM. Well, as everyone says, *Performance tuning is an art*. There is no tool that maximizes performance gain in all scenarios; because environments differ, performance has to be tuned accordingly.

The earlier chapters talked about paravirtualized drivers available with KVM. Para-virtualized drivers are designed for improving performance in virtualization. When we talk about KVM, the paravirtualization drivers are virtio drivers. Virtio drivers are not limited to KVM hypervisors though. We will start with virtio drivers and then will dive into different subsystem tuning and best practices.

We will cover the following topics:

- CPU and memory tuning
- Understanding NUMA, CPU, and memory tuning with NUMA
- Disk and block I/O tuning
- Network tuning
- KVM best practices

VirtIO

In the virtualization world, a comparison is always made with bare-metal systems. Paravirtualized drivers enhance the performance of guests and try to retain near-bare-metal performance. It is recommended to use paravirtualized drivers for fully virtualized guests, especially when the guest is running with I/O-heavy tasks and applications. Virtio is an API for virtual IO and was developed by Rusty Russell in support of his own virtualization solution, called `lguest`. Virtio was introduced to achieve a common framework for hypervisors for IO virtualization.

In short, when we use paravirtualized drivers, the guest operating system is aware that it's running on a hypervisor and includes drivers that act as the front end. The front end drivers are part of the guest system. When there are emulated devices and someone wants to implement backend drivers for these devices, hypervisors do this job. The frontend and backend drivers communicate through a path that is nothing but virtio. KVM uses virtio drivers as paravirtualized device drivers. This is also available for Windows guest machines running on KVM hosts:

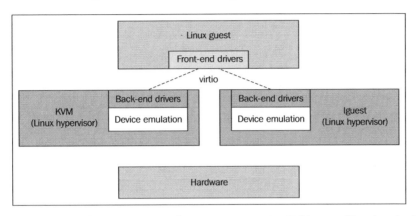

Source: `http://www.ibm.com/developerworks/library/l-virtio/`

There are mainly two layers (virt queue and virtual ring) to support communication between the guest and the hypervisor.

Virt queue and virtual ring (vring) is the transport mechanism implementation in virtio. Virt queue (virtio) is the queue interface that attaches the frontend and backend drivers. Each virtio device has its own virt queues and requests from guest systems are put into these virtual queues. Each Virt queue has its own ring, called a vring, which is where the memory is mapped between the qemu and guest. You can find the source for the various front end drivers within the `./drivers` subdirectory of the Linux kernel. There are different virtio drivers available for use in a KVM guest.

The devices are emulated in QEMU, and the drivers are part of the Linux kernel, or an extra package for Windows guests. Some examples of device/driver pairs:

- `virtio-net`: The virtio network device is a virtual Ethernet card. Virtio-net provides the driver for this.
- `virtio-blk`: The virtio block device is a simple virtual block device (that is, a disk). Virtio-blk provides the block device driver for the virtual block device.
- `virtio-balloon`: The virtio memory balloon device is a device for managing guest memory.

- virtio-scsi: The virtio SCSI host device groups together one or more disks and allows communicating to them using the SCSI protocol.

- virtio-console: The virtio console device is a simple device for data input and output between the guest and host userspace.

- virtio-rng: The virtio entropy device supplies high-quality randomness for guest use, and so on.

In general you should make use of these virtio devices in your KVM setup for better performance.

To know more about the virtio specification refer to http://docs.oasis-open.org/virtio/virtio/v1.0/virtio-v1.0.html.

CPU tuning

I would like to reiterate that vCPUs are POSIX threads in the KVM host. You can allocate vCPUs for guest systems according to your needs. However, to get the maximum or optimal performance, it is always better to allocate required virtual CPUs for each guest based on the expected load of the guest operating system. There is nothing wrong with allocating more than is needed; however, it may cause scaling issues in future, when considering the host system as a single unit serving all configured guests.

There is also a misconception that the number of vCPUs defined by all of the guest systems should be less than the total number of CPUs available in the HOST system. To expand further on this thought, if the total number of CPUs available in the HOST system is 32, some people think they can only define eight vCPUs each if they defined four guests in the system. There is no rule like that. Generally speaking, these vCPUs are lightweight processes running in your KVM hosts that get scheduled by the Linux scheduler based on the scheduling policy currently in place, which is supposed to treat all the processes running in the system in a fair way.

That said, KVM supports overcommitting virtualized CPUs. The rule that has to be applied here is that virtualized CPUs can be overcommitted as far as the load limits of guest virtual machines allow. However, real attention has to be paid here, otherwise it can badly hurt the performance if the vCPU load is increased near to 100%.

The number of vCPUs

Considering the performance impact of vCPU allocation or overcommitting, you should make sure the number of vCPUs (SMP guest) assigned for a single system does not exceed the total number of physical cores in the KVM host. For example: if the physical system has eight cores, you should not assign more than eight vCPUs to a single guest. If you do so, there is a huge possibility of significant performance degradation. There is nothing wrong with assigning eight vCPUs to a single guest in this scenario; this should work as expected. As mentioned earlier, these rules will fit best when the guest system load is limited or less than 100%. A word of caution here on overcommitting CPUs: you should not overcommit CPUs in your production environments without validating the worst cases that can occur. We say the CPUs are overcommitted when the sum of vCPUs for all guest systems defined in a KVM host is greater than the number of host CPUs on the system. You overcommit CPUs with one or multiple guests if the total number of vCPUs is greater than the number of host CPUs. So test well before you implement this in production systems. Client utilities such as virt-manager give a warning (Figure 2) when you try to overcommit the number of vCPUs.

For example, in our system, there are four available CPUs, so when I try to allocate more than four vCPUs, I get a warning that says **Overcommitting vCPUs can hurt performance**, as shown in the following screenshot:

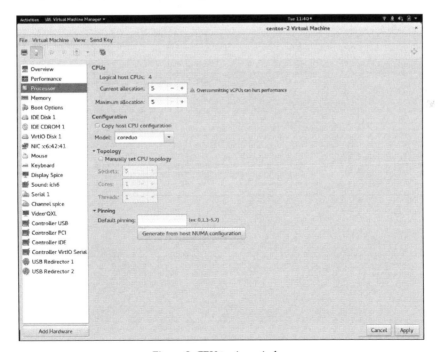

Figure 2: CPU tuning window

When we look at the preceding screenshot showing the CPU/processor configuration of a guest system, there are four main parts:

- The Number of vCPUs
- Configuration
- Topology
- Pinning

We just covered the first in the preceding paragraphs.

Let's move on to the second part: CPU configuration.

CPU configuration

Use this option to select the **CPU configuration type**, based on the desired CPU model. Expand the list to see available options, or click the **Copy host CPU configuration** button to detect and apply the physical host's CPU model and configuration. Once you select a CPU configuration, the available features/instructions of the CPU are displayed and can be individually enabled/disabled in the CPU Features list.

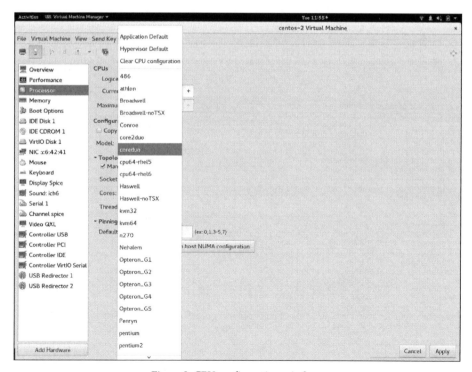

Figure 3: CPU configuration window

Depending on the version of the KVM software you have on your system, the available CPU configuration also differs. In my system (Fedora 22), I have the previously listed (Figure 3) CPU configuration. This option gives the flexibility of allocating the desired CPU model to the virtual machine. There is also an option (**Copy host CPU configuration**) that can copy the KVM host CPU model and configuration to the guest. Depending on the virt-manager version in use, you may get the option in the virt-manager GUI to individually select/deselect the CPU features for the CPU configuration you selected. One of the best practices is to copy the host CPU configuration over the manual configuration:

```
humble-lap $ virsh capabilities
<capabilities>

  <host>
    <uuid>bf4a43ce-e99c-4bc5-b2f2-8aacfcfcd552</uuid>
    <cpu>
      <arch>x86_64</arch>
      <model>Broadwell</model>
      <vendor>Intel</vendor>
      <topology sockets='1' cores='2' threads='2'/>
      <feature name='invtsc'/>
      <feature name='abm'/>
      <feature name='pdpe1gb'/>
      <feature name='rdrand'/>
      <feature name='f16c'/>
      <feature name='osxsave'/>
      <feature name='pdcm'/>
      <feature name='xtpr'/>
      <feature name='tm2'/>
      <feature name='est'/>
      <feature name='smx'/>
      <feature name='vmx'/>
      <feature name='ds_cpl'/>
      <feature name='monitor'/>
      <feature name='dtes64'/>
      <feature name='pbe'/>
      <feature name='tm'/>
      <feature name='ht'/>
      <feature name='ss'/>
      <feature name='acpi'/>
      <feature name='ds'/>
      <feature name='vme'/>
      <pages unit='KiB' size='4'/>
      <pages unit='KiB' size='2048'/>
    </cpu>
```

Figure 4: Host CPU feature list

CPU topology

The third stage in CPU tuning is the CPU topology configuration, as shown in Figure 5. You can configure the number of sockets, cores, and threads for your virtual machine, as shown:

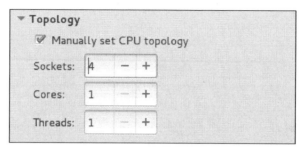

Figure 5: CPU topology

Although your environment may dictate other requirements, selecting the desired number of sockets, but with only a single core and a single thread, usually gives the best performance results and is the recommended setting.

CPU pinning

The fourth tuning option is vCPU pinning. When it comes to the performance tuning part of CPU, one of the best known techniques is vCPU pinning. Let's discuss this option in more detail. Obviously, wrong vCPU pinning can have a great impact on performance and can badly affect your KVM setup. First of all, why is pinning needed? The process of pinning specific vCPUs on a physical CPU can increases the CPU hit ratio. Whenever you pin a vCPU to a physical host CPU or subset of CPUs, you have to consider whether you are working on a NUMA (**Non Uniform Memory Access**)-capable system or not. If the system is NUMA-capable, extra care should be taken while doing the pinning process. Large performance improvements can be obtained by adhering to the system's specific NUMA topology. The **Generate from host NUMA configuration** option helps us to automatically generate a pinning configuration that is valid for the host. However, if the system is not NUMA-capable, you may encounter a message similar to that seen in the following screenshot when you try to generate the aforementioned configuration:

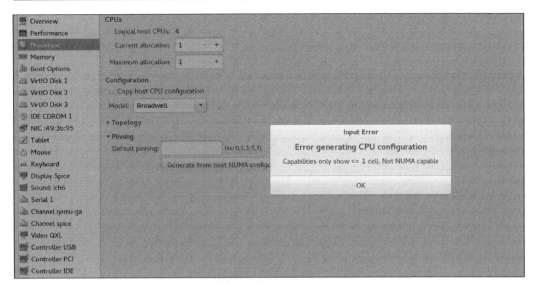

Figure 6: Generating from the NUMA configuration

We will discuss more about NUMA configurations and vCPU tuning later in this chapter. Confirmation of NUMA availability can be done by methods discussed in the following sections.

The numactl command

The first option to confirm NUMA availability uses the `numactl` command as shown next:

```
humble-lap $ numactl --hardware
available: 1 nodes (0)
node 0 cpus: 0 1 2 3
node 0 size: 7668 MB
node 0 free: 673 MB
node distances:
node    0
  0:   10
```

Figure 7: numactl hardware

It lists only one node. Even though this conveys the unavailability of NUMA, further clarification can be done by running the following command:

```
humble-lap $ cat /sys/kernel/debug/sched_features
```

This will *not* list NUMA flags if the system is not NUMA-aware. If the system is NOT NUMA-capable, the **Generate from host NUMA configuration** option will result in an error.

As a best practice, what you should remember here is, *do not use this option if the guest system has more vCPUs than a single NUMA node where it's running*. Even if the NUMA is available, the vCPUs are bound to the NUMA node and not to a particular physical CPU. We will discuss NUMA aware CPU tuning later in this chapter.

Till now, I have been using the term **CPU Pinning**; this is nothing but the process of setting the "affinity" between the vCPU and the physical CPU of the host, so that the vCPU will be executing in that physical CPU only. Use virsh vcpupin command for a 1:1 binding of vCPU to a physical CPU or to a subset of physical CPUs:

```
[humble-lap ]$ virsh vcpupin --help
  NAME
    vcpupin - control or query domain vcpu affinity

  SYNOPSIS
    vcpupin <domain> [--vcpu <number>] [--cpulist <string>] [--config] [--live] [--current]

  DESCRIPTION
    Pin domain VCPUs to host physical CPUs.

  OPTIONS
    [--domain] <string>  domain name, id or uuid
    --vcpu <number>  vcpu number
    --cpulist <string>  host cpu number(s) to set, or omit option to query
    --config         affect next boot
    --live           affect running domain
    --current        affect current domain

[humble-lap ]$
```

Figure 8: virsh vCPUpin help command output

There are couple of best practices when doing vCPU pinning:

- If the number of guest vCPUs is more than the single NUMA node CPUs, don't go for the default pinning option we discussed earlier.

- If the physical CPUs are spread across different NUMA nodes, it is always better to create multiple guests and pin vCPUs of each guest to physical CPUs in the same NUMA node. This is because accessing different NUMA nodes, or running across multiple NUMA nodes, significantly degrades performance for physical and virtualized tasks.

Reference: `https://docs.fedoraproject.org/en-US/Fedora/13/html/` `Virtualization_Guide/ch25s06.html` for more details.

Let us look at the steps of vCPU pinning:

1. Execute virsh node info to gather details about host CPU configuration.

```
humble-lap $ virsh nodeinfo
CPU model:          x86_64
CPU(s):             4
CPU frequency:      2895 MHz
CPU socket(s):      1
Core(s) per socket: 2
Thread(s) per core: 2
NUMA cell(s):       1
Memory size:        7852832 KiB
```

Figure 9: virsh nodeinfo command output

2. The next step is to get the CPU topology by executing command virsh capabilities and check the section tagged `<topology>`:

```
<topology>
  <cells num='1'>
    <cell id='0'>
      <memory unit='KiB'>7852832</memory>
      <pages unit='KiB' size='4'>1963208</pages>
      <pages unit='KiB' size='2048'>0</pages>
      <distances>
        <sibling id='0' value='10'/>
      </distances>
      <cpus num='4'>
        <cpu id='0' socket_id='0' core_id='0' siblings='0-1'/>
        <cpu id='1' socket_id='0' core_id='0' siblings='0-1'/>
        <cpu id='2' socket_id='0' core_id='1' siblings='2-3'/>
        <cpu id='3' socket_id='0' core_id='1' siblings='2-3'/>
      </cpus>
    </cell>
  </cells>
</topology>
```

Figure 10: virsh capabilities topology

Figure 10 shows that NUMA is not available in this system (<cell id='0'>).

3. Once we have identified the topology of our host, the next step is to start pinning the vCPUs. Let's first check the current affinity or pinning configuration with the guest named `centos-1` that has four vCPUs:

```
humble-lap $  virsh vcpupin centos-1
VCPU: CPU Affinity
----------------------------------------
   0: 0-3
   1: 0-3
   2: 0-3
   3: 0-3

humble-lap $ █
```

Figure 11: virsh vCPUpin info

The output in figure 11 means the guest vCPUs can run any of the physical CPUs (0-3). The method we use now to pin vCPUs is known as `static` placement, as seen in the guest XML file:

`<vCPU placement='static'>4</vCPU>`

4. Let us pin vCPU 1 to CPU 3 of the host:

```
humble-lap $ virsh vcpupin centos-1 1 3

humble-lap $ virsh vcpupin centos-1
VCPU: CPU Affinity
----------------------------------------
   0: 0-3
   1: 3
   2: 0-3
   3: 0-3

humble-lap $ virsh dumpxml centos-1
<domain type='kvm' id='2'>
  <name>centos-1</name>
  <uuid>4fe91628-1bdc-4765-8f01-d6387400c4c9</uuid>
  <memory unit='KiB'>2097152</memory>
  <currentMemory unit='KiB'>2097152</currentMemory>
  <vcpu placement='static'>4</vcpu>
  <cputune>
    <vcpupin vcpu='1' cpuset='3'/>
  </cputune>
```

Figure 12: virsh vCPUpin process

The vCPU with id 1 is pinned to the physical CPU with ID 3. The output in figure-12 verifies that the vCPU pin on running VM completed successfully. To know more about the placement options available in the vCPU tag, refer: `http://libvirt.org/formatdomain.html#elementsCPUAllocation`.

Notice the CPU affinity listed in the `virsh` command and the`<cputune>` tag in the XML dump of the running guest. As the XML tag says, this comes under the CPU tuning section of the guest. It is also possible to configure a set of physical CPUs for a particular vCPU instead of a single physical CPU. For more details on vCPU pinning, please refer to `http://libvirt.org/formatdomain.html#elementsCPUTuning`.

There are a couple of things to remember. vCPU pinning can improve performance; however, it depends on the host configuration and the other settings on the system. Make sure you do enough tests and validate the settings.

Let us try to change the vCPU pinning again:

```
humble-lap $ virsh vcpupin centos-1 0 3

humble-lap $ virsh vcpupin centos-1 1 2

humble-lap $ virsh vcpupin centos-1 2 3

humble-lap $ virsh vcpupin centos-1 3 1

humble-lap $ virsh vcpupin centos-1
CPU: CPU Affinity
----------------------------------------
  0: 3
  1: 2
  2: 3
  3: 1
```

Figure 13: virsh vCPUpin process - 2

You can also make use of virsh vcpuinfo to verify the pinning.

- The output of the `vcpuinfo` command is as follows:

```
 humble-lap $ virsh vcpuinfo
error: command 'vcpuinfo' requires <domain> option
 humble-lap $ virsh vcpuinfo centos-1
VCPU:              0
CPU:               3
State:             running
CPU time:          8.7s
CPU Affinity:      ---y

VCPU:              1
CPU:               2
State:             running
CPU time:          7.2s
CPU Affinity:      --y-

VCPU:              2
CPU:               3
State:             running
CPU time:          9.9s
CPU Affinity:      ---y

VCPU:              3
CPU:               1
State:             running
CPU time:          5.6s
CPU Affinity:      -y--
```

Figure 14: virsh vcpunfo verification

- virsh dumpxml output of the guest looks like the following:

```
<vcpu placement='static'>4</vCPU>
<cputune>
    <vcpupin vCPU='1' CPUset='2'/>
    <vcpupin vCPU='2' CPUset='3'/>
    <vcpupin vCPU='3' CPUset='1'/>
    <vcpupin vCPU='0' CPUset='3'/>
</cputune>
```

One more attribute called `emulatorpin` can be a sub-attribute to the `<cputune>` element. We will discuss `emulatorpin` in detail when we discuss NUMA.

Let us now explore the memory tuning options.

Working with memory

Memory is a precious resource for most environments, isn't it? Thus, the efficient use of memory should be achieved by tuning it. The first rule in optimizing KVM memory performance is not to allocate more resources to a guest during setup than it will use!

We will discuss the following in greater detail:

- Memory allocation
- Memory tuning
- Memory backing

Memory allocation

Let us start by how to allocate memory for a virtual system or guest. To make the allocation process simple, we will consider the libvirt client virt-manager again. Memory allocation can be done from the window shown in the following screenshot.

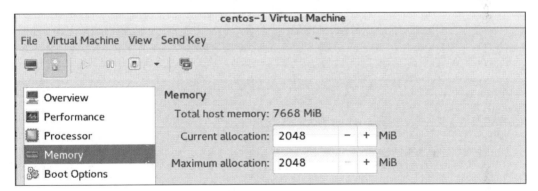

Figure 15: Memory allocation window

As you can see in the preceding figure, there are two main options: **Current allocation** and **Maximum allocation**:

- **Maximum allocation**: The runtime maximum memory allocation of the guest. This is the maximum memory that can be allocated to the guest when it's running

- **Current allocation**: The actual allocation of memory for the guest. This value can be less than the maximum allocation, to allow for ballooning up the guest's memory on the fly

```
--snip-- from http://libvirt.org/formatdomain.
html#elementsMemoryAllocation
<domain>
    ...
    <maxMemory slots='16' unit='KiB'>1524288</maxMemory>
    <memory unit='KiB'>524288</memory>
    <currentMemory unit='KiB'>524288</currentMemory>
    ...
</domain>
```

The `virsh` command can be used to tune these parameters or configurations. The relevant `virsh` commands are `setmem` and `setmaxmem`. The following screenshot shows the command options and parameter explanation:

```
[ humble-lap ]$ virsh setmem --help
  NAME
    setmem - change memory allocation

  SYNOPSIS
    setmem <domain> <size> [--config] [--live] [--current]

  DESCRIPTION
    Change the current memory allocation in the guest domain.

  OPTIONS
    [--domain] <string>  domain name, id or uuid
    [--size] <number>  new memory size, as scaled integer (default KiB)
    --config         affect next boot
    --live           affect running domain
    --current        affect current domain

[ humble-lap ]$ virsh setmaxmem --help
  NAME
    setmaxmem - change maximum memory limit

  SYNOPSIS
    setmaxmem <domain> <size> [--config] [--live] [--current]

  DESCRIPTION
    Change the maximum memory allocation limit in the guest domain.

  OPTIONS
    [--domain] <string>  domain name, id or uuid
    [--size] <number>  new maximum memory size, as scaled integer (default KiB)
    --config         affect next boot
    --live           affect running domain
    --current        affect current domain
```

Figure 16: virsh setmem/setmaxmem options

If NUMA is present the process of memory tuning can be a little tricky. We will discuss that in the NUMA section.

Memory tuning

The memory tuning options are added under <memtune> of the guest configuration file.

The guest XML representation of memory tuning can be represented as follows:

```
<domain>
    ...
  <memtune>
    <hard_limit unit='G'>1</hard_limit>
    <soft_limit unit='M'>128</soft_limit>
    <swap_hard_limit unit='G'>2</swap_hard_limit>
    <min_guarantee unit='bytes'>67108864</min_guarantee>
  </memtune>
    ...
</domain>
```

 Refer to http://libvirt.org/formatdomain. html#elementsMemoryTuning for more details.

The virt admin can configure the memory settings of a guest manually. If <memtune> configuration is omitted, the default memory settings apply for a guest. The virsh command in play here is:

```
# virsh memtune <virtual_machine> --parameter size
```

parameter can have any of the following values; this best practice is well documented in the man page:

```
--snip -- from virsh man page
  --hard-limit
  The maximum memory the guest can use.
  --soft-limit
  The memory limit to enforce during memory contention.
  --swap-hard-limit
```

The maximum memory plus swap the guest can use. This has to be more
than hard-limit value provided.

                    --min-guarantee

  The guaranteed minimum memory allocation for the guest.

--/snip--

The default/current values that are set for the memtune parameter can be fetched as
shown next:

```
[humble-lap ]$ virsh list
 Id    Name                                State
--------------------------------------------------------
 2        centos-1                         running

[humble-lap ]$ virsh memtune centos-1
hard_limit      : 9007199254740988
soft_limit      : 9007199254740988
swap_hard_limit: 9007199254740988

[humble-lap ]$ 
```

Figure 17: virsh memtune value listing

As mentioned in the same man page:

> "For QEMU/KVM, the parameters are applied to the QEMU process as a whole.
> Thus, when counting them, one needs to add up guest RAM, guest video RAM,
> and some memory overhead of QEMU itself. The last piece is hard to determine so
> one needs guess and try. For each tunable, it is possible to designate that unit the
> number is in on input, using the same values as for <memory>. For backwards
> compatibility, output is always in KiB."

When setting hard_limit, one should not set this value too low, because the
guest/domain may get killed by the kernel if this value is too low. To determine
the memory needed for a process to run is an undecidable problem.

To know more about how to set these parameters, please see the help output for the
memtune command in the following screenshot:

```
humble-lap $ virsh help memtune
  NAME
    memtune - Get or set memory parameters

  SYNOPSIS
    memtune <domain> [--hard-limit <number>] [--soft-limit <number>]
[--swap-hard-limit <number>] [--min-guarantee <number>] [--config]
[--live] [--current]

  DESCRIPTION
    Get or set the current memory parameters for a guest domain.
    To get the memory parameters use following command:

    virsh # memtune <domain>

  OPTIONS
    [--domain] <string>  domain name, id or uuid
    --hard-limit <number>  Max memory, as scaled integer (default Ki
B)
    --soft-limit <number>  Memory during contention, as scaled integ
er (default KiB)
    --swap-hard-limit <number>  Max memory plus swap, as scaled inte
ger (default KiB)
    --min-guarantee <number>  Min guaranteed memory, as scaled integ
er (default KiB)
    --config       affect next boot
    --live         affect running domain
    --current      affect current domain

humble-lap $ █
```

Figure 18: virsh memtune help

As we have covered memory allocation and tuning, the final option is memory backing.

Memory backing

Following is the guest XML representation of memory backing:

```
<domain>
    ...
  <memoryBacking>
    <hugepages>
    <page size="1" unit="G" nodeset="0-3,5"/>
    <page size="2" unit="M" nodeset="4"/>
    </hugepages>
    <nosharepages/>
```

```
          <locked/>
    </memoryBacking>

      ...
    </domain>
```

You may have noticed there are three main options for memory backing: hugepages, nosharepages, and locked.

Let us go through them one by one, starting with locked.

locked

As mentioned in earlier chapters, in a KVM environment, the guest memory lies in the process address space of the qemu-kvm process in the KVM host. These guest memory pages can be swapped out by the Linux kernel at any time based on the requirement the host has. locked helps us here! If you have set the memory backing option of guest to locked, the host will not swap out memory pages that belong to the virtual system or guest. The virtual memory pages in the host system memory are locked when this option is enabled:

```
<memoryBacking>
    <locked/>
</memoryBacking>
```

Note that, when setting locked, a hard_limit must be set in the <memtune> element to the maximum memory configured for the guest, plus any memory consumed by the process itself.

nosharepages

Following is the XML representation of nosharepages from guest configuration file:

```
<memoryBacking>
    <nosharepages/>
</memoryBacking>
```

There are different mechanisms that can enable sharing of memory when the memory pages are identical. Techniques such as KSM (kernel same page merging) share pages among guest systems. The nosharepages option instructs the hypervisor to disable shared pages for this guest. I.e. setting nosharepages prevents the host from merging the same memory used among guests.

hugepages

The third and final option is `hugepages`; which can be represented in XML format as follows:

```
<memoryBacking>
</hugepages>
</memoryBacking>
```

Hugepages were introduced in the Linux kernel to improve the performance of memory management. Memory is managed in blocks known as **pages**. Different architectures (i386, ia64) support different page sizes. x86 CPUs usually address memory in 4 KB pages, but they are capable of using larger 2 MB to 1 GB pages known as **hugepages**. CPUs have a built-in **memory management unit** (**MMU**) that contains a list of these pages. The pages are referenced through page tables and each page has a reference in the page table. When a system wants to handle a huge amount of memory, there are mainly two options. One of them involves increasing the number of page table entries in the hardware MMU. The second method increases the default page size. If we opt for the first method of increasing the page table entries, it is really expensive. The hardware MMU in a modern processor only supports hundreds or thousands of page table entries and will struggle when it deals with lots of page table entries or manipulations based on a high number of entries.

The second and more efficient method when dealing with large amounts memory management is *hugepages* or increased page sizes. The page tables used by 2 MB pages are suitable for managing multiple gigabytes of memory, whereas the page tables of 1 GB pages are best for scaling to terabytes of memory. Hugepages can significantly increase performance, particularly for large memory-intensive workloads. Most of the known Linux distributions are able to more effectively manage large amounts of memory by increasing the page size through the use of hugepages. A process can use hugepage memory support to improve performance by increasing CPU cache hits against the **Translation LookAside Buffer** (**TLB**). You already know guest systems are simply processes in a Linux system, thus the KVM guests are eligible to do the same.

 A **TLB** is a cache used for virtual-to-physical address translations. Typically, this is a very scarce resource on processors. Operating systems try to make the best use of a limited number of TLB resources. This optimization is more critical now, as bigger and bigger physical memories (several GB) are more readily available.

The aforementioned XML entries for hugepages instruct the hypervisor that the guest should have its memory allocated using hugepages instead of the normal native page size. If the system is NUMA capable, latest version of libvirt can set hugpages specifically for each NUMA node. The <page> element was introduced by libvirt to satisfy this. It has one compulsory attribute 'size' which specifies that hugepages should be used (especially useful on systems supporting hugepages of different sizes).We will discuss this in detail later, when we discuss CPU and memory tuning in NUMA-capable systems.

Before we move on, we should also mention **Transparent Hugepages (THP)**. THP is an abstraction layer that automate the hugepage size allocation base on the application request.

Transparent Hugepage support can be entirely disabled, or can only be enabled inside MADV_HUGEPAGE regions (to avoid the risk of consuming more memory resources), or enabled system-wide. There are three main options for configuring THP in a system: always, madvise, and never:

```
humble-lap $ cat/sys/kernel/mm/transparent_hugepage/enabled always
[madvise] never

humble-lap $
```

From the above output, we can see that the current THP setting in my system is madvise. The other options can be enabled by the following method:

```
echo always >/sys/kernel/mm/transparent_hugepage/enabled
echo madvise >/sys/kernel/mm/transparent_hugepage/enabled
echo never >/sys/kernel/mm/transparent_hugepage/enabled
```

In short, what these values meant are enabled` value can be set to:

- always: Always use THP
- madvise: Use hugepages only in virtual memory areas (VMAs) marked with MADV_HUGEPAGE
- never: Disable the feature

System settings for performance are automatically optimized by THP. By allowing all free memory to be used as a cache, performance is increased. It is possible to use static hugepages when THP is in place or in other way THP won't prevent using static method. However, when static hugepages are not used, KVM will use transparent hugepages instead of the regular 4 Kb page size. The advantages we get by using hugepages for a KVM guest's memory are that less memory is used for page tables and TLB misses are reduced; obviously, this increases performance. But keep in mind that when using hugepages for guest memory, you can no longer swap or balloon guest memory.

Let us have a quick look at how to use static hugepages in your KVM setup:

```
[ humble-lap ]$ cat /proc/meminfo |grep -i huge
AnonHugePages:          0 kB
HugePages_Total:        0
HugePages_Free:         0
HugePages_Rsvd:         0
HugePages_Surp:         0
Hugepagesize:        2048 kB
[ humble-lap ]$
```

In the above screenshot, we can see that the hugepage size in this system is 2 MB.

1. View the current hugepages value by running the following command or fetch it from `sysfs`, as shown next:

    ```
    [ humble-lap ]$ cat /proc/sys/vm/nr_hugepages
    0
    [ humble-lap ]$
    ```

2. From `sysfs` use the `sysctl -a |grep huge` command:

```
vm.hugepages_treat_as_movable = 0
vm.hugetlb_shm_group = 0
vm.nr_hugepages = 0
vm.nr_hugepages_mempolicy = 0
vm.nr_overcommit_hugepages = 0
```

3. As the hugepage size is 2 MB here, we can set hugepages in increments of 2 MB. To set the number of hugepages to 26,000, use the following command:

```
#echo 26000 > /proc/sys/vm/nr_hugepages
```

Total memory assigned for hugepages cannot be used by applications that are not hugepage aware. I.e, if you over alocate hugepages normal fuctioning of the host system can get affected.

4. To make it persistent, you can use the following:

```
# sysctl -w vm.nr_hugepages=<number of hugepages>
```

5. Then, mount the hugepages and restart the libvirtd service:

```
# mount -t hugetlbfs hugetlbfs /dev/hugepages
# sysctl start libvirtd
```

```
[ humble-lap ]$ mount |grep huge
cgroup on /sys/fs/cgroup/hugetlb type cgroup (rw,nosuid,nodev,noexec,relatime,huget
lb)
hugetlbfs on /dev/hugepages type hugetlbfs (rw,relatime,seclabel)
[ humble-lap ]$ cd /dev/hugepages/
[ humble-lap ]$ ls
libvirt
[ humble-lap ]$ cd libvirt/
[ humble-lap ]$ ls
qemu
```

6. Restart the hugepage-configured guest (`<memoryBacking></hugepages></memoryBacking>`). The VM will now start using the hugepages. Verify this using the command `cat /proc/meminfo |grep -i huge` on the host..

Getting acquainted with Kernel Same Page merging

According to the KVM official documentation:

> *KSM is a memory-saving deduplication feature that merges anonymous (private) pages (not pagecache ones). Although it started this way, KSM is currently suitable for more than Virtual Machine use, as it can be useful to any application that generates many instances of the same data*

```
http://www.Linux-kvm.org/page/KSM
```

As is well understood from the earlier quote, KSM is a feature that allows sharing identical pages between the different processes running in the system. We may presume that the identical pages may exist due to certain reasons—for example, if there are multiple processes spawned from the same binary or something similar. There is no rule like that though. KSM scans these identical memory pages and consolidates a **Copy on write (COW)** shared page. Well, if you don't know what I meant by COW, it is nothing but a mechanism by which, when there is an attempt to change a memory region that is shared and common to more than one process, the process that requests the change gets a new copy and the changes are saved in it. The same applies here. Even though the consolidated COW shared page is accessible by all the processes, whenever a process tries to change the content (here a write to the page), the process gets a new copy with the changes. By now, you will have understood that, by using KSM, we can reduce physical memory consumption. In the KVM context, this can really add value, because guest systems are qemu-kvm processes in the system and there is a huge possibility that all the VM processes will have a good amount of similar memory.

For the KSM to work, the process/application has to register its memory pages with KSM. In KVM land, KSM allows guests to share identical memory pages, thus achieving an improvement in memory consumption. Most of the shared pages are usually common libraries, or other identical, high-use data. This shared page or memory is marked as "copy on write". In short, KSM avoids memory duplication and it's really useful when similar guest operating systems are present in a KVM environment.

From the preceding theory, it's obvious that KSM provides enhanced memory speed and utilization. Mostly, this common shared data is stored in the cache or in main memory, which causes fewer cache misses for the KVM guests. Also, KSM can reduce the overall memory footprint of guests so that in one way, it allows the user to do memory overcommitting in a KVM setup, thus supplying greater utilization of available resources. However we have to keep in mind that KSM requires more CPU resources to identify the duplicate pages and to perform tasks such as sharing/merging.

Previously, I mentioned that the processes have to mark the "pages" to show that they are eligible candidates for KSM to operate. The marking can be done by a process based on the `MADV_MERGEABLE` flag, which we will discuss in the next section. You can explore the use of this flag from the `madvise` man page:

```
--snip  -- from #man 2 madvise
```

MADV_MERGEABLE (since Linux 2.6.32)

Enable Kernel Samepage Merging (KSM) for the pages in the range specified by addr and length. The kernel regularly scans those areas of user memory that have been marked as mergeable, looking for pages with identical content. These are replaced by a single write-protected page (that is automatically copied if a process later wants to update the content of the page). KSM merges only private anonymous pages (see mmap(2)).

The KSM feature is intended for applications that generate many instances of the same data (e.g., virtualization systems such as KVM). It can consume a lot of processing power; use with care. See the Linux kernel source file Documentation/vm/ksm.txt for more details.

The MADV_MERGEABLE and MADV_UNMERGEABLE operations are available only if the kernel was configured with CONFIG_KSM.

So, the kernel has to be configured with KSM, For example:

```
humble-lap $ cat /etc/redhat-release
Fedora release 22 (Twenty Two)
humble-lap $ uname -r
4.2.3-200.fc22.x86_64
humble-lap $ cat /boot/config-4.2.3-200.fc22.x86_64 |grep CONFIG_KSM
CONFIG_KSM=y
humble-lap $ dnf install ksm
```

Figure 20: KSM capability checking in the kernel

To explore KSM further, we will discuss the packages available and the options to configure KSM.

KSM packages and files

The KSM package in Fedora 22 provides the following files. Service configuration files and binaries such as `ksmctl` and `ksmtuned` are also part of this package:

```
humble-lap $ rpm -ql ksm
/etc/ksmtuned.conf
/etc/sysconfig/ksm
/usr/lib/systemd/system/ksm.service
/usr/lib/systemd/system/ksmtuned.service
/usr/libexec/ksmctl
/usr/sbin/ksmtuned
humble-lap $
```

Figure 21 : Listing KSM package files

The information about the KSM service can be fetched from the `sysfs` filesystem. There are different files available in this location, reflecting the current KSM status. These are updated dynamically by the kernel, and it has a precise record of KSM usage and statistics:

```
humble-lap $ ls /sys/kernel/mm/ksm/*
/sys/kernel/mm/ksm/full_scans
/sys/kernel/mm/ksm/merge_across_nodes
/sys/kernel/mm/ksm/pages_shared
/sys/kernel/mm/ksm/pages_sharing
/sys/kernel/mm/ksm/pages_to_scan
/sys/kernel/mm/ksm/pages_unshared
/sys/kernel/mm/ksm/pages_volatile
/sys/kernel/mm/ksm/run
/sys/kernel/mm/ksm/sleep_millisecs
humble-lap $
```

Figure 22: sysfs entries for KSM

In an upcoming section, we will discuss the `ksmtuned` service and its configuration variables. As `ksmtuned` is a service to control KSM, its configuration variables are analogous to the files we see in the `sysfs` filesystem. We will list the files present in `sysfs` here, with a small note about what each means:

- `full_scans`: Full scans run
- `merge_across_nodes`: Whether pages from different NUMA nodes can be merged
- `pages_shared`: Total pages shared

- `pages_sharing`: Pages presently shared
- `pages_to_scan`: Pages not scanned
- `pages_unshared`: Pages no longer shared
- `pages_volatile`: Number of volatile pages
- `run`: Whether the KSM process is running
- `sleep_millisecs`: Sleep milliseconds

It is also possible to tune these parameters with the flexible `virsh` command. The `virsh node-memory-tune` command does this job for you. For example, the following specifies the number of pages to scan before the shared memory service goes to sleep:

```
# virsh node-memory-tune --shm-pages-to-scan number
```

As with any other service, the `ksmtuned` service also has logs stored in a log file, `/var/log/ksmtuned`. KSM tuning activity is stored in this log file if the `DEBUG=1` line is added in the `/etc/ksmtuned.conf` file.

Refer to `https://www.kernel.org/doc/Documentation/vm/ksm.txt` for more details.

Once we start the KSM service as shown next, you can watch the values get changed depending on the KSM service in action:

```
#systemctl start ksm
```

The KSM service starts a kernel thread called `ksmd` as verified here:

```
[humble-lap ]$ systemctl status ksm
● ksm.service - Kernel Samepage Merging
   Loaded: loaded (/usr/lib/systemd/system/ksm.service; enabled; vendor preset: enabled)
   Active: active (exited) since Fri 2015-11-20 14:57:49 IST; 3h 21min ago
  Process: 1327 ExecStart=/usr/libexec/ksmctl start (code=exited, status=0/SUCCESS)
 Main PID: 1327 (code=exited, status=0/SUCCESS)
   CGroup: /system.slice/ksm.service

Warning: Journal has been rotated since unit was started. Log output is incomplete or unavailable.
[humble-lap ]$ ps aux |grep ksm
root        39  0.0  0.0      0      0 ?        SN   14:56   0:00 [ksmd]
```

Figure 23: ksm service command and ps command output

Once the KSM service is started, watch the changes by querying `sysfs` as shown in Figure 24. You can see some of the values getting changed when KSM is active:

```
humble-lap $ cat /sys/kernel/mm/ksm/*
0
1
1084
24585
100
118769
1338
1
20
humble-lap $ cat /sys/kernel/mm/ksm/*
0
1
1084
24585
100
118742
1365
1
20
humble-lap $ cat /sys/kernel/mm/ksm/*
0
1
1084
24585
100
118741
1366
1
20
humble-lap $ cat /sys/kernel/mm/ksm/full_scans
10
humble-lap $ cat /sys/kernel/mm/ksm/*
10
1
1084
24584
100
118714
1394
1
20
humble-lap $
```

Figure 24: sysfs entries for the KSM service

Let us explore the `ksmtuned` service in more detail. The `ksmtuned` service is designed in such a way that it goes through a cycle of actions and adjusts KSM; this cycle of actions will continue in a loop. Whenever a guest system is created or destroyed, libvirt will notify the `ksmtuned` service.

The `/etc/ksmtuned.conf` file is the configuration file for the `ksmtuned` service. The following file output is the default `ksmtuned.conf` file:

Here is a brief explanation of the configuration parameters available. You can see these configuration parameters match with the KSM files in `sysfs`:

```
# Configuration file for ksmtuned.
# How long ksmtuned should sleep between tuning adjustments
# KSM_MONITOR_INTERVAL=60

# Millisecond sleep between ksm scans for 16Gb server.
# Smaller servers sleep more, bigger sleep less.
# KSM_SLEEP_MSEC=10

#KSM_NPAGES_BOOST - is added to the `npages` value, when `free memory`
is less than `thres`.
# KSM_NPAGES_BOOST=300

# KSM_NPAGES_DECAY - is the value given is subtracted to the `npages`
value, when `free memory` is greater than `thres`.
# KSM_NPAGES_DECAY=-50

# KSM_NPAGES_MIN - is the lower limit for the `npages` value.
# KSM_NPAGES_MIN=64

#KSM_NPAGES_MAX - is the upper limit for the `npages` value.
# KSM_NPAGES_MAX=1250

# KSM_THRES_COEF - is the RAM percentage to be calculated in parameter
`thres`.
# KSM_THRES_COEF=20

# KSM_THRES_CONST - If this is a low memory system, and the `thres`
value is less than `KSM_THRES_CONST`, then reset `thres` value to
`KSM_THRES_CONST` value.
# KSM_THRES_CONST=2048
```

These configuration parameters in the `/etc/ksmtuned.conf` file instruct the KSM action. For example, npages sets how many pages KSM will scan before ksmd goes to sleep. It will be set at `/sys/kernel/mm/ksm/pages_to_scan.thres` sets the activation threshold, in kbytes. A KSM cycle is triggered when the thres value is added to the sum of all qemu-kvm processes when RSZ exceeds the total system memory. This parameter is the equivalent in Kbytes of the percentage defined in the `KSM_THRES_COEF` parameter.

Well, KSM is designed to improve performance and to allow memory overcommits. It serves this purpose in most environments; however, KSM may introduce a performance overhead in some setups or environments. Also, there is a concern that KSM may open a channel that could potentially be used to leak information across guests. If you have these concerns or if you see/experience KSM is not helping to improve the performance of your workload, KSM can be disabled.

To disable KSM , stop the `ksmtuned` and `ksm` services in your system by executing:

```
#systemctl stop ksm
#systemctl stop ksmtuned
```

Till now, we have gone through different tuning options for **CPU** and **memory**. We have covered the available options and their basic usage. However, we should keep pushing CPU and memory tuning in NUMA-aware systems. Even though we touched on NUMA tuning for CPU and memory earlier, we skipped some features; let's cover them now.

Tuning CPU and memory with NUMA

Before we start tuning CPU and memory for NUMA-capable systems, let's see what NUMA is and how it works.

What is NUMA?

NUMA is an abbreviation for **Non Uniform Memory Access**:

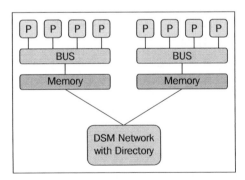

Figure 25: Reference from Wikipedia

Think about NUMA as a system where you have more than one system bus, each serving a small set of processors and associated memory. Each group of processors has its own memory and possibly its own I/O channels. It may not possible to stop or prevent access across these groups. Each of these groups is known as a NUMA node.

In this concept, if a process/thread is running on a NUMA node, the memory on the same node is normally called local memory and memory residing on another node is known as foreign/remote memory. This implementation is different from the **SMP (Symmetric Multiprocessor System)**, where the access time for all of the memory is the same for all the CPUs.

There exists something called the NUMA ratio, a measure of how quickly a CPU can access local memory compared to how quickly it can access remote/foreign memory. For example, if the NUMA ratio is 2.0, then it takes twice as long for a CPU to access remote memory. If the NUMA ratio is 1, it is symmetric multiprocessing (SMP). The greater the ratio, the more it costs to access the memory of other nodes. Before we explore tuning in more depth, let's discuss exploring the NUMA topology of a system. One of the easiest ways to show the current NUMA topology is via the numactl command:

```
[ humble-numaserver ]$ numactl -H
available: 2 nodes (0-1)
node 0 cpus: 0 2 4 6 8 10 12 14 16 18 20 22 24 26 28 30
node 0 size: 131026 MB
node 0 free: 114933 MB
node 1 cpus: 1 3 5 7 9 11 13 15 17 19 21 23 25 27 29 31
node 1 size: 131072 MB
node 1 free: 112458 MB
node distances:
node   0   1
  0:  10  20
  1:  20  10
[ humble-numaserver ]$
```

Figure 26: numactl output

The above numactl output conveys that there are 32 CPUs in the system and they belong to the two NUMA nodes. It also lists the memory associated with each NUMA node and the node distance. When we discussed vCPU pinning, we displayed the topology of the system using `virsh` capabilities. This command can give further details, as shown next:

```xml
<topology>
  <cells num='2'>
    <cell id='0'>
      <memory unit='KiB'>134171180</memory>
      <pages unit='KiB' size='4'>33542795</pages>
      <pages unit='KiB' size='2048'>0</pages>
      <distances>
        <sibling id='0' value='10'/>
        <sibling id='1' value='20'/>
      </distances>
      <cpus num='16'>
        <cpu id='0' socket_id='0' core_id='0' siblings='0,16'/>
        <cpu id='2' socket_id='0' core_id='1' siblings='2,18'/>
        <cpu id='4' socket_id='0' core_id='2' siblings='4,20'/>
        <cpu id='6' socket_id='0' core_id='3' siblings='6,22'/>
        <cpu id='8' socket_id='0' core_id='4' siblings='8,24'/>
        <cpu id='10' socket_id='0' core_id='5' siblings='10,26'/>
        <cpu id='12' socket_id='0' core_id='6' siblings='12,28'/>
        <cpu id='14' socket_id='0' core_id='7' siblings='14,30'/>
        <cpu id='16' socket_id='0' core_id='0' siblings='0,16'/>
        <cpu id='18' socket_id='0' core_id='1' siblings='2,18'/>
        <cpu id='20' socket_id='0' core_id='2' siblings='4,20'/>
        <cpu id='22' socket_id='0' core_id='3' siblings='6,22'/>
        <cpu id='24' socket_id='0' core_id='4' siblings='8,24'/>
        <cpu id='26' socket_id='0' core_id='5' siblings='10,26'/>
        <cpu id='28' socket_id='0' core_id='6' siblings='12,28'/>
        <cpu id='30' socket_id='0' core_id='7' siblings='14,30'/>
      </cpus>
    </cell>
    <cell id='1'>
      <memory unit='KiB'>134217728</memory>
      <pages unit='KiB' size='4'>33554432</pages>
      <pages unit='KiB' size='2048'>0</pages>
      <distances>
        <sibling id='0' value='20'/>
        <sibling id='1' value='10'/>
      </distances>
      <cpus num='16'>
        <cpu id='1' socket_id='1' core_id='0' siblings='1,17'/>
        <cpu id='3' socket_id='1' core_id='1' siblings='3,19'/>
        <cpu id='5' socket_id='1' core_id='2' siblings='5,21'/>
        <cpu id='7' socket_id='1' core_id='3' siblings='7,23'/>
        <cpu id='9' socket_id='1' core_id='4' siblings='9,25'/>
        <cpu id='11' socket_id='1' core_id='5' siblings='11,27'/>
        <cpu id='13' socket_id='1' core_id='6' siblings='13,29'/>
        <cpu id='15' socket_id='1' core_id='7' siblings='15,31'/>
        <cpu id='17' socket_id='1' core_id='0' siblings='1,17'/>
        <cpu id='19' socket_id='1' core_id='1' siblings='3,19'/>
        <cpu id='21' socket_id='1' core_id='2' siblings='5,21'/>
        <cpu id='23' socket_id='1' core_id='3' siblings='7,23'/>
        <cpu id='25' socket_id='1' core_id='4' siblings='9,25'/>
        <cpu id='27' socket_id='1' core_id='5' siblings='11,27'/>
        <cpu id='29' socket_id='1' core_id='6' siblings='13,29'/>
        <cpu id='31' socket_id='1' core_id='7' siblings='15,31'/>
      </cpus>
    </cell>
  </cells>
</topology>
```

Figure 27: NUMA topology of a system

To get a graphical view of the NUMA topology (please refer to the following figure), you can make use of a command called `lstopo`, that is available with the `hwloc-gui` package in Red Hat-based systems:

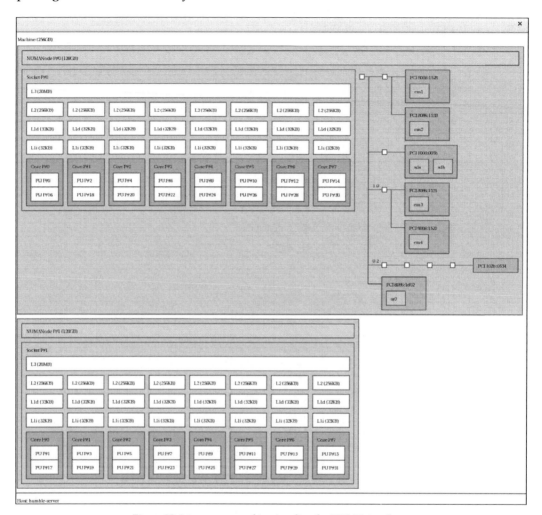

Figure 28: istopo command to visualize the NUMA topology

This screenshot also shows the PCI devices associated with the NUMA nodes. For example, em* (network interface) devices are attached to the NUMA node 0. Once we have the NUMA topology of the system and understand it, we can start tuning it especially for KVM virtualized setup.

NUMA memory allocation policies

The XML representation of NUMA tuning is as follows. You can see that tuning
NUMA introduces a new element tag called `numatune`:

```
<domain>
  ...
    <numatune>
      <memory mode="strict" nodeset="1-4,^3"/>
    </numatune>
  ...
</domain>
```

This is also configurable via the `virsh` command, as shown next:

```
[humble-lap ]$ virsh numatune --help
  NAME
    numatune - Get or set numa parameters

  SYNOPSIS
    numatune <domain> [--mode <string>] [--nodeset <string>] [--config] [--live] [--current]

  DESCRIPTION
    Get or set the current numa parameters for a guest domain.
    To get the numa parameters use following command:

    virsh # numatune <domain>

  OPTIONS
    [--domain] <string>  domain name, id or uuid
    --mode <string>  NUMA mode, one of strict, preferred and interleave
or a number from the virDomainNumatuneMemMode enum
    --nodeset <string>  NUMA node selections to set
    --config          affect next boot
    --live            affect running domain
    --current         affect current domain

[humble-lap ]$ 
```

Figure 29: virsh numatune output

numatune

The XML representation of this tag can be shown as follows:

```
<domain>
  ...
    <numatune>
      <memory mode="strict" nodeset="1-4,^3"/>
```

```
        <memnode cellid="0" mode="strict" nodeset="1"/>
        <memnode cellid="2" mode="preferred" nodeset="2"/>
    </numatune>
    . . .
</domain>
```

Even though the element called `numatune` is optional, it is provided to tune the performance of the NUMA host by controlling the NUMA policy for the domain process. The main sub-tags of this optional element are `memory` and `nodeset`. Some notes on these sub tags follow:

- memory: The optional `memory` element specifies how to allocate memory for the domain process on a NUMA host. It contains several optional attributes. The attribute mode is `interleave`, `strict`, or `preferred`; the default is `strict`.

  Three policy types define how memory is allocated from the nodes in a system:
  - Strict : The default operation is for the allocation to fall back to other NUMA nodes if the memory cannot be allocated on the target node. The `strict` policy means that the allocation will fail if the memory cannot be allocated on the target node.
  - Interleave: Memory pages are allocated across nodes specified by a `nodemask`, but are allocated in a round-robin fashion.
  - Preferred: Memory is allocated from a single preferred memory node. If sufficient memory is not available, memory can be allocated from other nodes.

- nodeset: The `nodeset` attribute specifies NUMA nodes, using the same syntax as the `cpuset` attribute for the vCPU element. `nodeset` is a list of NUMA nodes used by the host for running the domain. Its syntax is a comma-separated list, with - for ranges and ^ to exclude a node.

One of the important attributes here is `placement`:

"Attribute placement can be used to indicate the memory placement mode for domain process, its value can be either "static" or "auto", defaults to placement of vCPU, or "static" if nodeset is specified. "auto" indicates the domain process will only allocate memory from the advisory nodeset returned from querying numad, and the value of attribute nodeset will be ignored if it's specified. If placement of vCPU is 'auto', and numatune is not specified, a default numatune with placement 'auto' and mode 'strict' will be added implicitly."

Reference: `http://libvirt.org/formatdomain.html#elementsNUMATuning`.

If we expand the earlier strings or if we conclude these hierarchies, we will arrive at the following summary:

There are implicit inheritance rules between the `placement` mode you use for `<vcpu>` and `<numatune>`:

- The placement mode for `<numatune>` defaults to the same placement mode as `<vcpu>` or to `static` if `<nodeset>` is specified
- Similarly, the placement mode for `<vcpu>` defaults to the same placement mode as`<numatune>` or to `static` if `<cpuset>` is specified

This means that CPU tuning and memory tuning for domain processes can be specified and defined separately, but they can also be configured to be dependent on the other's placement mode.

There are some more things to consider when thinking about vCPU pinning in the NUMA context. We discussed the basis of vCPU pinning earlier in this chapter. In short, it gives similar advantages to task pinning on bare-metal systems. It increases cache efficiency. One example of this is an environment where all vCPU threads are running on the same physical socket, therefore sharing an L3 cache domain. When we discussed vCPU pinning, we said we should take care of some fundamental tuning issues when NUMA is present, because combining vCPU pinning with `numatune` can avoid NUMA misses. The performance impacts of NUMA misses are significant, generally starting at a 10% performance hit or higher. vCPU pinning and `numatune` should be configured together. As a use case, if the virtual machine is performing storage or network I/O tasks, it can be beneficial to pin all vCPUs and memory to the same physical socket that is physically connected to the I/O adapter.

emulatorpin

We pointed out that `emualtorpin` can fall into the CPU tune element. The XML representation of this would be as follows:

```
<domain>
  ...
    <cputune>
    ….．
      <emulatorpin cpuset="1-3"/>
      ….．
    </cputune>
  ...
</domain>
```

The `emulatorpin` element is optional and is used to pin the emulator (qemu-kvm) to a host physical CPU. This does not include vCPU or IO threads from the VM. It contains one required attribute CPU set specifying the physical CPUs to pin to. The `<emulatorpin>` tag provides a method of setting a precise affinity to emulator thread processes. As a result, vhost threads running on the same subset of physical CPUs and memory, will benefit from cache locality. If this is omitted, `emulator` is pinned to all the physical CPUs of the host system by default.

> Please note that `<vcpupin>`, `<numatune>`, and `<emulatorpin>` should be configured together to achieve optimal, deterministic performance when you tune a NUMA-capable system. Before we leave this section, there are a couple more things to cover: guest system NUMA topology and hugepage memory backing with NUMA.

Guest NUMA topology can be specified using the `<numa>` element in the guest XML configuration; some call this virtual NUMA:

```
<CPU>
    ...
  <numa>
    <cell id='0' CPUs='0-3' memory='512000' unit='KiB'/>
    <cell id='1' CPUs='4-7' memory='512000' unit='KiB'
memaccess='shared'/>
  </numa>
    ...
</CPU>
```

Guest NUMA topology can be specified using the `<numa>` tag inside the `<cpu>` tag in the guest virtual machine's XML. Each cell element specifies a NUMA cell or a NUMA node. The `<cpus>` tag specifies the CPU or range of CPUs that are part of the node. Memory specifies the node memory in kibibytes (that is, blocks of 1,024 bytes). Also, the optional attribute `memaccess` can control whether the memory is to be mapped as "shared" or "private". This is valid only for hugepages-backed memory. Each cell or node is assigned a cellid or nodeid in increasing order, starting from 0.

Previously, we discussed the `memorybacking` element, which can be specified to use hugepages in guest configurations. When NUMA is present in a setup, the optional `nodeset` attribute may come in handy as it ties a given guest's NUMA nodes to certain hugepage sizes:

```
<memoryBacking>
    <hugepages>
        <page size="1" unit="G" nodeset="0-3,5"/>
        <page size="2" unit="M" nodeset="4"/>
    </hugepages>
</memoryBacking>
```

In simple terms, hugepages from the host can be allocated to multiple guest NUMA nodes using the preceding configuration. The <page> element is introduced to satisfy the requirement. It has one compulsory attribute `size` which specifies that hugepages should be used (especially useful on systems supporting hugepages of different sizes). The default unit for the size attribute is kilobytes (a multiplier of 1,024). If you want to use a different unit, use the optional `unit` attribute. This can optimize memory performance, as guest NUMA nodes can be moved to host NUMA nodes as required, while the guest can continue to use the hugepages allocated by the host.

NUMA tuning also has to consider the NUMA node locality for PCI devices, especially when a PCI device is being passed through to the guest from the host. If the relevant PCI device is affiliated to a remote numa node, this can affect data transfer and thus hurt performance.

The easiest way to display the NUMA topology and PCI device affiliation is using the `istop` command that we discussed earlier. The non-graphic form of the same command can also be used to discover this configuration. Please refer to earlier sections.

KSM and NUMA

We discussed KSM in enough detail in previous sections. KSM is capable of detecting that a system is using NUMA memory and controlling merging pages across different NUMA nodes. If you remember, we encountered a `sysfs` entry called `merge_across_node` when we fetched KSM entries from `sysfs`. We can use this parameter to control the merging of pages belonging to different NUMA nodes.

```
[ humble-numaserver ]$ cat /sys/kernel/mm/ksm/merge_across_nodes
1
[ humble-numaserver ]$
```

By default, pages from all nodes can be merged together. When this parameter is set to zero, only pages from the same node are merged.

In general, unless you are oversubscribing or overcommitting the system memory, you will get better runtime performance by disabling KSM sharing.

When KSM merges across nodes on a NUMA host with multiple guest virtual machines, guests and CPUs from more distant nodes can suffer a significant increase in access latency to the merged KSM page.

Obviously, you know the guest XML entry (the `memorybacking` element) for asking the hypervisor to disable shared pages for the guest. If you don't remember, please read the memory tuning section for details of this element. Even though we can configure NUMA manually, there exists something called Automatic NUMA balancing. We did mention it earlier. Let's see what this concept involves.

Automatic NUMA balancing

The main aim of automatic NUMA balancing is to improve the performance of different applications running in a NUMA-aware system. The strategy behind its design is simple: an application will generally perform best when the threads of its processes are accessing memory on the same NUMA node where the threads are scheduled by the kernel. Automatic NUMA balancing moves tasks (threads or processes) closer to the memory they are accessing. It also moves application data to memory closer to the tasks that reference it. This is all done automatically by the kernel when automatic NUMA balancing is active. Automatic NUMA balancing will be enabled when booted on hardware with NUMA properties. The main conditions or criteria are:

- `numactl --hardware`: Shows multiple nodes
- `cat /sys/kernel/debug/sched_features`: Shows NUMA in the flags

To illustrate the second point:

```
[ humble-numaserver ]$ cat /sys/kernel/debug/sched_features

GENTLE_FAIR_SLEEPERS START_DEBIT NO_NEXT_BUDDY LAST_BUDDY CACHE_HOT_BUDDY
WAKEUP_PREEMPTION ARCH_POWER NO_HRTICK NO_DOUBLE_TICK LB_BIAS NONTASK_
POWER TTWU_QUEUE NO_FORCE_SD_OVERLAP RT_RUNTIME_SHARE NO_LB_MIN NUMA
NUMA_FAVOUR_HIGHER NO_NUMA_RESIST_LOWER
```

We can check whether it is enabled in the system via the following method:

```
[ humble-numaserver ]$ cat /proc/sys/kernel/numa_balancing
1
[ humble-numaserver ]$
```

Obviously, we can disable Automatic NUMA balancing via

```
# echo 0 > /proc/sys/kernel/numa_balancing
```

The Automatic NUMA balancing mechanism works based on the number of algorithms and data structures. The internals of this method are based on the following:

- NUMA hinting page faults
- NUMA page migration
- Task grouping
- Fault statistics
- Task placement
- Pseudo-interleaving, and so on

> For more details, refer to: `http://events.Linuxfoundation.org/sites/events/files/slides/summit2014_riel_chegu_w_0340_automatic_numa_balancing_0.pdf`

Any further explanation of these concepts is beyond the scope of this book. The preceding presentation provides details about how these parameters are applied and performance benchmarking. Please note that manual NUMA tuning of applications will override automatic NUMA balancing, disabling the periodic unmapping of memory, NUMA faults, migration, and automatic NUMA placement of those applications. Also, in some cases, system-wide manual NUMA tuning is preferred.

One of the best practices or recommendations for a KVM guest is to limit its resource, to the amount of resources on a single NUMA node. Put simply, this avoids unnecessarily splitting resources across NUMA nodes, which can degrade performance.

Understanding numad and numastat

There is a daemon to control efficient use of CPU and memory on systems with NUMA topology. numad is known as the **Automatic NUMA Affinity Management Daemon**. It monitors NUMA topology and resource usage within a system in order to dynamically improve NUMA resource allocation and management;

> *numad is a user-level daemon that provides placement advice and process management for efficient use of CPUs and memory on systems with NUMA topology.*

> *Numad is a system daemon that monitors NUMA topology and resource usage.*
> *It will attempt to locate processes for efficient NUMA locality and affinity,*
> *dynamically adjusting to changing system conditions. Numad also provides*
> *guidance to assist management applications with initial manual binding of CPU*
> *and memory resources for their processes. Note that numad is primarily intended*
> *for server consolidation environments, where there might be multiple applications*
> *or multiple virtual guests running on the same server system. Numad is most*
> *likely to have a positive effect when processes can be localized in a subset of the*
> *system's NUMA nodes. If the entire system is dedicated to a large in-memory*
> *database application, forexample, especially if memory accesses will likely remain*
> *unpredictable, numad will probably not improve performance.*

Please keep in mind that, when numad is enabled, its behavior overrides the default behavior of automatic NUMA balancing. To adjust and align the CPUs and memory resources automatically according to the NUMA topology, we need to run numad. To use numad as an executable, just run:

```
# numad
```

You can check whether this is started as shown:

```
[ humble-numaserver ]$ ps aux |grep numad
root    9170  0.0  0.0  93596  2828 ?       Ssl  Nov17   06:49 numad
```

Once the numad binary is executed it will start the alignment as shown next. In my system, I have the following virtual machines running.

```
[ humble-numaserver ]$ virsh list
Id  Name                     State
----------------------------------------------------
12  rhel7.0                  running
17  rhel7-atomic3            running
19  rhel7-atomic2            running
20  rhel7-atomic1            running
24  fedora21                 running
25  rhel7.0-2                running
```

If you watch the `numad` actions in the `/var/log/numad` log file, you can see similar messages!

```
Tue Nov 17 06:49:43 2015: Changing THP scan time in /sys/kernel/mm/
transparent_hugepage/khugepaged/scan_sleep_millisecs from 10000 to 1000
ms.
Tue Nov 17 06:49:43 2015: Registering numad version 20140225 PID 9170
Tue Nov 17 06:49:45 2015: Advising pid 1479 (qemu-kvm) move from nodes
(0-1) to nodes (1)
Tue Nov 17 06:49:47 2015: Including PID: 1479 in CPUset: /sys/fs/cgroup/
CPUset/machine.slice/machine-qemu\x2dfedora21.scope/emulator
Tue Nov 17 06:49:48 2015: PID 1479 moved to node(s) 1 in 3.33 seconds
Tue Nov 17 06:49:53 2015: Advising pid 20129 (qemu-kvm) move from nodes
(0-1) to nodes (0)
Tue Nov 17 06:49:54 2015: Including PID: 20129 in CPUset: /sys/fs/cgroup/
CPUset/machine.slice/machine-qemu\x2drhel7\x2datomic3.scope/emulator
Tue Nov 17 06:49:54 2015: PID 20129 moved to node(s) 0 in 0.84 seconds
Tue Nov 17 11:03:06 2015: Advising pid 2194 (qemu-kvm) move from nodes
(0-1) to nodes (0)
Tue Nov 17 11:03:06 2015: Including PID: 2194 in CPUset: /sys/fs/cgroup/
CPUset/machine.slice/machine-qemu\x2drhel7\x2datomic1.scope/emulator
Tue Nov 17 11:03:07 2015: PID 2194 moved to node(s) 0 in 0.31 seconds
```

From the preceding messages, it is understood some actions were performed by `numad` when we started the binary. You can use the `numastat` command, covered in an upcoming section, to monitor the difference before and after running the `numad` service.

`numad` will be running in your system until stopped with the following command:

```
# numad -i 0
```

Please remember, stopping `numad` does not remove the changes it has made to improve NUMA affinity. If system use changes significantly, running `numad` again will adjust the affinity to improve performance under the new conditions. Now let's move on to `numastat`.

"`numastat` - Show per-NUMA-node memory statistics for processes and the operating system"

The numactl package provides the numactl binary/command and the numad package provides the numad binary/command:

```
[ humble-numaserver ]$ numastat -c qemu-kvm

Per-node process memory usage (in MBs)
PID              Node 0 Node 1 Total
--------------   ------ ------ -----
1479 (qemu-kvm)      10   8865  8875
2119 (qemu-kvm)     667     77   744
2194 (qemu-kvm)    1465      0  1465
18404 (qemu-kvm)     30     25    54
20129 (qemu-kvm)   2182      0  2182
32548 (qemu-kvm)     34     16    50
--------------   ------ ------ -----
Total              4389   8982 13371
```

Figure 30: numastat command output for qemu-kvm process

The multiple memory tuning options we used has to be thoroughly tested using different workloads before moving the VM to production.

Before we jump on to the next topic, a word of caution! It is harder to live-migrate a pinned guest across hosts, because a similar set of backing resources/configurations may not be available on the destination or target host where the VM is getting migrated. For example, the target host may have a different NUMA topology. You should consider this fact when you tune a KVM environment. Automatic NUMA balancing may help, to a certain extent, the need for manually pinning guest resources, though.

Disk and block I/O tuning

We will start with disk options, transport, and image formats. Later we move onto block I/O tuning.

The virtual disk of a VM can be either block device or image file.

For better VM performace a block device based virtual disk is preferred over a image file that resides on a remote file system like NFS, GlusterFS, etc. However, we cannot ignore that the file backend helps the virt admin to better manage guest disks and it is immensely helpful in some scenarios. From our experience, we have noticed most users make use of disk image files, especially when performance is not much of a concern. Keep in mind that the total number of virtual disks that can be attached to a VM has a limit. At the same time, there is no restriction on mixing and using block devices and files and using them as storage disks for the same guest.

As mentioned earlier, a guest treats the virtual disk as its storage. When an application inside a guest operating system writes data to the local storage of the guest system, it has to pass through a couple of layers. That said, this I/O request has to traverse through the filesystem on the storage and the I/O subsystem of the guest operating system. After that, the qemu-kvm process passes it to the hypervisor from the guest OS. Once I/O is within the relam of the hypervisor, it starts processing the I/O like any other applications running in the host operating system. Here you can see the number of layers the I/O has to pass through to complete an I/O. Hence the block device backend performs better than the image file backend.

The following are our observations on disk backends and file or image based virtual disks:

- A file image is part of host filesystem and; it creates an additional resource demand for I/O operations compared to the block device backend

- Using sparse image files helps to over allocate host storage but its usage will reduce the performance of virtual disk

- Improper partitioning of guest storage when using disk image files can cause unnecessary I/O operations. Here we are mentioning about the alignment of standard partition units

At the start of this chapter, we discussed virtio drivers, which give better performance. So, it's recommended you use the virtio disk bus when configuring the disk rather than the IDE bus. The `virtio_blk` driver uses the VirtIO API to provide high performance for storage I/O device, thus increasing storage performance especially in large enterprise storage systems. We discussed different storage formats available in earlier chapters; however, the main ones are the `raw` and `qcow` formats. The best performance will be achieved when you are using the `raw` format. There is obviously a performance overhead delivered by the format layer when using `qcow`. Because the format layer has to perform some operations at times. for example if you want to grow a `qcow` image, it has to allocate the new cluster and so on. However `qcow` would be an option if you want to make use of features such as snapshots. These extra facilities are provided with the image format, `qcow`. Some performance comparisons can be found at `http://www.Linux-kvm.org/page/Qcow2`.

For more details on `qcow`, refer to `https://people.gnome.org/~markmc/qcow-image-format.html` and `https://en.wikipedia.org/wiki/Qcow`.

There are three options that can be considered for I/O tuning:

- Cache Mode
- I/O mode
- I/O tuning.

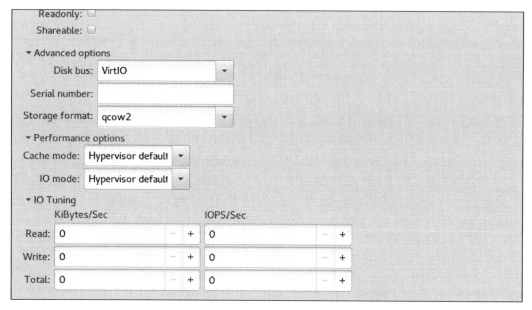

Virtual disk configuration

Cache mode

The next figure comes in handy when we think about different cache settings and their effect on I/O when originating from guest systems:

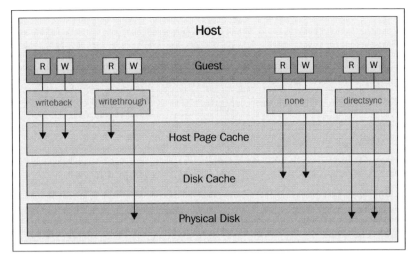

Disk cache modes

The following are the different cache modes:

- **None**: Maybe you have heard about the flag called `O_DIRECT`; it allows process to specify performing I/O without using the OS cache layer. The `cache=none` option is analogous to that. When this option has been set, the host page cache is bypassed and I/O happens directly between the `qemu-kvm userspace` buffers and the underlying storage device. That said, I/O from the guest is not cached on the host, but may be kept in a `writeback` disk cache. Use this option for guests with large I/O requirements. `cache=none` is considered to be the best choice. Also this is the only option to support migration.

- **writethrough**: This matches the semantics of `O_DSYNC`. The I/O from the guest is cached on the host but written through to the physical medium. In this scenario, writes are reported as completed only when the data has been committed to the storage device. Even though it assures data integrity, this mode is slower and prone to scaling problems. But this mode can be an option when a small number of guests with lower I/O requirements is in place. This cache mode is suggested for guests that do not support a `writeback` cache where migration is not needed.

- **writeback**: In this scenario, I/O from the guest is cached on the host. The hostpage cache is used and writes are reported to the guest as completed when placed in the hostpage cache; the normal page cache management will handle commitment to the storage device.

- **directsync**: Similar to `writethrough` but I/O from the guest bypasses the host page cache. In this configuration, the writes are reported as completed only when the data has been committed to the `cache=writeback` storage device, and when it is also desirable to bypass the host page cache.

- **unsafe**: The host may cache all disk I/O, and sync requests from guests are ignored, similarly to the mode. It's unsafe because there is a huge risk of data loss in the event there is a host failure. However, this may come in handy when doing a guest installation or similar tasks.

- **default**: If no cache mode is specified, the system's default settings are chosen.

The cache option settings can reflect in the guest XML as follows:

```
<disk type='file' device='disk'>
<driver name='qemu' type='raw'cache='writeback'/>
```

But the final configuration is I/O mode.

I/O mode

The XML representation of I/O mode configuration is similar to the following:

```
<disk type='file' device='disk'>
<driver name='qemu' type='raw'io='threads'/>
```

There are three main options available for I/O mode:

- `IO=native`: This mode refers to an asynchronous kernel I/O (AIO) with direct I/O options. This is expected to perform better on block devices; however when we use this option it requires `cache=none/directsync` to be set. If this cache option is not set, libvirt will fallback to `io=threads` mode.

- `IO=threads`: The default is host user-mode-based threads, which can be set by the `io=threads` option. This asynchronous IO mode is expected to perform better on file systems.

- `IO=default`: The default will be taken into account. In short, you should consider using `io=native` for block device-based VMs.

I/O tuning

Limiting the disk I/O of each guest may be required especially, when multiple guests exist in your setup. This is because, if only one guest is keeping the host system busy with the number of disk I/Os generated from it, it's not fair! Generally speaking, it is the system/virt administrator's responsibility to ensure all the running guests gets enough resources to work on—in other words, **Quality of Service (QOS)**! This is to be guaranteed. Even though disk I/O is not the only resource that has to be considered to guarantee this, this has some importance. This tuning can prevent a guest system from over-utilizing shared resources and impacting the performance of other guests systems coexisting in the same hypervisor. This is really a requirement, especially when the host system is serving a VPS or a similar kind of service. KVM gives the flexibility to do I/O throttling independently to each block device attached to a guest and supports limits on throughput and I/O operations.

This can be achieved via the `virsh blkdeviotune` command. The different options that can be set using this command are displayed next:

```
[humble-lap ]$ virsh blkdeviotune --help
  NAME
    blkdeviotune - Set or query a block device I/O tuning parameters.

  SYNOPSIS
    blkdeviotune <domain> <device> [--total-bytes-sec <number>] [--read
-bytes-sec <number>] [--write-bytes-sec <number>] [--total-iops-sec <nu
mber>] [--read-iops-sec <number>] [--write-iops-sec <number>] [--total-
bytes-sec-max <number>] [--read-bytes-sec-max <number>] [--write-bytes-
sec-max <number>] [--total-iops-sec-max <number>] [--read-iops-sec-max
<number>] [--write-iops-sec-max <number>] [--size-iops-sec <number>] [-
-config] [--live] [--current]

  DESCRIPTION
    Set or query disk I/O parameters such as block throttling.

  OPTIONS
    [--domain] <string>  domain name, id or uuid
    [--device] <string>  block device
    --total-bytes-sec <number>  total throughput limit in bytes per sec
ond
    --read-bytes-sec <number>  read throughput limit in bytes per secon
d
    --write-bytes-sec <number>  write throughput limit in bytes per sec
ond
    --total-iops-sec <number>  total I/O operations limit per second
    --read-iops-sec <number>  read I/O operations limit per second
    --write-iops-sec <number>  write I/O operations limit per second
    --total-bytes-sec-max <number>  total max in bytes
    --read-bytes-sec-max <number>  read max in bytes
    --write-bytes-sec-max <number>  write max in bytes
    --total-iops-sec-max <number>  total I/O operations max
    --read-iops-sec-max <number>  read I/O operations max
    --write-iops-sec-max <number>  write I/O operations max
    --size-iops-sec <number>  I/O size in bytes
    --config        affect next boot
    --live          affect running domain
    --current       affect current domain
```

virsh blkdeviotune command

Details about parameters such as `total-bytes-sec`, `read-bytes-sec`, `write-bytes-sec`, `total-iops-sec`, and so on, are well understood from the preceding command output and also documented in the `virsh` command man page.

For example, to throttle disk `vdb` on a `virtual machine` called `centos-1` to 2000 I/O operations per second and 50 MB-per-second throughput, run this command:

```
# virsh blkdeviotune centos-1 vdb --total-iops-sec 2000 --total-bytes-sec
52428800
```

Networking tuning in KVM

What I have seen in most KVM environment is that all the network traffic from a guest will take a single network path. There won't be any traffic segregation, which causes congestion in most KVM setups. As a first step for network tuning, I would advise trying different networks or dedicated networks for management, backups, or live migration. But when you have more than one network interface for your traffic, please try to avoid multiple network interfaces for the same network or segment. If this is at all in play, apply some network tuning that is common for such setups; for example, use `arp_filter` to prevent ARP Flux, an undesirable condition that can occur in both hosts and guests and is caused by the machine responding to ARP requests from more than one network interface:

```
echo 1 > /proc/sys/net/ipv4/conf/all/arp_filter or edit /etc/sysctl.conf
to make this setting persistent.
```

For more information on arp flux please refer to `http://Linux-ip.net/html/ether-arp.html#ether-arp-flux`.

The next tuning can be done on the driver level; that said, by now we know that virtio drivers give better performance compared to emulated device APIs. So, obviously using the `virtio_net` driver in guest systems should be taken into account. When we use the `virtio_net` driver, it has a backend driver in `qemu` that takes care of the communication initiated from the guest network. Even if this was performing better, some more enhancements in this area introduced a new driver called `vhost_net`.`vhost_net` is a character device that can be used to reduce the number of system calls involved in virtio networking. In other words, vhost provides in-kernel virtio devices for KVM (`https://lwn.net/Articles/346267/`). Even though `vhost` is a common framework that can be used by different drivers, the network driver, `vhost_net`, was one of the first drivers. The following screenshot will make this clearer:

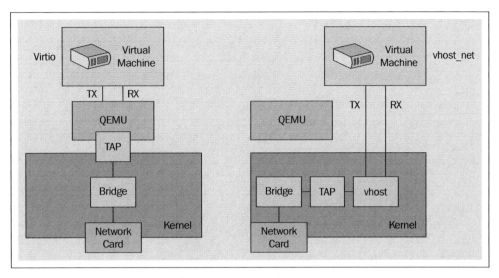

Source: `access.redhat.com`

As you may have noticed, the number of context switches is really reduced with the new path of communication. The good news is that there is no extra configuration required in guest systems to support `vhost` because there is no change to the frontend driver.

`vhost_net` reduces copy operations, lowers latency and CPU usage, and thus yields better performance. First of all, the kernel module called `vhost_net` (refer to the screenshot in the next section) has to be loaded in the system. As this is a character device inside the host system, it creates a device file called `/dev/vhost-net` on the host. This character device serves as the interface for configuring the `vhost-net` instance.

How to turn it on?

When QEMU is launched with `-netdev tap,vhost=on`, it opens `/dev/vhost-net` and initializes the `vhost-net` instance with several `ioctl()` calls. This initialization process binds `qemu` with a `vhost-net` instance, along with other operations such as feature negotiations and so on:

```
[humble-lap ]$ lsmod |grep vhost
vhost_net              20480  1
vhost                  32768  1 vhost_net
macvtap                20480  1 vhost_net
tun                    28672  4 vhost_net
[humble-lap ]$ modinfo vhost_net
filename:       /lib/modules/4.2.3-200.fc22.x86_64/kernel/drivers/vhost/vhost_net.ko.xz
alias:          devname:vhost-net
alias:          char-major-10-238
description:    Host kernel accelerator for virtio net
author:         Michael S. Tsirkin
license:        GPL v2
version:        0.0.1
srcversion:     1EDC0A4AEC45D8F033A71FE
depends:        vhost,tun,macvtap
intree:         Y
vermagic:       4.2.3-200.fc22.x86_64 SMP mod_unload
signer:         Fedora kernel signing key
sig_key:        6B:32:69:BB:F8:47:97:01:C8:03:15:FB:5F:36:8A:F9:24:52:07:BE
sig_hashalgo:   sha256
parm:           experimental_zcopytx:Enable Zero Copy TX; 1 -Enable; 0 - Disable (int)
[humble-lap ]$
[humble-lap ]$ modinfo --parameters vhost_net
experimental_zcopytx:Enable Zero Copy TX; 1 -Enable; 0 - Disable (int)
[humble-lap ]$ █
```

vhost kernel module information

A snip from my KVM host is shown next:

```
--snip-- of qemu-kvm process

...

-netdev tap,fd=25,id=hostnet0,vhost=on,vhostfd=27 -device virtio-net-pci,
netdev=hostnet0,id=net0,mac=52:54:00:49:3b:95,bus=pci.0,addr=0x3

--/snip--
```

One of the parameters available with the `vhost_net` module is `experimental_zcopytx`. What does it do? This parameter controls something called `Bridge Zero Copy Transmit`. Let's see what this means:

```
--snip-- from http://www.google.com/patents/US20110126195
```

"A system for providing a zero copy transmission in virtualization environment includes a hypervisor that receives a guest operating system (OS) request pertaining to a data packet associated with a guest application, where the data packet resides in a buffer of the guest OS or a buffer of the guest application and has at least a partial header created during the networking stack processing. The hypervisor further sends, to a network device driver, a request to transfer the data packet over a network via a network device, where the request identifies the data packet residing in the buffer of the guest OS or the buffer of the guest application, and the hypervisor refrains from copying the data packet to a hypervisor buffer."

If your environment uses large packet sizes, this parameter configuration may have a noticeable effect. The host CPU overhead is reduced by configuring this parameter when the guest communicates to the external network. This does not affect the performance in the following scenarios:

- Guest to guest communication
- Guest to host
- Small packet workloads

Also, the performance improvement can be obtained by enabling multi queue virtio-net (`https://fedoraproject.org/wiki/Features/MQ_virtio_net`).

One of the bottlenecks when using `virtio-net` was its single RX and TX queue. Even though there are more vCPUs, the networking throughput was affected by this limitation. Guests cannot transmit or retrieve packets in parallel as `virtio-net` has only one TX and RX queue. To solve this limitation, multi queue virtio net was developed. Till this implementation happened virtual NICs could not utilize the multi queue support that is available in the Linux kernel. `tap/virtio-net backend` had to serialize the co-current transmission/receiving request, which comes from different CPUs that caused the performance overhead.

This bottleneck is lifted by introducing multiqueue support in both frontend and backend drivers. This also helps guests scale with more vCPUs.

To start a guest with two queues, you could specify the `queues` parameters to both `tap` and `virtio-net`, as follows:

```
#qemu-kvm -netdev tap,queues=2,... -device virtio-net-pci,queues=2,...
```

The equivalent guest XML is as follows:

```
<interface type='network'>
    <source network='default'/>
    <model type='virtio'/>
    <driver name='vhost' queues='M'/>
</interface>
```

Where 'M' can be 1 to 8, as the kernel supports up to eight queues for a multi-queue tap device. Once it's configured for qemu, inside the guest, we need to enable multi queue support by the ethtool command. Enable the multi queue through ethtool (where the value of K is from 1 to M) by:

```
#ethtool -L eth0 combined 'K'
```

Multi Queue virtio-net provides the greatest performance benefit when:

- Traffic packets are relatively large.
- The guest is active on many connections at the same time, with traffic running between guests, guest to host, or guest to an external system.
- The number of queues is equal to the number of vCPUs. This is because multi-queue support optimizes RX interrupt affinity and TX queue selection in order to make a specific queue private to a specific vCPU.

In spite of these, please test the impact in your setup, because the CPU consumption will be greater in this scenario even though the network throughput is impressive.

Other networking tuning options are **device assignment** and **Single Root IO Virtualization(SR-IOV)**. Device assignment is nothing but directly assigning a host physical NIC to the guest system. Obviously, this can result in better performance, but please note that the device won't be usable for hosts and other guest systems. Please refer to the previous chapters for more information on how to do device assignment and SR-IOV in KVM land:

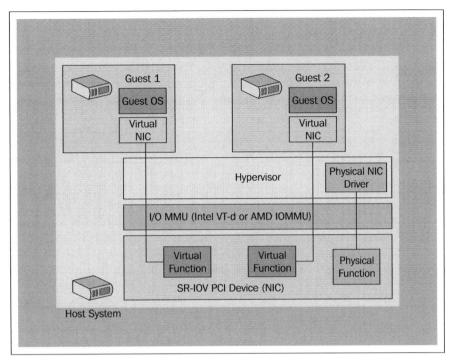

SR-IOV picture

Additional references:

https://fedoraproject.org/wiki/Features/KVM_PCI_Device_Assignment

https://fedoraproject.org/wiki/Features/SR-IOV

KVM guest time-keeping best practices

There are different mechanisms for time keeping. One of the best known techniques is **Network Time Protocol (NTP)** .This is a networking protocol for clock synchronization between computer systems over packet-switched, variable-latency data networks. One thing that needs to be considered in a virtualization environment is the maxim that the guest time should be in sync with the hypervisor/host, because it affects lots of guest operations and can cause unpredictable results if they are not in sync.

There are different ways to achieve time sync, however; it depends on the setup you have. I have seen people using NTP, setting the system clock from the hardware clock using `hwclock -s` and so on. The first thing that needs to be considered here is trying to make the KVM host time in sync and stable. You can use NTP-like protocols to achieve this. Once it's in place, the guest time has to be kept in sync. Even though there are different mechanisms for doing that, the best option would be using `kvm-clock`!

kvm-clock

`kvm-clock` is also known as a virtualization-aware (paravirtualized) clock device. When `kvm-clock` is in use, the guest asks the hypervisor about the current time, guaranteeing both stable and accurate timekeeping. The functionality is achieved by the guest registering a page and sharing the address with the hypervisor. This is a shared page between the guest and the hypervisor. The hypervisor keeps updating this page unless it is asked to stop. The guest can simply read this page whenever it wants time information. However, please note that the hypervisor should support `kvm-clock` for the guest to use it. For more details, you can reference https://lkml.org/lkml/2010/4/15/355.

You can verify whether `kvm_clock` is loaded inside the guest via the following method:

```
[root@kvmguest ]$ dmesg |grep kvm-clock
[   0.000000] kvm-clock: Using msrs 4b564d01 and 4b564d00
[   0.000000] kvm-clock: CPU 0, msr 4:27fcf001, primary CPU clock
[   0.027170] kvm-clock: CPU 1, msr 4:27fcf041, secondary CPU clock
....
[   0.376023] kvm-clock: CPU 30, msr 4:27fcf781, secondary CPU clock
[   0.388027] kvm-clock: CPU 31, msr 4:27fcf7c1, secondary CPU clock
[   0.597084] Switched to clocksource kvm-clock
```

Further verification on, currently the guest uses it as a clock source can be done by:

```
[root@kvmguest ]$  cat /sys/devices/system/clocksource/clocksource0/
current_clocksource
kvm-clock
[root@kvmguest ]$
```

So, use `kvm_clock` (it's a recommended practice) to achieve the best result!

Summary

In this chapter, we went through the performance tuning aspects of a KVM setup. Starting with the virtio framework, we went through various subsystems, such as CPU and memory, disk and block I/O, network time keeping, and tuning possibilities. We also covered NUMA concepts, Hugepages, KSM, and the tuning that can be applied with it. Performance has to be measured and you have to come up with the best options to match your scenario.

In the next chapter, we will discuss how to migrate your virtual machines running on foreign hypervisors to the KVM hypervisor using the `virt-v2v` tool. We will also discuss physical machine-to-virtual machine migration in the next chapter.

14

V2V and P2V Migration Tools

V2V is a process in which you move VMs that are virtualized on one vendor's virtualization platform to another, whereas P2V involves moving all the data from a physical system to a virtualized infrastructure in order to gain all the flexibility and cost-saving benefits of virtualization. In this chapter, you will learn how to migrate virtual machines running on foreign hypervisors to a KVM hypervisor using a virt-v2v tool. You will also learn how to migrate physical machines to virtual machines and then run them on the cloud.

Introducing the virt-v2v utility

virt-v2v is a special command-line utility, using which we can convert VMs from a foreign hypervisor to run on a KVM hypervisor managed by libvirt, OpenStack, oVirt, and **Red Hat Enterprise Virtualization (RHEV)**. virt-p2v is a companion tool of virt-v2v that comes as an ISO or CD image to help a physical machine's conversion to a virtual machine.

However, is a special utility to convert a virtual machine from one platform to another or physical to virtual server conversion really required? Can't we just copy the bits residing on a physical disk to a virtual disk, such as dd + nc? This might be the question in your mind. If it is, then it's a valid question indeed.

System conversion using utilities such as dd and nc works. You will be able to migrate the systems from virtual to virtual, as well as physical to virtual, but with partial success. It also involves a lot of manual work, so there is a high chance of failure.

To automate the conversion process, a specialized tool is required as virtual to virtual or physical to virtual system conversions are not just copying bits from one disk to another, along with copying data from one location to another. It is very important to inject KVM paravirtualized drivers and modify some internal low-level guest operating system configurations. virt-v2v does automation of all the manual work involved in the system conversion. You just need to run the command and it will perform all the necessary actions to successfully and quickly migrate the systems.

virt-v2v can currently convert RHEL4, RHEL 5, RHEL 6, RHEL 7, Windows XP, Windows Vista, Windows 7, Windows Server 2003, Windows Server 2008 virtual machines running on Xen, VMware ESX, and physical systems to KVM hypervisors.

The following source hypervisors are currently supported by virt-v2v:

- libvirt-managed Xen
- VMware vSphere ESX/ESXi — versions 3.5, 4.0, 4.1, 5.0, 5.1, and 5.5

How does virt-v2v work?

In order to convert a virtual machine from foreign hypervisors to run on KVM hypervisors, the virt-v2v utility performs the following steps:

1. Retrieve guest configuration (xml) from the hypervisor
2. Export a disk image
3. Modify the disk image
4. Create a guest on the target hypervisor

virt-v2v connects to the target hypervisor using libvirt, retrieves the specified virtual machine configuration and disk path, and then transfers the disk image over the network to the conversion server. Next, we will modify this image to install a virtio driver (network and block). We will then update the guest operating system configuration to match the KVM environment that includes updating the /etc/fstab and xorg.conf file, rebuilding initrd, removing blkid.tab, and finally creating a guest on the target KVM host.

Getting the virt-v2v utility

The virt-v2v utility is shipped as an RPM package. The package is available in the Fedora base channel. To install it, we will use the `dnf` package manager by running the following command:

```
#dnf install virt-v2v
```

The system on which the virt-v2v package is installed is referred to as the virt-v2v conversion server. It can be installed on a virtual or physical system.

Preparing for the v2v conversion

virt-v2v has a number of possible input and output modes, which are selected using the `-i` and `-o` options. The input is the source hypervisor and the output is the destination hypervisor. If you want to convert the virtual machine from VMware, select VMware as the input and choose the destination where you want to run the virtual machine upon conversion. It can be oVirt, glance, or a standalone KVM host. The following diagram depicts a typical virtual to virtual migration procedure:

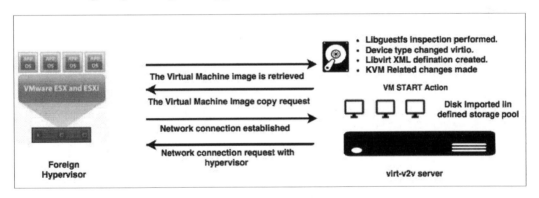

The following are the prerequisites of a V2V migration using the virt-v2v utility.

Guest operating system-specific prerequisites:

- **Linux**: Make sure that the Linux operating system running on the system is supported by virt-v2v and the kernel in use contains the virtio drivers. You can quickly check whether the virtio drivers are present in the kernel or not by running the following command:

```
#lsmod | grepvirtio
virtio              4977  0
```

If the output of the preceding command is blank, it means that the virtio drivers are not present in the kernel that you are using on the system. You may want to upgrade the kernel to the latest version.

- **Windows**: Make sure that the following checklist is followed:

    ◦ Install the `libguestfs-winsupport` package on the host running virt-v2v. This package provides support for NTFS, which is used by many Windows systems.

    ◦ Install the `virtio-win` package on the host running virt-v2v. This package provides paravirtualized block and network drivers for Windows guests:

      ```
      # yum install libguestfs-winsupportvirtio-win on virt- v2v
      conversion server.
      ```

    ◦ Disable the **Anti-Virus (AV)** software if any installed, as in some circumstances it may prevent new drivers that virt-v2v installs from working.

    ◦ Disable Group Policy before doing the conversion, as in some circumstances it may prevent new drivers that virt-v2v installs, from working.

Source hypervisor-specific prerequisites:

- **KVM**: Ensure that SSH is enabled and listening on the default port. Root login over SSH must be allowed. Make sure that the `PermitRootLogin` directive set to `yes` in `/etc/ssh/sshd_config`.

- **VMware vSphere**: Make sure that the following checklist is followed:

    ◦ Remove VMware-Tools installed on the system

    ◦ Enable SSH access to the system with permit root login

    ◦ virt-v2v directly talks to vCenter in order to perform the conversion, so you need either administrator-user credentials or a user with a custom non-administrator role, with a minimum set of permissions to access datastores and virtual machine configurations

- **XEN Virtualization**: The conversion guest must have access to the packages repository as new kernel and drivers need to be downloaded, and SSH should be enabled.

Conversion process

During the conversion, depending on the source hypervisor selection, the virt-v2v utility performs the following actions:

- Removes the kernel package if it's a paravirtualized guest
- Removes the the Xen drivers, such as xen_net, xen_blk, and so on
- If the guest has several kernels installed, it will find out the newest kernel containing virtio drivers
- If the new kernel supports virtio, replace the network driver with virtio_net and block driver with virtio_blk; otherwise use non-virtio drivers
- Replaces the display driver with *cirrus*
- Updates the `/etc/fstab` configuration of modprobe
- Makes sure that initrd can boot the real root device

To convert a virtual machine, the syntax is as follows:

```
# virt-v2v -i<input target> -o <output target> -os<output storage>
# virt-v2v -ic<libvirtURI><guest name> -o <output target>  -os<output
storage > --network <network>
```

virt-v2v has number of possible options to customize the output, `--no-trim all` says not to trim the resulted disk. `-of` is to change the output disk format. For a complete list of the parameters available with virt-v2v, refer to the virt-v2v main page, available here: `http://libguestfs.org/virt-v2v.1.html`.

> Performing live v2v is not supported yet. Ensure that the virtual machine is stopped prior to running the v2v conversion process on it.

VMware guest conversion

Let's see how to move virtual machines from the VMware vSphere platform to a KVM hypervisor.

Converting a VMware vSphere guest to a standalone KVM host

To convert a virtual machine to a standalone KVM host, perform the following steps:

1. Run the following command, using values from your system. In this example, `esxhost1.example.com` is the VMware vCenter server, `VM001` is the name of the virtual machine, and `/var/tmp` is the local repository to store the image:

    ```
    # virt-v2v -ic vpx://admin@esxhost1.example.com/Datacenter/esxi
    "vm001" -o local -os /var/tmp
    ```

2. On running this command, virt-v2v will ask for the password for `admin@esx.example.com`. You can enter the password interactively or by using the `--password-file` option.

> In non-production environments, the VMware vCenter server may have a nonvalid certificate, for example, a self-signed certificate. In this case, certificate checking can be explicitly disabled by adding `?no_verify=1` to the connection URI, as shown in the following example:
>
> `... -ic esx://esx.example.com?no_verify=1`

The conversion process will take some time to complete. You will be shown the progress and the conversion step that is currently in progress on the console. The time to complete the process depends on the virtual machine disk size and the network bandwidth. As the disk is transferred over the network, it is recommended to have at least 1 G Ethernet link.

On successful completion, virt-v2v will create a new libvirt domain XML file and disk image in the `/var/tmp` directory. You can define the virtual machine using `virsh define <xml file path>` and it will be listed in your virt-manager and other libvirt connections.

Converting a VMware vSphere guest to oVirt

The procedure is same as the previous one, except you need to point the output storage to your oVirt export storage domain:

1. Create an NFS export domain. Attach this to the oVirt data center. Make sure that the host acting as the virt-v2v conversion server has access it.

2. Shut down the virtual machine and uninstall VMware Tools on the guest operating system.

3. Now convert the virtual machines using the following command:

```
virt-v2v -icvpx://admin@esxhost1.example.com/Datacenter/esxi
"vm002   -o rhev -osovirt.nfs:/export_domain --network ovirt
```

Here:

- ° -ic: This is the URI of your ESX host.

- ° -o: This is the output method. No explicit method is available for oVirt; however, the RHEV method works out of box.

- ° -os: This is the output storage, the NFS export storage domain path, where you wish to save the converted virtual machine image. The domain must be in a format, for example, `ovirt.nfs:/export_domain`.

- ° -network: This is the network where the virtual machine will be mapped.

 Optionally, you can create a virt-v2v profile. It is very useful when a large number of virtual machine migrations are planned.

4. Import the virtual machine from the export storage domain into oVirt.

Converting a VMware vSphere guest to an OpenStack-Glance repository

The procedure to convert a VMware guest to OpenStack is a bit different than converting to an oVirt or standalone KVM host. You will first need to install the OpenStack-Glance package on the virt-v2v conversion host and set the environment variables pointing to the OpenStack keystone API and its access credentials. The steps are outlined as follows:

1. Install the Glance service client binary and tools on the virt-v2v conversion server:

```
# dnf install python-glanceclient
```

2. Copy the `/root/keystonerc_admin` file from your OpenStack controller node to the virt-v2v conversion server and source it:

```
#source /root/keystonerc_admin
#cat /root/keystonerc_admin
export OS_USERNAME=admin
export OS_TENANT_NAME=admin
export OS_PASSWORD=my_password
export OS_AUTH_URL=http://192.0.2.1:5000/v2.0/
```

3. Set the `LIBGUESTFS_BACKEND` method to `direct`:

```
# export LIBGUESTFS_BACKEND=direct
```

4. Now you can run virt-v2v:

```
# virt-v2v -ic 'vpx://vcenter1.example.com/datacentername/
esxihost1.example.com?no_verify=1' "guestvm1" -o glance
```

5. Enter your vCenter administrator password when prompted. This process can take a long time.

6. Once the conversion is completed, log in to your OpenStack Dashboard and confirm that the image has been uploaded in **Project | Compute | Images**.

Xen guest conversion

virt-v2v does not yet natively support converting virtual machines from Citrix's Xen-based virtualization. However you can use virt-v2v for converting virtual machines running on old Xen implementations in CentOS5 or similar hosts that is managed by libvirt.

The following things are to be checked before initiating conversion:

- Make sure that the virtual machine that needs to be migrated to the KVM hypervisor has access to the YUM repository in order to download a non-Xen kernel and some other stuff.

- Make sure that the SSH connection is enabled on Xen Dom0.

- Once you confirm the preceding options, you can start converting your Xen virtual machines using the following commands.

The following are the different targets to which a Xen VM can be converted:

- To convert a Xen virtual machine to a KVM standalone host, run the following command:

```
# virt-v2v -ic 'xen+ssh://root@xen.example.com' rhel5-1-xen' -o
local -os /v2vconvert/ -on rhel5-1-kvm
```

This command will convert a virtual machine named `rhel5-1-xen` to a local KVM hypervisor. Store its disk in the `/v2vconvert` directory and renames it as `rhel5-1-kvm`. In virt-manager, it will be listed `rhel5-1-kvm`.

- To convert a Xen virtual machine to an oVirt virtual data center, run the following command:

```
virt-v2v -icxen+ssh://root@xen.example.com' -o rhev -osstorage.
example.com:/exportdomain --network ovirt rhel5-2-xen
```

This command will convert the virtual machine named `rhel5-2-xen` to the oVirt format and store it in an oVirt export storage domain-backed `storage.example.com:/exportdomain` NFS share.

- To convert a Xen virtual machine to an OpenStack Glance image repository, run the following command:

```
virt-v2v -icxen+ssh://root@xen.example.com'  -o glance rhel5-3-xen
```

 Make sure that you export your `openstackkeystonerc_admin` file before initiating conversion of the virtual machine.

This command will convert the virtual machine named `rhel5-3-xen` to your OpenStack Glance image repository.

Converting standalone KVM guests to an oVirt Virtualization platform and the OpenStack cloud

In order to convert guests from a standalone KVM system to oVirt, perform the following steps:

1. Create an NFS export domain. Attach this to the oVirt data center. Make sure that the host acting as virt-v2v conversion server has access it.

2. Shut down the virtual machine. Make sure that SSH is enabled on the host.

3. Convert the virtual machine using the following command:

```
#virt-v2v -icqemu+ssh://root@kvmhost.example.com/system -o rhev
-osstorage.example.com:/exportdomain --network ovirtguest_name
```

`kvmhost.example.com/system`: This is the KVM host from where the virtual machine needs to be migrated.

4. Import the virtual machine from the export storage domain into Ovirt.

    ○   To convert guests from a standalone KVM system to Glance, run the following command:

    ```
    #virt-v2v -icqemu+ssh://root@kvmhost.example.com/system -o
    rhev -o glance vm001
    ```

    This command will convert the `vm001` virtual machine Windows 7 guest to your OpenStack Glance image repository from the `kvmhost.example.com` host.

A few things to note here are as follows:

*   Make sure that you export your `openstackkeystonerc_admin` file before initiating conversion of the virtual machine
*   Make sure that `ibguestfs-winsupport` and `virto-win` packages are installed on the virt-v2v conversion server

Troubleshooting virt-v2v related issues

Here are a few points to keep in mind while troubleshooting virt-v2v:

*   Ensure that the required v2v packages are installed on the virt-v2v conversion server. For example, libguestfs-winsupport and virtio-win are installed when a Windows guest migration is planned.
*   Ensure that SSH is enabled on the source host machine.
*   Make sure that the Export Storage domain has enough space to accommodate new virtual machines.
*   Verify that the virt-v2v command syntax that is being used is correct. The virt-v2v man page has a detailed explanation of each parameter and examples are also included.

Everything fine, but the migration is still failing?

In such a situation, enabling virt-v2v debug logs will be helpful. Virt-v2v debug logs can be enabled by prefixing the virt-v2v command with the following environment variables:

```
LIBGUESTFS_TRACE=1
LIBGUESTFS_DEBUG=1
```

The following is what the command will look like:

```
#LIBGUESTFS_TRACE=1 LIBGUESTFS_DEBUG=1 virt-v2v -icxen+ssh://root@vmhost.
example.com -o rhev -osstorage.example.com:/exportdomain --network
ovirtguest_name   2>&1 | tee virt-v2v.log
```

Physical system to virtual conversion

virt-v2v can to talk to a foreign hypervisor to obtain a VM's virtual hardware information and metadata. But when the source is a physical system, virt-v2v cannot gather information on hardware. To solve this virt-v2v relies on a small bootable image to run a tool named virt-p2v on the physical host. virt-p2v sends the physical system's data over SSH to the virt-v2v host, which then convert it to a VM on the target hypervisor.

Creating a virt-p2v bootable image

virt-p2v bootable media is unfortunately not available on any official Fedora site for download. You will need build it on your own using either the virt-p2v-make-disk (http://libguestfs.org/virt-p2v-make-disk.1.html) or virt-p2v-make-kickstart (http://libguestfs.org/virt-p2v-make-kickstart.1.html) utilities. Both these utilities are part of the virt-v2v package. Perform the following steps in order to create a virt-p2v bootable image:

1. Write a virt-p2v bootable USB key on /dev/sdX:

    ```
    #virt-p2v-make-disk -o /dev/sdX fedora-22
    ```

    This command will write the virt-p2v to /dev/sdX USB drive and make it bootable.

2. Create a virt-p2v bootable ISO and burn on DVD:

    ```
    #virt-p2v-make-kickstart fedora
    ```

    This will build a kickstart file for Fedora. The kickstart file will be called p2v.ks and is located in the current directory.

3. Once you have the `kickstart` file, you can use *livecd-creator(8)* (http://man.he.net/man8/livecd-creator) to make a live CD:

```
#livecd-creator p2v.ks
```

This http://oirase.annexia.org/virt-p2v/ directory contains the unofficial virt-p2v ISOs and PXE boot images. You may use them if you don't wish to build virt-p2v on your own.

The resulting virt-p2v tool allows you to convert physical hosts into virtual machines. This is accomplished by the network booting the physical host with the virt-p2v boot image, which then copies the disk image and network configuration to the virt-v2v server for conversion.

Can we convert any physical computers to virtual using virt-v2v?

Many a times, you must have thought whether it is possible to convert a physical computer to a virtual system using virt-v2v. It depends on the physical system configuration. I have tested converting many physical computers and it worked absolutely fine. However, there are some restrictions that apply to P2V. To perform a P2V conversion, your physical system must have the following prerequisites:

- They must have at least 512 MB of RAM.
- They cannot have any volumes larger than 2040 GB.
- virt-v2v supports P2V conversion for computers based on the x86 or x86_64 architecture. You won't able able convert computers with Itanium architecture–based operating systems.
- Computers with their root filesystem root on a software RAID md device cannot be converted to virtual machines.
- The operating system installed on the computer must be supported to run as a guest on KVM.
- They must have at least one Ethernet connection.

If your physical computer meets the preceding basic hardware requirements, it will successfully boot the P2V client. The following diagram depicts a typical physical to virtual migration:

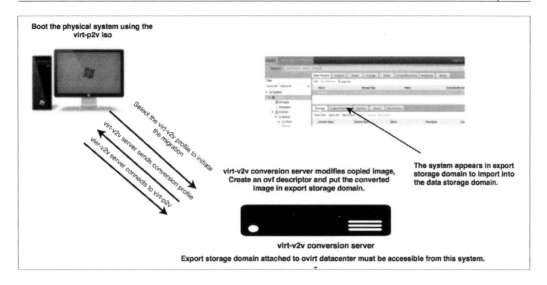

Boot the physical system using the virt-p2v iso

Select the virt-v2v profile to initiate the migration

virt-v2v server sends conversion profile

vier-v2v server connects to virt-p2v

virt-v2v conversion server modifies copied image, Create an ovf descriptor and put the converted image in export storage domain.

The system appears in export storage domain to import into the data storage domain.

virt-v2v conversion server

Export storage domain attached to ovirt datacenter must be accessible from this system.

Booting a physical system using a virt-p2v bootable disk for conversion

The following are the steps to convert a physical system to a virtual system. The following steps should be run in the same sequence as documented:

1. Boot the physical system using virt-p2v. The virt-p2v client comes with a sleek and minimal, yet complete configuration GUI. The first dialog looks similar to the following image:

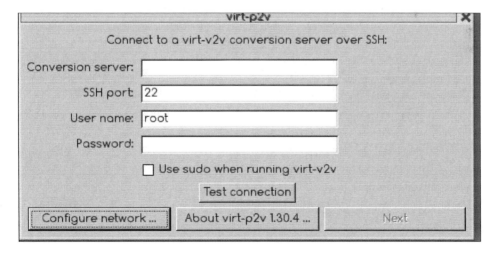

Connect to a virt-v2v conversion server over SSH:

Conversion server:

SSH port: 22

User name: root

Password:

☐ Use sudo when running virt-v2v

Test connection

Configure network ...   About virt-p2v 1.30.4 ...   Next

2. The virt-p2v looks for a DHCP server for network confirmation from DHCP. If there is no DHCP server on the network, click on the **Configure Network** button and press *Enter* to open the **Network Connections** dialog box:

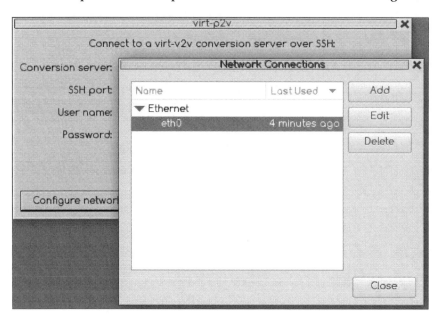

3. On completing the network configuration, enter the details of the conversion server: the hostname, SSH port number, remote username, and either the password or SSH identity (private key) URL:

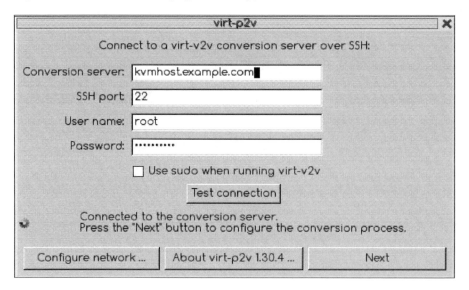

4. In order to perform the conversion, the virt-p2v needs root privileges on the virt-v2v conversion server. If the root SSH login is not allowed on the virt-v2v conversion server, tick the **Use sudo when running virt-v2v** checkbox to elevate privileges of the root user using sudo.

5. You must click on the **Test connection** button first to test the SSH connection for the conversion server. If this is successful, then click the **Next** button to move to the next button.

6. Clicking on the *Next* button will bring the main configuration of the virt-p2v client. The configuration is divided into four parts. Starting with the target profile, where you can specify the **Name** of the resulted virtual machine, **vCPU**, and **Memory** configurations.

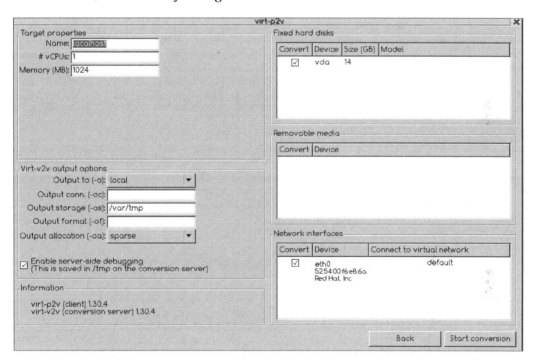

7. In the right-hand column, there are three panels that control which hard disks, removable media devices, and network interfaces will be created in the output guest. Normally, leaving these in the default settings is fine.

8. In the bottom left corner, **virt-v2v output options** is where you can specify the output target, output connection, output storage location, output format, and the end output allocation. By default, the output disk is set to **sparse**.

9. Specify the conversion target to the same as we used with the virt-v2v command and click the start button to initiate the conversion. You will get the progress dialog once the conversion is completed. The system is powered off automatically, as shown in the following image:

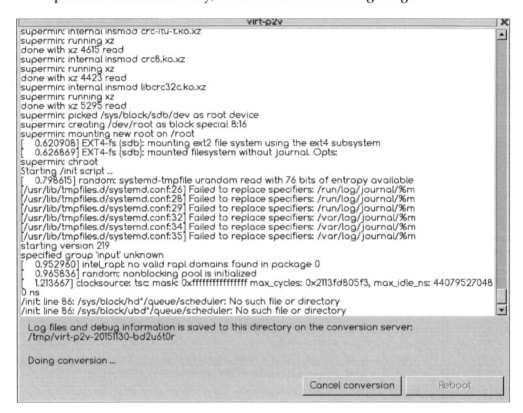

Converting virtual machines from unsupported virtualization platforms

If you have a virtual machine running on VirtualBox, Oracle VM, or any other unsupported virtualization platforms and wish to convert it to KVM then you have two options available.

The first option is to export the virtual machine from your virtualization platform to **open virtualization format** (**ova**). Copy this ova container to the virt-v2v conversion server and use ova as the input for the virt-v2v command:

```
#export pool=default
#virt-v2v -i ova -os $pool ovafile
```

This command will read the manifest bundled into the ova file, and create a virtual machine on the local standalone KVM host. The resulting disk image is stored in a libvirt storage pool, named `default`.

The second option is to consider the virtual machine as a physical system and use virt-p2v method to convert it.

Now you may have a question, how virt-v2v identify the guest operating system?

virt-v2v uses the virt-inspector utility to inspect the actual OS inside the guest image. This will detect the OS type (Windows/Linux), version (XP/2003/?), and other OS-dependent information.

List of input and output methods supported with virt-v2v

Input:

- `-i disk`: This is used to read from local disk images (mainly for testing).
- `-ilibvirt`: This is used to read from any libvirt source. As libvirt can connect to many different hypervisors, it is used to read guests from VMware, RHEL 5 Xen, and more. The `-ic` option selects the precise libvirt source.
- `-ilibvirtxml`: This is used to read from libvirt XML files. This is the method used by virt-p2v(1) behind the scenes.
- `-i ova`: This is used to read from a VMware ova source file.
- `-o glance`: This is used to write to OpenStack Glance.

Output:

- `-o libvirt`: This is used to write to any libvirt target. Libvirt can connect to local or remote KVM hypervisors. The `-oc` option selects the precise libvirt target.
- `-o local`: This is used to write to a local disk image with a local libvirt configuration file (mainly for testing).
- `-o qemu`: This writes to a local disk image with a shell script to boot the guest directly in qemu (mainly for testing).
- `-o rhev`: This is used to write to a RHEV-M/oVirt target. `-o vdsm` is only used when virt-v2v runs under VDSM control.

Summary

This chapter covered virtual to virtual and physical to virtual conversions using the virt-v2v utility, covering Windows and Linux system conversion. It also covered how to move a physical system to virtual and then to the cloud, and how to troubleshoot virt-v2v-related issues by enabling debug loggings.

Converting a Virtual Machine into a Hypervisor

KVM needs the virtualization extension (`# egrep '(vmx|svm)' /proc/cpuinfo`) of CPU to run as a hypervisor. This means that you need multiple bare metal systems to test the examples provided in this book, which is a challenge for most of the sysadmins. What if you can test everything using your laptop?

Introducing nested KVM

Nested KVM is technology that enables KVM to run virtual machines inside a virtual machine. This enables the virtualization extension available on a physical CPU inside a virtual CPU.

How to enable nested KVM?

By default, nested KVM is disabled.

Open `/etc/modprobe.d/kvm.conf` as root user using a text editor like vim. If the file does not exist create `/etc/modprobe.d/kvm.conf`:

- #Uncomment `kvm_intel` line if your CPU make is Intel
- #options `kvm_intel nested=1`
- #Uncomment `kvm_intel` line if your CPU make is AMD
- #options `kvm_amd nested=1`

Save the file and reboot the system. Once the system reboots verify nested by checking.

```
# cat /sys/module/kvm_intel/parameters/nested
Y
```

For AMD, the file to check is `/sys/module/kvm_intel/parameters/nested`:

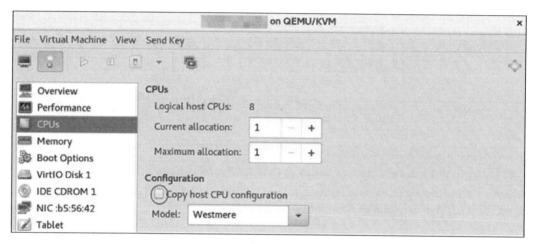

Fig - 1

After verifying nested status, change the CPU model of the VM to match host's CPU; that is, enable **Copy host CPU configuration** (*Fig-1*). Start the VM and execute `egrep '(vmx|svm)' /proc/cpuinfo` in the VM. You should be able to see vmx or svm in the output based on the host CPU model.

Your VM can now create its own virtual machines for the purpose of testing.

Index

A

**Advanced Message Queuing
  Protocol (AMQP)**
  about 337
  reference 337
Apache Software Foundation (ASF) 19
**Application Programming
  Interface (API) 21**
applications 245
aSPICE: Secure SPICE Client application
  download link 239
automated virtual machine deployment
  about 96
  oz, defining 99-101
  virt-builder, defining 96-99

B

Bare Metal 14
best practices, KVM guest time-keeping
  about 407, 408
  kvm-clock 408
binary translation
  reference 10
bridge
  about 106
  creating, with shared physical
    interfaces 131-133

C

cache mode, disk and block I/O tuning
  about 398, 399
  default 400
  directsync 400
  none 399

  unsafe 400
  writeback 400
  writethrough 399
CentOS 7 template
  preparing, with LAMP stack 188
clone provisioning method
  used, for deploying VMs 192, 193
Cloudstack 19
cluster 317
containers 7
controller 244
Copy on write (COW) shared page 377
core OpenStack components
  defining 336-338
CPU and memory
  tuning, with NUMA 383
CPU cores 64
CPU pinning
  about 360-362
  numactl command 361
CPU tuning
  about 356
  CPU configuration 358
  CPU pinning 360
  CPU topology 360
  number of vCPUs 357

D

data structures
  defining 37-40, 48-51
device assignment 406
device/driver pair examples, virtio
  virtio-balloon 355
  virtio-blk 355
  virtio-console 356

---

[431]

Made in the USA
San Bernardino,
CA